A WRITER'S DIARY

BOOKS BY VIRGINIA WOOLF

A Writer's Diary

BEING EXTRACTS FROM THE DIARY OF
VIRGINIA WOOLF

Edited by Leonard Woolf

A HARVEST/HBJ BOOK
HARCOURT BRACE JOVANOVICH
NEW YORK AND LONDON

Printed in the United States of America
    F G H I J

Library of Congress Cataloging in Publication Data
Woolf, Virginia (Stephen) 1882-1941.
    A writer's diary.
    (A Harvest book, HB 264)
    1. Woolf, Virginia (Stephen) 1882-1941.
I. Title.
[PR6045.072Z5   1973]   828'.9'1203 [B]   73-5737
ISBN 0-15-698380-X (pbk.)

CONTENTS

PREFACE

In 1915 Virginia Woolf began regularly to write a diary. She continued to do so until 1941 and the last entry is four days before her death. She did not write it regularly every day. There are sometimes entries daily for several days; more usually there is an entry every few days and then there will perhaps be a gap of a week or two. But the diary gives for 27 years a consecutive record of what she did, of the people whom she saw, and particularly of what she thought about those people, about herself, about life, and about the books she was writing or hoped to write. She wrote it on blank sheets of paper (8¼" by 10½", i.e. technically large post quarto). At first the sheets were clipped together with loose-leaf rings, but all the later diaries are in bound volumes. We used to have the sheets bound up in paper over boards, and the cover paper is nearly always one of the coloured, patterned Italian papers which we frequently used for binding books of poetry published by us in The Hogarth Press and of which she was very fond. We used to buy the paper for the sheets and have it bound up in books ready for her to use, and she wrote her novels in this kind of book as well as her diary. When she died, she left 26 volumes of diary written in this kind of book in her own hand.

The diary is too personal to be published as a whole during the lifetime of many people referred to in it. It is, I think, nearly always a mistake to publish extracts from diaries or letters, particularly if the omissions have to be made in order to protect the feelings or reputations of the living. The omissions almost always distort or conceal the true character of the diarist or letter-writer and produce spiritually what an Academy picture does materially, smoothing out the wrinkles, warts, frowns, and asperities. At the best and even unexpurgated, diaries give a distorted or one-sided portrait of the writer, because, as Virginia

Woolf herself remarks somewhere in these diaries, one gets into the habit of recording one particular kind of mood—irritation or misery, say—and of not writing one's diary when one is feeling the opposite. The portrait is therefore from the start unbalanced, and, if someone then deliberately removes another characteristic, it may well become a mere caricature.

Nevertheless the present book is composed of extracts from Virginia Woolf's diaries. She used her diary partly, in the normal way of diarists, to record what she did and what she thought about people, life, and the universe. But she also used it in a very individual way as a writer and artist. In it she communed with herself about the books she was writing or about future books which she intended to write. She discusses the day-to-day problems of plot or form, of character or exposition, which she encounters in each of her books as she conceives them or writes or revises them. Her position as an artist and the merits of her books are a subject of dispute, and no prudent man would claim to judge to a nicety the place which a contemporary writer will occupy in the pantheon of letters. Some critics are irritated and many less sophisticated readers are bewildered by her later novels. But no one denies that she was a serious artist and there are many people who, like Professor Bernard Blackstone, have no doubt that "she was a great artist," that "she did supremely well what no one else has attempted to do," and that her "world will survive as the crystal survives under the crushing rock-masses." * And it is relevant to what I have to say in this preface that many of the people who cannot understand or dislike or ridicule her novels agree that in *The Common Reader* and her other books of essays she showed herself to be a very remarkable literary critic.

I have been carefully through the 26 volumes of diary and have extracted and now publish in this volume practically everything which referred to her own writing. I have included also three other kinds of extract. The first consists of a certain number of passages in which she is obviously using the diary as a method of practising or trying out the art of writing. The

* *Virginia Woolf*, by Bernard Blackstone, pages 36, 37, and 38 (British Council & Longmans, Green, London, 1952).

second consists of a few passages which, though not directly or indirectly concerned with her writings, I have deliberately selected because they give the reader an idea of the direct impact upon her mind of scenes and persons, i.e. of the raw material of her art. Thirdly I have included a certain number of passages in which she comments upon the books she was reading.

The book throws light upon Virginia Woolf's intentions, objects, and methods as a writer. It gives an unusual psychological picture of artistic production from within. Its value and interest naturally depend to a great extent upon the value and interest of the product of Virginia Woolf's art. Unless I had agreed with Professor Blackstone, I would not have edited and published this book. She was, I think, a serious artist and all her books are serious works of art. The diaries at least show the extraordinary energy, persistence, and concentration with which she devoted herself to the art of writing and the undeviating conscientiousness with which she wrote and rewrote and again rewrote her books. *The Waves* seems to me a great work of art, far and away the greatest of her books. *To the Lighthouse* and *Between the Acts* should also, I think, live in their own right, while the other books, though on a lower level of achievement, are, as I said, "serious" and will always be worth reading and studying. I put forward this opinion, not as of any value, but as an explanation of my publishing the book.

In editing the diary I was in some doubt whether to indicate omissions. In the end I decided not to do so as a general rule. The omissions and the dots would have been so continual as to worry the reader. This leads me to revert to what I said above. The reader must remember that what is printed in this volume is only a very small portion of the diaries and that the extracts were embedded in a mass of matter unconnected with Virginia Woolf's writing. Unless this is constantly borne in mind, the book will give a very distorted view of her life and her character.

Virginia Woolf does not always indicate in the diary where she is when she is writing it and it is rarely of much importance that the reader should know. The following facts will probably clear up any doubt in any particular case. From 1915 to March,

1924, we lived at Hogarth House, Richmond. This in the diary
is often referred to simply as "Hogarth." At the same time we
also had a lease of Asheham House, near Lewes, in Sussex, referred to in the diary simply as "Asheham." We used Asheham
ordinarily only for week-ends and holidays. In 1919 the lease
of Asheham House came to an end and we bought Monks
House, Rodmell, near Lewes, moving into it in September,
1919. In 1924 we sold Hogarth House, Richmond, and took a
lease of 52 Tavistock Square, W.C.1, often referred to in the
diary as "Tavistock." We lived there from March, 1924, until
August, 1939, when we moved to 37 Mecklenburgh Square,
W.C.1. In 1940 the house in Mecklenburgh Square was so badly
damaged by bombs that all the furniture had to be removed
and we lived until Virginia Woolf's death in 1941 at Monks
House.

I append to this preface a glossary of names of persons used
in the diary which will help the reader to understand who is
being referred to in any particular passage.

LEONARD WOOLF

1 January, 1953

GLOSSARY OF NAMES
USED IN THE DIARY

Angelica	Angelica Bell, daughter of Vanessa Bell, married David Garnett.
Bob	R. C. Trevelyan
Bunny	David Garnett
Charleston	House near Lewes occupied by Clive and Vanessa Bell, about 8 miles from Monks House, Rodmell.
Clive	Clive Bell, husband of Vanessa
Dadie	G. W. Rylands
Desmond	Desmond MacCarthy
Duncan	Duncan Grant
Goldie	G. Lowes Dickinson
Gordon Square	The house, No. 46, where the Bells lived
Harold	Harold Nicolson
Hugh	Hugh Walpole
James	James Strachey
Julian	Julian Bell, son of Vanessa, killed in Spain
L.	Leonard Woolf
Lytton	Lytton Strachey
Maynard	John Maynard (later Lord) Keynes
Morgan	E. M. Forster
Nessa	Vanessa Bell, sister of Virginia Woolf
Ottoline or Ott	Lady Ottoline Morrell
Quentin	Quentin Bell, son of Vanessa
Roger	Roger Fry
Sibyl	Lady Colefax
Sydney	Sir Sydney Waterlow
Tilton	House near Lewes occupied by Maynard and Lydia Keynes, about 8 miles from Monks House, Rodmell.
Tom	T. S. Eliot
Vita	V. Sackville-West (Mrs. Harold Nicolson)

1918

Monday, August 4th

While waiting to buy a book in which to record my impressions first of Christina Rossetti, then of Byron, I had better write them here. For one thing I have hardly any money left, having bought Leconte de Lisle in great quantities. Christine has the great distinction of being a born poet, as she seems to have known very well herself. But if I were bringing a case against God she is one of the first witnesses I should call. It is melancholy reading. First she starved herself of love, which meant also life; then of poetry in deference to what she thought her religion demanded. There were two good suitors. The first indeed had his peculiarities. He had a conscience. She could only marry a particular shade of Christian. He could only stay that shade for a few months at a time. Finally he developed Roman Catholicism and was lost. Worse still was the case of Mr. Collins—a really delightful scholar—an unworldly recluse—a single-minded worshipper of Christina, who could never be brought into the fold at all. On this account she could only visit him affectionately in his lodgings, which she did to the end of her life. Poetry was castrated too. She would set herself to do the psalms into verse; and to make all her poetry subservient to the Christian doctrines. Consequently, as I think, she starved into austere emaciation a very fine original gift, which only wanted licence to take to itself a far finer form than, shall we say, Mrs. Browning's. She wrote very easily; in a spontaneous childlike kind of way one imagines, as is the case generally with a true gift; still undeveloped. She has the natural singing power. She thinks too. She has fancy. She could, one is profane enough to guess, have been ribald and witty. And, as a reward for all her sacrifices, she died in terror, uncertain of salvation. I confess though that I have only turned her poetry over, making my way inevitably to the ones I knew already.

Asheham diary drains off my meticulous observations of flowers, clouds, beetles and the price of eggs; and, being alone, there is no other event to record. Our tragedy has been the squashing of a caterpillar; our excitement the return of the servants from Lewes last night, laden with all L.'s war books and the English review for me, with Brailsford upon a League of Nations, and Katherine Mansfield on *Bliss*. I threw down *Bliss* with the exclamation, "She's done for!" Indeed I don't see how much faith in her as woman or writer can survive that sort of story. I shall have to accept the fact, I'm afraid, that her mind is a very thin soil, laid an inch or two deep upon very barren rock. For *Bliss* is long enough to give her a chance of going deeper. Instead she is content with superficial smartness; and the whole conception is poor, cheap, not the vision, however imperfect, of an interesting mind. She writes badly too. And the effect was as I say, to give me an impression of her callousness and hardness as a human being. I shall read it again; but I don't suppose I shall change. She'll go on doing this sort of thing, perfectly to her and Murry's satisfaction. I'm relieved now that they didn't come. Or is it absurd to read all this criticism of her personally into a story?

Anyhow I was very glad to go on with my Byron. He has at least the male virtues. In fact, I'm amused to find how easily I can imagine the effect he had upon women—especially upon rather stupid or uneducated women, unable to stand up to him. So many, too, would wish to reclaim him. Ever since I was a child (as Gertler would say, as if it proved him a particularly remarkable person) I've had the habit of getting full of some biography and wanting to build up my imaginary figure of the person with every scrap of news I could find about him. During the passion, the name of Cowper or Byron or whoever it might be, seemed to start up in the most unlikely pages. And then, suddenly, the figure becomes distant and merely one of the usual dead. I'm much impressed by the extreme badness of B.'s poetry—such of it as Moore quotes with almost speechless admiration. Why did they think this Album stuff the finest fire of poetry? It reads hardly better than L. E. L. or Ella Wheeler Wilcox. And they dissuaded him from doing what he knew he could do, which was to write satire. He came home from the East with satires (parodies of Horace) in his bag and *Childe Harold*. He was persuaded that *Childe Harold* was the best poem ever written. But he never as a young man believed in his poetry; a proof, in such a confident dogmatic person, that he hadn't the gift. The Wordsworths and Keatses believe in that as much as they believe in anything. In his character, I'm often reminded a little of Rupert Brooke, though this is to Rupert's disadvantage. At any rate Byron had superb force; his letters prove it. He had in many ways a very fine nature too; though as no one laughed him out of his affectations he became more like Horace Cole than one could wish. He could only be laughed at by a woman, and they worshipped instead. I haven't yet come to Lady Byron, but I suppose, instead of laughing, she merely disapproved. And so he became Byronic.

Friday, August 8th

In the absence of human interest, which makes us peaceful and content, one may as well go on with Byron. Having indicated that I am ready, after a century, to fall in love with him, I suppose my judgment of Don Juan may be partial. It is the most readable poem of its length ever written, I suppose: a quality which it owes in part to the springy random haphazard galloping nature of its method. This method is a discovery by itself. It's what one has looked for in vain—an elastic shape which will hold whatever you choose to put into it. Thus he could write out his mood as it came to him; he could say whatever came into his head. He wasn't committed to be poetical; and thus escaped his evil genius of the false romantic and imaginative. When he is serious he is sincere: and he can impinge upon any subject he likes. He writes 16 cantos without once flogging his flanks. He had, evidently, the able witty mind of what my father Sir Leslie would have called a thoroughly masculine nature. I maintain that these illicit kinds of book are far

more interesting than the proper books which respect illusions
devoutly all the time. Still, it doesn't seem an easy example to
follow; and indeed like all free and easy things, only the skilled
and mature really bring them off successfully. But Byron was
full of ideas—a quality that gives his verse a toughness and
drives me to little excursions over the surrounding landscape
or room in the middle of my reading. And tonight I shall have
the pleasure of finishing him—though why considering that I've
enjoyed almost every stanza, this should be a pleasure I really
don't know. But so it always is, whether the book's a good book
or a bad book. Maynard Keynes admitted in the same way that
he always cuts off the advertisements at the end with one hand
while he's reading, so as to know exactly how much he has to
get through.

Monday, August 19th
  I finished by the way the *Electra* of Sophocles, which has
been dragging on down here, though it's not so fearfully difficult after all. The thing that always impresses me fresh is the
superb nature of the story. It seems hardly possible *not* to make
a good play of it. This perhaps is the result of having tradi-
tional plots which have been made and improved and freed
from superfluities by the polish of innumerable actors and
authors and critics, till it becomes like a lump of glass worn
smooth in the sea. Also, if everyone in the audience knows be-
forehand what is going to happen, much finer and subtler
touches will tell, and words can be spared. At any rate my feeling always is that one can't read too carefully, or attach enough
weight to every line and hint; and that the apparent bareness
is only on the surface. There does, however, remain the question of reading the wrong emotions into the text. I am generally
humiliated to find how much Jebb is able to see; my only
doubt is whether he doesn't see too much—as I think one might
do with a bad modern English play if one set to work. Finally,
the particular charm of Greek remains as strong and as difficult
to account for as ever. One feels the immeasurable difference
between the text and the translation with the first words. The
heroic woman is much the same in Greece and England. She

is of the type of Emily Brontë. Clytaemnestra and Electra are clearly mother and daughter, and therefore should have some sympathy, though perhaps sympathy gone wrong breeds the fiercest hate. E. is the type of woman who upholds the family above everything; the father. She has more veneration for tradition than the sons of the house; feels herself born of the father's side and not of the mother's. It's strange to notice how although the conventions are perfectly false and ridiculous, they never appear petty or undignified as our English conventions are constantly made to do. Electra lived a far more hedged in life than the women of the mid-Victorian age, but this has no effect upon her, except in making her harsh and splendid. She could not go out for a walk alone; with us it would be a case of a maid and a hansom cab.

Tuesday, September 10th

Though I am not the only person in Sussex who reads Milton, I mean to write down my impressions of *Paradise Lost* while I am about it. Impressions fairly well describes the sort of thing left in my mind. I have left many riddles unread. I have slipped on too easily to taste the full flavour. However I see, and agree to some extent in believing, that this full flavour is the reward of highest scholarship. I am struck by the extreme difference between this poem and any other. It lies, I think, in the sublime aloofness and impersonality of the emotion. I have never read Cowper on the sofa, but I can imagine that the sofa is a degraded substitute for *Paradise Lost*. The substance of Milton is all made of wonderful, beautiful and masterly descriptions of angels' bodies, battles, flights, dwelling places. He deals in horror and immensity and squalor and sublimity but never in the passions of the human heart. Has any great poem ever let in so little light upon one's own joys and sorrows? I get no help in judging life; I scarcely feel that Milton lived or knew men and women; except for the peevish personalities about marriage and the woman's duties. He was the first of the masculinists, but his disparagement rises from his own ill luck and seems even a spiteful last word in his domestic quarrels. But how smooth, strong and elaborate it all is! What poetry? I can conceive that even Shakespeare after this would seem a little troubled, personal, hot and imperfect. I can conceive that this is the essence, of which almost all other poetry is the dilution. The inexpressible fineness of the style, in which shade after shade is perceptible, would alone keep one gazing into it, long after the surface business in progress has been despatched. Deep down one catches still further combinations, rejections, felicities and masteries. Moreover, though there is nothing like Lady Macbeth's terror or Hamlet's cry, no pity or sympathy or intuition, the figures are majestic; in them is summed up much of what men thought of our place in the universe, of our duty to God, our religion.

1919

I mean to copy this out when I can buy a book, so I omit
the flourishes proper to the new year. It is not money this time
that I lack, but the capacity, after a fortnight in bed, to make
the journey to Fleet Street. Even the muscles of my right hand
feel as I imagine a servant's hand to feel. Curiously enough, I
have the same stiffness in manipulating sentences, though by
rights I should be better equipped mentally now than I was a
month ago. The fortnight in bed was the result of having a
tooth out, and being tired enough to get a headache—a long
dreary affair, that receded and advanced much like a mist on a
January day. One hour's writing daily is my allowance for the
next few weeks; and having hoarded it this morning I may
spend part of it now, since L. is out and I am much behindhand
with the month of January. I note however that this diary writing does not count as writing, since I have just re-read my year's
diary and am much struck by the rapid haphazard gallop at
which it swings along, sometimes indeed jerking almost intolerably over the cobbles. Still if it were not written rather faster
than the fastest type-writing, if I stopped and took thought, it
would never be written at all; and the advantage of the method
is that it sweeps up accidentally several stray matters which I
should exclude if I hesitated, but which are the diamonds of
the dustheap. If Virginia Woolf at the age of 50, when she sits
down to build her memoirs out of these books, is unable to
make a phrase as it should be made, I can only condole with her
and remind her of the existence of the fireplace, where she has
my leave to burn these pages to so many black films with red
eyes in them. But how I envy her the task I am preparing for
her! There is none I should like better. Already my 37th birth-

7

day next Saturday is robbed of some of its terrors by the thought.
Partly for the benefit of this elderly lady (no subterfuges will
then be possible: 50 is elderly, though I anticipate her protest
and agree that it is not old) partly to give the year a solid
foundation I intend to spend the evenings of this week of cap-
tivity in making out an account of my friendships and their
present condition, with some account of my friends' characters;
and to add an estimate of their work and a forecast of their
future works. The lady of 50 will be able to say how near to
the truth I come; but I have written enough for tonight (only
15 minutes, I see).

Wednesday, March 5th

Just back from four days at Asheham and one at Charleston.
I sit waiting for Leonard to come in, with a brain still running
along the railway lines, which unfits it for reading. But oh,
dear, what a lot I've got to read! The entire works of Mr.
James Joyce, Wyndham Lewis, Ezra Pound, so as to compare
them with the entire works of Dickens and Mrs. Gaskell; besides that George Eliot; and finally Hardy. And I've just done
Aunt Anny,* on a really liberal scale. Yes, since I wrote last
she has died, a week ago today to be precise, at Freshwater, and
was buried up at Hampstead yesterday, where six or seven years
ago we saw Richmond buried in a yellow fog. I suppose my feeling for her is half moonshine; or rather half reflected from other
feelings. Father cared for her; she goes down the last, almost, of
that old nineteenth century Hyde Park Gate world. Unlike
most old ladies she showed very little anxiety to see one; felt,
I sometimes think, a little painfully at the sight of us, as if we'd
gone far off and recalled unhappiness, which she never liked to
dwell on. Also, unlike most old Aunts she had the wits to feel
how sharply we differed on current questions; and this, perhaps,
gave her a sense, hardly existing with her usual circle, of age,
obsoleteness, extinction. For myself, though she need have had
no anxieties on this head, since I admired her sincerely; but
still the generations certainly look very different ways. Two

* Lady Ritchie, Thackeray's daughter.

or perhaps three years ago L. and I went to see her; found her much diminished in size, wearing a feather boa round her neck and seated alone in a drawing room almost the copy, on a smaller scale, of the old drawing room; the same subdued pleasant air of the eighteenth century and old portraits and old china. She had our tea waiting for us. Her manner was a little distant, and more than a little melancholy. I asked her about father, and she said how those young men laughed in a "loud melancholy way" and how their generation was a very happy one, but selfish; and how ours seemed to her fine but very terrible; but we hadn't any writers such as they had. "Some of them have just a touch of that quality; Bernard Shaw has; but only a touch. The pleasant thing was to know them all as ordinary people, not great men." And then a story of Carlyle and father; Carlyle saying he'd as soon wash his face in a dirty puddle as write journalism. She put her hand down, I remember, into a bag or box standing beside the fire, and said she had a novel, three quarters written, but couldn't finish it. Nor do I suppose it ever was finished; but I've said all I can say, dressing it up a trifle rosily, in *The Times* tomorrow. I have written to Hester, but how I doubt the sincerity of my own emotion!

Wednesday, March 19th

Life piles up so fast that I have no time to write out the equally fast rising mound of reflections, which I always mark down as they rise to be inserted here. I meant to write about the Barnetts and the peculiar repulsiveness of those who dabble their fingers self approvingly in the stuff of others' souls. The Barnetts were at any rate plunged to the elbow; red handed if ever philanthropists were, which makes them good examples; and then, unquestioning and unspeculative as they were, they give themselves away almost to the undoing of my critical faculty. Is it chiefly intellectual snobbery that makes me dislike them? Is it snobbery to feel outraged when she says "Then I came close to the Great Gates"—or reflects that God = good, devil = evil. Has this coarseness of grain any necessary connection with labour for one's kind? And then the smug vigour of

their self-satisfaction! Never a question as to the right of what
they do—always a kind of insensate forging ahead until, naturally, their undertakings are all of colossal size and portentous
prosperity. Moreover, could any woman of humour or insight
quote such paeans to her own genius? Perhaps the root of it all
lies in the adulation of the uneducated, and the easy mastery
of the will over the poor. And more and more I come to loathe
any dominion of one over another; any leadership, any imposi-
tion of the will. Finally, my literary taste is outraged by the
smooth way in which the tale is made to unfold into fullblown
success, like some profuse peony. But I only scratch the surface
of what I feel about these two stout volumes.*

Thursday, March 27th
. . . *Night and Day* which L. has spent the past two mornings and evenings in reading. I own that his verdict, finally pronounced this morning, gives me immense pleasure: how far one
should discount it, I don't know. In my own opinion *N. & D.*
is a much more mature and finished and satisfactory book than
The Voyage Out; as it has reason to be. I suppose I lay myself
open to the charge of niggling with emotions that don't really
matter. I certainly don't anticipate even two editions. And yet
I can't help thinking that, English fiction being what it is,
I compare for originality and sincerity rather well with most
of the modern. L. finds the philosophy very melancholy. It too
much agrees with what he was saying yesterday. Yet, if one is
to deal with people on a large scale and say what one thinks,
how can one avoid melancholy? I don't admit to being hopeless
though: only the spectacle is a profoundly strange one; and as
the current answers don't do, one has to grope for a new one,
and the process of discarding the old, when one is by no means
certain what to put in their place, is a sad one. Still, if you think
of it, what answers do Arnold Bennett or Thackeray, for instance, suggest? Happy ones—satisfactory solutions—answers one
would accept, if one had the least respect for one's soul? Now
I have done my last odious piece of typewriting, and when I

* *Rev. Canon S. A. Barnett; His Life, Work and Friends.* By his wife, Mrs.
Barnett, C.B.E. (Murray).

have scribbled this page, I shall write and suggest Monday as the day for coming up to lunch with Gerald.* I don't suppose I've ever enjoyed any writing so much as I did the last half of *Night and Day*. Indeed, no part of it taxed me as *The Voyage Out* did; and if one's own ease and interest promise anything good, I should have hopes that some people, at least, will find it a pleasure. I wonder if I shall ever be able to read it again? Is the time coming when I can endure to read my own writing in print without blushing—shivering and wishing to take cover?

Wednesday, April 2nd

Yesterday I took *Night and Day* up to Gerald and had a little half domestic half professional interview with him in his office. I don't like the Clubman's view of literature. For one thing it breeds in me a violent desire to boast: I boasted of Nessa and Clive and Leonard; and how much money they made. Then we undid the parcel and he liked the title but found that Miss Maud Annesley has a book called *Nights and Days*—which may make difficulties with Mudies. But he was certain he would wish to publish it; and we were altogether cordial; and I noticed how his hair is every blade of it white, with some space between the blades; a very sparsely sown field. I had tea at Gordon Square.

Saturday, April 12th

These ten minutes are stolen from *Moll Flanders*, which I failed to finish yesterday in accordance with my time sheet, yielding to a desire to stop reading and go up to London. But I saw London, in particular the view of white city churches and palaces from Hungerford Bridge through the eyes of Defoe. I saw the old women selling matches through his eyes; and the draggled girl skirting round the pavement of St. James's Square seemed to me out of *Roxana* or *Moll Flanders*. Yes, a great writer surely to be there imposing himself on me after 200 years. A great writer—and Forster † has never read his books! I was beckoned by Forster from the Library as I approached.

* Gerald Duckworth, publisher, half-brother of V. W.
† E. M. Forster.

We shook hands very cordially; and yet I always feel him shrinking sensitively from me, as a woman, a clever woman, an up to date woman. Feeling this I commanded him to read Defoe, and left him, and went and got some more Defoe, having bought one volume at Bickers on the way.

Thursday, April 17th

However one may abuse the Stracheys their minds remain a source of joy to the end; so sparkling, definite and nimble. Need I add that I reserve the qualities I most admire for people who are not Stracheys? It is so long since I have seen Lytton that I take my impression of him too much from his writing, and his paper upon Lady Hester Stanhope was not one of his best. I could fill this page with gossip about people's articles in the *Athenaeum;* since I had tea with Katherine * yesterday and Murry † sat there mud-coloured and mute, livening only when we talked his shop. He has the jealous partiality of a parent for his offspring already. I tried to be honest, as if honesty were part of my philosophy, and said how I disliked Grantorte on whistling birds, and Lytton and so on. The male atmosphere is disconcerting to me. Do they distrust one? despise one? and if so why do they sit on the whole length of one's visit? The truth is that when Murry says the orthodox masculine thing about Eliot, for example, belittling my solicitude to know what he said of me, I don't knuckle under; I think what an abrupt precipice cleaves asunder the male intelligence, and how they pride themselves upon a point of view which much resembles stupidity. I find it much easier to talk to Katherine; she gives and resists as I expect her to; we cover more ground in much less time; but I respect Murry. I wish for his good opinion. Heinemann has rejected K. M.'s stories; and she was oddly hurt that Roger had not invited her to his party. Her hard composure is much on the surface.

Easter Sunday, April 20th

In the idleness which succeeds any long article, and Defoe is the second leader this month, I got out this diary and read,

* Katherine Mansfield.   † J. Middleton Murry.

as one always does read one's own writing, with a kind of guilty intensity. I confess that the rough and random style of it, often so ungrammatical, and crying for a word altered, afflicted me somewhat. I am trying to tell whichever self it is that reads this hereafter that I can write very much better; and take no time over this; and forbid her to let the eye of man behold it. And now I may add my little compliment to the effect that it has a slapdash and vigour and sometimes hits an unexpected bull's eye. But what is more to the point is my belief that the habit of writing thus for my own eye only is good practice. It loosens the ligaments. Never mind the misses and the stumbles. Going at such a pace as I do I must make the most direct and instant shots at my object, and thus have to lay hands on words, choose them and shoot them with no more pause than is needed to put my pen in the ink. I believe that during the past year I can trace some increase of ease in my professional writing which I attribute to my casual half hours after tea. Moreover there looms ahead of me the shadow of some kind of form which a diary might attain to. I might in the course of time learn what it is that one can make of this loose, drifting material of life; finding another use for it than the use I put it to, so much more consciously and scrupulously, in fiction. What sort of diary should I like mine to be? Something loose knit and yet not slovenly, so elastic that it will embrace anything, solemn, slight or beautiful that comes into my mind. I should like it to re-semble some deep old desk, or capacious hold-all, in which one flings a mass of odds and ends without looking them through. I should like to come back, after a year or two, and find that the collection had sorted itself and refined itself and coalesced, as such deposits so mysteriously do, into a mould, transparent enough to reflect the light of our life, and yet steady, tranquil compounds with the aloofness of a work of art. The main requi-site, I think on re-reading my old volumes, is not to play the part of censor, but to write as the mood comes or of anything whatever; since I was curious to find how I went for things put in haphazard, and found the significance to lie where I never saw it at the time. But looseness quickly becomes slovenly. A little effort is needed to face a character or an incident which needs to be recorded. Nor can one let the pen write without guidance; for fear of becoming slack and untidy like Vernon Lee. Her ligaments are too loose for my taste.

Monday, May 12th

We are in the thick of our publishing season; Murry, Eliot * and myself are in the hands of the public this morning. For this reason, perhaps, I feel slightly but decidedly depressed. I read a bound copy of *Kew Gardens* through; having put off the evil task until it was complete. The result is vague. It seems to me slight and short; I don't see how the reading of it impressed Leonard so much. According to him it is the best short piece I have done yet; and this judgment led me to read the *Mark on the Wall* and I found a good deal of fault with that. As Sydney Waterlow once said, the worst of writing is that one depends so much upon praise. I feel rather sure that I shall get none for this story; and I shall mind a little. Unpraised, I find it hard to start writing in the morning; but the dejection lasts only 30 minutes, and once I start I forget all about it. One should aim, seriously, at disregarding ups and downs; a compliment here, silence there; Murry and Eliot ordered, and not me; the central fact remains stable, which is the fact of my own pleasure in the art. And these mists of the spirit have other causes, I expect; though they are deeply hidden. There is some ebb and flow of the tide of life which accounts for it; though what produces either ebb or flow I'm not sure.

Tuesday, June 10th

I must use up the fifteen minutes before dinner in going on again, in order to make up the great gap. We are just in from the Club; from ordering a reprint of the *Mark on the Wall* at the Pelican Press; and from tea with James. His news is that Maynard in disgust at the peace terms has resigned, kicked the dust of office off him and is now an academic figure at Cambridge. But I must really sing my own praises, since I left off at the point when we came back from Asheham to find the hall

* T. S. Eliot.

table stacked, littered, with orders for *Kew Gardens*. They strewed the sofa and we opened them intermittently through dinner and quarrelled, I'm sorry to say, because we were both excited, and opposite tides of excitement coursed in us, and they were blown to waves by the critical blast of Charleston. All these orders—150 about, from shops and private people—come from a review in the *Lit. Sup.* presumably by Logan, in which as much praise was allowed me as I like to claim. And 10 days ago I was stoically facing complete failure! The pleasure of success was considerably damaged, first by our quarrel, and second by the necessity of getting some 90 copies ready, cutting covers, printing labels, glueing backs, and finally despatching, which used up all spare time and some not spare till this moment. But how success showered during those days! Gratuitously, too, I had a letter from Macmillan in New York, so much impressed by *The Voyage Out* that they want to read *Night and Day*. I think the nerve of pleasure easily becomes numb. I like little sips, but the psychology of fame is worth considering at leisure. I fancy one's friends take the bloom off. Lytton lunched here on Saturday with the Webbs, and when I told him my various triumphs, did I imagine a little shade, instantly dispelled, but not before my rosy fruit was out of the sun. Well, I treated his triumphs in much the same way. I can't feel gratified when he expatiates upon a copy of *Eminent Victorians* lined and initialled "M" or "H" by Mr. or Mrs. Asquith. Yet clearly the thought produced a comfortable glow in him. The luncheon was a success. We ate in the garden and Lytton sported very gracefully and yet with more than his old assurance over the conversation. "But I'm *not* interested in Ireland—"

Saturday, July 19th

One ought to say something about Peace day, I suppose, though whether it's worth taking a new nib for that purpose I don't know. I'm sitting wedged into the window and so catch almost on my head the steady drip of rain which is pattering on the leaves. In ten minutes or so the Richmond procession begins. I fear there will be few people to applaud the town councillors dressed up to look dignified and march through the streets. I've a sense of holland covers on the chairs; of being left behind when everyone's in the country. I'm desolate, dusty, and disillusioned. Of course we did not see the procession. We have only marked the bins of refuse on the outskirts. Rain held off till some half hour ago. The servants had a triumphant morning. They stood on Vauxhall Bridge and saw everything. Generals and soldiers and tanks and nurses and bands took two hours in passing. It was they said the most splendid sight of their lives. Together with the Zeppelin raid it will play a great part in the history of the Boxall family. But I don't know—it seems to me a servants' festival; something got up to pacify and placate "the people"—and now the rain's spoiling it; and perhaps some extra treat will have to be devised for them. That's the reason of my disillusionment I think. There's something calculated and politic and insincere about these peace rejoicings. Moreover they are carried out with no beauty and not much spontaneity. Flags are intermittent; we have what the servants, out of snobbishness, I think, insisted upon buying, to surprise us. Yesterday in London the usual sticky stodgy conglomerations of people, sleepy and torpid as a cluster of drenched bees, were crawling over Trafalgar Square, and rocking about the pavements in the neighbourhood. The one pleasant sight I saw was due rather to the little breath of wind than to decorative skill; some long tongue-shaped streamers attached to the top of the Nelson column licked the air, furled and unfurled, like the gigantic tongues of dragons, with a slow, rather serpentine beauty. Otherwise theatres and music-halls were studded with stout glass pincushions which, rather prematurely, were all radiant within—but surely light might have shown to better advantage. However night was sultry and magnificent so far as that went, and we were kept awake some time after getting into bed, by the explosion of rockets which for a second made our room bright. (And now, in the rain, under a grey brown sky, the bells of Richmond are ringing—but church bells only recall weddings and Christian services.) I can't deny that I feel a little mean at writing so lugubriously; since we're all supposed to keep up the belief that we're glad and enjoying ourselves. So on a birthday, when for some reason things have gone wrong, it was a point of honour in the nursery to pretend. Years later one could confess what a horrid fraud it seemed; and if, years later, these docile herds will own up that they too saw through it, and will have no more of it—well—should I be more cheerful? I think the dinner at the 1917 Club, and Mrs. Besant's speech rubbed the gilt, if there were any grains remaining, effectually off the gingerbread. Hobson was sardonic. She—a massive and sulky featured old lady, with a capacious head, however, thickly covered with curly white hair—began by comparing London, lit up and festive, with Lahore. And then she pitched into us for our maltreatment of India, she, apparently, being "them" and not "us." But I don't think she made her case very solid, though superficially it was all believable, and the 1917 Club applauded and agreed. I can't help listening to speaking as though it were writing and thus the flowers, which she brandished now and again, looked terribly artificial. It seems to me more and more clear that the only honest people are the artists, and that these social reformers and philanthropists get so out of hand and harbour so many discreditable desires under the disguise of loving their kind, that in the end there's more to find fault with in them than in us. But if I were one of them?

Sunday, July 20th

Perhaps I will finish the account of the peace celebrations. What herd animals we are after all!—even the most disillusioned. At any rate, after sitting through the procession and the peace bells unmoved, I began after dinner to feel that if something was going on, perhaps one had better be in it. I routed up poor L. and threw away my Walpole. First lighting a row of glass lamps and seeing that the rain was stopped, we went out just before tea. Explosions had for some time promised fireworks. The doors of the public house at the corner were open and the room crowded; couples waltzing; songs being shouted, waveringly, as if one must be drunk to sing. A troop of little boys with lanterns were parading the green, beating sticks. Not many shops went to the expense of electric light. A woman of the upper classes was supported dead drunk between two men partially drunk. We followed a moderate stream flowing up the Hill. Illuminations were almost extinct half way up, but we kept on till we reached the terrace. And then we did see something—not much indeed, for the damp had deadened the chemicals. Red and green and yellow and blue balls rose slowly into the air, burst, flowered into an oval of light, which dropped in minuter grains and expired. There were hazes of light at different points. Rising over the Thames, among trees, these rockets were beautiful; the light on the faces of the crowd was strange; yet of course there was grey mist muffling everything and taking the blaze off the fire. It was a melancholy thing to see the incurable soldiers lying in bed at the Star and Garter with their backs to us, smoking cigarettes and waiting for the noise to be over. We were children to be amused. So at eleven we went home and saw from my study Ealing do its best to rejoice, and indeed one fire balloon went so high that L. believed it a star; but there were nine showing. Today the rain has left us in no doubt that any remaining festivities are to be completely quenched.

Tuesday, October 21st

This is Trafalgar day and yesterday is memorable for the appearance of *Night and Day*. My six copies reached me in the morning and five were despatched, so that I figure the beaks of five friends already embedded. Am I nervous? Oddly little; more excited and pleased than nervous. In the first place, there it is, out and done with; then I read a bit and liked it; then I have a kind of confidence, that the people whose judgment I value will probably think well of it, which is much reinforced by the knowledge that even if they don't, I shall pick up and start another story on my own. Of course, if Morgan and Lytton and the others should be enthusiastic, I should think the better of myself. The bore is meeting people who say the usual things. But on the whole I see what I'm aiming at; what I feel is that this time I've had a fair chance and done my best; so that I can be philosophic and lay the blame on God.

Thursday, October 23rd

The first fruits of *Night and Day* must be entered. "No doubt a work of the highest genius"—Clive Bell. Well, he might not have liked it: he was critical of *The Voyage Out*. I own I'm pleased: yet not convinced that it is as he says. However, this is a token that I'm right to have no fears. The people whose judgment I respect won't be so enthusiastic as he is, but they'll come out decidedly on that side, I think.

Thursday, October 30th

I have the excuse of rheumatism for not writing more; and my hand tired of writing, apart from rheumatism. Still, if I could treat myself professionally as a subject for analysis I could make an interesting story of the past few days, of my vicissitudes about *N. and D.* After Clive's letter came Nessa's—unstinted praise; on top of that Lytton's: enthusiastic praise; a grand triumph; a classic; and so on; Violet's * sentence of eulogy followed; and then, yesterday morning, this line from Morgan "I like it less than *The Voyage Out*." Though he spoke also of great admiration and had read in haste and proposed re-reading, this rubbed out all the pleasure of the rest. Yes, but to continue. About 3 in the afternoon I felt happier and easier on account of his blame than on account of the others' praise—as if one were in the human atmosphere again, after a blissful roll among elastic clouds and cushiony downs. Yet I suppose I value Morgan's opinion as much as anybody's. Then there's a column in *The Times* this morning; high praise; and intelligent too; saying among other things that *N. and D.*, though it has less brilliance on the surface, has more depth than the other; with which I agree. I hope this week will see me through the reviews; I should like intelligent letters to follow; but I want to be writing little stories; I feel a load off my mind all the same.

Thursday, November 6th

Sydney and Morgan dined with us last night. On the whole, I'm glad I sacrificed a concert. The doubt about Morgan and *N. and D.* is removed; I understand why he likes it less than *V.O.*; and, in understanding, see that it is not a criticism to discourage. Perhaps intelligent criticism never is. All the same, I shirk writing it out, because I write so much criticism. What

* Violet Dickinson, an old friend.

he said amounted to this: *N. and D.* is a strictly formal and classical work; that being so one requires, or he requires, a far greater degree of lovability in the characters than in a book like *V.O.*, which is vague and universal. None of the characters in *N. and D.* is lovable. He did not care how they sorted themselves out. Neither did he care for the characters in *V.O.*, but there he felt no need to care for them. Otherwise, he admired practically everything; his blame does not consist in saying that *N. and D.* is less remarkable than t'other. O and beauties it has in plenty—in fact, I see no reason to be depressed on his account. Sydney said he had been completely upset by it and was of opinion that I had on this occasion "brought it off." But what a bore I'm becoming! Yes, even old Virginia will skip a good deal of this; but at the moment it seems important. The *Cambridge Magazine* repeats what Morgan said about dislike of the characters; yet I am in the forefront of contemporary literature. I'm cynical about my figures, they say; but directly they go into detail, Morgan, who read the Review sitting over the gas fire, began to disagree. So all critics split off, and the wretched author who tries to keep control of them is torn asunder. For the first time this many years I walked along the river bank between ten and eleven. Yes, it's like the shut up house I once compared it to; the room with its dust sheets on the chairs. The fishermen are not out so early; an empty path; but a large aeroplane on business. We talked very rarely, the proof being that we (I anyhow) did not mind silences. Morgan has the artist's mind; he says the simple things that clever people don't say; I find him the best of critics for that reason. Suddenly out comes the obvious thing that one has overlooked. He is in trouble with a novel of his own, fingering the keys but only producing discords so far.

Friday, December 5th

Another of these skips, but I think the book draws its breath steadily if with deliberation. I reflect that I've not opened a Greek book since we came back; hardly read outside my review books, which proves that my time for writing has not been mine at all. I'm almost alarmed to find how intensely I'm specialised.

My mind turned by anxiety, or other cause, from its scrutiny of blank paper, is like a lost child—wandering the house, sitting on the bottom step to cry. *Night and Day* flutters about me still, and causes great loss of time. George Eliot would never read reviews, since talk of her books hampered her writing. I begin to see what she meant. I don't take praise or blame excessively to heart, but they interrupt, cast one's eyes backwards, make one wish to explain or investigate. Last week I had a cutting paragraph to myself in *Wayfarer;* this week Olive Heseltine applies balm. But I had rather write in my own way of *Four Passionate Snails* than be, as K. M. maintains, Jane Austen over again.

1920

The day after my birthday; in fact I'm 38, well, I've no doubt
I'm a great deal happier than I was at 28; and happier today
than I was yesterday having this afternoon arrived at some idea
of a new form for a new novel. Suppose one thing should open
out of another—as in an unwritten novel—only not for 10 pages
but 200 or so—doesn't that give the looseness and lightness I
want; doesn't that get closer and yet keep form and speed, and
enclose everything, everything? My doubt is how far it will
enclose the human heart—Am I sufficiently mistress of my dialogue to net it there? For I figure that the approach will be
entirely different this time: no scaffolding; scarcely a brick to
be seen; all crepuscular, but the heart, the passion, humour,
everything as bright as fire in the mist. Then I'll find room for
so much—a gaiety—an inconsequence—a light spirited stepping
at my sweet will. Whether I'm sufficiently mistress of things—
that's the doubt; but conceive(?) *Mark on the Wall, K.G.* and
Unwritten Novel taking hands and dancing in unity. What
the unity shall be I have yet to discover; the theme is a blank
to me; but I see immense possibilities in the form I hit upon
more or less by chance two weeks ago. I suppose the danger is
the damned egotistical self; which ruins Joyce and Richardson
to my mind: is one pliant and rich enough to provide a wall for
the book from oneself without its becoming, as in Joyce and
Richardson, narrowing and restricting? My hope is that I've
learnt my business sufficiently now to provide all sorts of enter-
tainments. Anyhow, I must still grope and experiment but this
afternoon I had a gleam of light. Indeed, I think from the ease
with which I'm developing the unwritten novel there must be
a path for me there.

Wednesday, February 4th

The mornings from 12 to 1 I spend reading *The Voyage Out*. I've not read it since July 1913. And if you ask me what I think I must reply that I don't know—such a harlequinade as it is— such an assortment of patches—here simple and severe—here frivolous and shallow—here like God's truth—here strong and free flowing as I could wish. What to make of it, Heaven knows. The failures are ghastly enough to make my cheeks burn—and then a turn of the sentence, a direct look ahead of me, makes them burn in a different way. On the whole I like the young woman's mind considerably. How gallantly she takes her fences —and my word, what a gift for pen and ink! I can do little to amend, and must go down to posterity the author of cheap witticisms, smart satires and even, I find, vulgarisms—crudities rather —that will never cease to rankle in the grave. Yet I see how people prefer it to *N. and D.* I don't say admire it more, but find it a more gallant and inspiring spectacle.

Tuesday, March 9th

In spite of some tremors I think I shall go on with this diary for the present. I sometimes think that I have worked through the layer of style which suited it—suited the comfortable bright hour after tea; and the thing I've reached now is less pliable. Never mind; I fancy old Virginia, putting on her spectacles to read of March 1920 will decidedly wish me to continue. Greetings! my dear ghost; and take heed that I don't think 50 a very great age. Several good books can be written still; and here's the bricks for a fine one. To return to the present owner of the name, on Sunday I went up to Campden Hill to hear the Schubert quintet—to see George Booth's house—to take notes for my story—to rub shoulders with respectability—all these reasons took me there and were cheaply gratified at 7/6.

Whether people see their own rooms with the devastating clearness that I see them, thus admitted once for one hour, I doubt. Chill superficial seemliness; but thin as a March glaze of ice on a pool. A sort of mercantile smugness. Horsehair and mahogany is the truth of it; and the white panels, Vermeer reproductions, Omega table and variegated curtains rather a snobbish disguise. The least interesting of rooms; the compromise; though of course that's interesting too. I took against the family system. Old Mrs. Booth enthroned on a sort of commode in widow's dress; flanked by devoted daughters; with grandchildren somehow symbolical cherubs. Such neat dull little boys and girls. There we all sat in our furs and white gloves.

Saturday, April 10th

I'm planning to begin *Jacob's Room* next week with luck. (That's the first time I've written that.) It's the spring I have in my mind to describe; just to make this note—that one scarcely notices the leaves out on the trees this year, since they seem never entirely to have gone—never any of that iron blackness of the chestnut trunks—always something soft and tinted; such as I can't remember in my life before. In fact, we've skipped a winter; had a season like the midnight sun; a new return to full daylight. So I hardly notice that chestnuts are out—the little parasols spread on our window tree; and the churchyard grass running over the old tombstones like green water.

Thursday, April 15th

My handwriting seems to be going to the dogs. Perhaps I confuse it with my writing. I said that Richmond * was enthusiastic over my James article? Well, two days ago, little elderly Walkley attacked it in *The Times,* said I'd fallen into H. J.'s worst mannerisms—hardbeaten "figures"—and hinted that I was a sentimental lady friend. Percy Lubbock was included too; but, rightly or wrongly, I delete the article from my mind with blushes, and see all my writing in the least becoming light. I suppose it's the old matter of "florid gush"—no doubt a true criticism, though the disease is my own, not caught from H. J., if that's any comfort. I must see to it though. *The Times* atmosphere brings it out; for one thing I have to be formal there, especially in the case of H. J., and so contrive an article rather like an elaborate design, which encourages ornament.

* Bruce Richmond, Editor of *Times Literary Supplement.*

Desmond, however, volunteered admiration. I wish one could make out some rule about praise and blame. I predict that I'm destined to have blame in any quantity. I strike the eye; and elderly gentlemen in particular get annoyed. *An Unwritten Novel* will certainly be abused: I can't foretell what line they'll take this time. Partly, it's the "writing well" that sets people off —and always has done, I suppose, "Pretentious" they say; and then a woman writing well, and writing in *The Times*—that's the line of it. This slightly checks me from beginning *Jacob's Room*. But I value blame. It spurs one, even from Walkley; who is (I've looked him out) 65, and a cheap little gossip, I'm glad to think, laughed at, even by Desmond. But don't go forgetting that there's truth in it; more than a grain in the criticism that I'm damnably refined in *The Times;* refined and cordial; I don't think it's easy to help it; since, before beginning the H. J. article, I took a vow I'd say what I thought, and say it in my own way. Well, I've written all this page and not made out how to steady myself when the *Unwritten Novel* appears.

Tuesday, May 11th

It is worth mentioning, for future reference, that the creative power which bubbles so pleasantly in beginning a new book quiets down after a time, and one goes on more steadily. Doubts creep in. Then one becomes resigned. Determination not to give in, and the sense of an impending shape keep one at it more than anything. I'm a little anxious. How am I to bring off this conception? Directly one gets to work one is like a person walking, who has seen the country stretching out before. I want to write nothing in this book that I don't enjoy writing. Yet writing is always difficult.

Wednesday, June 23rd

I was struggling, at this time, to say honestly that I don't think Conrad's last book a good one. I have said it. It is painful (a little) to find fault there, where almost solely, one respects. I can't help suspecting the truth to be that he never sees anyone who knows good writing from bad, and then being a foreigner, talking broken English, married to a lump of a wife, he withdraws more and more into what he once did well, only piles it on higher and higher, until what can one call it but stiff melodrama. I would not like to find *The Rescue* signed Virginia Woolf. But will anyone agree with this? Anyhow nothing shakes my opinion of a book. Nothing—nothing. Only perhaps if it's the book of a young person—or of a friend—no, even so, I think myself infallible. Haven't I lately dismissed Murry's play, and exactly appraised K.'s story, and summed up Aldous Huxley; and doesn't it somehow wound my sense of fitness to hear Roger mangling these exact values?

Thursday, August 5th

Let me try to say what I think as I read *Don Quixote* after dinner—Principally that writing was then story telling to amuse people sitting round the fire without any of our devices for pleasure. There they sit, women spinning, men contemplative, and the jolly, fanciful, delightful tale is told to them, as to grown up children. This impresses me as the motive of D. Q.: to keep us entertained at all costs. So far as I can judge, the beauty and thought come in unawares: Cervantes scarcely conscious of serious meaning, and scarcely seeing D. Q. as we see him. Indeed that's my difficulty—the sadness, the satire, how far are they ours, not intended—or do these great characters have it in them to change according to the generation that looks at them? Much, I admit, of the tale-telling is dull—not much, only a little at the end of the first volume, which is obviously told as a story to keep one contented. So little said out, so much kept back, as if he had not wished to develop that side of the matter—the scene of the galley slaves marching is an instance of what I mean. Did C. feel the whole of the beauty and sadness of that as I feel it? Twice I've spoken of "sadness."

Is that essential to the modern view? Yet how splendid it is to unfurl one's sail and blow straight ahead on the gust of the great story telling, as happens all through the first part. I suspect the Fernando-Cardino-Lucinda story was a courtly episode in the fashion of the day, anyhow dull to me. I am also reading *Ghoa le Simple*—bright, effective, interesting, yet so arid and spick and span. With Cervantes everything there; in solution if you like; but deep, atmospheric, living people casting shadows solid, tinted as in life. The Egyptians, like most French writers, give you a pinch of essential dust instead, much more pungent and effective, but not nearly so surrounding and spacious. By God! What stuff I'm writing! Always these images. I write *Jacob* every morning now, feeling each day's work like a fence which I have to ride at, my heart in my mouth till it's over, and I've cleared, or knocked the bar out. (Another image, unthinking it was one. I must somehow get Hume's Essays and purge myself.)

Sunday, September 26th

But I think I minded more than I let on; for somehow *Jacob* has come to a stop, in the middle of that party too, which I enjoyed so much. Eliot coming on the heel of a long stretch of writing fiction (two months without a break) made me listless; cast shade upon me; and the mind when engaged upon fiction wants all its boldness and self-confidence. He said nothing—but I reflected how what I'm doing is probably being better done by Mr. Joyce. Then I began to wonder what it is that I am doing; to suspect, as is usual in such cases, that I have not thought my plan out plainly enough—so to dwindle, niggle, hesitate—which means that one's lost. But I think my two months of work are the cause of it, seeing that I now find myself veering round to Evelyn and even making up a paper upon Women, as a counterblast to Mr. Bennett's adverse views reported in the papers. Two weeks ago I made up *Jacob* incessantly on my walks. An odd thing, the human mind! so capricious, faithless, infinitely shying at shadows. Perhaps at the bottom of my mind, I feel that I'm distanced by L. in every respect.

Monday, October 25th (First day of winter time)

Why is life so tragic; so like a little strip of pavement over an abyss. I look down; I feel giddy; I wonder how I am ever to walk to the end. But why do I feel this: Now that I say it I don't feel it. The fire burns; we are going to hear the Beggar's Opera. Only it lies about me; I can't keep my eyes shut. It's a feeling of impotence; of cutting no ice. Here I sit at Richmond, and like a lantern stood in the middle of a field my light goes up in darkness. Melancholy diminishes as I write. Why then don't I write it down oftener? Well, one's vanity forbids. I want to appear a success even to myself. Yet I don't get to the bottom of it. It's having no children, living away from friends, failing to write well, spending too much on food, growing old. I think too much of whys and wherefores; too much of myself. I don't like time to flap round me. Well then, work. Yes, but I so soon tire of work—can't read more than a little, an hour's writing is enough for me. Out here no one comes in to waste time pleasantly. If they do, I'm cross. The labour of going to London is too great. Nessa's children grow up, and I can't have them in to tea, or go to the Zoo. Pocket money doesn't allow of much. Yet I'm persuaded that these are trivial things; it's life itself, I think sometimes, for us in our generation so tragic— no newspaper placard without its shriek of agony from someone. McSwiney this afternoon and violence in Ireland; or it'll be the strike. Unhappiness is everywhere; just beyond the door; or stupidity, which is worse. Still I don't pluck the nettle out of me. To write *Jacob's Room* again will revive my fibres, I feel. Evelyn is due; but I don't like what I write now. And with it all how happy I am—if it weren't for my feeling that it's a strip of pavement over an abyss.

1921

Tuesday, March 1st

I am not satisfied that this book is in a healthy way. Suppose one of my myriad changes of style is antipathetic to the material? or does my style remain fixed? To my mind it changes always. But no one notices. Nor can I give it a name myself. The truth is that I have an internal, automatic scale of values; which decides what I had better do with my time. It dictates "this half hour must be spent on Russian." "This must be given to Wordsworth." Or "Now I'd better darn my brown stockings." How I come by this code of values I don't know. Perhaps it's the legacy of puritan grandfathers. I suspect pleasure slightly. God knows. And the truth is also that writing, even here, needs screwing of the brain—not so much as Russian, but then half the time I learn Russian I look in the fire and think what I shall write tomorrow. Mrs. Flanders is in the orchard. If I were at Rodmell I should have thought it all out walking on the flats. I should be in fine writing trim. As it is Ralph,* Carrington † and Brett ‡ have this moment gone; I'm dissipated; we dine and go out to the Guild. I can't settle as I should to think of Mrs. Flanders in the orchard.

Sunday, March 6th

Nessa approves of *Monday or Tuesday*—mercifully; and thus somewhat redeems it in my eyes. But I now wonder a little what the reviewers will make of it—this time next month. Let me try to prophesy. Well, *The Times* will be kindly, a little cautious. Mrs. Woolf, they will say, must beware of virtuosity. She must beware of obscurity. Her great natural gifts etc. . . . She is at her best in the simple lyric, or in *Kew Gardens. An*

---

* Ralph Partridge.   † Mrs. Partridge.   ‡ Dorothy Brett.

Unwritten Novel is hardly a success. And as for *A Society,*
though spirited, it is too one-sided. Still Mrs. Woolf can always
be read with pleasure. Then, in the *Westminster, Pall Mall*
and other serious evening papers I shall be treated very shortly
with sarcasm. The general line will be that I am becoming too
much in love with the sound of my own voice; not much in
what I write; indecently affected; a disagreeable woman. The
truth is, I expect, that I shan't get very much attention anywhere. Yet, I become rather well known.

Friday, April 8th. 10 minutes to 11 a.m.
And I ought to be writing *Jacob's Room;* and I can't, and
instead I shall write down the reason why I can't—this diary
being a kindly blankfaced old confidante. Well, you see, I'm a
failure as a writer. I'm out of fashion: old: shan't do any better:
have no headpiece: the spring is everywhere: my book out
(prematurely) and nipped, a damp firework. Now the solid
grain of fact is that Ralph sent my book out to *The Times* for
review without date of publication in it. Thus a short notice
is scrambled through to be in "on Monday at latest," put in an
obscure place, rather scrappy, complimentary enough, but
quite unintelligent. I mean by that they don't see that I'm
after something interesting. So that makes me suspect that I'm
not. And thus I can't get on with *Jacob.* Oh and Lytton's book
is out and takes up three columns; praise I suppose. I do not
trouble to sketch this in order; or how my temper sank and
sank till for half an hour I was as depressed as I ever am. I
mean I thought of never writing any more—save reviews. To
rub this in we had a festival party at 41: to congratulate Lytton; which was all as it should be, but then he never mentioned
my book, which I suppose he has read; and for the first time I
have not his praise to count on. Now if I'd been saluted by the
Lit. Sup. as a mystery—a riddle, I shouldn't mind; for Lytton
wouldn't like that sort of thing, but if I'm as plain as day, and
negligible?
     Well, this question of praise and fame must be faced. (I
forgot to say that Doran has refused the book in America.) How
much difference does popularity make? (I'm putting clearly, I

may add, after a pause in which Lottie has brought in the milk and the sun has ceased to eclipse itself, that I'm writing a good deal of nonsense.) One wants, as Roger said very truly yesterday, to be kept up to the mark; that people should be interested and watch one's work. What depresses me is the thought that I have ceased to interest people—at the very moment when, by the help of the press, I thought I was becoming more myself. One does *not* want an established reputation, such as I think I was getting, as one of our leading female novelists. I have still, of course, to gather in all the private criticism, which is the real test. When I have weighed this I shall be able to say whether I am "interesting" or obsolete. Anyhow, I feel quite alert enough to stop, if I'm obsolete. I shan't become a machine, unless a machine for grinding articles. As I write, there rises somewhere in my head that queer and very pleasant sense of something which I want to write; my own point of view. I wonder, though, whether this feeling that I write for half a dozen instead of 1500 will pervert this?—make me eccentric— no, I think not. But, as I said, one must face the despicable vanity which is at the root of all this niggling and haggling. I think the only prescription for me is to have a thousand interests—if one is damaged, to be able instantly to let my energy flow into Russian, or Greek, or the press, or the garden, or people, or some activity disconnected with my own writing.

Sunday, April 9th

I must note the symptoms of the disease, so as to know it next time. The first day one's miserable; the second happy. There was an Affable Hawk * on me in the *New Statesman* which at any rate made me feel important (and it's that that one wants) and Simpkin Marshall rang up for a second fifty copies. So they must be selling. Now I have to stand all the twitching and teasing of private criticism which I shan't enjoy. There'll be Roger tomorrow. What a bore it all is!—and then one begins to wish one had put in other stories and left out the *Haunted House,* which may be sentimental.

* Desmond MacCarthy's pseudonym.

Tuesday, April 12th

I must hurriedly note more symptoms of the disease, so that I can turn back here and medicine myself next time. Well; I'd worn through the acute stage and come to the philosophic semi-depressed, indifferent, spent the afternoon taking parcels round the shops, going to Scotland Yard for my purse, when L. met me at tea and dropped into my ear the astonishing news that Lytton thinks the *String Quartet* "marvellous." This came through Ralph, who doesn't exaggerate, to whom Lytton need not lie; and did for a moment flood every nerve with pleasure, so much so that I forgot to buy my coffee and walked over Hungerford Bridge twanging and vibrating. A lovely blue evening too, the river sky colour. And then there was Roger who thinks I'm on the track of real discoveries and certainly not a fake. And we've broken the record of sales, so far. And I'm not nearly so pleased as I was depressed; and yet in a state of security; fate cannot touch me; the reviewers may snap; and the sales decrease. What I had feared was that I was dismissed as negligible.

Friday, April 29th

I ought to say something of Lytton. I have seen him oftener these last days than for a whole year perhaps. We have talked about his book and my book. This particular conversation took place in Verreys: gilt feathers: mirrors: blue walls and Lytton and I taking our tea and brioche in a corner. We must have sat well over an hour.

"And I woke last night and wondered where to place you," I said. "There's St. Simon and La Bruyère."

"Oh God," he groaned.

"And Macaulay," I added.

"Yes, Macaulay," he said. "A little better than Macaulay."

But not his man, I insisted. "More civilisation of course. And then you've only written short books."

"I'm going to do George IV next," he said.

"Well, but your place," I insisted.

"And yours?" he asked.

"I'm the 'ablest of living women novelists,' " I said. "So the *British Weekly* says."

"You influence me," he said.

And he said he could always recognise my writing though I wrote so many different styles.

"Which is the result of hard work," I insisted. And then we discussed histories; Gibbon; a kind of Henry James, I volunteered.

"Oh dear no—not in the least," he said.

"He has a point of view and sticks to it," I said. "And so do you. I wobble." But what is Gibbon?

"Oh, he's there all right," Lytton said. "Forster says he's an Imp. But he hadn't many views. He believed in 'virtue' perhaps."

"A beautiful word," I said.

"But just read how the hordes of barbarians devastated the City. It's marvellous. True, he was queer about the early Christians—didn't see anything in them at all. But read him. I'm going to next October. And I'm going to Florence, and I shall be very lonely in the evenings."

"The French have influenced you more than the English, I suppose," I said.

"Yes. I have their definiteness. I'm formed."

"I compared you with Carlyle the other day," I said. "I read the *Reminiscences*. Well, they're the chatter of an old toothless gravedigger compared with you; only then he has phrases."

"Ah yes, he has them," said Lytton. "But I read him to Norton and James the other day and they shouted—they wouldn't have it."

"I'm a little anxious though about 'mass.' "

"That's my danger, is it?"

"Yes. You may cut too fine," I said. "But it's a magnificent subject—George IV—and what fun, setting to work on it."

"And your novel?"

"Oh, I put in my hand and rummage in the bran pie."

"That's what's so wonderful. And it's all different."

"Yes, I'm 20 people."

"But one sees the whole from the outside. The worst of George IV is that no one mentions the facts I want. History must be written all over again. It's all morality—"

"And battles," I added.

And then we walked through the streets together, for I had to buy coffee.

Thursday, May 26th

I sat in Gordon Square yesterday for an hour and a half talking to Maynard. Sometimes I wish I put down what people say instead of describing them. The difficulty is that they say so little. Maynard said he liked praise; and always wanted to boast. He said that many men marry in order to have a wife to boast to. But, I said, it's odd that one boasts considering that no one is ever taken in by it. It's odd too that you, of all people, should want praise. You and Lytton are passed beyond boasting—which is the supreme triumph. There you sit and say nothing. I love praise, he said. I want it for the things I'm doubtful about. Then we got upon publishing, and the Hogarth press; and novels. Why should they explain what bus he took? he asked. And why shouldn't Mrs. Hilbery be sometimes the daughter of Katharine. Oh, it's a dull book, I know, I said; but don't you see you must put it all in before you can leave out. The best thing you ever did, he said, was your Memoir on George. You should pretend to write about real people and make it all up. I was dashed of course (and Oh dear what nonsense—for if George is my climax I'm a mere scribbler).

Saturday, August 13th

"Coleridge was as little fitted for action as Lamb, but on a different account. His person was of a good height, but as sluggish and solid as the other's was light and fragile. He had, perhaps, suffered it to look old before its time, for want of exercise. His hair was white at 50; and as he generally dressed in black and had a very tranquil demeanour, his appearance was gentlemanly, and for several years before his death was reverend. Nevertheless, there was something invincibly young in

the look of his face. It was round and fresh-coloured, with
agreeable features, and an open, indolent, goodnatured mouth.
This boy-like expression was very becoming in one who dreamed
and speculated as he did when he was really a boy, and who
passed his life apart from the rest of the world, with a book and
his flowers. His forehead was prodigious,—a great piece of placid
marble;—and his fine eyes, in which all the activity of his mind
seemed to concentrate, moved under it with a sprightly ease,
as if it was a pastime to them to carry all that thought.

"And it was pastime. Hazlitt said that Coleridge's genius
appeared to him like a spirit, all head and wings, eternally
floating about in etherialities. He gave me a different impression. I fancied him a goodnatured wizard, very fond of earth,
and conscious of reposing with weight enough in his easy chair,
but able to conjure his etherialities about him in the twinkling
of an eye. He could also change them by thousands and dismiss
them as easily when his dinner came. It was a mighty intellect
put upon a sensual body; and the reason he did little more
with it than talk and dream was that it is agreeable to such a
body to do little else. I do not mean that C. was a sensualist in
an ill sense . . ." which is all that I can take the trouble to
quote from Leigh Hunt's memoirs volume II page 223, sup-
posing I should want to cook this up again somewhere. L. H.
was our spiritual grandfather, a free man. One could have
spoken to him as to Desmond. A light man, I daresay, but
civilised, much more so than my grandfather in the flesh. These
free, vigorous spirits advance the world, and when one lights
on them in the strange waste of the past one says "Ah, you're
my sort"—a great compliment. Most people who died 100 years
ago are like strangers. One is polite and uneasy with them.
Shelley died with H.'s copy of *Lamia* in his hand. H. would receive it back from no other, and so burnt it on the pyre. Going
home from the funeral? H. and Byron laughed till they split.
This is human nature and H. doesn't mind owning to it. Then
I like his inquisitive human sympathies: history so dull because of its battles and laws; and sea voyages in books so dull
because the traveller will describe beauties instead of going

into the cabins and saying what the sailors looked like, wore, eat, said; how they behaved.

Lady Carlisle is dead. One likes people much better when they're battered down by a prodigious siege of misfortune than when they triumph. Such a stock of hope and gifts she set out with, and lost everything (so they say) and died of sleepy sickness, her 5 sons dead before her and the war crushing her hope for humanity.

Wednesday, August 17th

To while away the time till L. comes in from London, Fergusson, office etc., I may as well scribble. Really I think my scribbling is coming back. Here I have spent the whole day, off and on, making up an article—for Squire perhaps, because he wants a story, and because Mrs. Hawkesford has told Mrs. Thomsett that I am one of the, if not the, cleverest women in England. It's not nerve power so much as praise that has lacked, perhaps. Yesterday I was seized with the flux, as the Bible has it. Dr. Vallence was fetched, came after dinner, and paid a call. I wish I could write down his conversation. A mild, heavy lidded, little elderly man, son of a Lewes doctor, has always lived here, existing on a few broad medical truths learnt years ago, which he applies conscientiously. He can speak French, as it were, in words of one syllable. As both L. and I knew a good deal more than he did we got upon general topics—old Verrall and how he starved himself purposely to death. "I could have had him sent away," said Dr. V. meditatively. "He had been away once. His sister's away to this day—quite crazy, I believe —a bad family, very bad. I sat with him in your sitting room. We had to sit right into the chimney to get warm. I tried to interest him in chess. No. He didn't seem able to take an interest in anything. But he was too old—too weak. I couldn't send him away." So he starved himself to death, pottering about his garden.

Crossing his knees and touching his little moustache meditatively now and then, V. then asked me if I did anything? (He thought me a chronic invalid, a fine lady.) I said I wrote. "What, novels? Light things?" Yes, novels. "I have another lady novelist among my patients—Mrs. Dudeny. I've had to buck her up—to fulfil a contract, a contract for a new novel. She finds Lewes very noisy. And then we have Marion Crawford. . . . But Mr. Dudeny is the puzzle king. Give him any puzzle—he'll tell you the answer. He makes up the sort of puzzles shops print on their menus. He writes columns in the papers about puzzles."

"Did he help to answer puzzles in the war?" I asked.

"Well, I don't know about that. But a great many soldiers wrote to him—the puzzle king." Here he crossed his legs the opposite way. Finally he went and invited L. to join the Lewes Chess Club, which I should very much like to attend myself, these glimpses into different groups always fascinating me intolerably, for I shall never join the party of Dr. Vallence and the puzzle king.

Thursday, August 18th

Nothing to record; only an intolerable fit of the fidgets to write away. Here I am chained to my rock; forced to do nothing; doomed to let every worry, spite, irritation and obsession scratch and claw and come again. This is a day that I may not walk and must not work. Whatever book I read bubbles up in my mind as part of an article I want to write. No one in the whole of Sussex is so miserable as I am; or so conscious of an infinite capacity of enjoyment hoarded in me, could I use it. The sun streams (no, never streams; floods rather) down upon all the yellow fields and the long low barns; and what wouldn't I give to be coming through Firle woods, dirty and hot, with my nose turned home, every muscle tired and the brain laid up in sweet lavender, so sane and cool, and ripe for the morrow's task. How I should notice everything— the phrase for it coming the moment after and fitting like a glove; and then on the dusty road, as I ground my pedals, so my story would begin telling itself; and then the sun would be down; and home, and some bout of poetry after dinner, half read, half lived, as if the flesh were dissolved and through it the flowers burst red and white. There! I've written out half my irritation. I hear poor L. driving the lawn mower up and down,

for a wife like I am should have a latch to her cage. She bites!
And he spent all yesterday running round London for me. Still
if one is Prometheus, if the rock is hard and the gadflies pungent, gratitude, affection, none of the nobler feelings have
sway. And so this August is wasted.

Only the thought of people suffering more than I do at all
consoles; and that is an aberration of egotism, I suppose. I will
now make out a time table if I can to get through these odious
days.

Poor Mdlle. Lenglen, finding herself beaten by Mrs. Mal-
lory, flung down her racquet and burst into tears. Her vanity
I suppose is colossal. I daresay she thought that to be Mdlle.
Lenglen was the greatest thing in the world; invincible, like
Napoleon. Armstrong, playing in the test match, took up his
position against the gates and would not move, let the bowlers
appoint themselves, the whole game became farcical because
there was not time to play it out. But Ajax in the Greek play
was of the same temper—which we all agree to call heroic in
him. But then everything is forgiven to the Greeks. And I've
not read a line of Greek since last year, this time, too. But I
shall come back, if it's only in snobbery; I shall be reading
Greek when I'm old; old as the woman at the cottage door,
whose hair might be a wig in a play, it's so white, so thick.
Seldom penetrated by love for mankind as I am, I sometimes
feel sorry for the poor who don't read Shakespeare, and indeed
have felt some generous democratic humbug at the Old Vic,
when they played Othello and all the poor men and women
and children had him there for themselves. Such splendour and
such poverty. I am writing down the fidgets, so no matter if I
write nonsense. Indeed, any interference with the normal proportions of things makes me uneasy. I know this room too well
—this view too well—I am getting it all out of focus, because I
can't walk through it.

Monday, September 12th

I have finished *The Wings of the Dove*, and make this comment. His manipulation becomes so elaborate towards the end

that instead of feeling the artist you merely feel the man who is posing the subject. And then I think he loses the power to feel the crisis. He becomes merely excessively ingenious. This, you seem to hear him saying, is the way to do it. Now just when you expect a crisis, the true artist evades it. Never do the thing, and it will be all the more impressive. Finally, after all this juggling and arranging of silk pocket handkerchiefs, one ceases to have any feeling for the figure behind. Milly thus manipulated disappears. He overreaches himself. And then one can never read it again. The mental grasp and stretch are magnificent. Not a flabby or slack sentence, but much emasculated by this timidity or consciousness or whatever it is. Very highly American, I conjecture, in the determination to be highly bred, and the slight obtuseness as to what high breeding is.

Tuesday, November 15th

Really, really—this is disgraceful—15 days of November spent and my diary none the wiser. But when nothing is written one may safely suppose that I have been stitching books; or we have had tea at 4 and I have taken my walk afterwards; or I have had to read something for next day's writing, or I have been out late, come home with stencilling materials and sat down in excitement to try one. We went to Rodmell, and the gale blew at us all day; off arctic fields; so we spent our time attending to the fire. The day before this I wrote the last words of *Jacob*—on Friday November 4th to be precise, having begun it on April 16, 1920: allowing for 6 months interval due to *Monday or Tuesday* and illness, this makes about a year. I have not yet looked at it. I am struggling with Henry James's ghost stories for *The Times;* have I not just laid them down in a mood of satiety? Then I must do Hardy; then I want to write a life of Newnes; then I shall have to furbish up *Jacob;* and one of these days, if only I could find energy to tackle the Paston letters, I must start *Reading:* directly I've started *Reading* I shall think of another novel, I daresay. So that the only question appears to be—will my fingers stand so much scribbling?

Monday, December 19th

I will add a postscript, as I wait for my parcels to be wrapped up, on the nature of reviewing.

"Mrs. Woolf? I want to ask you one or two questions about your Henry James article.

"First (only about the right name of one of the stories).

"And now you use the word 'lewd.' Of course, I don't wish you to change it, but surely that is rather a strong expression to apply to anything by Henry James. I haven't read the story lately of course—but still, my impression is—"

"Well, I thought that when I read it: one has to go by one's impressions at the time."

"But you know the usual meaning of the word? It is—ah—*dirty*. Now poor dear old Henry James— At any rate, think it over and ring me up in 20 minutes." So I thought it over and came to the required conclusion in twelve minutes and a half. But what is one to do about it? He made it sufficiently clear not only that he wouldn't stand "lewd" but that he didn't much like anything else. I feel that this becomes more often the case, and I wonder whether to break off, with an explanation, or to pander, or to go on writing against the current. This last is probably right, but somehow the consciousness of doing that cramps one. One writes stiffly, without spontaneity. Anyhow, for the present I shall let it be, and meet my castigation with resignation. People will complain I'm sure, and poor Bruce fondling his paper like an only child dreads public criticism, is stern with me, not so much for disrespect to poor old Henry, but for bringing blame on the Supplement. And how much time I have wasted!

1922

Wednesday, February 15th

Of my reading I will now try to make some note. First Peacock: *Nightmare Abbey,* and *Crotchet Castle.* Both are so much better than I remember. Doubtless, Peacock is a taste acquired in maturity. When I was young, reading him in a railway carriage in Greece, sitting opposite Thoby,* I remember, who pleased me immensely by approving my remark that Meredith had got his women from Peacock, and that they were very charming women, then, I say, I rather had to prod my enthusiasm. Thoby liked it straight off. I wanted mystery, romance, psychology, I suppose. And now more than anything I want beautiful prose. I relish it more and more exquisitely. And I enjoy satire more. I like the scepticism of his mind more. I enjoy intellectuality. Moreover, fantasticality does a good deal better than sham psychology. One touch of red in the cheek is all he gives, but I can do the rest. And then they're so short; and I read them in little yellowish perfectly appropriate first editions.

The masterly Scott has me by the hair once more. *Old Mortality.* I'm in the middle; and have to put up with some dull sermons; but I doubt that he can be dull, because everything is so much in keeping—even his odd monochromatic landscape painting, done in smooth washes of sepia and burnt sienna. Edith and Henry too might be typical figures by an old master, put in exactly in the right place. And Cuddie and Mause are as usual marching straight away for all time, as lusty as life. But I daresay the lighting and the story telling business prevent him from going quite ahead with his fun as in the *Antiquary.*

* Thoby Stephen, V. W.'s brother.

To continue—certainly the later chapters are bare and grey, ground out too palpably; authorities, I daresay, interfering with the original flow. And Morton is a prig; and Edith a stick; and Evandale a brick; and the preacher's dulness I could take for granted. Still—still—I want to know what the next chapter brings, and these gallant old fellows can be excused practically anything.

How far can our historical portrait painters be trusted, seeing the difficulty I have in putting down the face of Violet Dickinson, whom I saw, for two hours, yesterday afternoon? One hears her talking in a swinging random way to Lottie in the hall, as she comes in. "Where's my marmalade? How's Mrs. Woolf? Better eh? Where is she?" meanwhile putting down coat and umbrella and not listening to a word. Then she seemed to me as she came in gigantically tall; tailor made; with a pearl dolphin with red tongue swinging from a black ribbon; rather stouter; with her white face, prominent blue eyes; nose with a chip off the end; and small beautifully aristocratic hands. Very well; but her talk? Since nature herself could give no account of it—since nature has wilfully left out some screw, what chance is there for me? Such nonsense putting old Ribblesdale and Horner on Boards—Ly. R. was an Astor—refused to let a penny of hers be invested. Your friend Miss Schreiner has gone to Bankok. Don't you remember all her boots and shoes in Eaton Square? To tell the truth I remembered neither Schreiner, her boots, or Eaton Square. Then Herman Norman is back and says things are in an awful mess at Teheran.

"He's my cousin," I said.

"How's that?" Off we went on to Normans. Leonard and Ralph were having tea meanwhile and sometimes intercepted a whiff of grapeshot. Now all this, properly strung together, would make a very amusing sketch in the style of Jane Austen. But old Jane, if she had been in the mood, would have given all the other things—no, I don't think she would; for Jane was not given to general reflections; one can't put in the shadows that appear curving round her, and giving her a sort of beauty. She quiets down—though believing the old doctrine that talk must be incessant—and becomes humane, generous; shows that humorous sympathy which brings everything into her scope—naturally; with a touch of salt and reality; she has the range of a good novelist, bathing things in their own atmosphere too, only all so fragmentary and jerky. She told me she had no wish to live. "I'm very happy," she said. "Oh yes, very happy—But why should I want to go on living? What is there to live for?" "Your friends?" "My friends are all dead." "Ozzie?" "Oh, he'd do just as well without me. I should like to tidy things up and disappear." "But you believe in immortality?" "No. I don't know that I do. Dust, ashes, I say." She laughed of course; and yet, as I say, has somehow the all round imaginative view which makes one believe her. Certainty I like—is love the word for these strange deep ancient affections, which began in youth and have got mixed up with so many important things? I kept looking at her large pleasant blue eyes, so candid and generous and hearty and going back to Fritham and Hyde Park Gate. But this doesn't make a picture, all the same. I feel her somehow to be the sketch for a woman of genius. All the fluid gifts have gone in; but not the bony ones.

Friday, February 17th

I've just had my dose of phenacetin—that is to say a mildly unfavourable review of *Monday or Tuesday* reported by Leonard from the *Dial*, the more depressing as I had vaguely hoped for approval in that august quarter. It seems as if I succeed nowhere. Yet, I'm glad to find, I have acquired a little philosophy. It amounts to a sense of freedom. I write what I like writing and there's an end on it. Moreover, heaven knows I get consideration enough.

Saturday, February 18th

Once more my mind is distracted from the thought of death. There was something about fame I had it in mind to say yesterday. Oh, I think it was that I have made up my mind that I'm not going to be popular, and so genuinely that I look upon disregard or abuse as part of my bargain. I'm to write what I like; and they're to say what they like. My only interest as a writer lies, I begin to see, in some queer individuality; not in strength, or passion, or anything startling, but then I say to myself, is not "some queer individuality" precisely the quality I respect? Peacock for example: Barrow; Donne; Douglas, in *Alone*, has a touch of it. Who else comes to mind immediately? Fitzgerald's Letters. People with this gift go on sounding long after the melodious vigorous music is banal. In proof of this, I read that a small boy, given a book by Marie Corelli for a Sunday school prize, at once killed himself; and the coroner remarked that one of her books was not what he himself would call "at all a nice book." So perhaps the *Mighty Atom* is dwindling away and *Night and Day* arising; though *The Voyage Out* seems at the moment most in esteem. That encourages me. After 7 years next April the *Dial* speaks of its superb artistry. If they say the same of *N. and D.* in 7 years I shall be content; but I must wait 14 for anyone to take *Monday or Tuesday* to heart. I want to read Byron's Letters, but I must go on with *La Princesse de Clèves*. This masterpiece has long been on my conscience. Me to talk of fiction and not to have read this classic! But reading classics is generally hard going. Especially classics like this one, which are classics because of their perfect taste, shapeliness, composure, artistry. Not a hair of its head is dishevelled. I think the beauty very great, but hard to appreciate. All the characters are noble. The movement is stately. The machinery a little cumbrous. Stories have to be told. Letters dropped. It is the action of the human heart and not of muscle or fate that we watch. But stories of noble human hearts have their movements unapproachable in other circumstances. There is a queer understated profundity in the relations between Madame de Clèves and her mother, for example. If I were reviewing it, I think I should take for my text beauty in character. Thank God though I am not reviewing it. Within the last few minutes I have skimmed the reviews in the *New Statesman;* between coffee and cigarette I read the *Nation;* now the best brains in England (metaphorically speaking) sweated themselves for I don't know how many hours to give me this brief condescending sort of amusement. When I read reviews I crush the column together to get at one or two sentences; is it a good book or a bad? And then I discount those two sentences according to what I know of the book and of the reviewer. But when I write a review I write every sentence as if it were going to be tried before three Chief Justices. I can't believe that I am crushed together and discounted. Reviews seem to me more and more frivolous. Criticism on the other hand absorbs me more and more. But after 6 weeks influenza my mind throws up no matutinal fountains. My note book lies by my bed unopened. At first I could hardly read for the swarm of ideas that rose involuntarily. I had to write them out at once. And this is great fun. A little air, seeing the buses go by, lounging by the river, will, please God, send the sparks flying again. I am suspended between life and death in an unfamiliar way. Where is my paper knife? I must cut Lord Byron.

Friday, June 23rd

Jacob, as I say, is being typed by Miss Green, and crosses the Atlantic on July 14th. Then will begin my season of doubts and ups and downs. I am guarding myself in this way. I am going to be well on with a story for Eliot, lives for Squire, and *Reading;* so that I can vary the side of the pillow as fortune inclines. If they say this is all a clever experiment, I shall produce *Mrs. Dalloway* in Bond Street as the finished product. If they say your fiction is impossible, I shall say what about Miss Ormerod, a fantasy. If they say "You can't make us care a damn for any of your figures," I shall say read my criticism then. Now what *will* they say about *Jacob?* Mad, I suppose: a disconnected rhapsody; I don't know. I will confide my view to this book on re-reading. On re-reading novels is the title of a very laborious, yet rather gifted article, for the *Supt.*

Wednesday, July 26th

On Sunday L. read through *Jacob's Room.* He thinks it my best work. But his first remark was that it was amazingly well written. We argued about it. He calls it a work of genius; he thinks it unlike any other novel; he says that the people are ghosts; he says it is very strange: I have no philosophy of life he says; my people are puppets, moved hither and thither by fate. He doesn't agree that fate works in this way. Thinks I should use my "method" on one or two characters next time; and he found it very interesting and beautiful, and without lapse (save perhaps the party) and quite intelligible. Pocky has so disturbed my mind that I cannot write this as formally as it deserves, for I was anxious and excited. But I am on the whole pleased. Neither of us knows what the public will think. There's no doubt in my mind that I have found out how to begin (at 40) to say something in my own voice; and that interests me so that I feel I can go ahead without praise.

Wednesday, August 16th

I should be reading *Ulysses,* and fabricating my case for and against. I have read 200 pages so far—not a third; and have been amused, stimulated, charmed, interested, by the first 2 or 3 chapters—to the end of the cemetery scene; and then puzzled, bored, irritated and disillusioned by a queasy undergraduate scratching his pimples. And Tom, great Tom, thinks this on a par with *War and Peace!* An illiterate, underbred book it seems to me; the book of a self taught working man, and we all know how distressing they are, how egotistic, insistent, raw, striking, and ultimately nauseating. When one can have the cooked flesh, why have the raw? But I think if you are anaemic, as Tom is, there is a glory in blood. Being fairly normal myself I am soon ready for the classics again. I may revise this later. I do not compromise my critical sagacity. I plant a stick in the ground to mark page 200.

For my own part I am laboriously dredging my mind for *Mrs. Dalloway* and bringing up light buckets. I don't like the feeling. I'm writing too quickly. I must press it together. I wrote 4 thousand words of *Reading* in record time, 10 days; but then it was merely a quick sketch of Pastons, supplied by books. Now I break off, according to my quick change theory, to write *Mrs. D.* (who ushers in a host of others, I begin to perceive). Then I do Chaucer; and finish the first chapter early in September. By that time, I have my Greek beginning perhaps, in my head; and so the future is all pegged out; and when *Jacob* is rejected in America and ignored in England, I shall be philo-sophically driving my plough fields away. They are cutting the corn all over the country, which supplies that metaphor, and perhaps excuses it. But I need no excuses, since I am not writing for the *Lit. Sup*. Shall I ever write for them again?

Tuesday, August 22nd

The way to rock oneself back into writing is this. First gentle exercise in the air. Second the reading of good literature. It is a mistake to think that literature can be produced from the raw. One must get out of life—yes, that's why I disliked so much the irruption of Sydney—one must become externalised; very, very concentrated, all at one point, not having to draw upon the scattered parts of one's character, living in the brain. Sydney comes and I'm Virginia; when I write I'm merely a sensibility. Sometimes I like being Virginia, but only when I'm scattered and various and gregarious. Now, so long as we are here, I'd like to be only a sensibility. By the way, Thackeray is good read-ing, very vivacious, with "touches" as they call them over the way at the Shanks', of astonishing insight.

Monday, August 28th

I am beginning Greek again, and must really make out some plan: today 28th: *Mrs. Dalloway* finished on Saturday 2nd Sept.: Sunday 3rd to Friday 8th; start Chaucer. Chaucer—that chapter, I mean, should be finished by Sept. 22nd. And then? Shall I write the next chapter of *Mrs. D.*—if she is to have a next chap-ter; and shall it be *The Prime Minister?* which will last till the week after we get back—say October 12th. Then I must be ready to start my Greek chapter. So I have from today, 28th, till 12th —which is just over 6 weeks—but I must allow for some interrup-tions. Now what have I to read? Some Homer: one Greek play: some Plato: Zimmern: Sheppard, as textbook: Bentley's Life: if done thoroughly, this will be enough. But which Greek play? and how much Homer, and what Plato? Then there's the an-thology. All to end upon the Odyssey because of the Eliza-bethans. And I must read a little Ibsen to compare with

Euripides—Racine with Sophocles—perhaps Marlowe with
Aeschylus. Sounds very learned; but really might amuse me;
and if it doesn't, no need to go on.

Wednesday, September 6th

My proofs * come every other day and I could depress myself
adequately if I went into that. The thing now reads thin and
pointless; the words scarcely dint the paper; and I expect to be
told I've written a graceful fantasy, without much bearing upon
real life. Can one tell? Anyhow, nature obligingly supplies me
with the illusion that I am about to write something good;
something rich and deep and fluent, and hard as nails, while
bright as diamonds.

I finished *Ulysses* and think it a mis-fire. Genius it has, I
think; but of the inferior water. The book is diffuse. It is brack-
ish. It is pretentious. It is underbred, not only in the obvious
sense, but in the literary sense. A first rate writer, I mean, respects writing too much to be tricky; startling; doing stunts.
I'm reminded all the time of some callow board school boy, full
of wits and powers, but so self-conscious and egotistical that he
loses his head, becomes extravagant, mannered, uproarious, ill
at ease, makes kindly people feel sorry for him and stern ones
merely annoyed; and one hopes he'll grow out of it; but as
Joyce is 40 this scarcely seems likely. I have not read it carefully; and only once; and it is very obscure; so no doubt I have
scamped the virtue of it more than is fair. I feel that myriads
of tiny bullets pepper one and spatter one; but one does not
get one deadly wound straight in the face—as from Tolstoy, for
instance; but it is entirely absurd to compare him with Tolstoy.

Thursday, September 7th

Having written this, L. put into my hands a very intelligent
review of *Ulysses,* in the American *Nation;* which, for the first
time, analyses the meaning; and certainly makes it very much
more impressive than I judged. Still I think there is virtue and
some lasting truth in first impressions; so I don't cancel mine.

* Of *Jacob's Room.*

I must read some of the chapters again. Probably the final beauty of writing is never felt by contemporaries; but they ought, I think, to be bowled over; and this I was not. Then again, I had my back up on purpose; then again I was over stimulated by Tom's praises.

Thursday, September 26th

Wittering. Morgan came on Friday; Tom on Saturday. My talk with Tom deserves writing down, but won't get it for the light is fading; and we cannot write talk down either, as was agreed at Charleston the other day. There was a good deal of talk about *Ulysses*. Tom said, "He is a purely literary writer. He is founded upon Walter Pater with a dash of Newman." I said he was virile—a he-goat; but didn't expect Tom to agree. Tom did though; and said he left out many things that were important. The book would be a landmark, because it destroyed the whole of the nineteenth century. It left Joyce himself with nothing to write another book on. It showed up the futility of all the English styles. He thought some of the writing beautiful. But there was no "great conception"; that was not Joyce's intention. He thought that Joyce did completely what he meant to do. But he did not think that he gave a new insight into human nature—said nothing new like Tolstoy. Bloom told one nothing. Indeed, he said, this new method of giving the psychology proves to my mind that it doesn't work. It doesn't tell as much as some casual glance from outside often tells. I said I had found *Pendennis* more illuminating in this way. (The horses are now cropping near my window; the little owl calling, and so I write nonsense.) So we go on to S. Sitwell, who merely explores his sensibility—one of the deadly crimes as Tom thinks: to Dostoievsky—the ruin of English literature, we agreed; Singe a fake; present state disastrous, because the form don't fit; to his mind not even promising well; he said that one must now be a very first rate poet to be a poet at all: When there were great poets, the little ones caught some of the glow, and were not worthless. Now there's no great poet. When was the last? I asked, and he said none that interested him since the time of Johnson. Browning he said was lazy: they are all lazy he said.

And Macaulay spoilt English prose. We agreed that people are now afraid of the English language. He said it came of being bookish, but not reading books enough. One should read all styles thoroughly. He thought D. H. Lawrence came off occasionally, especially in *Aaron's Rod,* the last book; had great moments; but was a most incompetent writer. He could cling tight to his conviction though. (Light now fails—7:10 after a bad rainy day.)

Wednesday, October 4th

I am a little uppish, though, and self assertive, because Brace wrote to me yesterday, "We think *Jacob's Room* an extraordinarily distinguished and beautiful work. You have, of course, your own method, and it is not easy to foretell how many readers it will have; surely it will have enthusiastic ones, and we delight in publishing it," or words to that effect. As this is my first testimony from an impartial person I am pleased. For one thing it must make *some* impression, as a whole; and cannot be wholly frigid fireworks. We think of publishing on October 27th. I daresay Duckworth is a little cross with me. I snuff my freedom. It is I think true, soberly and not artificially for the public, that I shall go on unconcernedly whatever people say. At last, I like reading my own writing. It seems to me to fit me closer than it did before. I have done my task here better than I expected. *Mrs. Dalloway* and the Chaucer chapter are finished: I have read 5 books of the Odyssey; *Ulysses;* and now begin Proust. I also read Chaucer and the Pastons. So evidently my plan of the two books running side by side is practicable and certainly I enjoy my reading with a purpose. I am committed to only one *Supt.* article—on essays—and that at my own time; so I am free. I shall read Greek now steadily and begin *The Prime Minister* on Friday morning. I shall read the Trilogy and some Sophocles and Euripides and a Plato dialogue: also the lives of Bentley and Jebb. At forty I am beginning to learn the mechanism of my own brain—how to get the greatest amount of pleasure and work out of it. The secret is I think always so to contrive that work is pleasant.

Saturday, October 14th

I have had two letters, from Lytton and Carrington, about *Jacob's Room,* and written I don't know how many envelopes; and here we are on the verge of publication. I must sit for my portrait to *John o' London's* on Monday. Richmond writes to ask that date of publication may be put ahead, so that they may notice it on Thursday. My sensations? they remain calm. Yet how could Lytton have praised me more highly? prophesies immortality for it as poetry; is afraid of my romance; but the beauty of the writing, etc. Lytton praises me too highly for it to give me exquisite pleasure; or perhaps that nerve grows dulled. I want to be through the splash and swimming in calm water again. I want to be writing unobserved. *Mrs. Dalloway* has branched into a book; and I adumbrate here a study of insanity and suicide; the world seen by the sane and the insane side by side—something like that. Septimus Smith? is that a good name? and to be more close to the fact than *Jacob:* but I think *Jacob* was a necessary step, for me, in working free. And now I must use this benignant page for making out a scheme of work.

I must get on with my reading for the Greek chapter. I shall finish *The Prime Minister* in another week—say 21st. Then I must be ready to start my Essay article for *The Times:* say on the 23rd. That will take say till 2nd November. Therefore I must now concentrate on Essays: with some Aeschylus, and I think begin Zimmern, making rather a hasty end of Bentley, who is not really much to my purpose. I think that clears the matter up—though *how* to read Aeschylus I don't quite know: quickly, is my desire, but that, I see, is an illusion.

As for my views about the success of *Jacob,* what are they? I think we shall sell 500; it will then go slowly and reach 800 by June. It will be highly praised in some places for "beauty"; will be crabbed by people who want human character. The only review I am anxious about is the one in the *Supt:* not that it will be the most intelligent, but it will be the most read and I can't bear people to see me clowned in public. The *W.G.**

* *Westminster Gazette.*

will be hostile; so, very likely, the *Nation*. But I am perfectly serious in saying that nothing budges me from my determination to go on, or alters my pleasure; so whatever happens, though the surface may be agitated, the centre is secure.

Tuesday, October 17th

As this is to be a chart of my progress I enter hastily here: one, a letter from Desmond who is halfway through, says "You have never written so well . . . I marvel and am puzzled"—or words to that effect: two, Bunny * rings up enthusiastic; says it is superb, far my best, has great vitality and importance: also he takes 36 copies, and says people already "clamour." This is not confirmed by the bookshops, visited by Ralph. I have sold under 50 today; but the libraries remain and Simpkin Marshall.

Sunday, October 29th

Miss Mary Butts being gone, and my head too stupid for reading, I may as well write here, for my amusement later perhaps. I mean I'm too riddled with talk and harassed with the usual worry of people who like and people who don't like *J.R.* to concentrate. There was *The Times* review on Thursday—long, a little tepid, I think—saying that one can't make characters in this way; flattering enough. Of course, I had a letter from Morgan in the opposite sense—the letter I've liked best of all. We have sold 650, I think; and have ordered a second edition. My sensations? as usual—mixed. I shall never write a book that is an entire success. This time the reviews are against me and the private people enthusiastic. Either I am a great writer or a nincompoop. "An elderly sensualist," the *Daily News* calls me. *Pall Mall* passes me over as negligible. I expect to be neglected and sneered at. And what will be the fate of our second thousand then? So far of course the success is much more than we expected. I think I am better pleased so far than I have ever been. Morgan, Lytton, Bunny, Violet, Logan,† Philip, ‡ have all written enthusiastically. But I want to be quit

---

* David Garnett.   † Logan Pearsall Smith.   ‡ Philip Morrell.

of all this. It hangs about me like Mary Butts' scent. I don't want to be totting up compliments, and comparing reviews. I want to think out *Mrs. Dalloway*. I want to foresee this book better than the others and get the utmost out of it. I expect I could have screwed *Jacob* up tighter, if I had foreseen; but I had to make my path as I went.

1923

Monday, June 4th

I'm over peevish in private, partly in order to assert myself.
I am a great deal interested suddenly in my book. I want to
bring in the despicableness of people like Ott.* I want to give
the slipperiness of the soul. I have been too tolerant often. The
truth is people scarcely care for each other. They have this
insane instinct for life. But they never become attached to anything outside themselves. Puff † said he loved his family and
had nothing whatever to knock over. He disliked cold indecency. So did Lord David. This must be a phrase in their set.
Puff said—I don't quite know what. I walked round the vegetable garden with him, passing Lytton flirting on a green seat;
and round the field with Sackville West, who said he was better,
and was writing a better novel, and round the lake with Menas-
seh (?) an Egyptian Jew, who said he liked his family and they
were mad and talked like books; and he said that they quoted
my writings (the Oxford youth) and wanted me to go and speak;
and then there was Mrs. Asquith. I was impressed. She is stone
white; with the brown veiled eyes of an aged falcon; and in
them more depth and scrutiny than I expected; a character,
with her friendliness and ease and decision. Oh if we could have
had Shelley's poems; and not Shelley the man! she said. Shelley
was quite intolerable, she pronounced; she is a rigid frigid puritan; and in spite of spending thousands on dress. She rides life,
if you like; and has picked up a thing or two, which I should
like to plunder and never shall. She led Lytton off and plucked
his arm, and hurried—and thought "people" pursued her; yet
was very affable with "people" when she had to be, and sat on

* Lady Ottoline Morrell. What follows describes a week-end at Garsington
where she and Philip Morrell lived.
† Anthony Asquith.

54

the window sill talking to a black shabby embroideress, to whom Ott. is being kind. That's one of her horrors—she's always being kind in order to say to herself at night, then Ottoline invites the poor little embroideress to her party and so to round off her own picture of herself. To sneer like this has a physical discomfort in it. She told me I looked wonderfully well, which I disliked. Why? I wonder. Because I had had a headache perhaps, partly. But to be well and use strength to get more out of life is, surely, the greatest fun in the world. What I dislike is feeling that I'm always taking care, or being taken care of. Never mind—work, work. Lytton says we have still 20 years before us. Mrs. Asquith said she loved Scott.

Wednesday, June 13th

There was Lady Colefax in her hat with the green ribbons. Did I say that I lunched with her last week? That was Derby Day and it rained, and all the light was brown and cold and she went on talking, talking, in consecutive sentences like the shavings that come from planes, artificial, but unbroken. It was not a successful party, Clive and Lytton and me. For Clive's back; and he dined here with Leo Myers the other night; and then I went to Golders Green and sat with Mary Sheepshanks in her garden and beat up the waters of talk, as I do so courageously, so that life mayn't be wasted. The fresh breeze went brushing all the thick hedges which divide the gardens. Somehow, extraordinary emotions possessed me. I forget now what. Often now I have to control my excitement—as if I were pushing through a screen; or as if something beat fiercely close to me. What this portends I don't know. It is a general sense of the poetry of existence that overcomes me. Often it is connected with the sea and St. Ives. Going to 46 continues to excite. The sight of two coffins in the Underground luggage office I daresay constricts all my feelings. I have the sense of the flight of time; and this shores up my emotions.

Tuesday, June 19th

I took up this book with a kind of idea that I might say something about my writing—which was prompted by glancing

at what K. M. said about her writing in *The Dove's Nest.* But
I only glanced. She said a good deal about feeling things deeply:
also about being pure, which I won't criticise, though of course
I very well could. But now what do I feel about *my* writing?—
this book, that is, *The Hours,** if that's its name? One must
write from deep feeling, said Dostoievsky. And do I? Or do I
fabricate with words, loving them as I do? No, I think not. In
this book I have almost too many ideas. I want to give life and
death, sanity and insanity; I want to criticise the social system,
and to show it at work, at its most intense. But here I may be
posing. I heard from Ka † this morning that she doesn't like
In the Orchard. At once I feel refreshed. I become anonymous,
a person who writes for the love of it. She takes away the motive
of praise, and lets me feel that without any praise I should be
content to go on. This is what Duncan said of his painting the
other night. I feel as if I slipped off all my ball dresses and stood
naked—which as I remember was a very pleasant thing to do.
But to go on. Am I writing *The Hours* from deep emotion? Of
course the mad part tries me so much, makes my mind squirt
so badly that I can hardly face spending the next weeks at it.
It's a question though of these characters. People, like Arnold
Bennett, say I can't create, or didn't in *Jacob's Room,* characters that survive. My answer is—but I leave that to the *Nation:*
it's only the old argument that character is dissipated into
shreds now; the old post-Dostoievsky argument. I daresay it's
true, however, that I haven't that "reality" gift. I insubstantise,
wilfully to some extent, distrusting reality—its cheapness. But
to get further. Have I the power of conveying the true reality?
Or do I write essays about myself? Answer these questions as I
may, in the uncomplimentary sense, and still there remains
this excitement. To get to the bones, now I'm writing fiction
again I feel my force glow straight from me at its fullest. After
a dose of criticism I feel that I'm writing sideways, using only
an angle of my mind. This is justification; for free use of the
faculties means happiness. I'm better company, more of a hu-

* Subsequently this title was altered to *Mrs. Dalloway.*
† Mrs. Arnold-Forster.

man being. Nevertheless, I think it most important in this book to go for the central things. Even though they don't submit, as they should, however, to beautification in language. No, I don't nail my crest to the Murrys, who work in my flesh after the manner of the jigger insect. It's annoying, indeed degrading, to have these bitternesses. Still, think of the eighteenth century. But then they were overt, not covert, as now.

I foresee, to return to *The Hours*, that this is going to be the devil of a struggle. The design is so queer and so masterful. I'm always having to wrench my substance to fit it. The design is certainly original and interests me hugely. I should like to write away and away at it, very quick and fierce. Needless to say, I can't. In three weeks from today, I shall be dried up.

Friday, August 17th

The question I want to debate here is the question of my essays: and how to make them into a book. The brilliant idea has just come to me of embedding them in Otway conversation. The main advantage would be that I could then comment and add what I had had to leave out, or failed to get in, e.g. the one on George Eliot certainly needs an epilogue. Also to have a setting for each would "make a book"; and the collection of articles is in my view an inartistic method. But then this might be too artistic; it might run away with me; it will take time. Nevertheless I should very much enjoy it. I should graze nearer my own individuality. I should mitigate the pomposity and sweep in all sorts of trifles. I think I should feel more at my ease. So I think a trial should be made. The first thing to do is to get ready a certain number of essays. There could be an introductory chapter. A family which reads the papers. The thing to do would be to envelop each essay in its own atmosphere. To get them into a current of life, and so to shape the book; to get a stress upon some main line—but what the line is to be, I can only see by reading them through. No doubt fiction is the prevailing theme. Anyhow the book should end with modern literature.

6	Jane Austen	*In order of time*
5	Addison	
14	Conrad	Montaigne
15	How it strikes a	Evelyn
	contemporary	Defoe
11	The Russians	Sheridan
4	Evelyn	Sterne
7	George Eliot	Addison
13	Modern Essays	Jane Austen
10	Henry James	Charlotte Brontë
	Re-reading novels	George Eliot
8	Charlotte Brontë	The Russians
2	Defoe	The Americans
12	Modern Novels	Thoreau
	Greeks	Emerson
9	Thoreau	Henry James
	Emerson	Modern Fiction
3	Sheridan?	On re-reading novels
2	Sterne?	Essays
1*a*	Old Memoirs	How it strikes a
		contemporary

These are, roughly, the headings.

Wednesday, August 29th

I've been battling for ever so long with *The Hours*, which is proving one of my most tantalising and refractory of books. Parts are so bad, parts so good; I'm much interested; can't stop making it up yet—yet. What is the matter with it? But I want to freshen myself, not deaden myself, so will say no more. Only I must note this odd symptom; a conviction that I shall go on, see it through, because it interests me to write it.

Thursday, August 30th

I was called, I think, to cut wood; we have to shape logs for the stove, for we sit in the lodge every night and my goodness, the wind! Last night we looked at the meadow trees, flinging about, and such a weight of leaves that every brandish seems the end. Only a strewing of leaves from the lime tree, though, this morning. I read such a white dimity rice pudding chapter of Mrs. Gaskell at midnight in the gale *Wives and Daughters,* I think: it must be better than old wives' tale all the same. You see, I'm thinking furiously about Reading and Writing. I have no time to describe my plans. I should say a good deal about *The Hours* and my discovery: how I dig out beautiful caves behind my characters: I think that gives exactly what I want; humanity, humour, depth. The idea is that the caves shall connect and each comes to daylight at the present moment. Dinner!

Wednesday, September 5th

And I'm slightly dashed by the reception of my Conrad conversation, which has been purely negative. No one has mentioned it. I don't think M. or B. quite approved. Never mind; to be dashed is always the most bracing treatment for me. A cold douche should be taken (and generally is) before beginning a book. It invigorates; makes one say "Oh all right. I write to please myself" and so go ahead. It also has the effect of making me more definite and outspoken in my style, which I imagine all to the good. At any rate, I began for the fifth but last time, I swear, what is now to be called *The Common Reader;* and did the first page quite moderately well this morning. After all this stew, it's odd how, as soon as I begin, a new aspect, never all this two or three years thought of, at once becomes clear; and gives the whole bundle a new proportion. To curtail, I shall really investigate literature with a view to answering certain questions about ourselves. Characters are to be merely views: personality must be avoided at all costs. I'm sure my Conrad adventure taught me this. Directly you specify hair, age etc. something frivolous, or irrelevant gets into the book, Dinner!

Monday, October 15th

I am now in the thick of the mad scene in Regent's Park. I find I write it by clinging as tight to fact as I can, and write perhaps 50 words a morning. This I must rewrite some day. I think the design is more remarkable than in any of my books.

I daresay I shan't be able to carry it out. I am stuffed with ideas for it. I feel I can use up everything I've ever thought. Certainly, I'm less coerced than I've yet been. The doubtful point is, I think, the character of Mrs. Dalloway. It may be too stiff, too glittering and tinselly. But then I can bring innumerable other characters to her support. I wrote the 100th page today. Of course, I've only been feeling my way into it—up till last August anyhow. It took me a year's groping to discover what I call my tunnelling process, by which I tell the past by instalments, as I have need of it. This is my prime discovery so far; and the fact that I've been so long finding it proves, I think, how false Percy Lubbock's doctrine is—that you can do this sort of thing consciously. One feels about in a state of misery— indeed I made up my mind one night to abandon the book— and then one touches the hidden spring. But lor' love me! I've not re-read my great discovery, and it may be nothing important whatsoever. Never mind. I own I have my hopes for this book. I am going on writing it now till, honestly, I can't write another line. Journalism, everything, is to give way to it.

1924

Monday, May 26th

London is enchanting. I step out upon a tawny coloured magic carpet, it seems, and get carried into beauty without raising a finger. The nights are amazing, with all the white porticos and broad silent avenues. And people pop in and out, lightly, divertingly like rabbits; and I look down Southampton Row, wet as a seal's back or red and yellow with sunshine, and watch the omnibuses going and coming and hear the old crazy organs. One of these days I will write about London, and how it takes up the private life and carries it on, without any effort. Faces passing lift up my mind; prevent it from settling, as it does in the stillness at Rodmell.

But my mind is full of *The Hours*. I am now saying that I will write at it for 4 months, June, July, August and September, and then it will be done, and I shall put it away for three months, during which I shall finish my essays; and then that will be—October, November, December—January; and I shall revise it January February March April; and in April my essays will come out, and in May my novel. Such is my programme. It is reeling off my mind fast, and free now; as ever since the crisis of August last, which I count the beginning of it, it has gone quick, being much interrupted though. It is becoming more analytical and human I think; less lyrical; but I feel as if I had loosed the bonds pretty completely and could pour everything in. If so—good. Reading it remains. I aim at 80,000 words this time. And I like London for writing it, partly because, as I say, life upholds one; and with my squirrel cage mind it's a great thing to be stopped circling. Then to see human beings freely and quickly is an infinite gain to me. And I can dart in and out and refresh my stagnancy.

Here we are at Rodmell, and I with 20 minutes to fill in before dinner. A feeling of depression is on me, as if we were old and near the end of all things. It must be the change from London and incessant occupation. Then, being at a low ebb with my book—the death of Septimus—and I begin to count myself a failure. Now the point of the Press is that it entirely prevents brooding; and gives me something solid to fall back on. Anyhow, if I can't write, I can make other people write; I can build up a business. The country is like a convent. The soul swims to the top. Julian * has just been and gone, a tall young man who, inveterately believing myself to be young as I do, seems to me like a younger brother; anyhow we sit and chatter, as easily as can be. It's all so much the same—his school continues Thoby's school. He tells me about boys and masters as Thoby used to. It interests me just in the same way. He's a sensitive, very quick witted, rather combative boy; full of Wells, and discoveries and the future of the world. And, being of my own blood, easily understood. Going to be very tall, and go to the Bar, I daresay. Nevertheless, in spite of the grumbling with which this began, honestly I don't feel old; and it's a question of getting up my steam again in writing. If only I could get into my vein and work it thoroughly, deeply, easily, instead of hacking at this miserable 200 words a day. And then, as the manuscript grows I have the old fear of it. I shall read it and find it pale. I shall prove the truth of Murry's saying, that there's no way of going on after *Jacob's Room*. Yet if this book proves anything, it proves that I can only write along those lines, and shall never desert them, but explore further and further and shall, heaven be praised, never bore myself an instant. But this slight depression—what is it? I think I could cure it by crossing the channel and writing nothing for a week. I want to see something going on busily without help from me: a French market town for example. Indeed, have I the energy, I'll cross to Dieppe; or compromise by exploring Sussex on a motor bus. August ought to be hot. Deluges descend. We

* Julian Bell, son of Vanessa.

sheltered under a haystack today. But oh the delicacy and complexity of the soul—for haven't I begun to tap her and listen to her breathing after all? A change of house makes me oscillate for days. And that's life; that's wholesome. Never to quiver is the lot of Mr. Allinson, Mrs. Hawkesford and Jack Squire. In two or three days, acclimatised, started, reading and writing, no more of this will exist. And if we didn't live venturously, plucking the wild goat by the beard, and trembling over precipices, we should never be depressed, I've no doubt; but already should be faded, fatalistic and aged.

Sunday, August 3rd

But it's a question of work. I am already a good deal pulled together by sticking at my books: my 250 words at fiction first, and then a systematic beginning, I daresay the 80th, upon *The Common Reader,* who might be finished in a flash I think, did I see the chance to flash and have done with it. But there's a lot of work in these things. It strikes me, I must now read *Pilgrim's Progress:* Mrs. Hutchinson. And should I demolish Richardson? whom I've never read. Yes, I'll run through the rain into the house and see if *Clarissa* is there. But that's a block out of my day and a long long novel. Then I must read the *Medea.* I must read a little translated Plato.

Friday, August 15th

Into all these calculations, broke the death of Conrad, followed by a wire from the *Lit. Sup.* earnestly asking me kindly to do a leader on him, which flattered and loyal, but grudgingly, I did; and it's out; and that number of the *Lit. Sup.* corrupted for me (for I can't, and never shall be able to, read my own writings. Moreover, now little Walkley's on the war path again I expect a bite next Wednesday). Yet I have never never worked so hard. For, having to do a leader in five days, I made hay after tea—and couldn't distinguish tea hay from morning hay either. So doesn't this give me two extra hours for critical works anyhow (as Logan calls them)? So I'm trying it—my fiction before lunch and then essays after tea. For I see that *Mrs. Dalloway* is going to stretch beyond October. In my forecasts

I always forget some most important intervening scenes: I think I can go straight at the grand party and so end; forgetting Septimus, which is a very intense and ticklish business, and jumping Peter Walsh eating his dinner, which may be some obstacle too. But I like going from one lighted room to another, such is my brain to me; lighted rooms; and the walks in the fields are corridors; and now today I'm lying thinking. By the way, why is poetry wholly an elderly taste? When I was 20, in spite of Thoby who used to be so pressing and exacting, I could not for the life of me read Shakespeare for pleasure; now it lights me as I walk to think I have two acts of *King John* tonight, and shall next read *Richard II*. It is poetry that I want now—long poems. Indeed I'm thinking of reading the Seasons. I want the concentration and the romance, and the words all glued together, fused, glowing; have no time to waste any more on prose. Yet this must be the very opposite to what people say. When I was 20 I liked eighteenth century prose; I liked Hakluyt, Merimée. I read masses of Carlyle, Scott's life and letters, Gibbon, all sorts of two volume biographies, and Shelley. Now it's poetry I want, so I repent like a tipsy sailor in front of a public house. . . . I don't often trouble now to describe cornfields and groups of harvesting women in loose blues and reds, and little staring yellow frocked girls. But that's not my eyes' fault: coming back the other evening from Charleston, again all my nerves stood upright, flushed, electrified (what's the word?) with the sheer beauty—beauty astounding and superabounding. So that one almost resents it, not being capable of catching it all and holding it all at the moment. One's progress through life is made immensely interesting by trying to grasp all these developments as one passes. I feel as if I were putting out my fingers tentatively on (here is Leonard, who has ordered me a trap in which to drive Dadie * to Tilton † tomorrow) either side as I grope down a tunnel, rough with odds and ends. And I don't describe encounters with herds of Alderneys any more—though this would have been necessary some years ago— how they barked and belled like stags round Grizzle; and how

---

* G. W. Rylands.   † A house near Firle rented by J. M. Keynes.

I waved my stick and stood at bay; and thought of Homer as they came flourishing and trampling towards me; some mimic battle. Grizzle grew more and more insolent and excited and skirmished about yapping. Ajax? That Greek, for all my ignorance, has worked its way into me.

Sunday, September 7th

It is a disgrace that I write nothing, or if I write, write sloppily, using nothing but present participles. I find them very useful in my last lap of *Mrs. D.* There I am now—at last at the party, which is to begin in the kitchen, and climb slowly upstairs. It is to be a most complicated, spirited, solid piece, knitting together everything and ending on three notes, at different stages of the staircase, each saying something to sum up Clarissa. Who shall say these things? Peter, Richard, and Sally Seton perhaps: but I don't want to tie myself down to that yet. Now I do think this might be the best of my endings and come off, perhaps. But I have still to read the first chapters, and confess to dreading the madness rather; and being clever. However, I'm sure I've now got to work with my pick at my seam, if only because my metaphors come free, as they do here. Suppose one can keep the quality of a sketch in a finished and composed work? That is my endeavour. Anyhow, none can help and none can hinder me any more. I've been in for a shower of compliments too from *The Times*, Richmond rather touching me by saying that he gives way to my novel with all the will in the world. I should like him to read my fiction, and always suppose he doesn't.

There I was swimming in the highest ether known to me and thinking I'd finish by Thursday; Lottie suggests to Karin we'd like to have Ann; Karin interprets my polite refusal to her own advantage and comes down herself on Saturday, blowing everything to smithereens. More and more am I solitary; the pain of these upheavals is incalculable; and I can't explain it either. . . . Here I am with my wrecked week—for how serene and lovely like a Lapland night was our last week together—feeling that I ought to go in and be a good aunt—which I'm not by nature; ought to ask Daisy what she wants; and by

rights I fill these moments full of Mrs. Dalloway's party for
tomorrow's writing. The only solution is to stay on alone over
Thursday and try my luck. A bad night (K.'s doing again) may
partly account. But how entirely I live in my imagination; how
completely depend upon spurts of thought, coming as I walk,
as I sit; things churning up in my mind and so making a perpetual pageant, which is to be my happiness. This brew can't
sort with nondescript péople. These wails must now have
ending, partly because I cannot see, and my hand shakes, having carried my bag from Lewes, where I sat on the Castle top,
where an old man was brushing leaves, and told me how to cure
lumbago; you tie a skein of silk round you; the silk costs three-
pence. I saw British canoes, and the oldest plough in Sussex
1750 found at Rodmell, and a suit of armour said to have been
worn at Seringapatam. All this I should like to write about, I
think. And of course children are wonderful and charming
creatures. I've had Ann in talking about the white seal and
wanting me to read to her. And how Karin manages to be so
aloof I can't think. There's a quality in their minds to me
very adorable; to be alone with them, and see them day to
day would be an extraordinary experience. They have what no
grown up has—that directness—chatter, chatter, chatter, on Ann
goes, in a kind of world of her own, with its seals and dogs;
happy because she's going to have cocoa tonight, and go blackberrying tomorrow. The walls of her mind all hung round with
such bright vivid things, and she doesn't see what we see.

Friday, October 17th
It is disgraceful. I did run upstairs thinking I'd make time
to enter that astounding fact—the last words of the last page of
Mrs. Dalloway, but was interrupted. Anyhow, I did them a
week ago yesterday. "For there she was," and I felt glad to be
quit of it, for it has been a strain the last weeks, yet fresher in
the head; with less I mean of the usual feeling that I've shaved
through and just kept my feet on the tight rope. I feel indeed
rather more fully relieved of my meaning than usual—whether
this will stand when I re-read is doubtful. But in some ways

this book is a feat; finished without break from illness, which is an exception; and written really in one year; and finally, written from the end of March to the 8th October without more than a few days' break for writing journalism. So it may differ from the others. Anyhow, I feel that I have exorcised the spell which Murry and others said I had laid myself under after *Jacob's Room*. The only difficulty is to hold myself back from writing others. My cul de sac, as they called it, stretches so far and shows such vistas. I see already the Old Man.

It strikes me that in this book I practise writing; do my scales; yes and work at certain effects. I daresay I practised *Jacob* here; and *Mrs. D.* and shall invent my next book here; for here I write merely in the spirit—great fun it is too, and old V. of 1940 will see something in it too. She will be a woman who can see, old V., everything—more than I can, I think. But I'm tired now.

Saturday, November 1st

I must make some notes of work; for now I must buckle to. The question is how to get the two books done. I am going to skate rapidly over *Mrs. D.*, but it will take time. No: I cannot say anything much to the point, for what I must do is to experiment next week; how much revision is needed, and how much time it takes. I am very set on getting my essays out before my novel. Yesterday I had tea in Mary's room and saw the red lighted tugs go past and heard the swish of the river: Mary in black with lotus leaves round her neck. If one could be friendly with women, what a pleasure—the relationship so secret and private compared with relations with men. Why not write about it? Truthfully? As I think, the diary writing has greatly helped my style; loosened the ligatures.

Tuesday, November 18th

What I was going to say was that I think writing must be formal. The art must be respected. This struck me reading some of my notes here, for if one lets the mind run loose it becomes egotistic; personal, which I detest. At the same time the irregular fire must be there; and perhaps to loose it one must begin by being chaotic, but not appear in public like that. I am driving my way through the mad chapters of *Mrs. D.* My wonder is whether the book would have been better without them. But this is an afterthought, consequent upon learning how to deal with her. Always I think at the end, I see how the whole ought to have been written.

Saturday, December 13th

I am now galloping over *Mrs. Dalloway,* re-typing it entirely from the start, which is more or less what I did with the *V.O.*: a good method, I believe, as thus one works with a wet brush over the whole, and joins parts separately composed and gone dry. Really and honestly I think it the most satisfactory of my novels (but have not read it cold-bloodedly yet). The reviewers will say that it is disjointed because of the mad scenes not connecting with the Dalloway scenes. And I suppose there is some superficial glittery writing. But is it "unreal"? Is it mere accomplishment? I think not. And as I think I said before, it seems to leave me plunged deep in the richest strata of my mind. I can write and write and write now: the happiest feeling in the world.

Monday, December 21st

Really it is a disgrace—the number of blank pages in this book. The effect of London on diaries is decidedly bad. This is I fancy the leanest of them all, and I doubt that I can take it to Rodmell, or if I did, whether I could add much. Indeed it has been an eventful year, as I prophesied; and the dreamer of January 3rd has dreamt much of her dream true; here we are in London, with Nelly alone, Dadie gone it is true, but Angus to replace him. What emerges is that changing houses is not so cataclysmic as I thought; after all, one doesn't change body or brain. Still I am absorbed in "my writing," putting on a spurt to have *Mrs. D.* copied for L. to read at Rodmell; and then in I dart to deliver the final blows to *The Common Reader,* and then—and then I shall be free. Free at least to write out one or two more stories which have accumulated. I am less and less sure that they *are* stories, or what they are. Only I do feel fairly sure that I am grazing as near as I can to my own ideas, and getting a tolerable shape for them. I think there is less and less wastage. But I have my ups and downs.

1925

Wednesday, January 6th

Rodmell was all gale and flood; these words are exact. The river overflowed. We had 7 days' rain out of 10. Often I could not face a walk. L. pruned, which needed heroic courage. My heroism was purely literary. I revised *Mrs. D.*, the chillest part of the whole business of writing, the most depressing—exacting. The worst part is at the beginning (as usual) where the aeroplane has it all to itself for some pages and it wears thin. L. read it; thinks it my best—but then has he not *got* to think so? Still I agree. He thinks it has more continuity than *J.'s R.*, but is difficult owing to the lack of connection, visible, between the two themes. Anyhow it is sent off to Clark's, and proofs will come next week. This is for Harcourt Brace, who has accepted without seeing and raised me to 15 p.c.

Tuesday, April 8th

I am under the impression of the moment, which is the complex one of coming back home from the South of France to this wide dim peaceful privacy—London (so it seemed last night) which is shot with the accident I saw this morning—a woman crying oh, oh, oh, faintly, pinned against the railings with a motor car on top of her. All day I have heard that voice. I did not go to her help; but then every baker and flower seller did that. A great sense of the brutality and wildness of the world remains with me—there was this woman in brown walking along the pavement—suddenly a red film car turns a somersault, lands on top of her and one hears this oh, oh, oh. I was on my way to see Nessa's new house and met Duncan in the square, but as he had seen nothing he could not in the least feel what I felt, or Nessa either, though she made some effort to connect it with Angelica's accident last spring. But I assured her it was only a passing brown woman; and so we went over the house composedly enough.

Since I wrote, which is these last months, Jacques Raverat has died; after longing to die; and he sent me a letter about *Mrs. Dalloway* which gave me one of the happiest days of my life. I wonder if this time I have achieved something? Well, nothing anyhow compared with Proust, in whom I am embedded now. The thing about Proust is his combination of the utmost sensibility with the utmost tenacity. He searches out these butterfly shades to the last grain. He is as tough as catgut and as evanescent as a butterfly's bloom. And he will, I suppose, both influence me and make me out of temper with every sentence of my own. Jacques died, as I say; and at once the siege of emotions began. I got the news with a party here—Clive, Bee How, Julia Strachey, Dadie. Nevertheless, I do not any longer feel inclined to doff the cap to death. I like to go out of the room talking, with an unfinished casual sentence on my lips. That is the effect it had on me—no leavetakings, no submission, but someone stepping out into the darkness. For her though the nightmare was terrific. All I can do now is to keep natural with her, which is I believe a matter of considerable importance. More and more do I repeat my own version of Montaigne—"It's life that matters."

I am waiting to see what form of itself Cassis will finally cast up in my mind. There are the rocks. We used to go out after breakfast and sit on the rocks, with the sun on us. L. used to sit without a hat, writing on his knee. One morning he found a sea urchin—they are red with spikes which quiver slightly. Then we would go and walk in the afternoon, right up over the hill, into the woods, where one day we heard the motor cars and discovered the road to La Ciotat just beneath. It was stony, steep and very hot. We heard a great chattering birdlike noise once and I bethought me of the frogs. The ragged red tulips were out in the fields; all the fields were little angular shelves cut out of the hill and ruled and ribbed with vines; and all red, and rosy and purple here and there with the spray of some

fruit tree in bud. Here and there was an angular white or
yellow or blue washed house, with all its shutters tightly closed,
and flat paths round it, and once rows of stocks; an incom-
parable cleanness and definiteness everywhere. At La Ciotat
great orange ships rose up out of the blue water of the little
bay. All these bays are very circular and fringed with the pale
coloured plaster houses, very tall, shuttered, patched and
peeled, now with a pot and tufts of green on them, now with
clothes, drying; now an old old woman looking. On the hill,
which is stony as a desert, the nets were drying; and then in
the streets children and girls gossiped and meandered all in pale
bright shawls and cotton frocks, while the men picked up the
earth of the main square to make a paved court of it. The Hotel
Cendrillon is a white house with red tiled floors, capable of
housing perhaps 8 people. And then the whole hotel atmosphere provided me with many ideas: oh so cold, indifferent,
superficially polite, and exhibiting such odd relationships; as if
human nature were now reduced to a kind of code, which it
has devised to meet these emergencies, where people who do
not know each other meet and claim their rights as members
of the same tribe. As a matter of fact, we got into touch all
round; but our depths were not invaded. But L. and I were
too too happy, as they say; if it were now to die etc. Nobody
shall say of me that I have not known perfect happiness, but
few could put their finger on the moment, or say what made it.
Even I myself, stirring occasionally in the pool of content,
could only say But this is all I want; could not think of anything better; and had only my half superstitious feeling at the
Gods who must when they have created happiness, grudge it.
Not if you get it in unexpected ways, though.

Sunday, April 19th

It is now after dinner, our first summertime night, and the
mood for writing has left me, only just brushed me and left
me. I have not achieved my sacred half hour yet. But think—
in time to come I would rather read something here than reflect that I did polish off Mr. Ring Lardner successfully. I'm

out to make £300 this summer by writing and build a bath and hot water range at Rodmell. But hush, hush—my books tremble on the verge of coming out and my future is uncertain. As for forecasts—it's just on the cards *Mrs. Dalloway* is a success (Harcourt thinks it "wonderful") and sells 2,000. I don't expect it. I expect a slow silent increase of fame, such as has come about, rather miraculously, since *J.'s R.* was published. My value mounting steadily as a journalist, though scarcely a copy sold. And I am not very nervous—rather; and I want as usual to dig deep down into my new stories without having a looking glass flashed in my eyes—Todd, to wit; Colefax to wit et cetera.

Monday, April 20th

One thing, in considering my state of mind now, seems to me beyond dispute; that I have, at last, bored down into my oil well, and can't scribble fast enough to bring it all to the surface. I have now at least 6 stories welling up in me, and feel, at last, that I can coin all my thoughts into words. Not but what an infinite number of problems remain; but I have never felt this rush and urgency before. I believe I can write much more quickly; if writing it is—this dash at the paper of a phrase, and then the typing and retyping—trying it over; the actual writing being now like the sweep of a brush; I fill it up afterwards. Now suppose I might become one of the interesting—I will not say great—but interesting novelists? Oddly, for all my vanity, I have not until now had much faith in my novels, or thought them my own expression.

Monday, April 27th

The Common Reader was out on Thursday: this is Monday and so far I have not heard a word about it, private or public; it is as if one tossed a stone into a pond and the waters closed without a ripple. And I am perfectly content, and care less than I have ever cared, and make this note just to remind me next time of the sublime progress of my books. I have been sitting to Vogue, the Becks that is, in their mews, which Mr. Woolner

built as his studio, and perhaps it was there he thought of my
mother, whom he wished to marry, I think. But my present reflection is that people have any number of
Second selves
is what I mean.
states of consciousness: and I should like to
investigate the party consciousness, the frock
consciousness etc. The fashion world at the
Becks—Mrs. Garland was there superintending a display—is
certainly one; where people secrete an envelope which connects
them and protects them from others, like myself, who am outside the envelope, foreign bodies. These states are very difficult
(obviously I grope for words) but I'm always coming back to
it. The party consciousness, for example: Sybil's consciousness. You must not break it. It is something real. You must
keep it up—conspire together. Still I cannot get at what I mean.
Then I meant to dash off Graves before I forget him.

Friday, May 1st
This is a note for future reference, as they say. *The Common
Reader* came out 8 days ago and so far not a single review has
appeared, and nobody has written to me or spoken to me about
it, or in any way acknowledged the fact of its existence; save
Maynard, Lydia, and Duncan. Clive is conspicuously dumb;
Mortimer has flu and can't review it; Nancy saw him reading
it, but reported no opinion; all signs which point to a dull chill
depressing reception; and complete failure. I have just come
through the hoping fearing stage and now see my disappointment floating like an old bottle in my wake and am off on fresh
adventures. Only if the same thing happens to *Dalloway* one
need not be surprised. But I must write to Gwen.

Monday, May 4th
This is the temperature chart of a book. We went to Cambridge, and Goldie said he thought me the finest living critic:
said, in his jerky angular way: "Who wrote that extraordinarily
good article on the Elizabethans two or three months ago in the
Lit. Sup.?" I pointed to my breast. Now there's one sneering
review in *Country Life,* almost inarticulate with feebleness,

trying to say what a Common reader is, and another, says Angus, in the *Star*, laughing at Nessa's cover. So from this I prognosticate a good deal of criticism on the ground that I'm obscure and odd; and some enthusiasm; and a slow sale, and an increased reputation. Oh yes, my reputation increases.

Saturday, May 9th

As for *The Common Reader*, the *Lit. Sup.* had close on two columns sober and sensible praise—neither one thing nor the other—my fate in *The Times*. And Goldie writes that he thinks "this is the best criticism in English—humorous, witty and profound." My fate is to be treated to all extremes and all mediocrities. But I never get an enthusiastic review in the *Lit. Sup.* And it will be the same for *Dalloway*, which now approaches.

Thursday, May 14th

I meant to register more of my books' temperatures. *C.R.* does not sell; but is praised. I was really pleased to open the *Manchester Guardian* this morning and read Mr. Fausset on the Art of V. W.; brilliance combined with integrity; profound as well as eccentric. Now if only *The Times* would speak out thus, but *The Times* mumbles and murmurs like a man sucking pebbles. Did I say that I had nearly two mumbling columns on me there? But the odd thing is this: honestly I am scarcely a shade nervous about *Mrs. D.* Why is this? Really I am a little bored, for the first time, at thinking how much I shall have to talk about it this summer. The truth is that writing is the profound pleasure and being read the superficial. I'm now all on the strain with desire to stop journalism and get on to *To the Lighthouse*. This is going to be fairly short; to have father's character done complete in it; and mother's; and St. Ives; and childhood; and all the usual things I try to put in—life, death, etc. But the centre is father's character, sitting in a boat, reciting We perished, each alone, while he crushes a dying mackerel. However, I must refrain. I must write a few little stories first and let the *Lighthouse* simmer, adding to it between tea and dinner till it is complete for writing out.

Friday, May 15th

Two unfavourable reviews of *Mrs. D.* (*Western Mail* and *Scotsman*); unintelligible, not art etc. and a letter from a young man in Earls Court. "This time you have done it—you have caught life and put it in a book . . ." Please forgive this outburst, but further quotation is unnecessary; and I don't think I should bother to write this if I weren't jangled. What by? The sudden heat, I think, and the racket of life. It is bad for me to see my own photograph.

Wednesday, May 19th

Well, Morgan admires. This is a weight off my mind. Better than *Jacob* he says: was sparing of words; kissed my hand, and on going said he was awfully pleased, very happy (or words to that effect) about it. He thinks—but I won't go into detailed criticism; I shall hear more; and this is only about the style being simpler, more like other people's this time.

Monday, June 1st

Bank holiday, and we are in London. To record my books' fates slightly bores me; but now both are floated, and *Mrs. D.* doing surprisingly well. 1070 already sold. I recorded Morgan's opinion; then Vita was a little doubtful; then Desmond, whom I see frequently about his book, dashed all my praise by saying that Logan thought the *C.R.* well enough, but nothing more. Desmond has an abnormal power for depressing me. He takes the edge off life in some extraordinary way. I love him; but his balance and goodness and humour, all heavenly in themselves, somehow diminish lustre. I think I feel this not only about my work but about life. However, now comes Mrs. Hardy to say that Thomas reads, and hears the *C.R.* read, with "great pleasure." Indeed, save for Logan, and he's a salt-veined American, I have had high praise. Also Tauchnitz asks about them.

Sunday, June 14th

A disgraceful confession—this is Sunday morning and just after ten, and here I am sitting down to write diary and not fiction or reviews, without any excuse, except the state of my mind. After finishing those two books, though, one can't concentrate directly on a new one; and then the letters, the talk, the reviews, all serve to enlarge the pupil of my mind more and more. I can't settle in, contract, and shut myself off. I've written 6 little stories, scrambled them down untidily and have thought out, perhaps too clearly, *To the Lighthouse*. And both books so far are successful. More of *Dalloway* has been sold this month than of *Jacob* in a year. I think it possible we may sell 2,000. The *Common* one is making money this week. And I get treated at great length and solemnity by old gentlemen.

Thursday, June 18th

No, Lytton does not like *Mrs. Dalloway,* and, what is odd, I like him all the better for saying so, and don't much mind. What he says is that there is a discordancy between the ornament (extremely beautiful) and what happens (rather ordinary —or unimportant). This is caused, he thinks, by some discrepancy in Clarissa herself: he thinks she is disagreeable and limited, but that I alternately laugh at her and cover her, very remarkably, with myself. So that I think as a whole, the book does not ring solid; yet, he says, it is a whole; and he says sometimes the writing is of extreme beauty. What can one call it but genius? he said! Coming when, one never can tell. Fuller of genius, he said, than anything I had done. Perhaps, he said, you have not yet mastered your method. You should take something wilder and more fantastic, a framework that admits of anything, like *Tristram Shandy*. But then I should lose touch with emotions, I said. Yes, he agreed, there must be reality for you to start from. Heaven knows how you're to do it. But he thought me at the beginning, not at the end. And he said the *C.R.* was divine, a classic, *Mrs. D* being, I fear, a flawed stone. This is very personal, he said, and old fashioned perhaps; yet I think there is some truth in it, for I remember the night at Rodmell when I decided to give it up, because I found Clarissa in some way tinselly. Then I invented her memories. But I think some distaste for her persisted. Yet, again, that was true to

my feeling for Kitty and one must dislike people in art without its mattering, unless indeed it is true that certain characters
detract from the importance of what happens to them. None
of this hurts me, or depresses me. It's odd that when Clive and
others (several of them) say it is a masterpiece, I am not much
exalted; when Lytton picks holes, I get back into my working
fighting mood, which is natural to me. I
July 20th. Have   don't see myself a success. I like the sense of
sold about 1530.   effort better. The sales collapsed completely
                       for three days; now a little dribble begins
again. I shall be more than pleased if we sell 1500. It's now
1250.

                                              Saturday, June 27th
   A bitter cold day, succeeding a chilly windy night, in which
were lit all the Chinese lanterns of Roger's garden party. And
I do not love my kind. I detest them. I pass them by. I let them
break on me like dirty rain drops. No longer can I summon up
that energy which, when it sees one of these dry little shapes
floating past, or rather stuck on the rock, sweeps round them,
steeps them, infuses them, nerves them, and so finally fills them
and creates them. Once I had a gift for doing this, and a passion,
and it made parties arduous and exciting. So when I wake early
now I luxuriate most in a whole day alone; a day of easy natural
poses, a little printing; slipping tranquilly off into the deep
water of my own thoughts navigating the underworld; and then
replenishing my cistern at night with Swift. I am going to write
about Stella and Swift for Richmond, as a sign of grace, after
sweeping guineas off the *Vogue* counter. The first fruit of the
C.R. (a book too highly praised now) is a request to write for
the *Atlantic Monthly*. So I am getting pushed into criticism. It
is a great standby—this power to make large sums by formulat-
ing views on Stendhal and Swift. (But while I try to write, I
am making up *To the Lighthouse*—the sea is to be heard all
through it. I have an idea that I will invent a new name for
my books to supplant "novel." A new —— by Virginia Woolf.
But what? Elegy?)

Monday, July 20th

Here the door opened and Morgan came in to ask us out to lunch with him at the Etoile, which we did, though we had a nice veal and ham pie at home (this is in the classic style of journalists). It comes of Swift perhaps, the last words of which I have just written, and so fill up time here. I should consider my work list now. I think a little story, perhaps a review, this fortnight; having a superstitious wish to begin *To the Lighthouse* the first day at Monk's House. I now think I shall finish it in the two months there. The word "sentimental" sticks in my gizzard (I'll write it out of me in a story—Ann Watkins of New York is coming on Wednesday to enquire about my stories). But this theme may be sentimental; father and mother and child in the garden; the death; the sail to the Lighthouse. I think, though, that when I begin it I shall enrich it in all sorts of ways; thicken it; give it branches—roots which I do not perceive now. It might contain all characters boiled down; and childhood; and then this impersonal thing, which I'm dared to do by my friends, the flight of time and the consequent break of unity in my design. That passage (I conceive the book in 3 parts. 1. at the drawing room window; 2. seven years passed; 3. the voyage) interests me very much. A new problem like that breaks fresh ground in one's mind; prevents the regular ruts.

What shall I read at Rodmell? I have so many books at the back of my mind. I want to read voraciously and gather material for the *Lives of the Obscure*—which is to tell the whole history of England in one obscure life after another. Proust I should like to finish. Stendhal, and then to skirmish about hither and thither. These 8 weeks at Rodmell always seem capable of holding an infinite amount. Shall we buy the house at Southease? I suppose not.

Thursday, July 30th

I am intolerably sleepy and annulled and so write here. I do want indeed to consider my next book, but I am inclined to wait for a clearer head. The thing is I vacillate between a single

and intense character of father; and a far wider slower book—
Bob T.* telling me that my speed is terrific and distinctive. My
summer's wanderings with the pen have I think shown me one
or two new dodges for catching my flies. I have sat here, like
an improviser with his hands rambling over the piano. The
result is perfectly inconclusive and almost illiterate. I want to
learn greater quiet and force. But if I set myself that task,
don't I run the risk of falling into the flatness of *N. & D.*? Have
I got the power needed if quiet is not to become insipid? These
questions I will leave, for the moment, unanswered. So that
episode is over. But, dear me, I'm too dull to write and must
go and fetch Mr. Dobrée's novel and read it, I think. Yet I have
a thousand things to say. I think I might do something in *To
the Lighthouse,* to split up emotions more completely. I think
I'm working in that direction.

Saturday, September 5th

And why couldn't I see or feel that all this time I was getting a little used up and riding on a flat tyre? So I was, as it
happened; and fell down in a faint at Charleston, in the middle
of Q.'s birthday party; and then have lain about here, in that
odd amphibious life of headache, for a fortnight. This has
rammed a big hole in my 8 weeks which were to be stuffed so
full. Never mind. Arrange whatever pieces come your way.
Never be unseated by the shying of that undependable brute,
life, hag-ridden as she is by my own queer, difficult, nervous
system. Even at 43 I don't know its workings, for I was saying
to myself, all the summer, "I'm quite adamant now. I can go
through a tussle of emotions peaceably that two years ago, even,
would have raked me raw."

I have made a very quick and flourishing attack on *To the
Lighthouse,* all the same—22 pages straight off in less than a
fortnight. I am still crawling and easily enfeebled, but if I
could once get up steam again, I believe I could spin it off
with infinite relish. Think what a labour the first pages of

* R. C. Trevelyan.

Dalloway were! Each word distilled by a relentless clutch on my brain.

Monday, September 13th, perhaps

A disgraceful fact—I am writing this at 10 in the morning in bed in the little room looking into the garden, the sun beaming steady, the vine leaves transparent green, and the leaves of the apple tree so brilliant that, as I had my breakfast, I invented a little story about a man who wrote a poem, I think, comparing them with diamonds, and the spiders' webs, (which glance and disappear astonishingly) with something or other else; which led me to think of Marvell on a country life, so to Herrick and the reflection that much of it was dependent upon the town and gaiety—a reaction. However, I have forgotten the facts. I am writing this partly to test my poor bunch of nerves at the back of my neck—will they hold or give again, as they have done so often?—for I'm amphibious still, in bed and out of it; partly to glut my itch ("glut" an "itch"!) for writing. It is the great solace and scourge.

Tuesday, September 22nd

How my handwriting goes down hill! Another sacrifice to the Hogarth Press. Yet what I owe the Hogarth Press is barely paid by the whole of my handwriting. Haven't I just written to Herbert Fisher refusing to do a book for the Home University Series on Post-Victorian?—knowing that I can write a book, a better book, a book off my own bat, for the Press if I wish! To think of being battened down in the hold of those University Dons fairly makes my blood run cold. Yet I'm the only woman in England free to write what I like. The others must be thinking of series and editors. Yesterday I heard from Harcourt Brace that *Mrs. D.* and *C.R.* are selling 148 and 73 weekly—isn't that a surprising rate for the fourth month? Doesn't it portend a bathroom and a w.c., either here or Southease? I am writing in the watery blue sunset, the repentance of an ill tempered morose day, which vanished, the clouds, I have no doubt, showing gold over the downs, and leaving a soft gold fringe on the top there.

Tuesday, December 7th

I am reading the *Passage to India,* but will not expatiate here, as I must elsewhere. This book for the H.P. I think I will find some theory about fiction; I shall read six novels and start some hares. The one I have in view is about *perspective.* But I do not know. My brain may not last me out. I cannot think closely enough. But I can—if the *C.R.* is a test—beat up ideas and express them now without too much confusion. (By the way, Robert Bridges likes *Mrs. Dalloway;* says no one will read it; but it is beautifully written, and some more, which L., who was told by Morgan, cannot remember.)

I don't think it is a matter of "development" but something to do with prose and poetry, in novels. For instance Defoe at one end; E. Brontë at the other. Reality something they put at different distances. One would have to go into conventions; real life; and so on. It might last me—this theory—but I should have to support it with other things. And death—as I always feel—hurrying near. 43: how many more books? Katie * came here; a sort of framework of discarded beauty hung on a battered shape now. With the firmness of the flesh and the blue of the eye, the formidable manner has gone. I can see her as she was at 22 H.P.G.† 25 years ago; in a little coat and skirt; very splendid; eyes half shut; lovely mocking voice; upright; tremendous; shy. Now she babbles along.

"But no duke ever asked me, my dear Virginia. They called me the Ice Queen. And why did I marry Cromer? I loathed Egypt; I loathed invalids. I've had two very happy times in my life—childhood—not when I grew up, but later, with my boys' club, my cottage and my chow—and now. Now I have all I want. My garden—my dog."

I don't think her son enters in very largely. She is one of these cold eccentric great Englishwomen, enormously enjoying her rank and the eminence it lends her in St. John's Wood,

---

* Lady Cromer.
† 22 Hyde Park Gate where V. W. lived until the age of 17.

and now free to poke into all the dusty holes and corners, dressed like a charwoman, with hands like apes' and fingernails clotted with dirt. She never stops talking. She lacks much body to her. She has almost effused in mist. But I enjoyed it, though I think she has few affections and no very passionate interests. Now, having cried my cry, and the sun coming out, to write a list of Christmas presents.

1926

Tuesday, February 23rd

I am blown like an old flag by my novel. This one is *To the
Lighthouse.* I think it is worth saying for my own interest
that at last, at last, after that battle *Jacob's Room,* that agony—
all agony but the end—*Mrs. Dalloway,* I am now writing as fast
and freely as I have written in the whole of my life; more so—
20 times more so—than any novel yet. I think this is the proof
that I was on the right path; and that what fruit hangs in my
soul is to be reached there. Amusingly, I now invent theories
that fertility and fluency are the things: I used to plead for a
kind of close, terse effort. Anyhow this goes on all the morning:
and I have the devil's own work not to be flogging my brain
all the afternoon. I live entirely in it, and come to the surface
rather obscurely and am often unable to think what to say
when we walk round the Square, which is bad I know. Perhaps
it may be a good sign for the book though. Of course it is largely
known to me: but all my books have been that. It is, I feel that
I can float everything off now; and "everything" is rather a
crowd and weight and confusion in the mind.

Saturday, February 27th

I think I shall initiate a new convention for this book—beginning each day on a new page—my habit in writing serious literature. Certainly I have room to waste a little paper in this
year's book. As for the soul; why did I say I would leave it out?
I forget. And the truth is, one can't write directly about the
soul. Looked at, it vanishes; but look at the ceiling, at Grizzle,*
at the cheaper beasts in the Zoo which are exposed to walkers
in Regent's Park, and the soul slips in. It slipped in this after-

* A dog.

noon. I will write that I said, staring at the bison: answering L. absentmindedly: but what was I going to write?

Mrs. Webb's book has made me think a little what I could say of my own life. I read some of 1923 this morning, being headachy again, and taking a delicious draught of silence. But then there were causes in her life: prayer; principle. None in mine. Great excitability and search after something. Great content—almost always enjoying what I'm at, but with constant change of mood. I don't think I'm ever bored. Sometimes a little stale; but I have a power of recovery—which I have tested; and am now testing for the 50th time. I have to husband my head still very carefully: but then, as I said to Leonard today, I enjoy epicurean ways of society; sipping and then shutting my eyes to taste. I enjoy almost everything. Yet I have some restless searcher in me. Why is there not a discovery in life? Something one can lay hands on and say "This is it"? My depression is a harassed feeling. I'm looking: but that's not it—that's not it. What is it? And shall I die before I find it? Then (as I was walking through Russell Square last night) I see the mountains in the sky: the great clouds; and the moon which is risen over Persia; I have a great and astonishing sense of something there, which is "it." It is not exactly beauty that I mean. It is that the thing is in itself enough: satisfactory; achieved. A sense of my own strangeness, walking on the earth is there too: of the infinite oddity of the human position; trotting along Russell Square with the moon up there and those mountain clouds. Who am I, what am I, and so on: these questions are always floating about in me: and then I bump against some exact fact —a letter, a person, and come to them again with a great sense of freshness. And so it goes on. But on this showing, which is true, I think, I do fairly frequently come upon this "it"; and then feel quite at rest.

Tuesday, March 9th

As for Mary's * party, there, save for the usual shyness about powder, paint, shoes and stockings, I was happy, owing to the

* Mrs. St. John Hutchinson.

supremacy of literature. This keeps us sweet and sane. George Moore—me I mean.

He has a pink foolish face; blue eyes like hard marbles; a crest of snow-white hair; little unmuscular hands; sloping shoulders; a high stomach; neat, purplish well-brushed clothes; and perfect manners, as I consider them. That is to say he speaks without fear or dominance; accepting me on my merits; everyone on their merits. Still in spite of all uncowed, unbeaten, lively, shrewd. As for Hardy and Henry James, though, what shall one say?

"I am a fairly modest man; but I admit I think *Esther Waters* a better book than *Tess*. But what is there to be said for that man? He cannot write. He cannot tell a story. The whole art of fiction consists in telling a story. Now he makes a woman confess. How does he do it? In the third person—a scene that should be moving, impressive. Think how Tolstoi would have done it!"

"But," said Jack,* "*War and Peace* is the greatest novel in the world. I remember the scene where Natalia puts on a moustache and Rostov sees her for the first time as she is and falls in love with her."

"No, my good friend, there is nothing very wonderful in that. That is an ordinary piece of observation. But, my good friend (to me—half hesitating to call me this) what have you to say for Hardy? You cannot find anything to say. English fiction is the worst part of English literature. Compare it with the French—with the Russians. Henry James wrote some pretty little stories before he invented his jargon. But they were about rich people. You cannot write stories about rich people; because, I think he said, they have no instincts. But Henry James was enamoured of marble balustrades. There was no passion in any of his people. And Anne Brontë was the greatest of the Brontës and Conrad could not write," and so on. But this is out of date.

Saturday, March 20th

But what is to become of all these diaries, I asked myself yesterday. If I died, what would Leo make of them? He would

* Mr. St. John Hutchinson.

be disinclined to burn them; he could not publish them. Well, he should make up a book from them, I think; and then burn the body. I daresay there is a little book in them; if the scraps and scratching were straightened out a little. God knows. This is dictated by a slight melancholia, which comes upon me sometimes now and makes me think I am old; I am ugly. I am repeating things. Yet, as far as I know, as a writer I am only now writing out my mind.

Friday, April 30th

The last of a wet windy month, excepting the sudden opening of all the doors at Easter and the summer displayed blazing, as it always is, I suppose, only cloud hidden. I have not said anything about Iwerne Minster. Now it would amuse me to see what I remember it by. Cranbourne Chase: the stunted aboriginal forest trees, scattered, not grouped in cultivations; anemones, bluebells, violets, all pale, sprinkled about, without colour, livid, for the sun hardly shone. Then Blackmore Vale; a vast air dome and the fields dropped to the bottom; the sun striking, there, there; a drench of rain falling, like a veil streaming from the sky, there and there; and the downs rising, very strongly scarped (if that is the word) so that they were ridged and ledged; then an inscription in a church "sought peace and ensured it" and the question who wrote these sonorous stylistic epitaphs?—and all the cleanliness of Iwerne village, its happiness and well-being, making me ask, as we tended to sneer, still this is the right method, surely; and then tea and cream—these I remember: the hot baths; my new leather coat; Shaftesbury, so much lower and less commanding than my imagination, and the drive to Bournemouth and the dog and the lady behind the rock, and the view of Swanage, and coming home.

Yesterday I finished the first part of *To the Lighthouse*, and today began the second. I cannot make it out—here is the most difficult abstract piece of writing—I have to give an empty house, no people's characters, the passage of time, all eyeless and featureless with nothing to cling to: well, I rush at it, and at once scatter out two pages. Is it nonsense, is it brilliance? Why am I so flown with words and apparently free to do exactly what I like? When I read a bit it seems spirited too; needs compressing, but not much else. Compare this dashing fluency with *Mrs. Dalloway* (save the end). This is not made up; it is the literal fact.

Tuesday, May 25th

I have finished—sketchily I admit—the second part of *To the Lighthouse*—and may, then, have it all written over by the end of July. A record. 7 months, if it so turns out.

Sunday, July 25th

At first I thought it was Hardy, and it was the parlour maid, a small thin girl, wearing a proper cap. She came in with silver cake stands and so on. Mrs. Hardy talked to us about her dog. How long ought we to stay? Can Mr. Hardy walk much etc. I asked, making conversation, as I knew one would have to. She has the large sad lacklustre eyes of a childless woman; great docility and readiness, as if she had learnt her part; not great alacrity, but resignation, in welcoming more visitors; wears a sprigged voile dress, black shoes and a necklace. We can't go far now, she said, though we do walk every day, because our dog isn't able to walk far. He bites, she told us. She became more natural and animated about the dog, who is evidently the real centre of her thoughts—then the maid came in. Then again the door opened, more sprucely, and in trotted a little puffy-cheeked cheerful old man, with an atmosphere cheerful and business-like in addressing us, rather like an old doctor's or solicitor's, saying "Well now—" or words like that as he shook hands. He was dressed in rough grey with a striped tie. His nose has a joint in it and the end curves down. A round whitish face, the eyes now faded and rather watery, but the whole aspect cheerful and vigorous. He sat on a three-cornered chair (I am too jaded with all this coming and going to do more than gather facts) at a round table, where there were the cake stands and so on; a chocolate roll; what is called a good tea; but he only drank one cup, sitting on his three-cornered chair. He was extremely affable and aware of his duties. He did not let the talk stop or disdain making talk. He talked of father: said he had seen me, or it might have been my sister, but he thought it was me, in my cradle. He had been to Hyde Park Place—oh, Gate was it. A very quiet street. That was why my father liked it. Odd to think that in all these years he had never been down there again. He went there often. Your father took my novel— *Far from the Madding Crowd*. We stood shoulder to shoulder against the British public about certain matters dealt with in that novel. You may have heard. Then he said how some other novel had fallen through that was to appear—the parcel had been lost coming from France—not a very likely thing to happen, as your father said—a big parcel of manuscript; and he asked me to send my story. I think he broke all the Cornhill laws—not to see the whole book; so I sent it in chapter by chapter and was never late. Wonderful what youth is! I had it in my head doubtless, but I never thought twice about it. It came out every month. They were nervous, because of Miss Thackeray I think. She said she became paralysed and could not write a word directly she heard the press begin. I daresay it was bad for a novel to appear like that. One begins to think what is good for the magazine, not what is good for the novel.

"You think what makes a strong curtain," put in Mrs. Hardy jocularly. She was leaning upon the tea table, not eating—gazing out.

Then we talked about manuscripts. Mrs. Smith had found the MS of *F. from the M.C.* in a drawer during the war and sold it for the Red Cross. Now he has his MSS back and the printer rubs out all the marks. But he wishes they would leave them as they prove it genuine.

He puts his head down like some old pouter pigeon. He has a very long head; and quizzical bright eyes, for in talk they grow bright. He said when he was in the Strand 6 years ago he scarcely knew where he was and he used to know it all intimately. He told us that he used to buy second-hand books— nothing valuable—in Wyck Street. Then he wondered why Great James Street should be so narrow and Bedford Row so broad. He had often wondered about that. At this rate, London would soon be unrecognisable. But I shall never go there again. Mrs. Hardy tried to persuade him that it was an easy drive—only 6 hours or so. I asked if she liked it, and she said Granville

Barker had told her that when she was in the nursing home she had "the time of her life." She knew everyone in Dorchester but she thought there were more interesting people in London. Had I often been to Siegfried's * flat? I said no. Then she asked about him and Morgan, said he was elusive, as if they enjoyed visits from him. I said I heard from Wells that Mr. Hardy had been up to London to see an air raid. "What things they say!" he said. "It was my wife. There was an air raid one night when we stayed with Barrie. We just heard a little pop in the distance. The searchlights were beautiful. I thought if a bomb now were to fall on this flat how many writers would be lost." And he smiled, in his queer way, which is fresh and yet sarcastic a little; anyhow shrewd. Indeed, there was no trace to my think- ing of the simple peasant. He seemed perfectly aware of every- thing; in no doubt or hesitation; having made up his mind; and being delivered of all his work, so that he was in no doubt about that either. He was not interested much in his novels, or in anybody's novels: took it all easily and naturally. "I never took long with them" he said. "The longest was *The Dinnasts* (so pronounced)." "But that was really three books," said Mrs. Hardy. "Yes; and that took me six years; but not working all the time." "Can you write poetry regularly?" I asked (being beset with the desire to hear him say something about his books; but the dog kept cropping up. How he bit; how the in- spector came out; how he was ill; and they could do nothing for him). "Would you mind if I let him in?" asked Mrs. Hardy, and in came Wessex, a very tousled, rough brown and white mongrel; got to guard the house, so naturally he bites people, said Mrs. H. "Well, I don't know about that," said Hardy, perfectly natural, and not setting much stock by his poems either it seemed. "Did you write poems at the same time as your novels?" I asked. "No," he said. "I wrote a great many poems. I used to send them about, but they were always re- turned," he chuckled. "And in those days I believed in editors. Many were lost—all the fair copies were lost. But I found the notes and I wrote them from those. I was always finding them.

* Siegfried Sassoon.

I found one the other day; but I don't think I shall find any more.

"Siegfried took rooms near here and said he was going to work very hard, but he left soon.

"E. M. Forster takes a long time to produce anything—7 years," he chuckled. All this made a great impression of the ease with which he did things. "I daresay *Far from the Madding Crowd* would have been a great deal better if I had written it differently," he said. But as if it could not be helped and did not matter.

He used to go to the Lushingtons in Kensington Square and saw my mother there. "She used to come in and out when I was talking to your father."

I wanted him to say one word about his writing before we left and could only ask which of his books he would have chosen if, like me, he had had to choose one to read in the train. I had taken the *Mayor of Casterbridge*. "That's being dramatised," put in Mrs. Hardy, and then brought *Life's Little Ironies*.

"And did it hold your interest?" he asked. I stammered that I could not stop reading it, which was true, but sounded wrong. Anyhow, he was not going to be drawn and went off about giving a young lady a wedding present. "None of my books are fitted to be wedding presents," he said. "You must give Mrs. Woolf one of your books," said Mrs. Hardy, inevitably. "Yes I will. But I'm afraid only in the little thin paper edition," he said. I protested that it would be enough if he wrote his name (then was vaguely uncomfortable).

Then there was de la Mare. His last book of stories seemed to them such a pity. Hardy had liked some of his poems very much. People said he must be a sinister man to write such stories. But he is a very nice man—a very nice man indeed. He said to a friend who begged him not to give up poetry, "I'm afraid poetry is giving up me." The truth is he is a very kind man and sees anyone who wants to see him. He has 16 people for the day sometimes. "Do you think one can't write poetry if one sees people?" I asked. "One might be able to—I don't see why not. It's a question of physical strength," said Hardy.

But clearly he preferred solitude himself. Always however he said something sensible and sincere, and thus made the obvious business of compliment-giving rather unpleasant. He seemed to be free of it all; very active minded; liking to describe people; not to talk in an abstract way; for example Col. Lawrence, bicycling with a broken arm "held like that" from Lincoln to Hardy, listened at the door to hear if there was anyone there. "I hope he won't commit suicide," said Mrs. Hardy pensively, still leaning over the tea cups, gazing despondently. "He often says things like it, though he has never said quite that perhaps. But he has blue lines round his eyes. He calls himself Shaw in the army. No one is to know where he is. But it got into the papers." "He promised me not to go into the air," said Hardy. "My husband doesn't like anything to do with the air," said Mrs. Hardy.

Now we began to look at the grandfather clock in the corner. We said we must go—tried to confess we were only down for the day. I forgot to say that he offered L. whisky and water, which struck me that he was competent as a host and in every way. So we got up and signed Mrs. Hardy's visitors books; and Hardy took my *Life's Little Ironies* off and trotted back with it signed; and Woolf spelt Wolff, which I daresay had given him some anxiety. Then Wessex came in again. I asked if Hardy could stroke him. So he bent down and stroked him, like the master of the house. Wessex went on wheezing away.

There was not a trace anywhere of deference to editors, or respect for rank or extreme simplicity. What impressed me was his freedom, ease and vitality. He seemed very "Great Victorian" doing the whole thing with a sweep of his hand (they are ordinary smallish, curled up hands) and setting no great stock by literature; but immensely interested in facts; incidents; and somehow, one could imagine, naturally swept off into imagining and creating without a thought of its being difficult or remarkable; becoming obsessed; and living in imagination. Mrs. Hardy thrust his old grey hat into his hand and he trotted us out on to the road. "Where is that?" I asked him, pointing to a clump of trees on the down opposite, for his house is outside the town, with open country (rolling, massive downs, crowned with little tree coronets before and behind) and he said, with interest, "That is Weymouth. We see the lights at night—not the lights themselves, but the reflection of them." And so we left and he trotted in again.

Also I asked him if I might see the picture of Tess which Morgan had described, an old picture: whereupon he led me to an awful engraving of Tess coming into a room from a picture by Herkomer. "That was rather my idea of her," he said. But I said I had been told he had an old picture. "That's fiction," he said. "I used to see people now and then with a look of her."

Also Mrs. Hardy said to me "Do you know Aldous Huxley?" I said I did. They had been reading his book, which she thought "very clever." But Hardy could not remember it: said his wife had to read to him—his eyes were now so bad. "They've changed everything now," he said. "We used to think there was a beginning and a middle and an end. We believed in the Aristotelian theory. Now one of those stories came to an end with a woman going out of the room." He chuckled. But he no longer reads novels. The whole thing—literature, novels etc., all seemed to him an amusement, far away too, scarcely to be taken seriously. Yet he had sympathy and pity for those still engaged in it. But what his secret interests and activities are— to what occupation he trotted off when we left him—I do not know. Small boys write to him from New Zealand and have to be answered. They bring out a "Hardy number" of a Japanese paper, which he produced. Talked too about Blunden. I think Mrs. Hardy keeps him posted in the doings of the younger poets.

RODMELL *1926*

As I am not going to milk my brains for a week, I shall here write the first pages of the greatest book in the world. This is what the book would be that was made entirely solely and with integrity of one's thoughts. Suppose one could catch them before they became "works of art"? Catch them hot and sudden as they rise in the mind—walking up Asheham hill for instance. Of course one cannot; for the process of language is

slow and deluding. One must stop to find a word. Then, there
is the form of the sentence, soliciting one to fill it.

Art and thought

What I thought was this: if art is based on thought, what is the
transmuting process? I was telling myself the story of our visit
to the Hardys, and I began to compose it; that is to say to dwell
on Mrs. Hardy leaning on the table, looking out, apathetically,
vaguely, and so would soon bring everything into harmony
with that as the dominant theme. But the actual event was
different.

Next   *Writing by living people*

I scarcely ever read it. But, owing to his giving me the books,
am now reading *C.* by M. Baring. I am surprised to find it as
good as it is. But how good is it? Easy to say it is not a great
book. But what qualities does it lack? That it adds nothing to
one's vision of life, perhaps. Yet it is hard to find a serious flaw.
My wonder is that entirely second rate work like this, poured
out in profusion by at least 20 people yearly, I suppose, has so
much merit. Never reading it, I get into the way of thinking it
nonexistent. So it is, speaking with the utmost strictness. That
is, it will not exist in 2026; but it has some existence now,
which puzzles me a little. Now Clarissa bores me; yet I feel
this is important. And why?

My own brain

Here is a whole nervous breakdown in miniature. We came
on Tuesday. Sank into a chair, could scarcely rise; everything
insipid; tasteless, colourless. Enormous desire for rest. Wednesday—only wish to be alone in the open air. Air delicious—
avoided speech; could not read. Thought of my own power of
writing with veneration, as of something incredible, belonging
to someone else; never again to be enjoyed by me. Mind a
blank. Slept in my chair. Thursday. No pleasure in life whatsoever; but felt perhaps more attuned to existence. Character
and idiosyncrasy as Virginia Woolf completely sunk out.

Humble and modest. Difficulty in thinking what to say. Read automatically, like a cow chewing cud. Slept in chair. Friday: sense of physical tiredness; but slight activity of the brain. Beginning to take notice. Making one or two plans. No power of phrase-making. Difficulty in writing to Lady Colefax. Saturday (today) much clearer and lighter. Thought I could write, but resisted, or found it impossible. A desire to read poetry set in on Friday. This brings back a sense of my own individuality. Read some Dante and Bridges, without troubling to understand, but got pleasure from them. Now I begin to wish to write notes, but not yet novel. But today senses quickening. No "making up" power yet: no desire to cast scenes in my book. Curiosity about literature returning; want to read Dante, Havelock Ellis and Berlioz autobiography; also to make a looking glass with shell frame. These processes have sometimes been spread over several weeks.

Proportions changed

That in the evening, or on colourless days, the proportions of the landscape change suddenly. I saw people playing stool-ball in the meadow; they appeared sunk far down on a flat board; and the downs raised high up and mountainous round them. Detail was smoothed out. This was an extremely beautiful effect: the colours of the women's dresses also showing very bright and pure in the almost untinted surroundings. I knew, also, that the proportions were abnormal—as if I were looking between my legs.

Second-rate art

i.e. C., by Maurice Baring. Within it limits, it is not second rate, or there is nothing markedly so, at first go off. The limits are the proof of its non-existence. He can only do one thing; himself to wit; charming, clean, modest, sensitive Englishman. Outside that radius and it does not carry far nor illumine much, all is—as it should be—light, sure, proportioned, affecting even; told in so well bred a manner that nothing is exaggerated, all related, proportioned. I could read this for ever, I said. L. said one would soon be sick to death of it.

Wandervögeln

of the sparrow tribe. Two resolute, sunburnt, dusty girls in jerseys and short skirts, with packs on their backs, city clerks, or secretaries, tramping along the road in the hot sunshine at Ripe. My instinct at once throws up a screen, which condemns them: I think them in every way angular, awkward and self-assertive. But all this is a great mistake. These screens shut me out. Have no screens, for screens are made out of our own integument; and get at the thing itself, which has nothing whatever in common with a screen. The screen-making habit, though, is so universal that probably it preserves our sanity. If we had not this device for shutting people off from our sympathies we might perhaps dissolve utterly; separateness would be impossible. But the screens are in the excess; not the sympathy.

Returning health

This is shown by the power to make images; the suggestive power of every sight and word is enormously increased. Shakespeare must have had this to an extent which makes my normal state the state of a person blind, deaf, dumb, stone-stockish and fish-blooded. And I have it compared with poor Mrs. Bartholomew almost to the extent that Shakespeare has it compared with me.

Bank Holiday

Very fat woman, girl and man spend Bank Holiday—a day of complete sun and satisfaction—looking up family graves in the churchyard. 23 youngish men and women spend it tramping along with ugly black boxes on shoulders and arms, taking photographs. Man says to woman, "Some of these quiet villages don't seem to know it's Bank Holiday at all" in a tone of superiority and slight contempt.

The married relation

Arnold Bennett says that the horror of marriage lies in its "dailiness." All acuteness of relationship is rubbed away by this. The truth is more like this: life—say 4 days out of 7—becomes automatic; but on the 5th day a bead of sensation (between husband and wife) forms which is all the fuller and more sensitive because of the automatic customary unconscious days on either side. That is to say the year is marked by moments of great intensity. Hardy's "moments of vision." How can a relationship endure for any length of time except under these conditions?

Friday, September 3rd

Women in tea garden at Bramber—a sweltering hot day: rose trellises; white-washed tables; lower middle classes; motor omnibuses constantly passing; bits of grey stone scattered on a paper-strewn greensward, all that's left of the Castle.

Woman leaning over the table, taking command of the treat, attended by two elder women, whom she pays for to girl waitress (or marmalade coloured fat girl, with a body like the softest lard, destined soon to marry, but as yet only 16 or so).

WOMAN: What can we have for tea?
GIRL (*very bored, arms akimbo*): Cake, bread and butter, tea. Jam?
WOMAN: Have the wasps been troublesome? They get into the jam—(as if she suspected the jam would not be worth having).

Girl agrees.

WOMAN: Ah, wasps have been very prominent this year.
GIRL: That's right.

So she doesn't have jam.

This amused me, I suppose.
For the rest, Charleston, Tilton,* *To the Lighthouse,* Vita, expeditions: the summer dominated by a feeling of washing in boundless warm fresh air—such an August not come my way for years; bicycling; no settled work done, but advantage taken of air for going to the river or over the downs. The novel is now easily within sight of the end, but this, mysteriously,

* The Keynes's house.

comes no nearer. I am doing Lily on the lawn; but whether
it's her last lap, I don't know. Nor am I sure of the quality;
the only certainty seems to be that after tapping my antennae
in the air vaguely for an hour every morning I generally write
with heat and ease till 12:30; and thus do my two pages. So it
will be done, written over that is, in 3 weeks,
5th September.   I forecast, from today. What emerges? At this
moment I'm casting about for an end. The
problem is how to bring Lily and Mr. R. together and make a
combination of interest at the end. I am feathering about with
various ideas. The last chapter which I begin tomorrow is In
the Boat: I had meant to end with R. climbing on to the rock.
If so, what becomes of Lily and her picture? Should there be a
final page about her and Carmichael looking at the picture and
summing up R.'s character? In that case I lose the intensity of
the moment. If this intervenes between R. and the lighthouse,
there's too much chop and change, I think. Could I do it in a
parenthesis? So that one had the sense of reading the two things
at the same time?

I shall solve it somehow, I suppose. Then I must go on to the
question of quality. I think it may run too fast and free and so
be rather thin. On the other hand, I think it is subtler and more
human than *Jacob's Room* and *Mrs. Dalloway*. And I am encouraged by my own abundance as I write. It is proved, I think,
that what I have to say is to be said in this manner. As usual,
side stories are sprouting in great variety as I wind this up: a
book of characters; the whole string being pulled out from
some simple sentence, like Clara Pater's "Don't you find that
Barker's pins have no points to them?" I think I can spin out
all their entrails this way; but it is hopelessly undramatic. It
is all in oratio obliqua. Not quite all; for I have a few direct
sentences. The lyric portions of *To the Lighthouse* are collected
in the 10-year lapse and don't interfere with the text so much
as usual. I feel as if it fetched its circle pretty completely this
time; and I don't feel sure what the stock criticism will be.
Sentimental? Victorian?

Then I must begin to plan out my book on literature for the
Press. Six chapters. Why not groups of ideas, under some rough

heading—for example: Symbolism. God. Nature. Plot. Dialogue. Take a novel and see what the competent parts are. Separate this and bring under them instances of all the books which display them biggest. Probably this would pan out historically. One could spin a theory which would bring the chapters together. I don't feel that I can read seriously and exactly for it. Rather I want to sort out all the ideas that have accumulated in me.

Then I want to write a bunch of "Outlines" to make money (for under a new arrangement, we're to share any money over £200 that I make); this I must leave rather to chance, according to what books come my way. I am frightfully contented these last few days, by the way. I don't quite understand it. Perhaps reason has something to do with it.

Monday, September 13th

The blessed thing is coming to an end I say to myself with a groan. It's like some prolonged rather painful and yet exciting process of nature, which one desires inexpressibly to have over. Oh the relief of waking and thinking it's done—the relief and the disappointment, I suppose. I am talking of *To the Lighthouse*. I am exacerbated by the fact that I spent four days last week hammering out de Quincey, which has been lying about since June; so refused £30 to write on Willa Cather; and now shall be quit in a week I hope of this unprofitable fiction and could have wedged in Willa before going back. So I should have had £70 of my year's £200 ready made by October. (My greed is immense; I want to have £50 of my own in the Bank to buy Persian carpets, pots, chairs, etc.) Curse Richmond, Curse the Times, Curse my own procrastinations and nerves. I shall do Cobden Sanderson and Mrs. Hemans and make something by them however. As for the book—Morgan said he felt "This is a failure," as he finished the *Passage to India*. I feel—what? A little stale this last week or two from steady writing. But also a little triumphant. If my feeling is correct, this is the greatest stretch I've put my method to, and I think it holds. By this I mean that I have been dredging up more feelings and characters, I imagine. But Lord knows, until I look at my haul. This is only my own feeling in process. Odd how I'm haunted by that damned criticism of Janet Case's "it's all dressing . . . technique. (*Mrs. Dalloway*). *The Common Reader* has substance." But then in one's strained state any fly has liberty to settle and it's always the gadflies. Muir praising me intelligently has comparatively little power to encourage—when I'm working, that is—when the ideas halt. And this last lap, in the boat, is hard, because the material is not so rich as it was with Lily on the lawn. I am forced to be more direct and more intense. I am making more use of symbolism, I observe; and I go in dread of "sentimentality." Is the whole theme open to that charge? But I doubt that any theme is in itself good or bad. It gives a chance to one's peculiar qualities —that's all.

Thursday, September 30th

I wished to add some remarks to this, on the mystical side of this solicitude; how it is not oneself but something in the universe that one's left with. It is this that is frightening and exciting in the midst of my profound gloom, depression, boredom, whatever it is. One sees a fin passing far out. What image can I reach to convey what I mean? Really there is none, I think. The interesting thing is that in all my feeling and thinking I have never come up against this before. Life is, soberly and accurately, the oddest affair; has in it the essence of reality. I used to feel this as a child—couldn't step across a puddle once, I remember, for thinking how strange—what am I? etc. But by writing I don't reach anything. All I mean to make is a note of a curious state of mind. I hazard the guess that it may be the impulse behind another book.* At present my mind is totally blank and virgin of books. I want to watch and see how the idea at first ocurs. I want to trace my own process.

Tuesday, November 23rd

I am re-doing six pages of *Lighthouse* daily. This is not, I think, so quick as *Mrs. D*: but then I find much of it very

* Perhaps *The Waves* or *Moths* (Oct. 1929).

sketchy and have to improvise on the typewriter. This I find much easier than re-writing in pen and ink. My present opinion is that it is easily the best of my books: fuller than *J.'s R.* and less spasmodic, occupied with more interesting things than *Mrs. D.*, and not complicated with all that desperate accompaniment of madness. It is freer and subtler, I think. Yet I have no idea yet of any other to follow it: which may mean that I have made my method perfect and it will now stay like this and serve whatever use I wish to put it to. Before, some development of method brought fresh subjects in view, because I saw the chance of being able to say them. Yet I am now and then haunted by some semi-mystic very profound life of a woman, which shall all be told on one occasion; and time shall be utterly obliterated; future shall somehow blossom out of the past. One incident—say the fall of a flower—might contain it. My theory being that the actual event practically does not exist —nor time either. But I don't want to force this. I must make up my series book.

1927

Friday, January 14th

This is out of order, but I have no new book and so must record here (and it was here I recorded the beginning of the *Lighthouse*) must record here the end. This moment I have finished the final drudgery. It is now complete for Leonard to read on Monday. Thus I have done it some days under the year and feel thankful to be out of it again. Since October 25th I have been revising and retyping (some parts three times over) and no doubt I should work at it again; but I cannot. What I feel is that it is a hard muscular book, which at this age proves that I have something in me. It has not run out and gone flabby: at least such is my feeling before reading it over.

Sunday, January 23rd

Well Leonard has read *To the Lighthouse* and says it is much my best book and it is a "masterpiece." He said this without my asking. I came back from Knole and sat without asking him. He calls it entirely new—'a psychological poem' is his name for it. An improvement upon *Dalloway;* more interesting. Having won this great relief, my mind dismisses the whole thing, as usual, and I forget it and shall only wake up and be worried again over proofs and then when it appears.

Saturday, February 12th

X's prose is too fluent. I've been reading it and it makes my pen run. When I've read a classic I am curbed and—not castrated; no, the opposite; I can't think of the word at the moment. Had I been writing "Y——" I should have run off whole pools of this coloured water; and then (I think) found my own method of attack. It is my distinction as a writer I think to get this clear and my expression exact. Were I writing travels I should wait till some angle emerged and go for that. The method of writing smooth narration can't be right; things don't happen in one's mind like that. But she is very skilful and golden voiced. This makes me think that I have to read *To the Lighthouse* tomorrow and Monday, straight through in print; straight through, owing to my curious methods, for the first time. I want to read largely and freely once; then to niggle over details. I may note that the first symptoms of *Lighthouse* are unfavourable. Roger it is clear did not like "Time Passes"; Harpers and the Forum have refused serial rights; Brace writes, I think, a good deal less enthusiastically than of *Mrs. D.* But these opinions refer to the rough copy, unrevised. And anyhow I feel callous: L.'s opinion keeps me steady; I'm neither one thing nor the other.

Monday, February 21st

Why not invent a new kind of play; as for instance:

Woman thinks . . .
He does.
Organ plays.
She writes.
They say:
She sings.
Night speaks
They miss

I think it must be something on this line—though I can't now see what. Away from facts; free; yet concentrated; prose yet poetry; a novel and a play.

Monday, February 28th

But I intend to work harder and harder. If they—the respectables, my friends, advise me against the *Lighthouse*, I shall write memoirs; have a plan already to get historical manuscripts and write *Lives of the Obscure;* but why do I pretend I should take advice? After a holiday the old ideas will come to me as usual; seeming fresher, more important than ever;

and I shall be off again, feeling that extraordinary exhilaration, that ardour and lust of creation—which is odd, if what I create is, as it well may be, wholly bad.

Monday, March 14th

Faith Henderson * came to tea; and, valiantly beating the waters of conversation, I sketched the possibilities which an unattractive woman, penniless, alone, might yet bring into being. I began imagining the position—how she would stop a motor on the Dover road and so get to Dover; cross the channel etc. It struck me, vaguely, that I might write a Defoe narrative for fun. Suddenly between twelve and one I conceived a whole fantasy to be called "The Jessamy Brides"—why, I wonder? I have rayed round it several scenes. Two women, poor, solitary at the top of a house. One can see anything (for this is all fantasy) the Tower Bridge, clouds, aeroplanes. Also old men listening in the room over the way. Everything is to be tumbled in pell mell. It is to be written as I write letters at the top of my speed; on the ladies of Llangollen; on Mrs. Fladgate; on people passing. No attempt is to be made to realise the character. Sapphism is to be suggested. Satire is to be the main note—satire and wildness. The ladies are to have Constantinople in view. Dreams of golden domes. My own lyric vein is to be satirised. Everything mocked. And it is to end with three dots . . . so. For the truth is I feel the need of an escapade

Orlando leading to *The Waves*. (8 July 1933).

after these serious poetic experimental books whose form is always so closely considered. I want to kick up my heels and be off. I want to embody all those innumerable little ideas and tiny stories which flash into my mind at all seasons. I think this will be great fun to write; and it will rest my head before starting the very serious, mystical poetical work which I want to come next. Meanwhile, before I can touch the *Jessamy Brides,* I have to write my book on fiction and that won't be done till January, I suppose. I might dash off a page or two now and then by way of experiment. And it

* Wife of Hubert (later Sir Hubert) Henderson.

is possible that the idea will evaporate. Anyhow this records the odd horrid unexpected way in which these things suddenly create themselves—one thing on top of another in about an hour. So I made up *Jacob's Room* looking at the fire at Hogarth House; so I made up the *Lighthouse* one afternoon in the Square here.

Monday, March 21st

My brain is ferociously active. I want to have at my books as if I were conscious of the lapse of time; age and death. Dear me, how lovely some parts of the *Lighthouse* are! Soft and pliable, and I think deep, and never a word wrong for a page at a time. This I feel about the dinner party and the children in the boat; but not of Lily on the lawn. That I do not much like. But I like the end.

Sunday, May 1st

And then I remember how my book is coming out. People will say I am irreverent—people will say a thousand things. But I think, honestly, I care very little this time—even for the opinion of my friends. I am not sure if it is good; I was disappointed when I read it through the first time. Later I liked it. Anyhow it is the best I can do. But would it be a good thing to read my things when they are printed, critically? It is encouraging that in spite of obscurity, affectation and so on my sales rise steadily. We have sold, already, 1220 before publication, and I think it will be about 1500, which for a writer like I am is not bad. Yet, to show I am genuine, I find myself thinking of other things with absorption and forgetting that it will be out on Thursday.

Thursday, May 5th

Book out. We have sold (I think) 1690 before publication—twice *Dalloway*. I write however in the shadow of the damp cloud of *The Times Lit. Sup.* review, which is an exact copy of the *J.'s R., Mrs. Dalloway* review, gentlemanly, kindly, timid, praising beauty, doubting character, and leaving me moderately depressed. I am anxious about "Time Passes." Think the

whole thing may be pronounced soft, shallow, insipid, sentimental. Yet, honestly, I don't much care; want to be let alone
to ruminate.

Wednesday, May 11th

My book. What is the use of saying one is indifferent to
reviews when positive praise, though mingled with blame, gives
one such a start on, that instead of feeling dried up, one feels,
on the contrary, flooded with ideas? I gather from vague hints,
through Margery Joad, through Clive, that some people say it is
my best book. So far Vita praises; Dotty * enthuses; an unknown donkey writes. No one has yet read it to the end, I daresay; and I shall hover about, not anxious but worried for two
more weeks, when it will be over.

Monday, May 16th

The book. Now on its feet so far as praise is concerned. It
has been out 10 days: Thursday a week ago. Nessa enthusiastic—a sublime, almost upsetting spectacle. She says it is an
amazing portrait of mother; a supreme portrait painter; has
lived in it; found the rising of the dead almost painful. Then
Ottoline, then Vita, then Charlie, then Lord Olivier, then Tom-
mie, then Clive.

Saturday, June 18th

This is a terribly thin diary for some reason. Half the year
has been spent and left only these few sheets. Perhaps I have
been writing too hard in the morning to write here also. Three
weeks wiped out by headache. We had a week at Rodmell, of
which I remember various sights, suddenly unfolding before
me spontaneously (for example, the village standing out to sea
in the June night, houses seeming ships; the marsh a fiery
foam) and the immense comfort of lying there lapped in peace.
I lay out all day in the new garden, with the terrace. It is already being made. There were blue tits nested in the hollow
neck of my Venus. Vita came over one very hot afternoon and
we walked to the river with her. Pinker † now swims after

* Dorothy Wellesley, later Duchess of Wellington.
† A spaniel.

Leonard's stick. I read—any trash; Maurice Baring; sporting memoirs. Slowly ideas began trickling in; and then suddenly I rhapsodised (the night L. dined with the Apostles) and told over the story of the Moths, which I think I will write very quickly, perhaps in between chapters of that long impending book on fiction. Now the Moths will I think fill out the skeleton which I dashed in here; the play-poem idea; the idea of some continuous stream, not solely of human thought, but of the ship, the night etc., all flowing together: intersected by the arrival of the bright moths. A man and a woman are to be sitting at table talking. Or shall they remain silent? It is to be a love story; she is finally to let the last great moth in. The contrasts might be something of this sort; she might talk, or think, about the age of the earth; the death of humanity; then the moths keep on coming. Perhaps the man could be left absolutely dim. France: hear the sea; at night; a garden under the window. But it needs ripening. I do a little work on it in the evening when the gramophone is playing late Beethoven sonatas. (The windows fidget at their fastenings as if we were at sea.)

The Waves.

We saw Vita given the Hawthornden. A horrid show up, I thought: not of the gentry on the platform—Squire, Drinkwater, Binyon only—of us all; all of us chattering writers. My word! how insignificant we all looked! How can we pretend that we are interesting, that our works matter? The whole business of writing became infinitely distasteful. There was no one I could care whether he read, liked, or disliked "my writing." And no one could care for my criticism either; the mildness, the conventionality of them all struck me. But there may be a stream of ink in them that matters more than the look of them —so tightly clothed, mild and decorous—showed. I felt there was no one full grown mind among us. In truth, it was the thick dull middle class of letters that met, not the aristocracy.

Wednesday, June 22nd

Women haters depress me and both Tolstoi and Mrs. Asquith hate women. I suppose my depression is a form of vanity. But then so are all strong opinions on both sides. I hate Mrs. A's hard, dogmatic empty style. But enough: I shall write about her tomorrow. I write every day about something and have deliberately set apart a few weeks to money-making, so that I may put £50 in each of our pockets by September. This will be the first money of my own since I married. I never felt the need of it till lately. And I can get it, if I want it, but shirk writing for money.

Thursday, June 23rd

This diary shall batten on the leanness of my social life. Never have I spent so quiet a London summer. It is perfectly easy to slip out of the crush unobserved. I have set up my standard as an invalid and no one bothers me. No one asks me to do anything. Vainly, I have the feeling that this is of my choice, not theirs; and there is a luxury in being quiet in the heart of chaos. Directly I talk and exert my wits in talk I get a dull damp rather headachy day. Quiet brings me cool clear quick mornings, in which I dispose of a good deal of work and toss my brain into the air when I take a walk. I shall feel some triumph if I skirt a headache this summer.

Thursday, June 30th

Now I must sketch out the Eclipse.

About 10 on Tuesday night several very long trains, accurately filled (ours with civil servants) left Kings Cross. In our carriage were Vita, Harold, Quentin, L. and I. This is Hatfield I daresay, I said. I was smoking a cigar. Then again, This is Peterborough, L. said. Before it got dark we kept looking at the sky; soft fleecy; but there was one star, over Alexandra Park. Look, Vita, that's Alexandra Park, said Harold. The Nicolsons got sleepy; H. curled up with his head on V.'s knee. She looked like Sappho by Leighton, asleep; so we plunged through the midlands; made a very long stay at York. Then at 3 we got out our sandwiches and I came in from the W.C. to find Harold being rubbed clean of cream. Then he broke the china sandwich box. Here L. laughed without restraint. Then we had another doze, or the N.'s did; then here was a level crossing, at which were drawn up a long line of motor omnibuses and motors, all burning pale yellow lights. It was getting grey—still a fleecy mottled sky. We got to Richmond about 3:30; it was cold and the N.'s had a quarrel, Eddie said, about V.'s luggage. We went off in the omnibus, saw a vast castle (who does that belong to, said Vita, who is interested in castles). It had a front window added and a light I think burning. All the fields were aburn with June grasses and red tasselled plants none coloured as yet, all pale. Pale and grey too were the little uncompromising Yorkshire farms. As we passed one, the farmer and his wife and sister came out, all tightly and tidily dressed in black, as if they were going to church. At another ugly square farm, two women were looking out of the upper windows. These had white blinds drawn down half across them. We were a train of 3 vast cars, one stopping to let the others go on; all very low and powerful; taking immensely steep hills. The driver once got out and put a small stone behind our wheel—inadequate. An accident would have been natural; there were also many motor cars. These suddenly increased as we crept up to the top of Bardon Fell. Here were people camping beside their cars. We got out and found ourselves very high, on a moor, boggy, heathery, with butts for grouse shooting. There were grass tracks here and there and people had already taken up positions. So we joined them, walking out to what seemed the highest point looking over Richmond. One light burned down there. Vales and moors stretched, slope after slope, round us. It was like the Haworth country. But over Richmond, where the sun was rising, was a soft grey cloud. We could see by a gold spot where the sun was. But it was early yet. We had to wait, stamping to keep warm. Ray had wrapped herself in the blue striped blanket off a double bed. She looked incredibly vast and bedroomish. Saxon looked very old. Leonard kept looking at his watch. Four great red setters came leaping over the moor. There were sheep feeding behind us. Vita had tried to buy a guinea pig—Quentin advised a savage—so she observed the animals from time to time. There were thin places in the clouds and some complete holes. The question was whether the sun would show through a cloud or through one of these hollow places when the time came. We began to get anxious. We saw rays coming through the bottom of the clouds.

Then, for a moment, we saw the sun, sweeping—it seemed to be sailing at a great pace and clear in a gap; we had out our smoked glasses; we saw it crescent, burning red; next moment it had sailed fast into the cloud again; only the red streamers came from it; then only a golden haze, such as one has often seen. The moments were passing. We thought we were cheated; we looked at the sheep; they showed no fear; the setters were racing round; everyone was standing in long lines, rather dignified, looking out. I thought how we were like very old people, in the birth of the world—druids on Stonehenge; (this idea came more vividly in the first pale light though). At the back of us were great blue spaces in the cloud. These were still blue. But now the colour was going out. The clouds were turning pale; a reddish black colour. Down in the valley it was an extraordinary scrumble of red and black; there was the one light burning; all was cloud down there, and very beautiful, so delicately tinted. Nothing could be seen through the cloud. The 24 seconds were passing. Then one looked back again at the blue; and rapidly, very very quickly, all the colours faded; it became darker and darker as at the beginning of a violent storm; the light sank and sank; we kept saying this is the shadow; and we thought now it is over—this is the shadow; when suddenly the light went out. We had fallen. It was extinct. There was no colour. The earth was dead. That was the astonishing moment; and the next when as if a ball had rebounded the cloud took colour on itself again, only a sparky ethereal colour and so the light came back. I had very strongly the feeling as the light went out of some vast obeisance; something kneeling down and suddenly raised up when the colours came. They came back astonishingly lightly and quickly and beautifully in the valley and over the hills—at first with a miraculous glittering and ethereality, later normally almost, but with a great sense of relief. It was like recovery. We had been much worse than we had expected. We had seen the world dead. This was within the power of nature. Our greatness had been apparent too.

The colour for some moments was of the most lovely kind—fresh, various; here blue and there brown; all new colours, as if washed over and repainted.

Now we became Ray in a blanket, Saxon in a cap etc. We were bitterly cold. I should say that the cold had increased as the light went down. One felt very livid. Then—it was over till 1999. What remained was the sense of the comfort which we get used to, of plenty of light, and colour. This for some time seemed a definitely welcome thing. Yet when it became established all over the country, one rather missed the sense of its being a relief and a respite, which one had had when it came back after the darkness. How can I express the darkness? It was a sudden plunge, when one did not expect it; being at the mercy of the sky; our own nobility; the druids; Stonehenge; and the racing red dogs; all that was in one's mind. Also, to be picked out of one's London drawing room and set down on the wildest moors in England, was impressive. For the rest, I remember trying to keep awake in the gardens at York while Eddy talked and falling asleep. Asleep again in the train. It was hot and we were messy. The carriage was full of things. Harold was very kind and attentive. Eddy was peevish. Roast beef and pineapple chunks, he said. We got home at 8:30 perhaps.

Tuesday, September 18th

A thousand things to be written had I time: had I power. A very little writing uses up my capacity for writing.

Laughton Place and Philip Ritchie's * death.

These as it happened synchronised. When Vita was here 10 days ago we drove over to Laughton and I broke in and explored the house. It seemed, that sunny morning, so beautiful, so peaceful; and as if it had endless old rooms. So I come home boiling with the idea of buying it; and so fired L. that we wrote to the farmer, Mr. Russell, and waited, all on wires, edgy, excited for an answer. He came himself, after some days; and we were to go and see it. This arranged, and our hopes very high, I opened the *Morning Post* and read the death of Philip Ritchie. "He can't take houses, poor Philip" I thought. And then the usual procession of images went through my mind.

* Son of Lord Ritchie.

Also, I think for the first time, I felt this death leaves me an elderly luggard; makes me feel I have no right to go on; as if my life were at the expense of his. And I had not been kind; not asked him to dinner and so on. So the two feelings—about buying the house and his death—fought each other; and sometimes the house won and sometimes death won; and we went to see the house and it turned out unspeakably dreary; all patched and spoilt; with grained oak and grey paper; a sodden garden and a glaring red cottage at the back. I note the strength and vividness of feelings which suddenly break and foam away. Now I forget to think about Philip Ritchie.

One of these days, though, I shall sketch here, like a grand historical picture, the outlines of all my friends. I was thinking of this in bed last night and for some reason I thought I would begin with a sketch of Gerald Brenan. There may be something in this idea. It might be a way of writing the memoirs of one's own times during people's lifetimes. It might be a most amusing book. The question is how to do it. Vita should be Orlando, a young nobleman. There should be Lytton; and it should be truthful but fantastic. Roger. Duncan. Clive. Adrian. Their lives should be related. But I can think of more books than I shall ever be able to write. How many little stories come into my head! For instance: Ethel Sands not looking at her letters. What this implies. One might write a book of short significant separate scenes. She did not open her letters.

Tuesday, September 25th

On the opposite page I wrote notes for Shelley, I think, by mistake for my writing book.

Now let me become the annalist of Rodmell.

Thirty-five years ago, there were 160 families living here where there are now no more than 80. It is a decaying village, which loses its boys to the towns. Not a boy of them, said the Rev. Mr. Hawkesford,* is being taught to plough. Rich people wanting weekend cottages buy up the old peasants' houses for fabulous sums. Monks House was offered to Mr. H. for £400; we gave £700. He refused it, saying he didn't wish to own coun-

* Rector of Rodmell in 1927.

try cottages. Now Mr. Allison will pay £1,200 for a couple and we he said might get £2,000 for this. He (Hawkesford) is an old decaying man, run to seed. His cynicism and the pleasant turn it gives his simple worn out sayings amuses me. He is sinking into old age, very shabby, loose limbed, wearing black woollen mittens. His life is receding like a tide, slowly; or one figures him as a dying candle, whose wick will soon sink into the warm grease and be extinct. To look at, he is like some aged bird; a little, small featured face, with heavily lidded smoky bright eyes; his complexion is still ruddy; but his beard is like an unweeded garden. Little hairs grow weakly all over his cheeks and two strands are drawn, like pencil marks, across his bald head. He tumbles into an armchair and tells over his stock of old village stories which always have this slightly mocking flavour as though, completely unambitious and by no means successful himself, he recouped himself by laughing slyly at the humours of the more energetic. The outlay these flashy newcomers make on their field and farms makes him sardonic. But he won't raise a finger either way; likes his cup of Indian tea, which he prefers to China, and doesn't much mind what anybody thinks. He smokes endless cigarettes and his fingers are not very clean. Talking of his well, he said, "It would be a different thing if one wanted baths"—which for some 70 years, presumably, he has done without. Then he likes a little practical talk about Aladdin lamps, for instance, and how the Rector at Iford has a device by which he makes the globe of the Veritas lamp, which is cheaper, serve. It appears that the Aladdin costs 10d. and 2/-. But it blackens suddenly and is useless. Leaning over stiles, it is of lamp mantles that the two rectors talk. Or he will advise about making a garage; how Percy should cut a trench and then old Fears should line the walls with cement. That is what he advises; and I fancy many many hours of his life have passed hobnobbing with Percies and Fears about cement and trenches. Of his clerical character there is little visible. He would not buy Bowen * a riding school he said; her sister did that. He didn't believe in it. She has a school at Rottingdean, keeps 12 horses, employs grooms

* Miss Hawkesford

and has to be at it all day, Sundays included. But having expressed his opinion in the family conclave he would leave it at that. Mrs. H. would back Bowen. She would get her way. The Rector would slouch off to his study, where he does heaven knows what. I asked him if he had work to do: a question which amused him a little. Not work, he said; but a young woman to see. And then he settled into the armchair again and so sat out a visit of over an hour and a half.

Wednesday, October 5th

I write in the sordid doss house atmosphere of approaching departure. Pinker is asleep in one chair; Leonard is signing cheques at the little deal table under the glare of the lamp. The fire is covered with ashes, since we have been burning it all day and Mrs. B. never cleans. Envelopes lie in the grate. I am writing with a pen which is feeble and wispy; and it is a sharp fine evening with a sunset, I daresay.

We went to Amberley yesterday and think of buying a house there. For it is an astonishing forgotten lovely place, between water meadows and downs. So impulsive we both are, in spite of our years.

But we are not as old as Mrs. Gray, who came to thank us for our apples. She won't send to buy, as it looks like begging, since we never take money. Her face is cut into by wrinkles; they make weals across her. She is 86 and can never remember such a summer. In her youth it was so hot in April often that they couldn't bear a sheet on them. Her youth must have been almost the same time as my father's. She is 9 years younger, I make out; born in 1841. And what did she see of Victorian England I wonder.

I can make up situations, but I cannot make up plots. That is: if I pass a lame girl I can, without knowing I do it, instantly make up a scene: (now I can't think of one). This is the germ of such fictitious gift as I have. And by the way I get letter after letter about my books and they scarcely please me.

If my pen allowed, I should now try to make out a work table, having done my last article for the *Tribune,* and now being free again. And instantly the usual exciting devices enter my mind: a biography beginning in the year 1500 and continu-

ing to the present day, called *Orlando:* Vita; only with a change
about from one sex to another. I think, for a treat, I shall let
myself dash this in for a week, while . . .

Saturday, October 22nd

This is a book, I think I have said before, which I write after
tea. And my brain was full of ideas, but I have spent them on
Mr. Ashcroft and Miss Findlater, fervent admirers.

"I shall let myself dash this in for a week"—I have done
nothing, nothing, nothing else for a fortnight; and am launched
somewhat furtively but with all the more passion upon *Orlando:* a Biography. It is to be a small book and written by
Christmas. I thought I could combine it with Fiction, but once
the mind gets hot it can't stop: I walk making up phrases;
sit, contriving scenes; am in short in the thick of the greatest
rapture known to me; from which I have kept myself since last
February, or earlier. Talk of planning a book, or waiting for
an idea! Then one came in a rush; I said to pacify myself, being
bored and stale with criticism and faced with that intolerable
dull Fiction, "You shall write a page of a story for a treat; you
shall stop sharp at 11:30 and then go on with the Romantics."
I had very little idea what the story was to be about. But the
relief of turning my mind that way was such that I felt happier
than for months; as if put in the sun, or laid on a cushion; and
after two days entirely gave up my time chart and abandoned
myself to the pure delight of this farce; which I enjoy as much
as I've ever enjoyed anything; and have written myself into half
a headache and had to come to a halt, like a tired horse, and
take a little sleeping draught last night; which made our breakfast fiery. I did not finish my egg. I am writing *Orlando* half in a
mock style very clear and plain, so that people will understand
every word. But the balance between truth and fantasy must
be careful. It is based on Vita, Violet Trefusis, Lord Lascelles,
Knole, etc.

Sunday, November 20th

I will now snatch a moment from what Morgan calls "life" to
enter a hurried note. My notes have been few; life a cascade,
a glissade, a torrent; all together. I think on the whole this *is*

our happiest autumn. So much work; and success now; and life on easy terms; heaven knows what. My morning rushes, pell mell, from 10 to 1. I write so quick I can't get it typed before lunch. This I suppose is the main backbone of my autumn—*Orlando*. Never do I feel this, except for a morning or two, writing criticism. Today I began the third chapter. Do I learn anything? Too much of a joke perhaps for that; yet I like these plain sentences; and the externality of it for a change. It is too thin of course; splashed over the canvas; but I shall cover the ground by January 7th (I say) and then re-write.

Wednesday, November 30th

A hurried note about the lunch party, L. dining at the Cranium. An art of light talk; about people. Bogey Harris; Maurice Baring. B. H. "knows" everyone: that is no one. Freddy Fossle? Oh yes I know him; knows Lady so-and-so. Knows everyone: can't admit to not knowing. A polished, burnished diner out—Roman Catholic. In the middle M. Baring says: "But Lady B. died this morning." Sibyl says: "Say that again." "But R. M. was lunching with her yesterday," says Bogey. "Well it's in the papers she's dead," says M. B. Sibyl says: "But she was quite young. Lord Ivor asked me to meet the young man his daughter's to marry." "I know Lord Ivor," says, or would say, Bogey. "Well it's odd," says Sibyl, giving up the attempt to wrestle with the death of the young at a lunch party. So on to wigs: "Lady Charlie used to have hers curled by a sailor on deck before she got up," says Bogey. "Oh, I've known her all my life. Went yachting with them. Lady . . . eyebrows fell into the soup. Sir John Cook was so fat they had to hike him up. Once he got out of bed in the middle of the night and fell on the floor, where he lay 5 hours —couldn't move. B. M. sent me a pear by the waiter with a long letter." Talk of houses and periods. All very smooth and surface talk; depends on knowing people; not on saying anything interesting. Bogey's cheeks are polished daily.

Tuesday, December 20th

This is almost the shortest day and perhaps the coldest night of the year. We are in the black heart of a terrific frost. I notice that look of black atoms in a clear air, which for some reason I can never describe to my liking. The pavement was white with great powdery flakes the other night, walking back with Roger and Helen; this was from Nessa's last Sunday—last, I fear, for many a month. But I have as usual "no time": let me count the things I should be doing this deep winter's night with Leonard at his last lecture and Pinker asleep in her chair. I should be reading Bagenal's story; Julian's play; Lord Chesterfield's letters; and writing to Hubert (about a cheque from the *Nation*). There is an irrational scale of values in my mind which puts these duties higher than mere scribbling.

This flashed to my mind at Nessa's children's party last night. The little creatures acting moved my infinitely sentimental throat. Angelica so mature and composed; all grey and silver; such an epitome of all womanliness; and such an unopened bud of sense and sensibility; wearing a grey wig and a sea coloured dress. And yet oddly enough I scarcely want children of my own now. This insatiable desire to write something before I die, this ravaging sense of the shortness and feverishness of life, make me cling, like a man on a rock, to my one anchor. I don't like the physicalness of having children of one's own. This occurred to me at Rodmell; but I never wrote it down. I can dramatise myself a parent, it is true. And perhaps I have killed the feeling instinctively; or perhaps nature does.

I am still writing the third chapter of *Orlando*. I have had of course to give up the fancy of finishing by February and printing this spring. It is drawing out longer than I meant. I have just been thinking over the scene when O. meets a girl (Nell)in the Park and goes with her to a neat room in Gerrard Street. There she will disclose herself. They will talk. This will lead to a diversion or two about women's love. This will bring in O.'s night life; and her clients (that's the word). Then she will see Dr. Johnson and perhaps write (I want somehow to quote it) To all you Ladies. So I shall get some effect of years passing; and then there will be a description of the lights of the eighteenth century burning; and the clouds of the nineteenth century rising. Then on to the nineteenth. But I have not considered this. I want to write it all over hastily and so keep unity of tone, which in this book is very important. It has to be half laughing, half serious; with great splashes of exaggeration. Perhaps I shall pluck up courage to ask *The Times* for a rise. But could I write for my Annual I would never write for another paper. How extraordinarily unwilled by me but potent in its own right, by the way, *Orlando* was! as if it shoved everything aside to come into existence. Yet I see looking back just now to March that it is almost exactly in spirit, though not in actual facts, the book I planned then as an escapade; the spirit to be satiric, the structure wild. Precisely.

Yes, I repeat, a very happy, a singularly happy autumn.

Thursday, December 22nd

I just open this for a moment, being dull of the head, to enter a severe reprimand of myself to myself. The value of society is that it snubs one. I am meretricious, mediocre, a humbug; am getting into the habit of flashy talk. Tinsel it seemed last night at the Keynes. I was out of humour and so could see the transparency of my own sayings. Dadie said a true thing too; when V. lets her style get on top of her, one thinks only of that; when she uses clichés, one thinks what she means. But, he says, I have no logical power and live and write in an opium dream. And the dream is too often about myself.

Now with middle age drawing on and age ahead it is important to be severe on such faults. So easily might I become a harebrained egotistic woman, exacting compliments, arrogant, narrow, withered. Nessa's children (I always measure myself against her and find her much the largest, most humane of the two of us), think of her now with an admiration that has no envy in it; with some trace of the old childish feeling that we were in league together against the world; and how proud I am of her triumphant winning of all our battles; as she takes her way so nonchalantly, modestly, almost anonymously, past the goal, with her children round her; and only a little added tenderness (a moving thing in her) which shows me that she too feels wonder, surprise, at having passed so many terrors and sorrows safe. . . .

The dream is too often about myself. To correct this; and to forget one's own sharp absurd little personality, reputation and the rest of it, one should read; see outsiders; think more; write more logically; above all be full of work; and practise anonymity. Silence in company; or the quietest statement, not the showiest; is also "medicated" as the doctors say. It was an empty party, rather, last night. Very nice here, though.

1928

Tuesday, January 17th

Yesterday we went to Hardy's funeral. What did I think of?
Of Max Beerbohm's letter, just read; or a lecture to the Newn-
hamites about women's writing. At intervals some emotion
broke in. But I doubt the capacity of the human animal for
being dignified in ceremony. One catches a bishop's frown and
twitch; sees his polished shiny nose; suspects the rapt spectacled
young priest, gazing at the cross he carries, of being a humbug; catches Robert Lynd's distracted haggard eye; then thinks
of the mediocrity of X.; next here is the coffin, an overgrown
one; like a stage coffin, covered with a white satin cloth; bearers
elderly gentlemen rather red and stiff, holding to the corners;
pigeons flying outside, insufficient artificial light; procession to
poets corner; dramatic "In sure and certain hope of immortality" perhaps melodramatic. After dinner at Clive's Lytton
protested that the great man's novels are the poorest of poor
stuff; and can't read them. Lytton sitting or lying inert, with
his eyes shut, or exasperated with them open. Lady Strachey
slowly fading, but it may take years. Over all this broods for me
some uneasy sense of change and mortality and how partings
are deaths; and then a sense of my own fame—why should this
come over me? and then of its remoteness; and then the pressure of writing two articles on Meredith and furbishing up the
Hardy. And Leonard sitting at home reading. And Max's
letter; and a sense of the futility of it all.

Saturday, February 11th

I am so cold I can hardly hold the pen. The futility of it all
—so I broke off; and have indeed been feeling that rather persistently, or perhaps I should have written here. Hardy and
Meredith together sent me torpid to bed with headache. I

know the feeling now, when I can't spin a sentence and sit mumbling and turning; and nothing flits by my brain, which is as a blank window. So I shut my studio door and go to bed, stuffing my ears with rubber; and there I lie a day or two. And what leagues I travel in the time! Such "sensations" spread over my spine and head directly I give them the chance; such an exaggerated tiredness; such anguishes and despairs; and heavenly relief and rest; and then misery again. Never was anyone so tossed up and down by the body as I am, I think. But it is over; and put away. . . .

For some reason, I am hacking rather listlessly at the last chapter of *Orlando,* which was to have been the best. Always, always the last chapter slips out of my hands. One gets bored. One whips oneself up. I still hope for a fresh wind, and don't very much bother, except that I miss the fun, which was so tremendously lively all October, November and December. I have my doubts if it is not empty; and too fantastic to write at such length.

Saturday, February 18th

And I should be revising Lord Chesterfield at this moment, but I'm not. My mind is wool-gathering away about *Women and Fiction,* which I am to read at Newnham in May. The mind is the most capricious of insects—flitting, fluttering. I had thought to write the quickest most brilliant pages in *Orlando* yesterday—not a drop came, all, forsooth, for the usual physical reasons, which delivered themselves today. It is the oddest feeling: as if a finger stopped the flow of the ideas in the brain; it is unsealed and the blood rushes all over the place. Again, instead of writing *O.,* I've been racing up and down the whole field of my lecture. And tomorrow, alas, we motor; for I must get back into the book—which has brightened the last few days satisfactorily. Not that my sensations in writing are an infallible guide.

Sunday, March 18th

I have lost my writing board; an excuse for the anæmic state of this book. Indeed I only write now, in between letters, to say that *Orlando* was finished yesterday as the clock struck

one. Anyhow the canvas is covered. There will be three months
of close work needed, imperatively, before it can be printed;
for I have scrambled and splashed and the canvas shows through
in a thousand places. But it is a serene, accomplished feeling, to
write, even provisionally, the End, and we go off on Saturday,
with my mind appeased.

I have written this book quicker than any; and it is all a
joke; and yet gay and quick reading I think; a writer's holiday.
I feel more and more sure that I will never write a novel again.
Little bits of rhyme come in. So we go motoring across France
on Saturday and shall be back on April 17th for the summer.
Time flies—oh yes; that summer should be here again; and I
still have the faculty of wonder at it. The world swinging round
again and bringing its green and blue close to one's eyes.

Thursday, March 22nd

These are the last pages at the end of *Orlando* and it is
twenty-five minutes to one; and I have written everything I
have to write and on Saturday we go abroad.

Yes it's done—*Orlando*—begun on 8th October, as a joke;
and now rather too long for my liking. It may fall between
stools, be too long for a joke, and too frivolous for a serious
book. All this I dismiss from a mind avid only of green fields,
the sun, wine; sitting doing nothing. I have been for the last
6 weeks rather a bucket than a fountain; sitting to be shot
into by one person after another. A rabbit that passes across a
shooting gallery, and one's friends go pop-pop. Heaven be
praised, Sibyl today puts us off; which leaves Dadie only and a
whole day's solitude, please Heaven, tomorrow. But I intend to
control this rabbit-shooting business when I come back. And
money making. I hope to settle in and write one nice little
discreet article for £25 each month; and so live; without stress;
and so read—what I want to read. At 46 one must be a miser;
only have time for essentials. But I think I have made moral
reflections enough, and should describe people, save that, when
seen so colourlessly, by duty not wish, one's mind is a little
slack in taking notes.

Watery blowy weather; and this time next week we shall be in the middle of France.

Tuesday, April 17th

Home again, as foretold, last night, and to settle the dust in my mind, write here. We have been across France and back —every inch of that fertile field traversed by the admirable Singer. And now towns and spires and scenes begin to rise in my mind as the rest sinks. I see Chartres in particular, the snail, with its head straight, marching across the flat country, the most distinguished of churches. The rose window is like a jewel on black velvet. The outside is very intricate yet simple; elongated; somehow preserved from the fantastic and ornate. Grey weather dashed all over this; and I remember coming in at night in the wet often and hearing the rain in hotels. Often I was bobbing up and down on my two glasses of vin du pays. It was rather a rush and a cram—as these jumbled notes testify. Once we were high up on a mountain in a snow storm; and rather afraid of a long tunnel. Twenty miles often cut us off from civilisation. One wet afternoon we punctured in a mountain village and I went in and sat with the family—a nice scrupulous polite woman, a girl who was pretty, shy, had a friend called Daisy at Earlsfield. They caught trout and wild boars. Then on we went to Florac, where I found a book— Girardin's memoirs in the old bookcase that had been sold with the house. Always some good food and hot bottles at night. Oh and my prize—£40 from the French. And Julian. And one or two hot days and the Pont du Garde in the sun; and Les Beaux (this is where Dante got his idea of Hell, Duncan said) and mounting all the time steadily was my desire for words, till I envisaged a sheet of paper and pen and ink as something of miraculous desirability—could even relish the scratch as if it were a divine kind of relief to me. And there was St. Remy and the ruins in the sun. I forget now how it all went—how thing fitted to thing; but the eminences now emerge and I noticed how, talking to Raymond at the *Nation* this afternoon, we had already pitched on the high points. Before that, crossing the

graveyard * in the bitter windy rain, we saw Hope † and a
dark cultivated woman. But on they went past us, with the
waver of an eye. Next moment I heard "Virginia" and turned
and there was Hope coming back—"Jane ‡ died yesterday,"
she murmured, half asleep, talking distraught, "out of herself."
We kissed by Cromwell's daughter's grave, where Shelley used
to walk, for Jane's death. She lay dead outside the graveyard in
that back room where we saw her lately raised on her pillows,
like a very old person whom life has tossed up and left; exalted, satisfied, exhausted. Hope the colour of dirty brown
paper. Then to the office, then home to work here; and now to
work and work, as hard as I can.

Saturday, April 21st

And I find myself again in the old driving whirlwind of
writing against time. Have I ever written with it? But I vow
I won't spend longer at *Orlando,* which is a freak; it shall come
out in September, though the perfect artist would revoke and
rewrite and polish—infinitely. But hours remain over to be
filled with reading something or other—I'm not sure what.
What sort of summer do I desire? Now that I have £16 to
spend before July 1st (on our new system) I feel freer; can
afford a dress and a hat and so may go about, a little, if I want.
And yet the only exciting life is the imaginary one. Once I get
the wheels spinning in my head, I don't want money much, or
dress, or even a cupboard, a bed at Rodmell or a sofa.

Tuesday, April 24th

A lovely soaring summer day this; winter sent howling home
to his arctic. I was reading *Othello* last night and was impressed
by the volley and volume and tumble of his words; too many
I should say, were I reviewing for *The Times.* He put them
in when tension was slack. In the great scenes, everything fits
like a glove. The mind tumbles and splashes among words

---

* The graveyard at the back of Brunswick Square. Jane Harrison and Hope
Mirrlees lived in a house near by.
 † Hope Mirrlees.
 ‡ Jane Harrison.

when it is not being urged on; I mean, the mind of a very great master of words who is writing with one hand. He abounds. The lesser writers stint. As usual, impressed by Shakespeare. But my mind is very bare to words—English words—at the moment; they hit me, hard, I watch them bounce and spring. I've read only French for 4 weeks. An idea comes to me for an article on French; what we know of it.

Friday, May 4th

And now there's the Femina prize to record before I go off this brilliant summer day to tea with Miss Jenkins in Doughty Street. I am going dutifully, not to snub the female young. But I shall be overpowering I doubt not. But it is a wonderful day.

The prize was an affair of dull stupid hours; a function; not alarming; stupefying. Hugh Walpole saying how much he disliked my books; rather, how much he feared for his own. Little Miss Robins, like a redbreast, creeping out. "I remember your mother—the most beautiful Madonna and at the same time the most complete woman of the world. Used to come and see me in my flat" (I see this as a summer visit on a hot day). "She never confided. She would suddenly say something so unexpected, from that Madonna face, one thought it *vicious.*" This I enjoyed; nothing else made much impression. Afterwards there was the horror of having looked ugly in cheap black clothes. I cannot control this complex. I wake at dawn with a start. Also the "fame" is becoming vulgar and a nuisance. It means nothing; yet takes one's time. Americans perpetually. Croly; Gaige; offers.

Thursday, May 31st

The sun is out again; I have half forgotten *Orlando* already, since L. has read it and it has half passed out of my possession; I think it lacks the sort of hammering I should have given it if I had taken longer; is too freakish and unequal, very brilliant now and then. As for the effect of the whole, that I can't judge. Not, I think, "important" among my works. L. says a satire.

L. takes *Orlando* more seriously than I had expected. Thinks it in some ways better than the *Lighthouse*: about more interesting things, and with more attachment to life and larger. The truth is I expect I began it as a joke and went on with it seriously. Hence it lacks some unity. He says it is very original. Anyhow I'm glad to be quit this time of writing "a novel"; and hope never to be accused of it again. Now I want to write some very closely reasoned criticism; book on fiction; an essay of some sort (but not Tolstoy for *The Times*). *Dr. Burney's Evening Party* I think for Desmond. And then? I feel anxious to keep the hatch down; not to let too many projects come in. Something abstract poetic next time—I don't know. I rather like the idea of these Biographies of living people. Ottoline suggests herself, but no. And I must tear up all that manuscript and write a great many notes and adventure out into the world.

June weather. Still, bright, fresh. Owing to the Lighthouse (car) I don't feel so shut in London as usual, and can imagine the evening on some moor now, or in France without the envy I used to have, in London on a fine evening. Also London itself perpetually attracts, stimulates, gives me a play and a story and a poem without any trouble, save that of moving my legs through the streets. I walked Pinker to Grays Inn Gardens this afternoon and saw—Red Lion Square: Morris's house; thought of them on winter evenings in the 50s; thought we are just as interesting; saw the Great Ormond Street where a dead girl was found yesterday; saw and heard the Salvation Army making Christianity gay for the people; a great deal of nudging and joking on the part of very unattractive young men and women; making it lively, I suppose; and yet, to be truthful, when I watch them I never laugh or criticise but only feel how strange and interesting this is; wonder what they mean by "Come to the Lord." I daresay exhibitionism accounts for some of it; the applause of the gallery; this lures boys to sing hymns; and kindles shop boys to announce in a loud voice that they are saved. It is what writing for the *Evening Standard* is for—and—I was going to say myself; but so far I have not done it.

Wednesday, June 20th

So sick of *Orlando* I can write nothing. I have corrected the proofs in a week; and cannot spin another phrase. I detest my own volubility. Why be always spouting words? Also I have almost lost the power of reading. Correcting proofs 5, 6 or 7 hours a day, writing in this and that meticulously, I have bruised my reading faculty severely. Take up Proust after dinner and put him down. This is the worst time of all. It makes me suicidal. Nothing seems left to do. All seems insipid and worthless. Now I will watch and see how I resurrect. I think I shall read something—say life of Goethe.

Wednesday, August 9th

. . . I write thus partly in order to slip the burden of writing narrative, as for instance, we came here * a fortnight ago. And we lunched at Charleston and Vita came and we were offered the field and we went to see the farm at Limekiln. Yet no doubt I shall be more interested, come 10 years, in facts; and shall want, as I do when I read, to be told details, details, so that I may look up from the page and arrange them too, into one of those makings up which seem so much truer done thus, from heaps of non-assorted facts, than now I can make them, when it is almost immediately under my eyes. It was a fine day last Monday, I rather think; and we drove through Ripe; and there was a girl and her feller at the gate in a narrow lane; and we had to interrupt them to turn the motor. I thought how the things they had been saying were dammed like a river, by our interruption; and they stood there half amused yet impatient, telling us to go to the left, but the road was up. They were glad when we went; yet gave us a flash of interest. Who are these people in their motor car: where are they going? and then this sunk beneath the mind and they forgot us completely. We went on. And then we reached the farm. The oasts had umbrella spokes poking out at the top; all was so ruined and faded. The Tudor farmhouse was almost blind; very small eyebrowed windows; old Stuart farmers must have peered out over the flat land, very dirty, ill kempt, like people in slums. But they had dignity; at least thick walls; fireplaces; and solidity; whereas now the house is lived in by

* Monks House, Rodmell.

one old weedy pink faced man, who flung himself in his arm-chair—go where you like—go anywhere, he said, loose jointed, somehow decayed, like the hop oasts; and damp like the mildewed carpets, and sordid, like the beds with the pots sticking out under them. The walls were sticky; the furniture mid-Victorian; little light came through. It was all dying, decaying; and he had been there 50 years and it will drop to pieces, since there is not enough beauty or strength to make anyone repair it.

Saturday, August 12th

Shall I now continue this soliloquy, or shall I imagine an audience, which will make me describe? This sentence is due to the book on fiction which I am now writing—once more, O once more. It is a hand to mouth book. I scribble down whatever I can think of about Romance, Dickens etc. must hastily gorge on Jane Austen tonight and dish up something tomorrow. All this criticism however may well be dislodged by the desire to write a story. *The Moths* * hovers somewhere at the back of my brain. But Clive yesterday at Charleston said that there were no class distinctions. We had tea from bright blue cups under the pink light of the giant hollyhock. We were all a little drugged with the country; a little bucolic I thought. It was lovely enough—made me envious of its country peace; the trees all standing securely—why did my eye catch the trees? The look of things has a great power over me. Even now, I have to watch the rooks beating up against the wind, which is high, and still I say to myself instinctively "What's the phrase for that?" and try to make more and more vivid the roughness of the air current and the tremor of the rook's wing slicing as if the air were full of ridges and ripples and roughnesses. They rise and sink, up and down, as if the exercise rubbed and braced them like swimmers in rough water. But what a little I can get down into my pen of what is so vivid to my eyes, and not only to my eyes; also to some nervous fibre, or fanlike membrane in my species.

* Became *The Waves*.

Friday, August 31st

This is the last day of August and like almost all of them of extraordinary beauty. Each day is fine enough and hot enough for sitting out; but also full of wandering clouds; and that fading and rising of the light which so enraptures me in the downs; which I am always comparing to the light beneath an alabaster bowl. The corn is now stood about in rows of three, four or five solid shaped yellow cakes—rich, it seems, with eggs and spice; good to eat. Sometimes I see the cattle galloping "like mad" as Dostoievsky would say, in the brooks. The clouds—if I could describe them I would; one yesterday had flowing hair on it, like the very fine white hair of an old man. At this moment they are white in a leaden sky; but the sun behind the house is making the grass green. I walked to the racecourse today and saw a weasel.

Monday, September 10th

. . . I was amused to find that when Rebecca West says "men are snobs" she gets an instant rise out of Desmond: so I retorted on him with the condescending phrase used about women novelists' "limitations" in *Life and Letters*. But there was no acrimony in this. We talked with fertility; never working a seam dry. Do you suppose then that we are now coming like the homing rooks back to the tops of our trees? and that all this cawing is the beginning of settling in for the night? I seem to notice in several of my friends some endearing and affecting cordiality; and a pleasure in intimacy; as if the sun were sinking. Often that image comes to me with some sense of my physical state being colder now, the sun just off one; the old disc of one's being growing cooler—but it is only just beginning; and one will turn cold and silver like the moon. This has been a very animated summer; a summer lived almost too much in public. Often down here I have entered into a sanctuary; a nunnery; had a religious retreat; of great agony once; and always some terror; so afraid one is of loneliness; of seeing to the bottom of the vessel. That is one of the experiences I have had here in some Augusts; and got then to a consciousness of what I call "reality": a thing I see before me: something abstract; but residing in the downs or sky; beside which nothing matters; in which I shall rest and continue to exist. Reality I call it. And I fancy sometimes this is the most necessary thing to me: that which I seek. But who knows—once one takes a pen and writes? How difficult not to go making "reality" this and that, whereas it is one thing. Now perhaps this is my gift: this perhaps is what distinguishes me from other people: I think it may be rare to have so acute a sense of something like that—but again, who knows? I would like to express it too.

Saturday, September 22nd

This has been the finest, and not only finest, but loveliest, summer in the world. Still, though it blows, how clear and bright it is; and the clouds are opalescent; the long barns on my horizon mouse-coloured; the stacks pale gold. Owning the field has given a different orient to my feelings about Rodmell. I begin to dig myself in and take part in it. And I shall build another storey to the house if I make money. But the news of *Orlando* is black. We may sell a third that we sold of the *Lighthouse* before publication—not a shop will buy save in sixes and twelves. They say this is inevitable. No one wants biography. But it is a novel, says Miss Ritchie.*

But it is called biography on the title page, they say. It will have to go to the Biography shelf. I doubt therefore that we shall do more than cover expenses—a high price to pay for the fun of calling it a biography. And I was so sure it was going to be the one popular book! Also it should be 10/6 or 12/6, not 9/-. Lord! lord! Thus I must write some articles this winter, if we are to have nest eggs at the Bank. Down here I have flung myself tooth and nail on my fiction book, and should have finished the first draft but for Dorothy Osborne whom I'm dashing off. It will need entire re-writing but the grind is done—the rushing through book after book and now what shall I read? These novels have hung about me so long. Mercy it is to be quit of them; and shall I read English poetry, French memoirs —shall I read now for a book to be called "The Lives of the

* Miss Ritchie was the traveller.

Obscure"? And when, I wonder, shall I begin *The Moths?* Not
until I am pressed into it by those insects themselves. Nor have
I any notion what it is to be like—a completely new attempt I
think. So I always think.

Saturday, October 27th
    A scandal, a scandal, to let so much time slip and I leaning
on the Bridge watching it go. Only leaning has not been my
pose; running up and down, irritably, excitedly, restlessly. And
the stream viciously eddying. Why do I write these metaphors?
Because I have written nothing for an age. *Orlando* has been
published. I went to Burgundy with Vita. It flashed by. How
disconnected this is! My ambition is from this very moment, 8
minutes to 6, on Saturday evening, to attain complete concentration again. When I have written here, I am going to open
Fanny Burney's diaries and work solidly at that article which
poor Miss McKay cables about. I am going to read, to think. I
gave up reading and thinking on 26th September when I went
to France. I came back and we plunged into London and publishing. I am a little sick of *Orlando.* I think I am a little indifferent now what anyone thinks. Joy's life in the doing—I
murder, as usual, a quotation; I mean it's the writing, not the
being read, that excites me. And as I can't write while I'm
being read, I am always a little hollow hearted; whipped up;
but not so happy as in solitude. The reception, as they say,
surpassed expectation. Sales beyond our record for the first
week. I was floating rather lazily on praise, when Squire barked
in the *Observer,* but even as I sat reading him on the Backs last
Sunday in the showering red leaves and their illumination, I
felt the rock of self esteem untouched in me. "This doesn't
really hurt," I said to myself; even now; and sure enough, before evening I was calm, untouched. And now there's Hugh
in the *Morning Post* to spread the butter again, and Rebecca
West—such a trumpet call of praise—that's her way—that I feel
a little sheepish and silly. And now no more of that I hope.
    Thank God, my long toil at the women's lecture is this
moment ended. I am back from speaking at Girton, in floods of
rain. Starved but valiant young women—that's my impression.

Intelligent, eager, poor; and destined to become schoolmistresses in shoals. I blandly told them to drink wine and have a room of their own. Why should all the splendour, all the luxury of life be lavished on the Julians and the Francises, and none on the Phares and the Thomases? There's Julian not much relishing it, perhaps. I fancy sometimes the world changes. I think I see reason spreading. But I should have liked a closer and thicker knowledge of life. I should have liked to deal with real things sometimes. I get such a sense of tingling and vitality from an evening's talk like that; one's angularities and obscurities are smoothed and lit. How little one counts, I think: how little anyone counts; how fast and furious and masterly life is; and how all these thousands are swimming for dear life. I felt elderly and mature. And nobody respected me. They were very eager, egotistical, or rather not much impressed by age and repute. Very little reverence or that sort of thing about. The corridors of Girton are like vaults in some horrid high church cathedral—on and on they go, cold and shiny, with a light burning. High Gothic rooms: acres of bright brown wood; here and there a photograph.

Wednesday, November 7th

And this shall be written for my own pleasure. But that phrase inhibits me; for if one writes only for one's own pleasure, I don't know what it is that happens. I suppose the convention of writing is destroyed: therefore one does not write at all. I am rather headachy and dimly obscured with sleeping draught. This is the aftermath (what does that mean?—Trench, whom I open idly apparently says nothing) of *Orlando*. Yes, yes: since I wrote here I have become two inches and a half higher in the public view. I think I may say that I am now among the well known writers. I had tea with Lady Cunard— might have lunched or dined any day. I found her in a little cap telephoning. It was not her atmosphere—this of solitary talk. She is too shrewd to expand and needs society to make her rash and random which is her point. Ridiculous little parakeet faced woman; but not quite sufficiently ridiculous. I kept wishing for superlatives; could not get the illusion to flap its wings.

Flunkeys, yes: but a little drab and friendly. Marble floor, yes:
but no glamour; no tune strumming, for me at least. And the
two of us sitting there had almost to be conventional and flat—
reminds me of Sir Thomas Browne—the greatest book of our
times—said a little flatly by a woman of business, to me who
don't believe in that kind of thing unless launched with cham-
pagne and garlands. Then in came Lord Donegall, a glib Irish
youth, dark, sallow, slick, on the Press. "Don't they treat you
like a dog?" I said. "No, not at all," he replied, astonished that
a marquis could be treated like a dog by anyone. And then
we went up and up to see pictures on stairs, in ballrooms and
finally to Lady C.'s bedroom, hung entirely with flower pieces.
The bed has its triangular canopy of rose red silk; the windows,
looking on the Square, are hung with green brocade. Her
poudreuse—like mine only painted and gilt—stood open with
gold brushes, looking glasses, and there on her gold slippers
were neatly laid gold stockings. All this paraphernalia for one
stringy old hop o' my thumb. She set the two great musical
boxes playing and I said did she lie in bed and listen to them?
But no. She has nothing fantastic in that way about her. Money
is important. She told me rather sordid stories of Lady Sackville never visiting her without fobbing something off on her—
now a bust, worth £5, for which she paid £100: now a brass
knocker. "And then her talk—I didn't care for it . . ." Somehow I saw into these sordid commonplace talks and could not
sprinkle the air with gold dust easily. But no doubt she has
her acuity, her sharp peck at life; only how adorable, I thought,
as I tiptoed home in my tight shoes, in the fog, in the chill,
could one open one of these doors that I still open so venturously, and find a live interesting real person, a Nessa, a Duncan, a Roger. Someone new, whose mind would begin vibrating.
Coarse and usual and dull these Cunards and Colefaxes are—
for all their astonishing competence in the commerce of life.

    And I cannot think what to write next. I mean the situation
is, this *Orlando* is of course a very quick brilliant book. Yes,
but I did not try to explore. And must I always explore? Yes I
think so still. Because my reaction is not the usual. Nor can I
even after all these years run it off lightly. *Orlando* taught me

how to write a direct sentence; taught me continuity and narrative and how to keep the realities at bay. But I purposely avoided of course any other difficulty. I never got down to my depths and made shapes square up, as I did in the *Lighthouse*.

Well but *Orlando* was the outcome of a perfectly definite, indeed overmastering, impulse. I want fun. I want fantasy. I want (and this was serious) to give things their caricature value. And still this mood hangs about me. I want to write a history, say of Newnham or the women's movement, in the same vein. The vein is deep in me—at least sparkling, urgent. But is it not stimulated by applause? overstimulated? My notion is that there are offices to be discharged by talent for the relief of genius: meaning that one has the play side; the gift when it is mere gift, unapplied gift; and the gift when it is serious, going to business. And one relieves the other.

Yes, but *The Moths?* That was to be an abstract mystical eyeless book: a playpoem. And there may be affectation in being too mystical, too abstract; saying Nessa and Roger and Duncan and Ethel Sands admire that; it is the uncompromising side of me; therefore I had better win their approval.

Again, one reviewer says that I have come to a crisis in the matter of style: it is now so fluent and fluid that it runs through the mind like water.

That disease began in the *Lighthouse*. The first part came fluid—how I wrote and wrote!

Shall I now check and consolidate, more in the *Dalloway* and *Jacob's Room* style?

I rather think the upshot will be books that relieve other books: a variety of styles and subjects: for after all, that is my temperament, I think, to be very little persuaded of the truth of anything—what I say, what people say—always to follow, blindly, instinctively with a sense of leaping over a precipice —the call of—the call of—now, if I write *The Moths* I must come to terms with these mystical feelings.

X destroyed our Saturday walk: he is now mouldy and to me depressing. He is perfectly reasonable and charming. Nothing surprises, nothing shocks him. He has been through it all, one feels. He has come out rolled, smoothed, rather sodden, rather creased and jumbled, like a man who has sat up all night in a third class railway carriage. His fingers are stained yellow with cigarettes. One tooth in the lower jaw is missing. His hair is dank. His eyes more than ever dubious. He has a hole in his blue sock. Yet he is resolute and determined—that's what I find so depressing. He seems to be sure that it is his view that is the right one: ours vagaries, deviations. And if his view is the right one, God knows there is nothing to live for: not a greasy biscuit. And the egotism of men surprises and shocks me even now. Is there a woman of my acquaintance who could sit in my armchair from 3 to 6:30 without the semblance of a suspicion that I may be busy, or tired, or bored; and so sitting could talk, grumbling and grudging, of her difficulties, worries; then eat chocolates, then read a book, and go at last, apparently self-complacent and wrapped in a kind of blubber of misty self-salutation? Not the girls at Newnham or Girton. They are far too spry; far too disciplined. None of that self confidence is their lot.

Wednesday, November 28th

Father's birthday. He would have been 96, 96, yes, today; and could have been 96, like other people one has known: but mercifully was not. His life would have   1928 entirely ended mine. What would have happened? No   1832 writing, no books;—inconceivable.

I used to think of him and mother daily; but writing the *Lighthouse* laid them in my mind. And now he comes back sometimes, but differently. (I believe this to be true—that I was obsessed by them both, unhealthily; and writing of them was a necessary act.) He comes back now more as a contemporary. I must read him some day. I wonder if I can feel again, I hear his voice, I know this by heart?

So the days pass and I ask myself sometimes whether one is not hypnotised, as a child by a silver globe, by life; and whether this is living. It's very quick, bright, exciting. But superficial perhaps. I should like to take the globe in my hands and feel it quietly, round, smooth, heavy, and so hold it, day

after day. I will read Proust I think. I will go backwards and
forwards.

   As for my next book, I am going to hold myself from writing till I have it impending in me: grown heavy in my mind
like a ripe pear; pendant, gravid, asking to be cut or it will fall.
The Moths still haunts me, coming, as they always do, un-
bidden, between tea and dinner, while L. plays the gramophone. I shape a page or two; and make myself stop. Indeed I
am up against some difficulties. Fame to begin with. *Orlando*
has done very well. Now I could go on writing like that—the
tug and suck are at me to do it. People say this was so spontaneous, so natural. And I would like to keep those qualities if
I could without losing the others. But those qualities were
largely the result of ignoring the others. They came of writing
exteriorly; and if I dig, must I not lose them? And what is my
own position towards the inner and the outer? I think a kind of
ease and dash are good;—yes: I think even externality is good;
some combination of them ought to be possible. The idea has
come to me that what I want now to do is to saturate every
atom. I mean to eliminate all waste, deadness, superfluity: to
give the moment whole; whatever it includes. Say that the
moment is a combination of thought; sensation; the voice of
the sea. Waste, deadness, come from the inclusion of things that
don't belong to the moment; this appalling narrative business
of the realist: getting on from lunch to dinner: it is false, unreal, merely conventional. Why admit anything to literature
that is not poetry—by which I mean saturated? Is that not my
grudge against novelists? that they select nothing? The poets
succeeding by simplifying: practically everything is left out. I
want to put practically everything in: yet to saturate. That is
what I want to do in *The Moths*. It must include nonsense,
fact, sordidity: but made transparent. I think I must read Ibsen
and Shakespeare and Racine. And I will write something about
them; for that is the best spur, my mind being what it is; then
I read with fury and exactness; otherwise I skip and skip; I am
a lazy reader. But no: I am surprised and a little disquieted by
the remorseless severity of my mind: that it never stops reading and writing; makes me write on Geraldine Jewsbury, on

Hardy, on Women—is too professional, too little any longer a dreamy amateur.

Tuesday, December 18th

L. has just been in to consult about a 3rd edition of *Orlando*. This has been ordered; we have sold over 6,000 copies; and sales are still amazingly brisk—150 today for instance; most days between 50 and 60; always to my surprise. Will they stop or go on? Anyhow my room is secure. For the first time since I married, 1912-1928—16 years, I have been spending money. The spending muscle does not work naturally yet. I feel guilty; put off buying, when I know that I should buy; and yet have an agreeable luxurious sense of coins in my pocket beyond my weekly 13/- which was always running out, or being encroached upon.

1929

Friday, January 4th

Now is life very solid or very shifting? I am haunted by the two contradictions. This has gone on for ever; will last for ever; goes down to the bottom of the world—this moment I stand on. Also it is transitory, flying, diaphanous. I shall pass like a cloud on the waves. Perhaps it may be that though we change, one flying after another, so quick, so quick, yet we are somehow successive and continuous we human beings, and show the light through. But what is the light? I am impressed by the transitoriness of human life to such an extent that I am often saying a farewell—after dining with Roger for instance; or reckoning how many more times I shall see Nessa.

Thursday, March 28th

It is a disgrace indeed; no diary has been left so late in the year. The truth was that we went to Berlin on 16th January, and then I was in bed for three weeks afterwards and then could not write, perhaps for another three, and have spent my energy since in one of my excited outbursts of composition—writing what I made up in bed, a final version of *Women and Fiction*.

And as usual I am bored by narrative. I want only to say how I met Nessa in Tottenham Court Road this afternoon, both of us sunk fathoms deep in that wash of reflection in which we both swim about. She will be gone on Wednesday for 4 months. It is queer how instead of drawing apart, life draws us together. But I was thinking a thousand things as I carried my teapot, gramophone records and stockings under my arm. It is one of those days that I called "potent" when we lived in Richmond.

Perhaps I ought not to go on repeating what I have always

138

said about the spring. One ought perhaps to be forever finding new things to say, since life draws on. One ought to invent a fine narrative style. Certainly there are many new ideas always forming in my head. For one, that I am going to enter a nunnery these next months; and let myself down into my mind; Bloomsbury being done with. I am going to face certain things. It is going to be a time of adventure and attack, rather lonely and painful I think. But solitude will be good for a new book. Of course, I shall make friends. I shall be external outwardly. I shall buy some good clothes and go out into new houses. All the time I shall attack this angular shape in my mind. I think *The Moths* (if that is what I shall call it) will be very sharply cornered. I am not satisfied though with the frame. There is this sudden fertility which may be mere fluency. In old days books were so many sentences absolutely struck with an axe out of crystal: and now my mind is so impatient, so quick, in some ways so desperate.

Sunday, May 12th

Here, having just finished what I call the final revision of *Women and Fiction* * so that L. can read it after tea, I stop; surfeited. And the pump, which I was so sanguine as to think ceased, begins again. About *Women and Fiction* I am not sure —a brilliant essay?—I daresay: it has much work in it, many opinions boiled down into a kind of jelly, which I have stained red as far as I can. But I am eager to be off—to write without any boundary coming slick in one's eyes: here my public has been too close; facts; getting them malleable, easily yielding to each other.

Tuesday, May 28th

Now about this book, *The Moths*. How am I to begin it? And what is it to be? I feel no great impulse; no fever; only a great pressure of difficulty. Why write it then? Why write at all? Every morning I write a little sketch, to amuse myself. I am not saying, I might say, that these sketches have any rele-

* *A Room of One's Own.*

vance. I am not trying to tell a story. Yet perhaps it might be done in that way. A mind thinking. They might be islands of light—islands in the stream that I am trying to convey; life itself going on. The current of the moths flying strongly this way. A lamp and a flower pot in the centre. The flower can always be changing. But there must be more unity between each scene than I can find at present. Autobiography it might be called. How am I to make one lap, or act, between the coming of the moths, more intense than another; if there are only scenes? One must get the sense that this is the beginning; this the middle; that the climax—when she opens the window and the moth comes in. I shall have the two different currents—the moths flying along; the flower upright in the centre; a perpetual crumbling and renewing of the plant. In its leaves she might see things happen. But who is she? I am very anxious that she should have no name. I don't want a Lavinia or a Penelope: I want "she." But that becomes arty, Liberty greenery yallery somehow: symbolic in loose robes. Of course I can make her think backwards and forwards; I can tell stories. But that's not it. Also I shall do away with exact place and time. Anything may be out of the window—a ship—a desert—London.

Sunday, June 23rd

It was very hot that day, driving to Worthing to see Leonard's mother, my throat hurt me. Next morning I had a headache—so we stayed on at Rodmell till today. At Rodmell I read through *The Common Reader;* and this is very important—I must learn to write more succinctly. Especially in the general idea essays like the last, "How it strikes a Contemporary," I am horrified by my own looseness. This is partly that I don't think things out first; partly that I stretch my style to take in crumbs of meaning. But the result is a wobble and diffusity and breathlessness which I detest. One must correct *A Room of One's Own* very carefully before printing. And so I pitched into my great lake of melancholy. Lord how deep it is! What a born melancholic I am! The only way I keep afloat is by working. A note for the summer—I must take more work than I can possibly get done.—No, I don't know what it comes from. Directly

I stop working I feel that I am sinking down, down. And as usual I feel that if I sink further I shall reach the truth. That is the only mitigation; a kind of nobility. Solemnity. I shall make myself face the fact that there is nothing—nothing for any of us. Work, reading, writing are all disguises; and relations with people. Yes, even having children would be useless.

However, I now begin to see *The Moths* rather too clearly, or at least strenuously, for my comfort. I think it will begin like this: dawn; the shells on a beach; I don't know—voices of cock and nightingale; and then all the children at a long table—lessons. The beginning. Well, all sorts of characters are to be there. Then the person who is at the table can call out anyone of them at any moment; and build up by that person the mood, tell a story; for instance about dogs or nurses; or some adventure of a child's kind; all to be very Arabian Nights; and so on: this shall be childhood; but it must not be *my* childhood; and boats on the pond; the sense of children; unreality; things oddly proportioned. Then another person or figure must be selected. The unreal world must be round all this—the phantom waves. The Moth must come in; the beautiful single moth. Could one not get the waves to be heard all through? Or the farmyard noises? Some odd irrelevant noises. She might have a book— one book to read in—another to write in—old letters. Early morning light—but this need not be insisted on; because there must be great freedom from "reality." Yet everything must have relevance.

Well all this is of course the "real" life; and nothingness only comes in the absence of this. I have proved this quite certainly in the past half hour. Everything becomes green and vivified in me when I begin to think of *The Moths*. Also, I think, one is much better able to enter into others'—

Monday, August 19th

I suppose dinner interrupted. And I opened this book in another train of mind—to record the blessed fact that for good or bad I have just set the last correction to *Women and Fiction*, or *A Room of One's Own*. I shall never read it again I suppose. Good or bad? Has an uneasy life in it I think: you feel the creature arching its back and galloping on, though as usual much is watery and flimsy and pitched in too high a voice.

Monday, September 10th

Leonard is having a picnic at Charleston and I am here—"tired." But why am I tired? Well I am never alone. This is the beginning of my complaint. I am not physically tired so much as psychologically. I have strained and wrung at journalism and proof correction; and underneath has been forming my Moth book. Yes, but it forms very slowly; and what I want is not to write it, but to think it for two or three weeks say—to get into the same current of thought and let that submerge everything. Writing perhaps a few phrases here at my window in the morning. (And they've gone to some lovely place—Hurstmonceux perhaps, in this strange misty evening;—and yet when the time came to go, all I wanted was to walk off into the hills by myself. I am now feeling a little lonely and deserted and defrauded, inevitably.) And every time I get into my current of thought I am jerked out of it. We have the Keynes; then Vita came; then Angelica and Eve; then we went to Worthington, then my head begins throbbing—so here I am, not writing—that does not matter, but not thinking, feeling or seeing—and seizing an afternoon alone as a treasure—Leonard appeared at the glass door at this moment; and they didn't go to Hurstmonceux or anywhere; and Sprott was there and a miner, so I missed nothing—one's first egotistical pleasure.

Really these premonitions of a book—states of soul in creating—are very queer and little apprehended . . .

And then I am 47: yes; and my infirmities will of course increase. To begin with my eyes. Last year, I think, I could read without spectacles; would pick up a paper and read it in a tube; gradually I found I needed spectacles in bed; and now I can't read a line (unless held at a very odd angle) without them. My new spectacles are much stronger than the old and when I take them off I am blinded for a moment. What other infirmities? I can hear, I think, perfectly: I think I could walk as well as ever. But then will there not be the change of life? And may that not be a difficult and even dangerous time? Obviously one can get over it by facing it with common sense—that it is a natural process; that one can lie out here and read; that one's faculties will be the same afterwards; that one has nothing to worry about in one sense—I've written some interesting books, can make money, can afford a holiday—Oh no; one has nothing to bother about; and these curious intervals in life—I've had many—are the most fruitful artistically—one becomes fertilised —think of my madness at Hogarth—and all the little illnesses— that before I wrote the *Lighthouse* for instance. Six weeks in bed now would make a masterpiece of *Moths*. But that won't be the name. Moths, I suddenly remember, don't fly by day. And there can't be a lighted candle. Altogether, the shape of the book wants considering—and with time I could do it. Here I broke off.

Wednesday, September 25th

Yesterday morning I made another start on *The Moths*, but that won't be its title; and several problems cry out at once to be solved. Who thinks it? And am I outside the thinker? One wants some device which is not a trick.

Friday, October 11th

And I snatch at the idea of writing here in order not to write *Waves* or *Moths* or whatever it is to be called. One thinks one has learnt to write quickly; and one hasn't. And what is odd, I'm not writing with gusto or pleasure: because of the concentration. I am not reeling it off; but sticking it down. Also, never, in my life, did I attack such a vague yet elaborate design; whenever I make a mark I have to think of its relation to a dozen others. And though I could go on ahead easily enough, I am always stopping to consider the whole effect. In particular is there some radical fault in my scheme? I am not quite satisfied with this method of picking out things in the room and being reminded by them of other things. Yet I can't at the moment divine anything which keeps so close to the original design and admits of movement. Hence, perhaps, these October days are to me a little strained and surrounded with silence. What I mean by this last word I don't quite know, since I have never stopped "seeing" people—Nessa and Roger, the Jeffers, Charles Buxton, and should have seen Lord David and am to see the Eliots—oh and there was Vita too. No, it's not physical silence; it's some inner loneliness—interesting to analyse if one could. To give an example—I was walking up Bedford Place is it—the straight street with all the boarding houses this afternoon—and I said to myself spontaneously, something like this. How I suffer. And no one knows how I suffer, walking up this street, engaged with my anguish, as I was after Thoby * died— alone; fighting something alone. But then I had the devil to fight, and now nothing. And when I come indoors it is all so silent—I am not carrying a great rush of wheels in my head— yet I am writing—oh and we are very successful—and there is —what I most love—change ahead. Yes, that last evening at Rodmell when Leonard came down against his will to fetch me, the Keynes came over. And Maynard is giving up the *Nation,* and so is Hubert † and so no doubt shall we. And it is autumn; and the lights are going up; and Nessa is in Fitzroy Street—in a great misty room with flaring gas and unsorted plates and glasses on the floor—and the Press is booming—and this celebrity business is quite chronic—and I am richer than I have ever been—and bought a pair of earrings today—and for all this, there is vacancy and silence somewhere in the machine. On the whole, I do not much mind; because what I like is to flash and dash from side to side, goaded on by what I call reality. If I never felt these extraordinarily pervasive strains—of unrest or rest or happiness or discomfort—I should float down into acquiescence. Here is something to fight; and when I wake early I say to myself Fight, fight. If I could catch the feeling, I would; the feeling of the singing of the real world, as one is driven by loneliness and silence from the habitable world; the sense that comes to me of being bound on an adventure; of being strangely free now, with money and so on, to do anything. I go to take theatre tickets (The Matriarch) and see a list of cheap excursions hanging there, and at once think that I will go to Stratford on Avon Mob Fair tomorrow—why not?—or to Ireland or to

* J. T. Stephen, brother of V. W. He died in 1906.
† Hubert Henderson, editor.

Edinburgh for a weekend. I daresay I shan't. But anything is possible. And this curious steed, life, is genuine. Does any of this convey what I want to say? But I have not really laid hands on the emptiness after all. It's odd, now I come to think of it— I miss Clive.

Wednesday, October 23rd

As it is true—I write only for an hour, then rush back feeling I cannot keep my brain on that spin any more—then typewrite, and am done by 12. I will here sum up my impressions before publishing *A Room of One's Own*. It is a little ominous that Morgan won't review it. It makes me suspect that there is a shrill feminine tone in it which my intimate friends will dislike. I forecast, then, that I shall get no criticism, except of the evasive jocular kind, from Lytton, Roger and Morgan; that the press will be kind and

He wrote yesterday, 3 Dec. and said he very much liked it.

talk of its charm and sprightliness; also I shall be attacked for a feminist and hinted at for a Sapphist; Sybil will ask me to luncheon; I shall get a good many letters from young women. I am afraid it will not be taken seriously. Mrs. Woolf is so accomplished a writer that all she says makes easy reading . . . this very feminine logic . . . a book to be put in the hands of girls. I doubt that I mind very much. The Moths; but I think it is to be waves, is trudging along; and I have that to refer to, if I am damped by the other. It is a trifle, I shall say; so it is; but I wrote it with ardour and conviction.

We dined last night with the Webbs and I had Eddy * and Dotty to tea. As for these mature dinner parties one has some friendly easy talk with one man—Hugh Macmillan †—about the Buchans and his own career; the Webbs are friendly but can't be influenced about Kenya; we sit in two lodging house rooms (the dining room had a brass bedstead behind a screen) eat hunks of red beef; and are offered whisky. It is the same enlightened, impersonal, perfectly aware of itself atmosphere. "My little boy shall have his toys"—but don't let that go any further

* E. Sackville-West.
† Afterwards Lord Macmillan.

—"that's what my wife says about my being in the Cabinet." No they have no illusions. And I compared them with L. and myself, and felt, (I daresay for this reason) the pathos, the symbolical quality of the childless couple; standing for something, united.

Saturday, November 2nd

Oh but I have done quite well so far with *Room of One's Own;* and it sells, I think; and I get unexpected letters. But I am more concerned with my *Waves.* I've just typed out my morning's work; and can't feel altogether sure. There is *something* there (as I felt about *Mrs. Dalloway*) but I can't get at it, squarely; nothing like the speed and certainty of the *Lighthouse: Orlando* mere child's play. Is there some falsity of method, somewhere? Something tricky?—so that the interesting things aren't firmly based? I am in an odd state; feel a cleavage; here's my interesting thing; and there's no quite solid table on which to put it. It might come in a flash, on re-reading—some solvent. I am convinced that I am right to seek for a station whence I can set my people against time and the sea—but Lord, the difficulty of digging oneself in there, with conviction. Yesterday I had conviction; it has gone today.

Saturday, November 30th

I fill in this page, nefariously; at the end of a morning's work. I have begun the second part of *Waves*—I don't know. I don't know. I feel that I am only accumulating notes for a book —whether I shall ever face the labour of writing it, God knows. From some higher station I may be able to pull it together—at Rodmell, in my new room. Reading the *Lighthouse* does not make it easier to write . . .

Sunday, December 8th

I read and read and finished I daresay 3 foot thick of MS. read carefully too; much of it on the border, and so needing thought. Now, with this load despatched, I am free to begin reading Elizabethans—the little unknown writers, whom I, so ignorant am I, have never heard of, Pullenham, Webb, Harvey.

This thought fills me with joy—no overstatement. To begin reading with a pen in my hand, discovering, pouncing, thinking of phrases, when the ground is new, remains one of my great excitements. Oh but L. will sort apples and the little noise upsets me; I can't think what I was going to say.

So I stopped writing, by which no great harm was done, and made out a list of Elizabethan poets. And I have, with great happiness, refused to write Rhoda Broughton, Ouida for de la Mare. That vein, popular as it is, witness Jane and Geraldine, is soon worked out in me. I want to write criticism. Yes, and one might make out an obscure figure or two. It was the Elizabethan prose writers I loved first and most wildly, stirred by Hakluyt, which father lugged home for me—I think of it with some sentiment—father tramping over the Library with his little girl sitting at H.P.G.* in mind. He must have been 65; I 15 or 16 then; and why I don't know but I became enraptured, though not exactly interested, but the sight of the large yellow page entranced me. I used to read it and dream of those obscure adventurers and no doubt practised their style in my copybook. I was then writing a long picturesque essay upon the Christian religion, I think; called Religio Laici, I believe, proving that man has need of a God; but the God was described in process of change; and I also wrote a history of Women; and a history of my own family—all very longwinded and Elizabethan in style.

RODMELL—*Boxing Day*

I find it almost incredibly soothing—a fortnight alone—almost impossible to let oneself have it. Relentlessly we have crushed visitors. We will be alone this once, we say; and really, it seems possible. Then Annie is to me very sympathetic. My bread bakes well. All is rather rapt, simple, quick, effective—except for my blundering on at *The Waves*. I write two pages of arrant nonsense, after straining; I write variations of every sentence; compromises; bad shots; possibilities; till my writing book is like a lunatic's dream. Then I trust to some inspiration on re-reading; and pencil them into some sense. Still I am not

* Hyde Park Gate, where the Stephen family lived when V. W. was a child.

satisfied. I think there is something lacking. I sacrifice nothing to seemliness. I press to my centre. I don't care if it all is scratched out. And there is something there. I incline now to try violent shots—at London—at talk—shouldering my way ruthlessly—and then, if nothing comes of it—anyhow I have examined the possibilities. But I wish I enjoyed it more. I don't have it in my head all day like the *Lighthouse* and *Orlando*.

1930

Sunday, January 12th

Sunday it is. And I have just exclaimed: "And now I can think of nothing else." Thanks to my pertinacity and industry, I can now hardly stop making up *The Waves*. The sense of this came acutely about a week ago on beginning to write the *Phantom Party:* now I feel that I can rush on, after 6 months' hacking, and finish: but without the least certainty how it's to achieve any form. Much will have to be discarded: what is essential is to write fast and not break the mood—no holiday, no interval if possible, till it is done. Then rest. Then re-write.

Sunday, January 26th

I am 48: we have been at Rodmell—a wet, windy day again; but on my birthday we walked among the downs, like the folded wings of grey birds; and saw first one fox, very long with his brush stretched; then a second; which had been barking, for the sun was hot over us; it leapt lightly over a fence and entered the furze—a very rare sight. How many foxes are there in England? At night I read Lord Chaplin's life. I cannot yet write naturally in my new room, because the table is not the right height and I must stoop to warm my hands. Everything must be absolutely what I am used to.

I forgot to say that when we made up our 6 months accounts, we found I had made about £3,020 last year—the salary of a civil servant: a surprise to me, who was content with £200 for so many years. But I shall drop very heavily I think. *The Waves* won't sell more than 2,000 copies. I am stuck fast in that book—I mean, glued to it, like a fly on gummed paper. Sometimes I am out of touch; but go on; then again feel that I have at last, by violent measures—like break-

It has sold about 6,500 today, Oct. 30th, 1931—after 3 weeks. But will stop now, I suppose.

ing through gorse—set my hands on something central. Perhaps I can now say something quite straight out; and at length; and need not be always casting a line to make my book the right shape. But how to pull it together, how to comport it—press it into one—I do not know; nor can I guess the end—it might be a gigantic conversation. The interludes are very difficult, yet I think essential; so as to bridge and also to give a background—the sea; insensitive nature—I don't know. But I think, when I feel this sudden directness, that it must be right: anyhow no other form of fiction suggests itself except as a repetition at the moment.

Sunday, February 16th

To lie on the sofa for a week. I am sitting up today in the usual state of unequal animation. Below normal, with spasmodic desire to write, then to doze. It is a fine cold day and if my energy and sense of duty persist, I shall drive up to Hampstead. But I doubt that I can write to any purpose. A cloud swims in my head. One is too conscious of the body and jolted out of the rut of life to get back to fiction. Once or twice I have felt that odd whirr of wings in the head, which comes when I am ill so often—last year for example at this time I lay in bed constructing *A Room of One's Own* (which sold 10,000 two days ago). If I could stay in bed another fortnight (but there is no chance of that) I believe I should see the whole of *The Waves*. Or of course I might go off on something different. As it is I half incline to insist upon a dash to Cassis; but perhaps this needs more determination than I possess; and we shall dwindle on here. Pinker is walking about the room looking for the bright patch—a sign of spring. I believe these illnesses are in my case—how shall I express it?—partly mystical. Something happens in my mind. It refuses to go on registering impressions. It shuts itself up. It becomes chrysalis. I lie quite torpid, often with acute physical pain—as last year; only discomfort this. Then suddenly something springs. Two nights ago Vita was here; and when she went I began to feel the quality of the evening—how it was spring coming: a silver light;

mixing with the early lamps; the cabs all rushing through the streets; I had a tremendous sense of life beginning; mixed with that emotion which is the essence of my feeling, but escapes description (I keep on making up the Hampton Court scene in *The Waves*—Lord how I wonder if I shall pull this book off! It is a litter of fragments so far). Well, as I was saying, between these long pauses, for I am swimming in the head and write rather to stabilise myself than to make a correct statement—I felt the spring beginning; and Vita's life so full and flush; and all the doors opening; and this is I believe the moth shaking its wings in me. I then begin to make up my story whatever it is; ideas rush in me; often though this is before I can control my mind or pen. It is no use trying to write at this stage. And I doubt if I can fill this white monster. I would like to lie down and sleep, but feel ashamed. Leonard brushed off his influenza in one day and went about his business feeling ill. Here am I still loafing, undressed, with Elly * coming tomorrow. But as I was saying, my mind works in idleness. To do nothing is often my most profitable way. I am reading Byron: Maurois: which sends me to *Childe Harold:* makes me speculate. How odd a mixture: the weakest sentimental Mrs. Hemans combined with trenchant bare vigour. How did they combine? And sometimes the descriptions in *C.H.* are "beautiful"; like a great poet. There are the three elements in Byron:

1. The romantic dark haired lady singing drawing room melodies to the guitar.

"Tambourgi! Tambourgi! thy 'larum afar
   Gives hope to the valiant and promise of war;"

"Oh! who is more brave than a dark Suliote,
   In his snowy camese and his shaggy capote"

—something manufactured; a pose; silliness.

2. Then there is the vigorous rhetorical, like his prose, and good as prose.

"Hereditary Bondsmen! know ye not
   Who would be free themselves must strike the blow?

* Elly Rendel, V. W.'s doctor.

By their right arms the conquest must be wrought?
Will Gaul or Muscovite redress ye? No!"

3. Then what rings to me truer, and is almost poetry.

"Dear Nature is the kindest mother still!
    Though always changing, in her aspect mild;
(All in Canto   From her bare bosom let me take my fill,
II of *C.H.*)   Her never-weaned, though not her favoured
        child.

To me by day or night she ever smiled,
Though I have marked her when none other hath,
And sought her more and more and loved her best in wrath."

4. And then there is of course the pure satiric, as in the description of a London Sunday; and
5. Finally (but this makes more than three) the inevitable half assumed half genuine tragic note, which comes as a refrain, about death and the loss of friends.

All thou could have of mine, stern Death! thou hast;
    The parent, Friend, and now the more than Friend:
Ne'er yet for me thine arrows flew so fast,
    And grief with grief continuing still to blend,
    Hath snatched the little joy that life had yet to lend.

These I think make him up; and make much that is spurious, vapid, yet very changeable, and then rich and with greater range than the other poets, could he have got the whole into order. A novelist, he might have been. It is odd however to read in his letters his prose and apparently genuine feeling about Athens: and to compare it with the convention he adopted in verse. (There is some sneer about the Acropolis.) But then the sneer may have been a pose too. The truth may be that if you are charged at such high voltage you can't fit any of the ordinary human feelings; must pose; must rhapsodise; don't fit in. He wrote in the Fun Album that his age was 100. And this is true, measuring life by feeling.

Monday, February 17th
And this temperature is up: but it has now gone down; and now

Thursday, February 20th

I must canter my wits if I can. Perhaps some character sketches.

Monday, March 17th

The test of a book (to a writer) is if it makes a space in which, quite naturally, you can say what you want to say. As this morning I could say what Rhoda said. This proves that the book itself is alive: because it has not crushed the thing I wanted to say, but allowed me to slip it in, without any compression or alteration.

Friday, March 28th

Yes, but this book is a very queer business. I had a day of intoxication when I said "Children are nothing to this": when I sat surveying the whole book complete and quarrelled with L. (about Ethel Smyth) and walked it off, felt the pressure of the form—the splendour, the greatness—as perhaps I have never felt them. But I shan't race it off in intoxication. I keep pegging away; and find it the most complex and difficult of all my books. How to end, save by a tremendous discussion, in which every life shall have its voice—a mosaic—I do not know. The difficulty is that it is all at high pressure. I have not yet mastered the speaking voice. Yet I think something is there; and I propose to go on pegging it down, arduously, and then rewrite, reading much of it aloud, like poetry. It will bear expansion. It is compressed I think. It is—whatever I make of it—a large and potential theme—which *Orlando* was not perhaps. At any rate, I have taken my fence.

Wednesday, April 9th

What I now think (about *The Waves*) is that I can give in a very few strokes the essentials of a person's character. It should be done boldly, almost as caricature. I have yesterday entered what may be the last lap. Like every piece of the book it goes by fits and starts. I never get away with it; but am tugged back. I hope this makes for solidity; and must look to my sentences. The abandonment of *Orlando* and *Lighthouse* is much checked

by the extreme difficulty of the form—as it was in *Jacob's Room*.
I think this is the furthest development so far; but of course it
may miss fire somewhere. I think I have kept stoically to the
original conception. What I fear is that the re-writing will have
to be so drastic that I may entirely muddle it somehow. It is
bound to be very imperfect. But I think it possible that I have
got my statues against the sky.

Sunday, April 13th

I read Shakespeare *directly* I have finished writing. When
my mind is agape and red-hot. Then it is astonishing. I never
yet knew how amazing his stretch and speed and word coining
power is, until I felt it utterly outpace and outrace my own,
seeming to start equal and then I see him draw ahead and do
things I could not in my wildest tumult and utmost press of
mind imagine. Even the less known plays are written at a speed
that is quicker than anybody else's quickest; and the words
drop so fast one can't pick them up. Look at this. "Upon a
gather'd lily almost wither'd." (That is a pure accident. I happen to light on it.) Evidently the pliancy of his mind was so
complete that he could furbish out any train of thought; and,
relaxing, let fall a shower of such unregarded flowers. Why
then should anyone else attempt to write? This is not "writing"
at all. Indeed, I could say that Shakespeare surpasses literature
altogether, if I knew what I meant.

Wednesday, April 23rd

This is a very important morning in the history of *The
Waves*, because I think I have turned the corner and see the
last lap straight ahead. I think I have got Bernard into the final
stride. He will go straight on now, and then stand at the door:
and then there will be a last picture of the waves. We are at
Rodmell and I daresay I shall stay on a day or two (if I dare)
so as not to break the current and finish it. O Lord and then
a rest; and then an article; and then back again to this hideous
shaping and moulding. There may be some joys in it all the
same.

Tuesday, April 29th

And I have just finished, with this very nib-ful of ink, the last sentence of *The Waves*. I think I should record this for my own information. Yes, it was the greatest stretch of mind I ever knew; certainly the last pages; I don't think they flop as much as usual. And I think I have kept starkly and ascetically to the plan. So much I will say in self-congratulation. But I have never written a book so full of holes and patches; that will need re-building, yes, not only re-modelling. I suspect the structure is wrong. Never mind. I might have done something easy and fluent; and this is a reach after that vision I had, the unhappy summer—or three weeks—at Rodmell, after finishing the *Lighthouse*. (And that reminds me—I must hastily provide my mind with something else, or it will again become pecking and wretched—something imaginative, if possible, and light; for I shall tire of Hazlitt and criticism after the first divine relief; and I feel pleasantly aware of various adumbrations in the back of my head; a life of Duncan; no, something about canvases glowing in a studio; but that can wait.)

P.M.   And I think to myself as I walk down Southampton Row, "And I have given you a new book."

Thursday, May 1st

And I have completely ruined my morning. Yes that is literally true. They sent a book from *The Times*, as if advised by Heaven of my liberty; and feeling my liberty wild upon me, I rushed to the cable and told Van Doren I would write on Scott. And now having read Scott, or the editor whom Hugh provides, I won't and can't; and have got into a fret trying to read it, and writing to Richmond to say I can't: have wasted the brilliant first of May which makes my skylight blue and gold; have only a rubbish heap in my head; can't read and can't write and can't think. The truth is, of course, I want to be back at *The Waves*. Yes that is the truth. Unlike all my other books in every way, it is unlike them in this, that I begin to re-write it, or conceive it again with ardour, directly I have done. I begin to see what I had in my mind; and want to begin cutting out masses of irrelevance and clearing, sharpening and making the good phrases shine. One wave after another. No room. And so on. But then we are going touring Devon and Cornwall on Sunday, which means a week off; and then I shall perhaps make my critical brain do a month's work for exercise. What could it be set to? Or a story?—no, not another story now . . .

Wednesday, August 20th

The Waves is I think resolving itself (I am at page 100) into a series of dramatic soliloquies. The thing is to keep them running homogeneously in and out, in the rhythm of the waves. Can they be read consecutively? I know nothing about that. I think this is the greatest opportunity I have yet been able to give myself; therefore I suppose the most complete failure. Yet I respect myself for writing this book—yes—even though it exhibits my congenital faults.

Monday, September 8th

I will signalise my return to life—that is writing—by beginning a new book, and it happens to be Thoby's birthday, I remark. He would have been, I think, 50 today. After coming out here I had the usual—oh how usual—headache; and lay, like a fibre of tired muscle on my bed in the sitting room, till yesterday. Now up again and on again; with one new picture in my mind; my defiance of death in the garden.

But the sentence with which this book was to open ran "Nobody has ever worked so hard as I do"—exclaimed in driving a paper fastener through the 14 pages of my Hazlitt just now. Time was when I dashed off these things all in the day's work. Now, partly because I must do them for America and make arrangements far ahead, I spend I daresay a ridiculous amount of time, more of trouble, on them. I began reading Hazlitt in January I think. And I am not sure that I have speared that little eel in the middle—that marrow—which is one's object in criticism. A very difficult business no doubt to find it, in all these essays; so many; so short; and on all subjects. Never mind; it shall go today; and my appetite for criticism is, oddly, whettened. I have some gift that way, were it not for the grind and the screw and the torture.

Tuesday, December 2nd

No, I cannot write that very difficult passage in *The Waves* this morning (how their lives hang lit up against the Palace) all because of Arnold Bennett and Ethel's * party. I can hardly get one word after another. There I was for 2 hours so it seemed, alone with B., in Ethel's little back room. And this meeting I am convinced was engineered by B. to "get on good terms with Mrs. Woolf"—when Heaven knows I don't care a rap if I'm on terms with B. or not. B. I say, because he can't say B. He

Soon after this A.B. went to France, drank a glass of water and died of typhoid. (March 30th. His funeral today.)

ceases; shuts his eyes; leans back; one waits. "Begin," he at last articulates quietly, without any fluster. But the method lengthens out intolerably a rather uninspired discourse. It's fun. I like the old creature. I do my best, as a writer, to detect signs of genius in his smoky brown eye: I see certain sensuality, power, I suppose; but O as he cackled out "What a blundering fool I am—what a baby—compared with Desmond MacCarthy—how clumsy—how could I attack professors?" This innocence is engaging; but would be more so if I felt him, as he infers, a "creative artist." He said that George Moore in *The Mummer's Wife* had shown him *The Five Towns*: taught him what to see there: has a profound admiration for G. M.; but despises him for boasting of his sexual triumphs. "He told me that a young girl had come to see him. And he asked her, as she sat on the sofa, to undress. And he said she took off all her clothes and let him look at her. . . . Now that I don't believe . . . But he is a prodigious writer—he lives for words. Now he's ill. Now he's an awful bore—he tells the same stories over and over. And soon people will say of me 'He's dead.' " I rashly said: "Of your books?" "No, of me," he replied, attaching, I suppose, a longer life than I do to his books.

* Ethel Sands.

"It's the only life," he said (this incessant scribbling, one word after another, one thousand words daily). "I don't want anything else. I think of nothing but writing. Some people are bored." "You have all the clothes you want, I suppose," I said. "And bath. And beds. And a yacht." "Oh yes, my clothes couldn't be better cut."

And at last I drew Lord David * in. And we taunted the old creature with thinking us refined. He said the gates of Hatfield were shut—"shut away from life." "But open on Thursdays," said Lord D. "I don't want to go on Thursdays," said B. "And you drop your aitches on purpose," I said, "thinking that you possess more 'life' than we do." "I sometimes tease," said B., "but I don't think I possess more life than you do. Now I must go home. I have to write one thousand words tomorrow morning." And this left only the scrag end of the evening; and this left me in a state where I can hardly drive my pen across the page.

Reflection: It is presumably a bad thing to look through articles, reviews, etc. to find one's own name. Yet I often do.

Thursday, December 4th

One word of slight snub in the *Lit. Sup.* today makes me determine, first, to alter the whole of *The Waves;* second, to put my back up against the public—one word of slight snub.

Friday, December 12th

This, I think, is the last day's breathing space I allow myself before I tackle the last lap of *The Waves.* I have had a week off—that is to say I have written three little sketches; and dawdled and spent a morning shopping and a morning, this morning, arranging my new table and doing odds and ends—but I think I have got my breath again and must be off for three or perhaps four weeks more. Then, as I think, I shall make one consecutive writing of *The Waves* etc.—the interludes—so as to work it into one—and then, oh dear, some must

* David Cecil.

be written again; and then, corrections; and then send to
Mabel; and then correct the type; and then give to Leonard.
Leonard perhaps shall get it some time late in March. Then
put away; then print, perhaps in June.

Monday, December 22nd

It occurred to me last night while listening to a Beethoven
quartet that I would merge all the interjected passages into
Bernard's final speech and end with the words O solitude:
thus making him absorb all those scenes and having no further
break. This is also to show that the theme effort, effort, domi-
nates: not the waves: and personality: and defiance: but I am
not sure of the effect artistically; because the proportions may
need the intervention of the waves finally so as to make a
conclusion.

RODMELL. *Saturday, December 27th*

But what's the use of talking about Bernard's final speech?
We came down on Tuesday and next day my cold was the
usual influenza and I am in bed with the usual temperature
and can't use my wits or, as is visible, form my letters. I daresay
two days will see me normal; but then the sponge behind my
forehead will be dry and pale—and so my precious fortnight
of exaltation and concentration is snatched; and I shall go back
to the racket and Nelly without a thing done. I clear myself
by thinking that I may evolve some thoughts. Meanwhile it
rains; Annie's child is ill; the dogs next door yap and yap;
all the colours are rather dim and the pulse of life dulled. I
moon torpidly through book after book: Defoe's *Tour;*
Rowan's autobiography; Benson's Memoirs; Jeans: in the
familiar way. The parson—Skinner—who shot himself emerges
like a bloody sun in a fog: a book worth, perhaps,
looking at again in a clearer mood. He shot him-
Diary of a   self in the beechwoods above his house; he spent
Somerset   a life digging up stones and reducing all places
rector.   to Camelodunum; quarrelled; bickered; yet loved
his sons; yet turned them out of doors—a clear hard picture
of one type of human life—the exasperated, unhappy, strug-

gling, intolerably afflicted. Oh and I've read Q. V.'s * letters;
and wonder what would happen had Ellen Terry been born
Queen. Complete disaster to the Empire? Q. V. entirely un-
aesthetic; a kind of Prussian competence and belief in herself
her only prominences; material; brutal to Gladstone; like a
mistress with a dishonest footman. Knew her own mind. But
the mind radically commonplace, only its inherited force and
cumulative sense of power making it remarkable.

Tuesday, December 30th

What it wants is presumably unity; but it is I think rather
good (I am talking to myself over the fire about *The Waves*).
Suppose I could run all the scenes together more?—by rhythms
chiefly. So as to avoid those cuts; so as to make the blood run
like a torrent from end to end—I don't want the waste that
the breaks give; I want to avoid chapters; that indeed is my
achievement, if any, here: a saturated unchopped completeness; changes of scene, of mind, of person, done without spilling a drop. Now if it could be worked over with heat and cur-
rency, that's all it wants. And I am getting my blood up (temp.
99). But all the same I went into Lewes and the Keynes came
to tea; and having got astride my saddle the whole world falls
into shape; it is this writing that gives me my proportions.

* Queen Victoria.

1931

Wednesday, January 7th
My head is not in the first spring of energy: this fortnight
has brought me no views of the lapping downs—no fields and
hedges—too many firelit houses and lit up pages and pen and
ink—curse my influenza. It is very quiet here—not a sound but
the hiss of the gas. Oh but the cold was too great at Rodmell.
I was frozen like a small sparrow. And I did write a few staggering sentences. Few books have interested me more to write
than *The Waves*. Why even now, at the end, I'm turning up a
stone or two: no glibness, no assurance; you see, I could perhaps do B.'s soliloquy in such a way as to break up, dig deep,
make prose move—yes I swear—as prose has never moved before; from the chuckle, the babble to the rhapsody. Something
new goes into my pot every morning—something that's never
been got at before. The high wind can't blow, because I'm
chopping and tacking all the time. And I've stored a few ideas
for articles: one on Gosse—the critic, as talker: the armchair
critic; one on Letters—one on Queens.

Now this is true: *The Waves* is written at such high pressure that I can't take it up and read it through between tea
and dinner; I can only write it for about one hour, from 10
to 11:30. And the typing is almost the hardest part of the
work. Heaven help me if all my little 80,000 word books are
going in future to cost me two years! But I shall fling off, like
a cutter leaning on its side, on some swifter, slighter adventure
—another *Orlando* perhaps.

Tuesday, January 20th
I have this moment, while having my bath, conceived an
entire new book *—a sequel to *A Room of One's Own*—about

* Eventually *Three Guineas*.

161

the sexual life of women: to be called Professions for Women
perhaps—Lord how exciting! This sprang out
of my paper to be read on Wednesday to Pippa's
society. Now for *The Waves*. Thank God—but
I'm very much excited.

(This is
Here and Now,
I think.
May '34.)

Friday, January 23rd

Too much excited, alas, to get on with *The Waves*. One
goes on making up "The Open Door," or whatever it is to be
called. The didactive demonstrative style conflicts with the
dramatic: I find it hard to get back inside Bernard again.

Monday, January 26th

Heaven be praised, I can truthfully say on this first day
of being 49 that I have shaken off the obsession of *Opening
the Door,* and have returned to *Waves:* and have this instant
seen the entire book whole, and now I can finish it—say in
under 3 weeks. That takes me to February 16th; then I propose, after doing Gosse, or an article perhaps, to dash off the
rough sketch of *Open Door,* to be finished by April 1st. (Easter
is April 3rd.) We shall then, I hope, have an Italian journey;
return say May 1st and finish *Waves,* so that the MS. can go
to be printed in June and appear in September. These are
possible dates anyhow. Yesterday at Rodmell we saw a magpie
and heard the first spring birds: sharp egotistical, like man.
A hot sun; walked over Caburn; home by Horley and saw three
men dash from a blue car and race without hats across a field.
We saw a silver and blue aeroplane in the middle of a field,
apparently unhurt, among trees and cows. This morning the
paper says three men were killed—the aeroplane dashing to
the earth. But we went on, reminding me of that epitaph in
the Greek anthology: when I sank, the other ships sailed on.

Monday, February 2nd

I think I am about to finish *The Waves*. I think I might
finish it on Saturday.

This is merely an author's note: never have I screwed my

brain so tight over a book. The proof is that I am almost incapable of other reading or writing. I can only flop wide once the morning is over. Oh Lord the relief when this week is over and I have at any rate the feeling that I have wound up and done with that long labour: ended that vision. I think I have just done what I meant; of course I have altered the scheme considerably; but my feeling is that I have insisted upon saying, by hook or by crook, certain things I meant to say. I imagine that the hookedness may be so great that it will be a failure from a reader's point of view. Well, never mind: it is a brave attempt. I think, something struggled for. Oh and then the delight of skirmishing free again—the delight of being idle and not much minding what happens; and then I shall be able to read again, with all my mind—a thing I haven't done these four months I daresay. This will have taken me 18 months to write: and we can't publish it till the autumn I suppose.

Wednesday, February 4th

A day ruined, for us both. L. has to go every morning at 10:15 to the Courts, where his jury is still called, but respited always till 10:15 the next day; and this morning, which should have dealt a formidable blow at *The Waves*—B. is within two days I think of saying O Death—was ruined by Elly, who was to have come at 9:30 sharp but did not come till 11. And it is now 12:30 and we sat talking about the period and professional women, after the usual rites with the stethoscope, seeking vainly the cause of my temperature. If we like to spend 7 guineas we might catch a bug—but we don't like. And so I am to eat Bemax and—the usual routine.

How strange and wilful these last exacerbations of *The Waves* are! I was to have finished it at Christmas.

Today Ethel * comes. On Monday I went to hear her rehearse. A vast Portland Place house with the cold wedding cake Adams plaster: shabby red carpets; flat surfaces washed

* Ethel Smyth.

with dull greens. The rehearsal was in a long room with a bow window looking on, in fact in, to other houses—iron staircases, chimneys, roofs—a barren brick outlook. There was a roaring fire in the Adams grate. Lady L. a now shapeless sausage, and Mrs. Hunter,* a swathed satin sausage, sat side by side on a sofa. Ethel stood at the piano in the window, in her battered felt, in her jersey and short skirt conducting with a pencil. There was a drop at the end of her nose. Miss Suddaby was singing the Soul, and I observed that she went through precisely the same attitudes of ecstasy and inspiration in the room as in a hall: there were two young or youngish men. Ethel's *pince nez* rode nearer and nearer the tip of her nose. She sang now and then; and once, taking the bass, made a cat squalling sound—but everything she does with such forthrightness, directness, that there is nothing ridiculous. She loses self-consciousness completely. She seems all vitalised; all energised. She knocks her hat from side to side. Strides rhythmically down the room to signify to Elizabeth that this is the Greek melody; strides back. Now the furniture moving begins, she said, referring to some supernatural gambols connected with the prisoner's escape, or defiance or death. I suspect the music is too literary—too stressed—too didactic for my taste. But I am always impressed by the fact that it is music—I mean that she has spun these coherent chords, harmonies, melodies out of her so practical vigorous student mind. What if she should be a great composer? This fantastic idea is to her the merest commonplace: it is the fabric of her being. As she conducts, she hears music like Beethoven's. As she strides and turns and wheels about to us perched mute on chairs she thinks this is about the most important event now taking place in London. And perhaps it is. Well—I watched the curiously sensitive, perceptive Jewish face of old Lady L. trembling like a butterfly's antennae to the sound. How sensitive to music old Jewesses are—how pliable, how supple. Mrs. Hunter sat like a wax figure, composed, upholstered, transfixed, with her gold chain purse.

* Ethel Smyth's sister.

Saturday, February 7th

Here in the few minutes that remain, I must record, heaven be praised, the end of *The Waves*. I wrote the words O Death fifteen minutes ago, having reeled across the last ten pages with some moments of such intensity and intoxication that I seemed only to stumble after my own voice, or almost, after some sort of speaker (as when I was mad) I was almost afraid, remembering the voices that used to fly ahead. Anyhow, it is done; and I have been sitting these 15 minutes in a state of glory, and calm, and some tears, thinking of Thoby and if I could write Julian Thoby Stephen 1881-1906 on the first page. I suppose not. How physical the sense of triumph and relief is! Whether good or bad, it's done; and, as I certainly felt at the end, not merely finished, but rounded off, completed, the thing stated—how hastily, how fragmentarily I know; but I mean that I have netted that fin in the waste of water which appeared to me over the marshes out of my window at Rodmell when I was coming to an end of *To the Lighthouse*.

What interests me in the last stage was the freedom and boldness with which my imagination picked up, used and tossed aside all the images, symbols which I had prepared. I am sure that this is the right way of using them—not in set pieces, as I had tried at first, coherently, but simply as images, never making them work out; only suggest. Thus I hope to have kept the sound of the sea and the birds, dawn and garden subconsciously present, doing their work under ground.

Saturday, March 28th

Arnold Bennett died last night; which leaves me sadder than I should have supposed. A lovable genuine man; impeded, somehow a little awkward in life; well meaning; ponderous; kindly; coarse; knowing he was coarse; dimly floundering and feeling for something else; glutted with success; wounded in his feelings; avid; thicklipped; prosaic intolerably; rather dignified; set upon writing; yet always taken in; deluded by splendour and success; but naive; an old bore; an egotist; much at the mercy of life for all his competence;

a shopkeeper's view of literature; yet with the rudiments, covered over with fat and prosperity and the desire for hideous Empire furniture; of sensibility. Some real understanding power, as well as a gigantic absorbing power. These are the sort of things that I think by fits and starts this morning, as I sit journalising; I remember his determination to write 1,000 words daily; and how he trotted off to do it that night, and feel some sorrow that now he will never sit down and begin methodically covering his regulation number of pages in his workmanlike beautiful but dull hand. Queer how one regrets the dispersal of anybody who seemed—as I say—genuine: who had direct contact with life—for he abused me; and I yet rather wished him to go on abusing me; and me abusing him. An element in life—even in mine that was so remote—taken away. This is what one minds.*

Saturday, April 11th
Oh I am so tired of correcting my own writing—these 8 articles—I have however learnt I think to dash: not to finick. I mean the writing is free enough; it's the repulsiveness of correcting that nauseates me. And the cramming in and the cutting out. And articles and more articles are asked for. Forever I could write articles.

But I have no pen—well, it will just make a mark. And not much to say, or rather too much and not the mood.

Wednesday, May 13th
Unless I write a few sentences here from time to time I shall, as they say, forget the use of my pen. I am now engaged in typing out from start to finish the 332 pages of that very condensed book *The Waves*. I do 7 or 8 daily; by which means I hope to have the whole complete by June 16th or thereabouts. This requires some resolution; but I can see no other way to make all the corrections and keep the lilt and join up and expand and do all the other final processes. It is like sweeping over an entire canvas with a wet brush.

* There is an entry in Arnold Bennett's diary for 1930 in which he records that he went to a dinner party at which V. W. was another guest, and adds: "Virginia is all right; other guests held their breath to listen to us."

Saturday, May 30th

No, I have just said, it being 12:45, I cannot write any more, and indeed I cannot: I am copying the death chapter; have re-written it twice. I shall go at it again and finish it, I hope, this afternoon. But how it rolls into a tight ball the muscles in my brain! This is the most concentrated work I have ever done—and oh the relief when it is finished. But also the most interesting.

p. 162. therefore halfway in 26 days. Shall finish by 1st July with luck.

Tuesday, June 23rd

And yesterday, 22nd June, when, I think, the days begin to draw in, I finished my re-typing of *The Waves*. Not that it is finished—oh dear no. For then I must correct the re-re-typing. This work I began on May 5th, and no one can say that I have been hasty or careless this time; though I doubt not the lapses and slovenliness are innumerable.

Tuesday, July 7th

O to seek relief from this incessant correction (I am doing the interludes) and write a few words carelessly. Still better, to write nothing; to tramp over the downs, blown like thistle, as irresponsible. And to get away from this hard knot in which my brain has been so tight spun—I mean *The Waves*. Such are my sentiments at half past twelve on Tuesday July 7th—a fine day I think—and everything, so the tag runs in my head, handsome about us.

Tuesday, July 14th

It is now twelve o'clock on the morning of July 14th—and Bob * has come in to ask me to sign a paper to get Palmer a pension. Bob says . . . mostly about his new house, washing basins, can he use a candle still to go to bed with; Bessy is moving in today; he is off to Italy for a month; will I send a copy of my new book to Count Moira, all Italians are Counts, once he showed four Counts round Cambridge; Palmer . . .

* R. C. Trevelyan.

. . . and so on: shuffling from foot to foot, taking his hat off and putting it on again, moving to the door and returning.

I had meant to say that I have just finished correcting the Hampton Court scene. (This is the final correction, please God!)

But my *Waves* account runs, I think, as follows:—

I began it, seriously, about September 10th 1929.

I finished the first version on April 10th 1930.

I began the second version on May 1st 1930.

I finished the second version on February 7th 1931.

I began to correct the second version on May 1st 1931, finished 22nd June 1931.

I began to correct the typescript on 25th June 1931.

Shall finish (I hope) 18th July 1931.

Then remain only the proofs.

Friday, July 17th

Yes, this morning I think I may say I have finished. That is to say I have once more, for the 18th time, copied out the opening sentences. L. will read it tomorrow; and

Which I
then lost.

I shall open this book to record his verdict. My own opinion—oh dear—it's a difficult book. I don't know that I've ever felt so strained. And I'm nervous, I confess, about L. For one thing he will be honest, more than usually. And it may be a failure. And I can't do any more. And I'm inclined to think it good but incoherent, inspissate; one jerk succeeding another. Anyhow it is laboured, compact. Anyhow I had a shot at my vision—if it's not a catch, it's a cast in the right direction. But I'm nervous. It may be small and finicky in general effect. Lord knows. As I say, repeating it to enforce the rather unpleasant little lift in my heart, I shall be nervous to hear what L. says when he comes out, say tomorrow night or Sunday morning, to my garden room, carrying the MS. and sits himself down and begins "Well!"

Sunday, July 19th

"It is a masterpiece," said L., coming out to my lodge this morning. "And the best of your books." This note I make;

adding that he also thinks the first 100 pages extremely difficult and is doubtful how far any common reader will follow.
But Lord! what a relief! I stumped off in the rain to make a
little round to Rat Farm in jubilation and am almost resigned
to the fact that a goat farm, with a house to be built, is now
in process on the slope near Northease.

Monday, August 10th

I have now—10:45—read the first chapter of *The Waves*,
and made no changes, save 2 words and 3 commas. Yes, anyhow this is exact and to the point. I like it. And see that for
once my proofs will be despatched with a few pencil strokes.
Now my brood mounts: I think "I am taking my fences . . .
We have asked Raymond. I am forging through the sea, in
spite of headache, in spite of bitterness. I may also get a ." *
I will now write a little at *Flush*.

Saturday, August 15th

I am in rather a flutter—proof reading. I can only read a
few pages at a time. So it was when I wrote it and Heaven
knows what virtue it has, this ecstatic book.

Sunday, August 16th

I should really apologise to this book for using it as I am
doing to write off my aimlessness; that is I am doing my
proofs—the last chapter this morning—and find that I must
stop after half an hour and let my mind spread, after these
moments of concentration. I cannot write my life of *Flush*,
because the rhythm is wrong. I think *The Waves* is anyhow
tense and packed; since it screws my brain up like this. And
what will the reviewers say? And my friends? They can't, of
course, find anything very new to say.

Monday, August 17th

Well now, it being just after 12:30, I have put the last corrections in *The Waves;* done my proofs; and they shall go
tomorrow—never, never to be looked at again by me, I imagine.

* The word is illegible.

Tuesday, September 22nd

And Miss Holtby says "It is a poem, more completely than any of your other books, of course. It is most rarely subtle. It has seen more deeply into the human heart, perhaps, than even *To the Lighthouse* . . ." and though I copy the sentence, because it is in the chart of my temperature, Lord, as I say, that temperature which was deathly low this time last week and then fever high, doesn't rise: is normal. I suppose I'm safe; I think people can only repeat. And I've forgotten so much. What I want is to be told that this is solid and means something. What it means I myself shan't know till I write another book. And I'm the hare, a long way ahead of the hounds my critics.

52 TAVISTOCK SQUARE. *Monday, October 5th*

A note to say I am all trembling with pleasure—can't go on with my Letter—because Harold Nicolson has rung up to say *The Waves* is a masterpiece. Ah Hah—so it wasn't all wasted then. I mean this vision I had here has some force upon other minds. Now for a cigarette and then a return to sober composition.

Well, to continue this egotistic diary: I am not terribly excited; no; at arms length more than usual; all this talk, because if the *W.* is anything it is an adventure which I go on alone; and the dear old *Lit. Sup:* who twinkles and beams and patronises—a long, and for *The Times,* kind and outspoken review—don't stir me very much. Nor Harold in *Action* either. Yes; to some extent; I should have been unhappy had they blamed, but Lord, how far away I become from all this; and we're jaded too, with people, with doing up parcels. I wonder if it is good to feel this remoteness—that is, that *The Waves* is not what they say. Odd, that they (*The Times*) should praise my characters when I meant to have none. But I'm jaded; I want my marsh, my down, a quiet waking in my airy bedroom. Broadcasting tonight; to Rodmell tomorrow. Next week I shall have to stand the racket.

Friday, October 9th

Really, this unintelligible book is being better "received" than any of them. A note in *The Times* proper—the first time this has been allowed me. And it sells—how unexpected, how odd that people can read that difficult grinding stuff!

Saturday, October 17th

More notes on *The Waves*. The sales, these past three days, have fallen to 50 or so: after the great flare up when we sold 500 in one day, the brushwood has died down, as I foretold. (Not that I thought we should sell more than 3,000.) What has happened is that the library readers can't get through it and are sending their copies back. So, I prophesy, it will now dribble along till we have sold 6,000 and then almost die, yet not quite. For it has been received, as I may say, quoting the stock phrases without vanity, with applause. All the provinces read enthusiastically. I am rather, in a sense, as the M.'s would say, touched. The unknown provincial reviewers say with almost one accord, here is Mrs. Woolf doing her best work; it can't be popular; but we respect her for so doing; and find *The Waves* positively exciting. I am in danger, indeed, of becoming our leading novelist, and not with the highbrows only.

Monday, November 16th

Here I will give myself the pleasure—shall I?—of copying a sentence or two from Morgan's unsolicited letter on *The Waves:*—

"I expect I shall write to you again when I have re-read *The Waves*. I have been looking in it and talking about it at Cambridge. It's difficult to express oneself about a work which one feels to be so very important, but I've the sort of excitement over it which comes from believing that one's encountered a classic."

I daresay that gives me more substantial pleasure than any letter I've had about any book. Yes, I think it does, coming from Morgan. For one thing it gives me reason to think I shall be right to go on along this very lonely path. I mean in the City today I was thinking of another book—about shopkeepers, and publicans, with low life scenes: and I ratified this sketch by Morgan's judgment. Dadie agrees too. Oh yes, between 50 and 60 I think I shall write out some very singular books, if I live. I mean I think I am about to embody at last the exact shapes my brain holds. What a long toil to reach this beginning —if *The Waves* is my first work in my own style! To be noted, as curiosities of my literary history: I sedulously avoid meeting Roger and Lytton whom I suspect do not like *The Waves*.

I am working very hard—in my way, to furbish up two long Elizabethan articles to front a new *Common Reader:* then I must go through the whole long list of those articles. I feel too, at the back of my brain, that I can devise a new critical method; something far less stiff and formal than these *Times* articles. But I must keep to the old style in this volume. And how, I wonder, could I do it? There must be some simpler, subtler, closer means of writing about books, as about people, could I hit upon it. (*The Waves* has sold more than 7,000.)

1932

Wednesday, January 13th

Oh but this is, as I always say, making an apology myself
to myself, not the first day of the year. It is the thirteenth, and
I am in one of those lassitudes and ebbs of life when I cannot
heave another word on to the wall. My word, what a heaving
The Waves was, that I still feel the strain!

Can we count on another 20 years? I shall be fifty on 25th,
Monday week that is: and sometimes feel that I have lived
250 years already, and sometimes that I am still the youngest
person in the omnibus. (Nessa said that she still always thinks
this, as she sits down.) And I want to write another four novels:
Waves, I mean; and the *Tap on the Door;* and to go through
English literature, like a string through cheese, or rather like
some industrious insect, eating its way from book to book,
from Chaucer to Lawrence. This is a programme, considering
my slowness, and how I get slower, thicker, more intolerant of
the fling and the rush, to last out my 20 years, if I have them.

Sunday, January 31st

Having just finished, as I say, the final version as I call it,
of my *Letter to a Young Poet*, I can take a moment's liberty.
From the cynical tone of this sentence I see that my finality is
not secure. Writing becomes harder and harder. Things I
dashed off I now compress and re-state. And for purposes which
I need not go into here, I want to use these pages for dialogue
for a time.

Monday, February 8th

Why did I ever say I would produce another volume of
Common Reader? It will take me week after week, month

after month. However a year spent—save for diversions in
Greece and Russia—in reading through English literature will
no doubt do good to my fictitious brain. Rest it anyhow. One
day, all of a rush, fiction will burst in. These remarks are
jotted down at the end of a long morning's work on Donne,
which will have to be done again, and is it worth the doing?
I wake in the night with the sense of being in an empty hall:
Lytton dead and those factories building. What is the point
of it—life—when I am not working—suddenly becomes thin,
indifferent. Lytton is dead, and nothing definite to mark it.
Also they write flimsy articles about him.

Thursday, February 11th

My mind is set running upon *A Knock on the Door* * (what's
its name?) owing largely to reading *Wells on Woman*—how
she must be ancillary and decorative in the world of the
future, because she has been tried, in 10 years, and has not
proved anything.

Tuesday, February 16th

And I have just "finished"—I use inverted commas ironi-
cally—my Donne, a great but I think well intentioned grind.
And I'm quivering and itching to write my—what's it to be
called?—"Men are like that"?—no, that's too patently feminist.
The sequel then, for which I have collected enough powder
to blow up St. Pauls. It is to have four pictures. And I must go
on with the *Common Reader*—for one thing, by way of proving
my credentials.

Tuesday, May 17th

What is the right attitude towards criticism? What ought I
to feel and say when Miss B. devotes an article in *Scrutiny* to
attacking me? She is young, Cambridge, ardent. And she says
I'm a very bad writer. Now I think the thing to do is to note
the pith of what is said—that I don't think—then to use the
little kick of energy which opposition supplies to be more

* Eventually *Three Guineas.*

vigorously oneself. It is perhaps true that my reputation will now decline. I shall be laughed at and pointed at. What should be my attitude—clearly Arnold Bennett and Wells took the criticism of their youngers in the wrong way. The right way is not to resent; not to be longsuffering and Christian and submissive either. Of course, with my odd mixture of extreme rashness and modesty (to analyse roughly) I very soon recover from praise and blame. But I want to find out an attitude. The most important thing is not to think very much about oneself. To investigate candidly the charge; but not fussily, not very anxiously. On no account to retaliate by going to the other extreme—thinking too much. And now that thorn is out—perhaps too easily.

Wednesday, May 25th

Now I have "finished" *David Copperfield*, and I say to myself can't I escape to some pleasanter atmosphere? Can't I expand and embalm and become a sentient living creature? Lord how I suffer! What a terrific capacity I possess for feeling with intensity—now, since we came back, I'm screwed up into a ball; can't get into step; can't make things dance; feel awfully detached; see youth; feel old; no, that's not quite it: wonder how a year or so perhaps is to be endured. Think, yet people do live; can't imagine what goes on behind faces. All is surface hard; myself only an organ that takes blows, one after another; the horror of the hard raddled faces in the flower show yesterday: the inane pointlessness of all this existence: hatred of my own brainlessness and indecision; the old treadmill feeling, of going on and on and on, for no reason: Lytton's death; Carrington's; a longing to speak to him; all that cut away, gone: . . . women: my book on professions: shall I write another novel; contempt for my lack of intellectual power; reading Wells without understanding; . . . society; buying clothes; Rodmell spoilt; all England spoilt: terror at night of things generally wrong in the universe; buying clothes; how I hate Bond Street and spending money on clothes: worst of all is this dejected barrenness. And my eyes hurt: and my hand trembles.

A saying of Leonard's comes into my head in this season of

complete inanity and boredom. "Things have gone wrong
somehow." It was the night C. killed herself. We were walking
along that silent blue street with the scaffolding. I saw all the
violence and unreason crossing in the air: ourselves small; a
tumult outside: something terrifying: unreason—shall I make
a book out of this? It would be a way of bringing order and
speed again into my world.

Thursday, May 26th

And now today suddenly the weight on my head is lifted
and I can think, reason, keep to one thing and concentrate.
Perhaps this is the beginning of another spurt. Perhaps I owe
it to my conversation with L. last night. I tried to analyse my
depression: how my brain is jaded with the conflict within of
two types of thought, the critical, the creative; how I am
harassed by the strife and jar and uncertainty without. This
morning the inside of my head feels cool and smooth instead of
strained and turbulent.

Tuesday, June 28th

Just "finished de Quincey." Thus am I trying to keep pace
with the days and deliver the second *C.R.* done on the last of
June, which I see with dismay is Thursday. I spent last summer thus toiling over *The Waves*. This is less severe by a long
chalk (what's the origin of that? cricket pitch? Billiards?). Anyhow it blazes; swoons; the heat. Royal, imperial, are the words
I fumble with in the Square. So hot yesterday—so hot, when
Prince Mirsky came with his fluent Russian lady: I mean she
was full of temperament; had the free gestures of the Slav:
but Mirsky was trap mouthed: opened and bit his remark to
pieces: has yellow misplaced teeth: wrinkles his forehead;
despair, suffering, very marked on his face. Has been in England, in boarding houses, for 12 years; now returns to Russia
"forever." I thought as I watched his eye brighten and fade
—soon there'll be a bullet through your head. That's one of
the results of war: this trapped cabin'd man. But that didn't
lubricate our tea.

Wednesday, June 29th

Whenever I suck my pen, my lip is covered with ink. And I have no ink with which to fill my pot; and it is 10 minutes past 12; and I have just finished Hardy; and I promise myself that the *C.R.* will be finally done by Wednesday next. And today is Sunday. Last night at 10 the Zeppelin came past with a string of light hanging from its navel. This consoled me for not having gone to the last night of the ballet. Now I have cleaned my table, which John inherits while I'm away. And I should now attack Ch. Rossetti. But Lord, how tired one gets of one's own writing.

Today is Wednesday and the *C.R.* I confess is not yet quite done. But then—well I had to re-write the last article, which I had thought so good, entirely. Not for many years shall I collect another bunch of articles.

Monday, July 11th

I will take a new pen and a new page to record the fact which is now a fact that I have slipped a green rubber band round *The Common Reader*, second series, and there it lies, at 10 minutes to one, ready to take upstairs. There is no sense of glory; only of drudgery done. And yet I daresay it's a nice enough book to read—I doubt that I shall write another like it all the same. I must find a quicker cut into books than this. But heaven be praised, not now. Now I'm taking a holiday. That is to say, what shall I write tomorrow? I can sit down and think.

Wednesday, July 13th

I have been sleeping over a promising novel. That's the way to write. I'm ruminating, as usual, how to improve my lot; and shall begin by walking, alone, in Regent's Park this afternoon. What I mean is why do a single thing one doesn't want to do—for instance buy a hat or read a book. Old Joseph Wright and old Lizzie Wright are people I respect. Indeed I do hope the second volume will come this morning. He was a maker of dialect dictionaries: he was a workhouse boy—his mother went charring. And he married Miss Lea a clergyman's daughter. And I've just read their love letters with respect.

And he said: "Always please yourself—then one person's happy
at any rate." And she said make details part of a whole—get
proportions right—contemplating marriage with Joe. Odd how
rare it is to meet people who say things that we ourselves could
have said. Their attitude to life much our own. Joe a very
thick sturdy man—"I am unique in certain respects," he said.
"We must leave some record of Joe and Lizzie to posterity."
Had his old working mother to Oxford. She thought All Souls
would make a good Co-op. Had a fist and struck boys. His
notion of learning. What is it? I sometimes would like to be
learned myself. About sounds and dialects. Still what use is it?
I mean, if you have that mind why not make something *beautiful*? Yes, but then the triumph of learning is that it leaves
something done solidly forever. Everybody knows now about
dialect, owing to his dictionary. He is a coarse, sturdy variety
of Sidney Webb and Walter Leaf—stockish, hairy; more humorous and forcible than either. Could work all night, wash
and work all next day. Miss Weisse, Tovey's lady, brought them
together—made Lizzie give up arranging the flowers in the
rectory and go to Oxford. She a woman of character. Wouldn't
accept Joe's offer of a job because he made her feel like a bear
at the end of a chain. But she married him. They were lost in
the woods by Virginia Water in 1896: and sat on a seat and
had an hour of great suffering, after which she accepted him
—they got on a baker's cart and were taken back to Miss Weisse.
An absorbing story. Joe knew all about servants. Joe taught
himself to read at 14: taught mill boys in a bedroom for 2d
a week: a surly but very sensitive man, apparently. Now this
is a testimony to Joe and Lizzie that I've been thinking how I
should have liked to see them—would now like to write to her.
A fine face with bright big eyes. Yes, but what happens in
volume two?

RODMELL. *Friday, August 5th*
     Yesterday L. came into my room at breakfast and said,
"Goldie * is dead." I never knew him well but had the com-

* G. Lowes Dickinson.

mon feeling that I have with those trusty Cambridge fellows: and was pleased, of course, by what he wrote of *The Waves:* and so came nearer. I get the strangest feeling now of our all being in the midst of some vast operation: of the splendour of this undertaking—life: of being capable of dying: an immensity surrounds me. No—I can't get it—shall let it brood itself into "a novel" no doubt. (It's thus I get the conception from which the book condenses.) At night L. and I talked of death again, the second time this year: how we may be like worms crushed by a motor car: what does the worm know of the car —how it is made? There may be a reason: if so not one we, as human beings, can grasp. Goldie had some mystic belief.

And now we have been to Lewes races and seen the fat lady in black with parts of her person spilling over the shooting seat on which her bulk is so insecurely poised: seen the riff raff of sporting society all lined up in their cars with the dickies bulging with picnic baskets: heard the bark of backers: seen for a second the pounding straining horses with red faced jockeys lashing them pound by. What a noise they made— what a sense of muscle hard and stretched—and beyond the downs this windy sunny day looked wild and remote; and I could rethink them into uncultivated land again.

Wednesday, August 17th

Now I think I have corrected the *C.R.* till I can correct no longer. And I have a few minutes' holiday before I need take the proofs in to L. Shall I then describe how I fainted again? That is the galloping hooves got wild in my head last Thursday night as I sat on the terrace with L. How cool it is after the heat! I said. We were watching the downs draw back into fine darkness after they had burnt like solid emerald all day. Now that was being softly finely veiled. And the white owl was crossing to fetch mice from the marsh. Then my heart leapt: and stopped: and leapt again: and I tasted that queer bitterness at the back of my throat; and the pulse leapt into my head and beat and beat, more savagely, more quickly. I am going to faint, I said, and slipped off my chair and lay on the grass. Oh no, I was not unconscious. I was alive: but possessed with this strug-

gling team in my head: galloping, pounding. I thought something will burst in my brain if this goes on. Slowly it muffled
itself. I pulled myself up and staggered, with what infinite
difficulty and alarm, now truly fainting and seeing the garden
painfully lengthened and distorted, back, back, back—how long
it seemed—could I drag myself?—to the house: and gained my
room and fell on my bed. Then pain, as of childbirth; and then
that too slowly faded; and I lay presiding, like a flickering
light, like a most solicitous mother, over the shattered splin-
tered fragments of my body. A very acute and unpleasant
experience.

Saturday, August 20th

A curious day in London yesterday. I said to myself standing
at L.'s window, Look at the present moment because it's not
been so hot for 21 years. There was a hot wind, as if one passed
over a kitchen, going from the studio to the Press. Outside
girls and young men lying in white on the square grass. So
hot we couldn't sit in the dining room. L. fetched and carried
and hardly let me walk upstairs carrying my own body. Coming back we had the car shut and the windscreen open—thus
sat in a hot rough gale which, as we came to the lanes and
woods, became deliciously cold and green. The coolest place is
the front seat of a car going at 40 or 50 miles with the windscreen open. Today, at 12:30, a wind rose: clouds descended;
now at 3:45 it's almost a normal warm summer day. For 10
days this heat has lasted. After my faint my head soon throbs;
or so I think. I think a little of dying suddenly and reflect,
Well then go about eating and drinking and laughing and
feeding the fish. Odd—the silliness one attributes to death—the
desire one has to belittle it and be found, as Montaigne said,
laughing with girls and good fellows. And L. is staking out the
dewpond and I am going in to be photographed. Three more
books appearing on Mrs. Woolf: which reminds me to make a
note, sometime, on my work.

A very good summer, this, for all my shying and jibbing,
my tremors this morning. Beautifully quiet, airy, powerful.
I believe I want this more humane existence for my next—to

spread carelessly among one's friends—to feel the width and amusement of human life: not to strain to make a pattern just yet: to be made supple, and to let the juice of usual things, talk, character, seep through me, quietly, involuntarily, before I say Stop and take out my pen. Yes, my thighs now begin to run smooth: no longer is every nerve upright. Yesterday we took plums to old Mrs. Grey. She is shrunk and sits on a hard chair in the corner. The door open. She twitches and trembles. Has the wild expressionless stare of the old. L. liked her despair: "I crawls up to bed hoping for the day; and I crawls down hoping for the night. I'm an ignorant old woman—can't write or read. But I prays to God every night to take me —oh to go to my rest. Nobody can say what pains I suffer. Feel my shoulder," and she began shuffling with a safety pin. I felt it. "Hard as iron; full of water, and my legs too." She pulled down her stocking. "The dropsy. I'm ninety-two; and all my brothers and sisters are dead; my daughter's dead; my husband is dead. . . ." She repeated her misery, her list of ills, over and over; could see nothing else; could only begin all over again; and kissed my hand, thanking us for our pound. This is what we make of our lives—no reading or writing— keep her alive with   * doctors when she wishes to die. Human ingenuity in torture is very great.

LONDON. *Sunday, October 2nd*

Yes, I will allow myself a new nib. Odd how coming back here upsets my writing mood. Odder still how possessed I am with the feeling that now, aged 50, I'm just poised to shoot forth quite free straight and undeflected my bolts whatever they are. Therefore all this flitter flutter of weekly newspapers interests me not at all. These are the soul's changes. I don't believe in ageing. I believe in forever altering one's aspect to the sun. Hence my optimism. And to alter now, cleanly and sanely, I want to shuffle off this loose living randomness: people; reviews; fame; all the glittering scales; and be withdrawn, and concentrated. So I shan't run about, just yet, buying

---

* Word illegible.

clothes, seeing people. We are off to Leicester tomorrow, to the Labour Party Conference. Then back to the fever of publishing. My *C.R.* doesn't cause me a single tremor. Nor Holtby's book.* I'm interested in watching what goes on for the moment without wishing to take part—a good frame of mind when one's conscious of power. Then I am backed now by the downs: the country: how happy L. and I are at Rodmell: what a free life that is—sweeping 30 or 40 miles; coming in when and how we like; sleeping in the empty house; dealing triumphantly with interruptions; and diving daily into that divine loveliness—always some walk; and the gulls on the purple plough; or going over to Tarring Neville—these are the flights I most love now—in the wide, the indifferent air. No being jerked, teased, tugged. And people come easily, flowering into intimacy in my room. But this is the past, or future. I am also reading D. H. L.† with the usual sense of frustration: and that he and I have too much in common—the same pressure to be ourselves: so that I don't escape when I read him: am suspended: what I want is to be made free of another world. This Proust does. To me Lawrence is airless, confined: I don't want this, I go on saying. And the repetition of one idea. I don't want that either. I don't want "a philosophy" in the least: I don't believe in other people's reading of riddles. What I enjoy (in the Letters) is the sudden visualisation: the great ghost springing over the wave (of the spray in Cornwall) but I get no satisfaction from his explanations of what he sees. And then it's harrowing: this panting effort after something: and "I have £6.10 left" and then Government hoofing him out, like a toad: and banning his book: the brutality of civilised society to this panting agonised man: and how futile it was. All this makes a sort of gasping in his letters. And none of it seems essential. So he pants and jerks. Then too I don't like strumming with two fingers—and the arrogance. After all, English has one million words: why confine yourself to 6? and praise yourself for so doing. But it's the preaching that rasps me. Like a person delivering judgment when only

* *Virginia Woolf,* by Winifred Holtby.   † D. H. Lawrence.

half the facts are there: and clinging to the rails and beating the cushion. Come out and see what's up here—I want to say. I mean it's so barren: so easy: giving advice on a system. The moral is, if you want to help, never systematise—not till you're 70: and have been supple and sympathetic and creative and tried out all your nerves and scopes. He died though at 45. And why does Aldous say he was an "artist"? Art is being rid of all preaching: things in themselves: the sentence in itself beautiful: multitudinous seas; daffodils that come before the swallow dares: whereas Lawrence would only say what proved something. I haven't read him of course. But in the Letters he can't listen beyond a point; must give advice; get you into the system too. Hence his attraction for those who want to be fitted: which I don't; indeed I think it a blasphemy this fitting of Carswells into a Lawrence system. So much more reverent to leave them alone: nothing else to reverence except the Carswellism of Carswell. Hence his schoolboy tweaking and smacking of anyone offered to him: Lytton, Bertie, Squire—all are suburban, unclean. His ruler coming down and measuring them. Why all this criticism of other people? Why not some system that includes the good? What a discovery that would be—a system that did not shut out.

Wednesday, November 2nd

He is a rattle headed, bolt eyed young man, raw boned, loose jointed, who thinks himself the greatest poet of all time. I daresay he is—it's not a subject that interests me enormously at the moment. What does? My own writing of course. I've just polished up the *L.S.* for *The Times*—a good one, I think, considering the currents that sway round that subject in *The Times* of all papers. And I have entirely remodelled my "Essay." It's to be an Essay-Novel, called *The Pargiters* *—and it's to take in everything, sex, education, life etc.: and come, with the most powerful and agile leaps, like a chamois, across precipices from 1880 to here and now. That's the notion anyhow, and I have been in such a haze and dream and intoxication,

---

* It became *The Years*.

declaiming phrases, seeing scenes, as I walk up Southampton Row that I can hardly say I have been alive at all, since 10th October.

Everything is running of its own accord into the stream, as with *Orlando*. What has happened of course is that after abstaining from the novel of fact all these years—since 1919—and *N. & D.* is dead—I find myself infinitely delighting in facts for a change, and in possession of quantities beyond counting: though I feel now and then the tug to vision, but resist it. This is the true line, I am sure, after *The Waves—The Pargiters*—this is what leads naturally on to the next stages—the essay-novel.

Monday, December 19th

Yes, today I have written myself to the verge of total extinction. Praised be I can stop and wallow in coolness and downs and let the wheels of my mind—how I beg them to do this— cool and slow and stop altogether. I shall take up *Flush* again, to cool myself. By Heaven, I have written 60,320 words since October 11th. I think this must be far the quickest going of any of my books: comes far ahead of *Orlando* or the *Lighthouse*. But then those 60 thousand will have to be sweated and dried into 30 or 40 thousand—a great grind to come. Never mind. I have secured the outline and fixed a shape for the rest. I feel, for the first time, No I mustn't take risks crossing the road, till the book is done. . . .

Yes, I will be free and entire and absolute and mistress of my life by October 1st, 1933. Nobody shall come here on their terms; or haul me off to them on theirs. Oh and I shall write a poet's book next. This one, however, releases such a torrent of fact as I did not know I had in me. I must have been observing and collecting these 20 years—since *Jacob's Room* anyhow. Such a wealth of things seen present themselves that I can't choose even—hence 60,000 words all about one paragraph. What I must do is to keep control; and not be too sarcastic; and keep the right degree of freedom and reserve. But oh how easy this writing is compared with *The Waves*! I wonder what the degree of carat-gold is in the two books. Of course this is external: but there's a good deal of gold—more than I'd thought—in externality. Anyhow, "what care I for my goose feather bed? I'm off to join the raggle taggle gipsies oh!" The gipsies, I say: not Hugh Walpole and Priestley—no. In truth *The Pargiters* is first cousin to *Orlando*, though the cousin is the flesh: *Orlando* taught me the trick of it. Now— oh but I must stop for 10 days at least—no 14—if not 21 days— now I must compose the 1880-1900 chapter, which needs skill. But I like applying skill I own. I am going to polish off my jobs: and tomorrow we go. A very fruitful varied and I think successful autumn—thanks partly to my tired heart: so I could impose terms: and I have never lived in such a race, such a dream, such a violent impulsion and compulsion—scarcely see- ing anything but *The Pargiters*.

RODMELL. *Friday, December 23rd*
    This is not the first day of the New Year: but the discrep- ancy may be forgiven.* I must write off my dejected rambling misery—having just read over the 30,000 words of *Flush* and come to the conclusion that they won't do. Oh what a waste— what a bore! Four months of work and heaven knows how much reading—not of an exalted kind either—and I can't see how to make anything of it. It's not the right subject for that length: it's too slight and too serious. Much good in it but would have to be much better. So here I am two days before Christmas pitched into one of my grey welters. True, it's partly over writing *The Pargiters*. But I can't get back into *Flush* ever, I feel: and L. will be disappointed; and the money loss too—that's a bore. I took it up impetuously after *The Waves* by way of a change: no forethought in me: and so got landed: it would need a month's hard work—and even then I doubt it. In that time I might have done Dryden and Pope. And I'm thus led to begin—no to end—the year with a doleful plaint. It is blazing hot; like spring, with the bees on the flowers. Never mind; this is not a reverse of the first order—not at all.

---

* Virginia Woolf kept her diary for each year in a separate manuscript book. This and the following entry are at the beginning of the 1933 book.

1933

This is in fact the last day of 1932, but I am so tired of pol-
ishing off *Flush*—such a pressure on the brain is caused by
doing ten pages daily—that I am taking a morning off and shall
use it here, in my lazy way, to sum up the whole of life . . .
the dew pond is filling; the goldfish are dead; it is a clear pale
blue eyed winter's day; and and—and my thoughts turn with
excitement to *The Pargiters,* for I long to feel my sails blow
out and to be careering with Elvira, Maggie and the rest over
the whole of human life. And indeed I cannot sum this up,
being tired in my head.

January 3rd, 1933

This is a little out of place,* but then so am I. We are up
for Angelica's party last night and I have half an hour to spend
before shooting in the new Lanchester (not ours—one lent)
back to Rodmell. We have been there just short of one fortnight and I ate myself into the heart of print and solitude—so
as to adumbrate a headache. And to wipe off the intensity of
concentration trying to re-write that abominable dog *Flush*
in 13 days, so as to be free—oh heavenly freedom—to write *The
Pargiters.* I insisted upon a night of chatter.

Thursday, January 5th

I am so delighted with my own ingenuity in having after
only ten years or so, made myself, in five minutes, a perfect
writing board, with pen tray attached, so that I can't ever again
fly into a fury bereft of ink and pen at the most critical moment
of a writer's life and see my sudden sentence dissipate itself
all for lack of a pen handy—and besides I'm so glad to be quit

* This entry is at the end of the 1932 manuscript book.

186

of page 100 of *Flush*—this the third time of writing that White-chapel scene, and I doubt if it's worth it, that I can't help dis-porting myself on this free blue page, which thank God in heaven, needs no re-writing. It is a wet misty day: my win-dows out here are all fog . . . if only because I'm in sublime reading fettle: seriously I believe that the strain of *The Waves* weakened my concentration for months—and then all that article compressing for the *C.R.* I am now at the height of my powers in that line, and have read, with close and powerful attention, some 12 or 15 books since I came here. What a joy—what a sense as of a Rolls Royce engine once more purring its 70 miles an hour in my brain. . . . I am also encouraged to read by the feeling that I am on the flood of creativeness in *The Pargiters*—what a liberation that gives one—as if every-thing added to that torrent—all books become fluid and swell the stream. But I daresay this is a sign only that I'm doing what is rather superficial and hasty and eager. I don't know. I've another week of *Flush* here, and then shall come to grips with my 20 years in one chapter problem. I visualise this book now as a curiously uneven time sequence—a series of great balloons, linked by straight narrow passages of narrative. I can take liberties with the representational form which I could not dare when I wrote *Night and Day*—a book that taught me much, bad though it may be.

Sunday, January 15th

I have come out here, our last morning, to write letters, so, naturally, I write this book. But then I haven't written a line these three weeks—only typed *Flush*, which, Heaven be praised, I "finished," almost without inverted commas, yesterday. Ah but my writing *Flush* has been gradually shoved out, as by a cuckoo born in the nest, by *The Pargiters*. How odd the mind's functions are! About a week ago, I began the making up of scenes—unconsciously: saying phrases to myself; and so, for a week, I've sat here, staring at the typewriter and speaking aloud phrases of *The Pargiters*. This becomes more and more maddening. It will however all be run off in a few days, when I let myself write again. I am reading Parnell. Yes; but this scene making increases the rate of my heart with uncomfortable rapidity. While I was forcing myself to do *Flush* my old headache came back—for the first time this autumn. Why should the *Ps.* make my heart jump; why should *Flush* stiffen the back of my neck? What connection has the brain with the body? Nobody in Harley Street could explain, yet the symptoms are purely physical and as distinct as one book is from the other.

Thursday, January 19th

It must be confessed that *The Pargiters* are like cuckoos in my nest—which should be *Flush.* I have only 50 pages to correct and send to Mabel; and these cursed scenes and dialogues will go on springing up in my head; and after correcting one page, I sit mooning for 20 minutes. I daresay this will increase the blood pressure when I come to write. But it is a tiresome bewildering distraction now.

Saturday, January 21st

Well, *Flush* lingers on and I cannot despatch him. That's the sad truth. I always see something I could press tighter or enwrap more completely. There's no trifling with words—can't be done: not when they're to stand "forever." So I am battening down my *Pargiters,* say till Wednesday—it shan't be later, I swear. And now I grow doubtful of the value of those figures. I'm afraid of the didactic: perhaps it was only that spurious passion that made me rattle away before Christmas. Anyhow I enjoyed it immensely and shall again—oh to be free, in fiction, making up my scenes again—however discreetly. Such is my cry this very fine cold January morning.

Thursday, January 26th

Well, *Flush* is, I swear, despatched. Nobody can say I don't take trouble with my little stories. And now, having bent my mind for 5 weeks sternly this way, I must unbend it the other—the Pargiter way. No critic ever gives full weight to the desire of the mind for change. Talk of being manysided—naturally one must go the other way. Now if I ever had the wits to go into the Shakespeare business I believe one would find the same law there—tragedy comedy and so on. Looming behind *The Pargiters* I can just see the shape of pure poetry beckoning me. But *The Pargiters* is a delightful solid possession to be enjoyed tomorrow. How bad I shall find it.

Thursday, February 2nd

Not that I much want a move in March, with *The Pargiters* on my hands. I am going however to work largely, spaciously, fruitfully on that book. Today I finished—rather more completely than usual—revising the first chapter. I am leaving out the interchapters—compacting them in the text: and project an appendix of dates. A good idea? And Galsworthy died two days ago, it suddenly struck me, walking just now by the Serpentine after calling on Mrs. W. (who's been dying—is recovering) with the gulls opening their scimitars—masses of gulls. Galsworthy's dead: and A. Bennett told me he simply couldn't stick Galsworthy. Had to praise Jack's books to Mrs. G. But I could say what I liked against Galsworthy. That stark man lies dead.

Saturday, March 25th

It is an utterly corrupt society I have just remarked, speaking in the person of Elvira Pargiter, and I will take nothing that it can give me etc. etc.: Now, as Virginia Woolf, I have to write—oh dear me what a bore—to the Vice Chancellor of Manchester University and say that I refuse to be made a Doctor of Letters. And to Lady Simon, who has been urgent in the matter and asks us to stay. Lord knows how I'm to put Elvira's language into polite journalese. What an odd coincidence! that real life should provide precisely the situation I was writing about. I hardly know which I am, or where: Virginia or Elvira: in the Pargiters or outside. We dined with Susan Lawrence two nights ago. A Mrs. Stocks of Manchester University was there. How delighted my husband will be to give you your degree in July! she began. And had rattled off a great deal about the delight of Manchester in seeing me honoured, before I had to pluck up courage and say: "But I won't take it." After that there was a general argument, with the Nevinsons, (Evelyn Sharp) Susan Lawrence etc. They all said they would take a degree from a University though not an honour from the state. They made me feel a little silly, priggish and perhaps extreme: but only superficially. Nothing would induce me to connive at all that humbug. Nor would it give me, even illicitly, any pleasure. I really believe that Nessa and I—she went with me and used my arguments about the silliness of honours for women—are without the publicity sense. Now for the polite letters. Dear Vice Chancellor—

Tuesday, March 28th

The polite letters have been sent. So far I have [not] had, nor could have had, any answer. No, thank Heaven, I need not emerge from my fiction in July to have a tuft of fur put on my head. It is the finest spring ever known—soft, hot, blue, misty.

Thursday, April 6th

Oh I'm so tired! I've written myself out over *The Pargiters*, this last lap. I've brought it down to Elvira in bed—the scene I've had in my mind ever so many months, but I can't write it now. It's the turn of the book. It needs a great shove to swing it round on its hinges. As usual, doubts rush in. I get it all too quick, too thin, too surface bright? Well, I'm too jaded to crunch it up, if that's so; and so shall bury it for a month— till we're back from Italy perhaps; and write on Goldsmith etc. meanwhile. Then seize on it fresh and dash it off in June, July, August, September. Four months should finish the first draft— 100,000 words, I think. 50,000 words written in 5 months— my record.

Thursday, April 13th

No I have worked myself too dry this time. There is not one idea left in the orange. But we go today and I shall sun, with only a few books. No, I will *not* write; I will *not* see people. A little nip from Gissing in the *T.L.S.* which I must answer. But indeed I can't find words—use the wrong ones—that's my state:

the familiar state after these three months writing—what fun that book is to me!

Tuesday, April 25th

That's all over—our ten days: and I wrote daily, almost, at Goldsmith—don't much see the point of my Goldsmiths and so on—and read Goldsmith, and so on. Yes: I should now be correcting *Flush* proofs—I doubt that little book to some extent: but I'm in a doubting mood: the scrambled mood of transience, for on Friday 5th we go to Siena; so I can't settle and make up my story, in which lies permanence. And as usual I want to seethe myself in something new—to break the mould of habit entirely and get that escape which Italy and the sun and the lounging and the indifference of all that to all this brings about. I rise, like a bubble out of a bottle. . . .

But *The Pargiters*. I think this will be a terrific affair. I must be bold and adventurous. I want to give the whole of the present society—nothing less: facts as well as the vision. And to combine them both. I mean, *The Waves* going on simultaneously with *Night and Day*. Is this possible? At present I have assembled 50,000 words of "real" life: now in the next 50 I must somehow comment; Lord knows how—while keeping the march of events. The figure of Elvira is the difficulty. She may become too dominant. She is to be seen only in relation to other things. This should give I think a great edge to both of the realities—this contrast. At present I think the run of events is too fluid and too free. It reads thin: but lively. How am I to get the depth without becoming static? But I like these problems, and anyhow there's a wind and a vigour in this naturalness. It should aim at immense breadth and immense intensity. It should include satire, comedy, poetry, narrative; and what form is to hold them all together? Should I bring in a play, letters, poems? I think I begin to grasp the whole. And it's to end with the press of daily normal life continuing. And there are to be millions of ideas but no preaching—history, politics, feminism, art, literature—in short a summing up of all I know, feel, laugh at, despise, like, admire, hate and so on.

Friday, April 28th

A mere note. We got out of the car last night and began walking down to the Serpentine. A summer evening. Chestnuts in their crinolines, bearing tapers; grey green water and so on. Suddenly L. bore off; and there was Shaw, dwindled shanks, white beard; striding along. We talked by a railing for 15 minutes. He stood with his arms folded, very upright, leaning back: teeth gold tipped. Just come from the dentist and "lured" out for a walk by the weather. Very friendly. That is his art, to make one think he likes one. A great spurt of ideas. "You forget that an aeroplane is like a car—it bumps—We went over the great wall—saw a little dim object in the distance. Of course the tropics are the place. The people are the original human beings. We are smudged copies. I caught the Chinese looking at us with horror—that we should be human beings! Of course the tour cost thousands: yet to see us you'd think we hadn't the price of the fare to Hampton Court. Lots of old spinsters had saved up for years to come. Oh but my publicity! It's terrifying. An hour's bombardment at every port. I made the mistake of accepting   * invitation. I found myself on a platform with the whole university round me. They began shouting We want Bernard Shaw. So I told them that every man at 21 must be a revolutionary. After that of course the police imprisoned them by dozens. I want to write an article for the *Herald* pointing out what Dickens said years ago about the folly of Parliament. Oh I could only stand the voyage by writing. I've written 3 or 4 books. I like to give the public full weight. Books should be sold by the pound. What a nice little dog. But aren't I keeping you and making you cold?" (touching my arm). Two men stopped along the path to look. Off he strode again on his dwindled legs. I said Shaw likes us. L. thinks he likes nobody. What will they say of Shaw in 50 years? He is 76 he said: too old for the tropics.

Last night—to relieve myself for a moment from correcting that silly book *Flush*—oh what a waste of time—I will record Bruno Walter. He is a swarthy, fattish man; not at all smart.

* There is a blank here in the manuscript.

Not at all the "great conductor." He is a little Slav, a little
Semitic. He is very nearly mad: that is, he can't get "the
poison" as he called it of Hitler out of him. "You must not
think of the Jews," he kept on saying. "You must think of
this awful reign of intolerance. You must think of the whole
state of the world. It is terrible—terrible. That this meanness,
that this pettiness, should be possible! Our Germany, which I
loved, with our tradition, our culture. We are now a disgrace."
Then he told us how you can't talk above a whisper. There are
spies everywhere. He had to sit in the window of his hotel in
Leipzig a whole day, telephoning. All the time soldiers were
marching. They never stop marching. And on the wireless,
between the turns, they play military music. Horrible, horrible! He hopes for the monarchy as the only hope. He will
never go back there. His orchestra had been in existence for
150 years: but it is the spirit of the whole that is awful. We
must band together. We must refuse to meet any German. We
must say that they are uncivilised. We will not trade with
them or play with them. We must make them feel themselves
outcasts—not by fighting them; by ignoring them. Then he swept
off to music. He has the intensity—genius?—which makes him live
everything he feels. Described conducting: must know every
player.

JUAN LES PINS. *Tuesday, May 9th*
Yes, I thought, I will make a note of that face—the face of
the woman stitching a very thin, lustrous green silk at a table
in the restaurant where we lunched at Vienne. She was like
fate—a consummate mistress of all the arts of self-preservation:
hair rolled and lustrous; eyes so nonchalant; nothing could
startle her; there she sat stitching her green silk with people
going and coming all the time; she not looking, yet knowing,
fearing nothing; expecting nothing—a perfectly equipped middle class Frenchwoman.
At Carpentras last night there was the little servant girl with
honest eyes, hair brushed in a flop and one rather black tooth.
I felt that life would crush her out inevitably. Perhaps 18, not
more; yet on the wheel, without hope; poor, not weak but

mastered—yet not enough mastered but to desire furiously travel, for a moment, a car. Ah but I am not rich, she said to me—which her cheap little stockings and shoes showed anyhow. Oh how I envy you, able to travel. You like Carpentras? But the wind blows ever so hard. You'll come again? That's the bell ringing. Never mind. Come over here and look at this. No, I've never seen anything like it. Ah yes, she always likes the English. ("She" was the other maid, with hair like some cactus in erection.) Yes I always like the English she said. The odd little honest face, with the black tooth, will stay on at Carpentras I suppose: will marry? will become one of those stout black women who sit in the door knitting? No: I foretell for her some tragedy: because she had enough mind to envy us the Lanchester.

PISA. *Friday, May 12th*

Yes, Shelley chose better than Max Beerbohm. He chose a harbour; a bay; and his home, with a balcony, in which Mary stood, looks out across the sea. Sloping sailed boats were coming in this morning—a windy little town, of high pink and yellow southern homes, not much changed I suppose: very full of the breaking of waves, very much open to the sea; and the rather desolate house standing with the sea just in front. Shelley, I suppose, bathed, walked, sat on the beach there; and Mary and Mrs. Williams had their coffee on the balcony. I daresay the clothes and the people were much the same. At any rate, a very good great man's house in its way. What is the word for full of the sea? Can't think tonight, sky high in a bedroom at the Nettano in Pisa, much occupied by French tourists. The Arno swimming past with the usual coffee coloured foam. Walked in the cloisters: this is true Italy, with the old dusty smell; people swarming in the streets; under the— what is the word for—I think the word for a street that has pillars is Arcade. Shelley's house waiting by the sea, and Shelley not coming, and Mary and Mrs. Williams watching from the balcony and then Trelawney coming from Pisa and burning the body on the shore—that's in my mind. All the colours here are white bluish marble against a very light saturated sky.

The tower leaning prodigiously. Clerical beggar at the door in a mock fantastic leather hat. The clergy walking. It was in these cloisters—Campo Santo—that L. and I walked 21 years ago and met the Palgraves and I tried to hide behind the pillars. And now we come in our car; and the Palgraves—are they dead, or very old? Now at any rate we have left the black country: the bald necked vulture country with its sprinkling of redroofed villas. This is the Italy one used to visit in a railway train with Violet Dickinson—taking the hotel bus.

SIENA. *Saturday, May 13th*
    Today we saw the most beautiful of views and the melancholy man. The view was like a line of poetry that makes itself; the shaped hill, all flushed with reds and greens; the elongated lines, cultivated every inch; old, wild, perfectly said, once and for all: and I walked up to a group and said What is that village? It called itself   *; and the woman with the blue eyes said, "Won't you come to my house and drink?" She was famished for talk. Four or five of them buzzed round us and I made a Ciceronian speech about the beauty of the country. But I have no money to travel with, she said, wringing her hands. We would not go to her house—a cottage on the side of the hill: and shook hands: hers were dusty: she wanted to keep them from me; but we all shook hands and I wished we had gone to her house, in the loveliest of all landscapes. Then, lunching by the river, among the ants, we met the melancholy man. He had five or six little fish in his hands, which he had caught in his hands. We said it was very beautiful country; and he said no, he preferred the town. He had been to Florence: no, he did not like the country. He wanted to travel, but had no money: worked at some village: no, he did not like the country, he repeated, with his gentle cultivated voice: no theatres, no pictures, only perfect beauty. I gave him 2 cigarettes; at first he refused, then offered us his six or seven little fish. But we could not cook them at Siena, we said. No, he agreed, and so we parted.

* Blank in manuscript.

It is all very well, saying one will write notes, but writing is a very difficult art. That is one has always to select: and I am too sleepy and hence merely run sand through my fingers. Writing is not in the least an easy art. Thinking what to write, it seems easy; but the thought evaporates, runs hither and thither. Here we are in the noise of Siena—the vast tunnelled arched stone town, swarmed over by chattering shrieking children.

Sunday, May 14th

Yes, I am reading—skipping—the *Sacred Fount*, about the most inappropriate of all books for this din—sitting by the open window, looking across heads and heads and heads—all Siena parading in grey and pink and the cars hooting. How finely run along those involuted threads? I don't.—that's the answer. I let 'em break. I only mark that the sign of a masterly writer is his power to break his mould callously. None of H. J.'s timid imitators have the vigour, once they've spun their sentence, to smash it. He has some native juice—figure: has driven his spoon deep into some stew of his own—some swarming mixture. That—his vitality—his vernacular—his pounce and grip and swing always spring fresh upon me, if at the same time I ask how could anyone, outside an orchis in a greenhouse, fabricate such an orchid's dream. Oh these Edwardian ladies with pale hair, these tailored "my dear men"! Yet compared to that vulgar old brute Creevey—L. is here bitten by a flea—H. J. is muscular, lean. No doubt the society of the Regent—the smell of brandy and bones, the painted velvet Lawrence women—the general laxity and lushness and vulgarity are here at their superlative. Of course the Shelleys, the Wordsworths, the Coleridges existed on the other side of the hedge. But when it comes gushing out of Creevey's page, it's for all the world like —something between Buckingham Palace, Brighton and the Queen's own italic style—so uncurbed, so weak: and how can one hope for a cure for a single person? There's all the dreary Lords and Ladies ogling and overeating; and plush and gilt;

and the Princess and the Prince—I think dissolution and obesity taking hold of the eighteenth century and swelling it into a puff ball efflorescence. 1860 is considerably more to the point.

Monday, May 15th

This should be all description—I mean of the little pointed green hills; and the white oxen and the poplars and the cypresses and the sculptured shaped infinitely musical, flushed green land from here to Abbazia *—that is where we went today; and couldn't find it and asked one after another of the charming tired peasants, but none had been 4 miles beyond their range, until we came to the stonebreaker and he knew. He could not stop work to come with us, because the inspector was coming tomorrow. And he was alone, alone, all day with no one to talk to. So was the aged Maria at the Abbazia. And she mumbled and slipped her words, as she showed us into the huge bare stone building; mumbled and mumbled, about the English—how beautiful they were. Are you a Contessa? she asked me. But she didn't like Italian country either. They seem stinted, dried up; like grasshoppers and with the manners of impoverished gentle people; sad, wise, tolerant, humorous. There was the man with the mule. He let the mule gallop away down the road. We are welcome, because we might talk; they draw round and discuss us after we're gone. Crowds of gentle kindly boys and girls always come about us and wave and touch their hats. And nobody looks at the view—except us —at the Euganean, bone white, this evening; then there's a ruddy red farm or two; and light islands swimming here and there in the sea of shadow—for it was very showery—then there are the black stripes of cypresses round the farm; like fur edges; and the poplars and the streams and the nightingales singing and sudden gusts of orange blossom; and white alabaster oxen with swinging chins—great flaps of white leather hanging under their noses—and infinite emptiness, loneliness, silence: never a new house, or a village; but only the vineyards and the olive trees, where they have always been. The hills

* Abbazia di Antimo at Montalcino.

go pale blue, washed very sharp and soft on the sky; hill after hill.

PIACENZA. *Friday, May 19th*

It's a queer thing that I write a date. Perhaps in this disoriented life one thinks, if I can say what day it is, then . . . Three dots to signify I don't know what I mean. But we have been driving all day from Lerici over the Apennines and it is now cold, cloistral, highly uncomfortable, in a vast galleried Italian inn, so ill provided with chairs that now at this present moment we are squatted, L. in a hard chair by his bed, I on the bed, in order to take advantage of the single light which burns between us. L. is writing directions to the Press. I am about to read Goldoni.

Lerici is hot and blue and we had a room with a balcony. There were Misses and Mothers—misses who had lost all chance of life long ago, and could with a gentle frown, a frown of mild sadness, confront a whole meal—arranged for the English—in entire silence, dressed as if for cold Sunday supper in Wimbledon. Then there's the retired Anglo-Indian, who takes shall we say Miss Toutchet for a walk, a breezy red faced man, very fond of evensong at the Abbey. She goes to the Temple; where "my brother" has rooms. Et cetera. Et cetera. Of the Apennines I have nothing to say—save that up on the top they're like the inside of a green umbrella: spine after spine: and clouds caught on the point of the stick. And so down to Parma; hot, stony, noisy; with shops that don't keep maps; and so on along a racing road, to Piacenza, at which we find ourselves now at 6 minutes to 9 P.M. This of course is the rub of travelling—this is the price paid for the sweep and the freedom—the dusting of our shoes and careering off tomorrow—and eating our lunch on a green plot beside a deep cold stream. It will be all over this day week—comfort—discomfort; and the zest and rush that no engagements, hours, habits give. Then we shall take them up again with more than the zest of travelling.

Sunday, May 21st

To write to keep off sleep—that is the exalted mission of

tonight—tonight sitting at the open window of a second-rate
inn in Draguignan—with plane trees outside, the usual single
noted bird, the usual loudspeaker. Everybody in France motors on Sunday; then sleeps it off at night. The hotel keepers
are gorged and scarcely stop playing cards. But Grasse was too
plethoric—we came on here late. We leave here early. I dip
into Creevey; L. into *Golden Bough*. We long for bed. This is
the tax for travelling—these sleepy uncomfortable hotel nights
—sitting on hard chairs under the lamp. But the seduction
works as we start—to Aix tomorrow—so home. And "home" becomes a magnet, for I can't stop making up the P's: can't live
without that intoxicant—though this is the loveliest and most
distracting alternative. But I'm full of holiday and want work
—ungrateful that I am!—and yet I want the hills near Fabbria
too and the hills near Siena—but no other hills—not these
black and green violent monotonous southern hills. We saw
poor Lawrence's Phoenix picked out in coloured pebbles at
Vence today among all the fretted lace tombs.

Tuesday, May 23rd

I have just said to myself if it were possible to write, those
white sheets would be the very thing, not too large or too
small. But I do not wish to write, except as an irritant. This
is the position. I sit on L.'s bed; he in the only armchair.
People tap up and down on the pavement. This is Vienne. It
is roasting hot—hotter and hotter it gets—and we are driving
through France; and it's Tuesday and we cross on Friday and
this strange interval of travel, of sweeping away from habita-
tion and habits will be over. On and on we go—through Aix,
through Avignon, on and on, under arches of leaves, over bare
sandy roads, under grey black hills with castles, beside vines:
and I'm thinking of the Pargiters: and L. is driving; and when
we come to poplars we get out and lunch by the river; and
then on; and take a cup of tea by the river: fetch our letters,
learn that Lady Cynthia Mosley is dead: picture the scene;
wonder at death; and drowse and doze in the heat, and decide
to sleep here—hotel de la Poste; and read another letter and
learn that the Book Society will probably take *Flush* and spec-

ulate what we shall do if we have £1,000 or £2,000 to spend. And what would these little burghers of Vienne, who are drinking coffee, do with that sum, I ask? The girl is a typist; the young men clerks. For some reason they start discussing hotels at Lyons, I think; and they haven't a penny piece between them; and all the men go into the urinal, one sees their legs; and the Morocco soldiers go in their great cloaks; and the children play ball and people stand lounging and everything becomes highly pictorial, composed, legs in particular—the odd angles they make: and the people dining in the hotel; and the queer air it all has, since we shall leave early tomorrow, of something designing Vienne on my mind, significantly. Now the draw of home, and freedom and no packing tells on us —oh to sit in an arm chair; and read and not have to ask for Eau Mineral, with which to brush our teeth!

52 TAVISTOCK SQUARE. *Tuesday, May 30th*
Yes, but of all things coming home from a holiday is undoubtedly the most damned. Never was there such aimlessness, such depression. Can't read, write or think. There's no climax here. Comfort yes: but the coffee's not so good as I expected. And my brain is extinct—literally hasn't the power to lift a pen. What one must do is to set it—my machine I mean—in the rails and give it a push. Lord—how I pushed yesterday to make it start running along Goldsmith again. There's that half finished article. Lord Salisbury said something about dished up speeches being like the cold remains of last night's supper. I see white grease on the pages of my article. Today it's a little warmer—tepid meat: a slab of cold mutton. It's coldish, dullish here. Yes, but I hear the clock tick and suspect, though I must not look, that the wheels are just beginning to turn on the rails. We go to Monks House for Whitsun, which is Monday —the suburban, the diminished Monks House, No, I can't look at *The Pargiters*. It's an empty snail shell. And I'm empty with a cold slab of a brain. Never mind. I shall dive head foremost into *The Pargiters*. And now I shall make my mind run along Italian—what's his name—Goldoni. A few verbs I think.

It occurs to me that this state, my depressed state, is the state in which most people usually are.

Wednesday, May 31st

I think I have now got to the point where I can write for four months straight ahead at *The Pargiters*. Oh the relief—the physical relief! I feel as if I could hardly any longer keep back—that my brain is being tortured by always butting against a blank wall—I mean *Flush,* Goldsmith, motoring through Italy. Now, tomorrow, I mean to run it off. And suppose only nonsense comes? The thing is to be venturous, bold, to take every possible fence. One might introduce plays, poems, letters, dialogues: must get the round, not only the flat. Not the theory only. And conversation: argument. How to do that will be one of the problems. I mean intellectual argument in the form of art: I mean how give ordinary waking Arnold Bennett life the form of art? These are rich hard problems for my four months ahead. And I don't know my own gifts at the moment. I'm disoriented completely after four weeks' holiday—no three—but tomorrow we go to Rodmell again. And I must fill up the chinks with reading—and don't want to settle down to books— Well, now I have to go up to Murray about my dress: and there's Ethel round the corner; but no letters; disorganisation from Whitsun again. I thought, driving through Richmond last night, something very profound about the synthesis of my being: how only writing composes it: how nothing makes a whole unless I am writing: now I have forgotten what seemed so profound. The rhododendron like coloured glass mounds at Kew. Oh the agitation, oh the discomfort of this mood.

And I am at once called out to draw lots in our Derby sweepstake. No favourite this year, they say.

Very well: the old Pargiters are beginning to run off: and I say oh to be done. I mean, writing is effort: writing is despair: and yet of course t'other day in the grilling heat at Rodmell I admit that the perspective—this I think was something like my profound thought at Richmond—shifts into focus: yes: the proportion is right: though I at the top suffer strain; suffer, as this morning, grim despair and shall O Lord when it comes to re-writing suffer an intensity of anguish ineffable (the word only means one can't express it); holding the thing;—all the things—the innumerable things—together.

Monday, July 10th

Bella * arrived and knocked her head upon the window of the car. She cut her nose and was dazed. And then I was in "one of my states"—how violent, how acute—and walked in Regents Park in black misery and had to summon my cohorts in the old way to see me through, which they have done more or less. A note made to testify to my own ups and downs: many of which go unrecorded though they are less violent I think than they used to be. But how familiar it was—stamping along the road, with gloom and pain constricting my heart: and the desire for death, in the old way, all for two I daresay careless words.

Thursday, July 20th

I am again in full flood with *The Pargiters* after a week of very scanty pages. The trouble is to get the meat pressed in: I mean to keep the rhythm and convey the meaning. It tends more and more, I think—at any rate the E.M. scenes—to drama. I think the next lap ought to be objective, realistic, in the manner of Jane Austen: carrying the story on all the time.

Saturday, August 12th

So naturally after Mrs. Nef I was so tired—I shivered and shook. I went to bed for 2 days and slept I daresay 7 hours, visiting the silent realms again. It strikes me—what are these sudden fits of complete exhaustion? I come in here to write: can't even finish a sentence; and am pulled under; now is this some odd effort; the subconscious pulling me down into her? I've been reading Faber on Newman; compared his account of a nervous breakdown; the refusal of some part of the mechanism; is that what happens to me? Not quite. Because I'm not

* Lady Southorn, sister of L. W.

evading anything. I long to write *The Pargiters*. No. I think the effort to live in two spheres: the novel; and life; is a strain. Nefs almost break me because they strain me so far from the other world; I only want walking and perfectly spontaneous childish life with L. and the accustomed when I'm writing at full tilt: to have to behave with circumspection and decision to strangers wrenches me into another region; hence the collapse.

Wednesday, August 16th

And owing to Sir Alan Cobham's flying and Angelica and Julian and fetching the boat I had another headache and bed and didn't see Ethel, but heard her voice and have 6 pages on the subject this morning, and didn't see the Wolves and am out here again * rubbing at *The Pargiters* and thinking Oh Lord how am I ever going to pull all that into shape. What a tremendous struggle it'll be! Never mind. I want to discuss Form, having been reading Turgenev. (But how my hand trembles after one of these headaches—can't lay hands on words or pens exactly—the habit has been broken.)

Form, then, is the sense that one thing follows another rightly. This is partly logic. T. wrote and re-wrote. To clear the truth of the unessential. But Dostoievsky would say that everything matters. But one can't read D. again. Now Shakespeare was constrained in form by the stage. (T. says one must find a new form for the old subject: but here, I suppose, uses the word differently.) The essential thing in a scene is to be preserved. How do you know what this is? How do we know if the D. form is better or worse than the T.? It seems less permanent. T.'s idea that the writer states the essential and lets the reader do the rest. D. to supply the reader with every possible help and suggestion. T. reduces the possibilities. The difficulty about criticism is that it is so superficial. The writer has gone so much deeper. T. kept a diary for Bozarov: wrote everything from his point of view. We have only 250 short pages. Our criticism is only a birds eye view of the pinnacle of an iceberg. The rest under water. One might begin it in this

---

* In her workroom at the end of Monks House garden.

way. The article might be more broken, less composed than
usual.

Thursday, August 24th

A week ago, on Friday to be precise, having got my mind
again, I dipped into *The Pargiters* and determined to sweat it
bare of flesh before going on, accumulating more scenes. I
am re-arranging too, all the first part, so as to bring it together.
The death happens in the first chapter now. I think I shall
reduce the size by half; it is however a little bare and jerky at
present. Moreover it is rather a rush and a strain. I have just
killed Mrs. P.: and can't shoot ahead to Oxford. For the truth
is these little scenes embroil one, just as in life; and one can't
switch off to a different mood all in a second. It seems to me
that the realness of the beginning is complete. I have a good
excuse for poetry in the second part, if I can take it. Rather an
interesting experiment—if I could see the same thing from two
different views. And now I have spent the morning reading
the Confession of Arsène Houssaye left here yesterday by
Clive. What a vast fertility of pleasure books hold for me! I
went in and found the table laden with books. I looked in
and sniffed them all. I could not resist carrying this one off and
broaching it. I think I could happily live here and read forever.

Saturday, September 2nd

Suddenly in the night I thought of *Here and Now* as a title
for the Pargiters. I think it better. It shows what I'm after and
does not compete with the Herries Saga, the Forsyte Saga and
so on. I have now done the first part; I mean compressed it,
shall, I think, compress Eleanor's day, and then what? The
rest does not admit of much compression. I think I have reduced it to 80,000 words perhaps: but it seems to me there
must be another 40, to come. 80 plus 40 equals 120,000. If so
it will be the longest of my little brood—longer than *Night and
Day* I imagine.

Tuesday, September 26th

Why not, one of these days, write a fantasy on the theme of
Crabbe?—a biographical fantasy—an experiment in biography.

I had so much of the most profound interest to write here—a dialogue of the soul with the soul—and I have let it all slip—why? Because of feeding the goldfish, of looking at the new pond, of playing bowls. Nothing remains now. I forget what it was about. Happiness. The perfect day, which was yesterday. And so on. Now I began the morning by telephoning corrections of *Twelfth Night,* to the *N.S.:* put in a comma, take out semi-colon; and so on. Then I come out here, having seen the carp, and write Turgenev.

Monday, October 2nd

It's October now; and we have to go to Hastings Conference tomorrow and Wednesday, to Vita, then back to London. I opened this in order to make one of my self-admonishments previous to publishing a book. *Flush* will be out on Thursday and I shall be very much depressed, I think, by the kind of praise. They'll say it's "charming," delicate, ladylike. And it will be popular. Well now I must let this slip over me without paying it any attention. I must concentrate on *The Pargiters* —or *Here and Now.* I must not let myself believe that I'm simply a ladylike prattler: for one thing it's not true. But they'll all say so. And I shall very much dislike the popular success of *Flush.* No, I must say to myself, this is a mere wisp, a veil of water; and so create, hardly, fiercely, as I feel now more able to do than ever before.

Sunday, October 29th

No, my head is too tired to go on with Bobby and Elvira—they're to meet at St. Paul's—this morning. I wish I could get it full and calm and unconscious. This last is difficult, owing to *Flush,* owing to the perpetual little spatter of comment that keeps me awake. Yesterday the *Granta* said I was now defunct. *Orlando, Waves, Flush* represent the death of a potentially great writer. This is only a rain drop, I mean the snub some little pimpled undergraduate likes to administer, just as he would put a frog in one's bed: but then there's all the letters and the requests for pictures—so many that, foolishly perhaps, I wrote a sarcastic letter to the *N.S.*—thus procuring more rain drops. This metaphor shows how tremendously important un-

consciousness is when one writes. But let me remember that
fashion in literature is an inevitable thing; also that one must
grow and change; also that I have, at last, laid hands upon my
philosophy of anonymity. My letter to the *N.S.* is the crude
public statement of a part of it. How odd last winter's revelation was! freedom; which now I find makes it quite easy for
me to refuse Sibyl's invitations, to take life much more strongly
and steadily. I will not be "famous," "great." I will go on
adventuring, changing, opening my mind and my eyes, refusing to be stamped and stereotyped. The thing is to free one's
self: to let it find its dimensions, not be impeded. And though
this as usual is only a pot shot, there is a great deal of substance
in it. October has been a bad month; but might have been
much worse without my philosophy.

Thursday, December 7th

I was walking through Leicester Square—how far from China
—just now when I read "Death of Noted Novelist" on the
posters. And I thought of Hugh Walpole. But it is Stella Benson. Then why write anything, immediately? I did not know
her; but have a sense of those fine patient eyes: the weak voice;
the cough; the sense of oppression. She sat on the terrace with
me at Rodmell. And now, so quickly, it is gone, what might
have been a friendship. Trusty and patient and very sincere
—I think of her; trying to cut through, in one of those difficult
evenings, to some deeper layer—certainly we could have reached
it, given the chance. I'm glad I stopped her at the door as she
got into her little car and asked her to call me Virginia—to
write to me. And she said: "There's nothing I should like better." But it's like the quenching of something—her death out
there in China; and I sitting here and writing about her and
so fugitive and yet so true; and no more to come. How mourn-
ful the afternoon seems, with the newspaper carts(?) dashing
up Kingsway, "Death of Noted Novelist" on the placard. A
very fine steady mind: much suffering; suppressed;—there
seems to be some sort of reproach to me in her death, as in
K. M.'s. I go on; and they cease. Why? Why not my name on
the posters? And I have a feeling of the protest each might

make: gone with their work unfinished—each so suddenly. Stella was 41. "I am going to send you my book" and so on. A dreary island she lived on, talking to colonels. A curious feeling, when a writer like S. B. dies, that one's response is diminished: *Here and Now* won't be lit up by her: it's life lessened. My effusion—what I send out—less porous and radiant —as if the thinking stuff were a web that were fertilised only by other people's (her that is) thinking it too: now lacks life.

Sunday, December 17th

I finished part 4 of *Here and Now* yesterday and therefore indulge in a contemplative morning. To freshen my memory of the war, I read some old diaries.

1934

Tuesday, January 16th

I have let all this time—three weeks at Monks—slip because I was there so divinely happy and pressed with ideas—another full flood of *Pargiters* or *Here and Now* (odd that Goldie's letter mentions that—*The Waves* is also here and now—I had forgotten). So I never wrote a word of farewell to the year; not a word describing the Keynes and the Jones; nothing about the walks I had ever so far into the downs; or the reading—Marvell of an evening, and the usual trash.

Sunday, February 18th

And I began *Here and Now* again this morning, Sunday, at the point where I left off all but three weeks ago for my headache. Here I note that from two to three weeks is the right space. It has not gone cold, as after six weeks: I still carry it in my mind, and can see how to revise. It has gone—the talk during the Raid—running all over the place, because I was tired; now I must press together; get into the mood and start again. I want to raise up the magic world all round me and live strongly and quietly there for six weeks. The difficulty is the usual one—how to adjust the two worlds. It is no good getting violently excited: one must combine.

Tuesday, April 17th

So jaded am I after last night that I cannot add a word to my *Sickert* or make out a sketch of the last chapters of *Here and Now*. A high price to pay for a hurried dinner at the Hutches: racing to *Macbeth;* talking to Dodo Macnaghten; then to Sir Fred Pollock on the stage of Sadlers Wells.

An idea about Shakespeare.

That the play demands coming to the surface—hence insists upon a reality which the novel need not have, but perhaps should have contact with the surface, coming to the top. This is working out my theory of the different levels in writing and how to combine them: for I begin to think the combination necessary. This particular relation with the surface is imposed on the dramatist of necessity: how far did it influence Shakespeare? Idea that one could work out a theory of fiction etc. on these lines; how many levels attempted, whether kept to or not.

Wednesday, May 9th

This, the 9th May, was our last day and fine. So we saw Warwickshire—but I've been reading the Monologue and note how oddly another style infects—at its best: thick green, thick leaves, stubby yellow stone houses and a fine sprinkling of Elizabethan cottages. All this led very harmoniously to Stratford on Avon; and all crabbers be damned—it is a fine, unselfconscious town, mixed, with eighteenth century and the rest all standing cheek by jowl. All the flowers were out in Shakespeare's garden. "That was where his study windows looked out when he wrote *The Tempest*," said the man. And perhaps it was true. Anyhow it was a great big house, looking straight at the large windows and the grey stone of the school chapel, and when the clock struck, that was the sound Shakespeare heard. I cannot without more labour than my roadrunning mind can compass describe the queer impression of sunny impersonality. Yes, everything seemed to say, this was Shakespeare's, had he sat and walked; but you won't find me, not exactly in the flesh. He is serenely absent—present; both at once; radiating round one; yes; in the flowers, in the old hall, in the garden; but never to be pinned down. And we went to the church and there was the florrid foolish bust, but what I had not reckoned for was the worn simple slab, turned the wrong way, Kind Friend for Jesus' sake forbear—again he seemed to be all air and sun smiling serenely; and yet down there one foot from me lay the little bones that had spread over the world this vast illumination. Yes, and then we walked round the church and all is simple and a little worn; the river slipping past the stone wall, with a red breadth from some flowering tree, and the edge of the turf unspoilt, soft and green and muddy and two casual nonchalant swans. The church and the school and the house are all roomy spacious places, resonant, sunny today, and in and out   *—yes, an impressive place; still living, and then the little bones lying there, which have created: to think of writing *The Tempest* looking out on that garden: what a rage and storm of thought to have gone over any mind; no doubt the solidity of the place was comfortable. No doubt he saw the cellars with serenity. And a few scented American girls and a good deal of parrot prattle from old gramophone discs at the birthplace, one taking up the story from the other. But isn't it odd, the caretaker at New Place agreed, that only one genuine signature of Shakespeare's is known; and all the rest, books, furniture, pictures etc. has completely vanished? Now I think Shakespeare was very happy in this, that there was no impediment of fame, but his genius flowed out of him and is still there, in Stratford. They were acting *As You Like It* I think in the theatre.

Duffers the biographers not to make more hum and melody out of New Place. I could, so I think. For the man told us that after the great grand-daughter's death there was a sale, and why shouldn't some of his things, he said, be lost, put away and come to light? Also, Queen H. Maria, Charles I's queen, stayed there at New Place with the grand-daughter(?) which shows how substantial it must have been. That he told us, and I had never heard. And he said Gaskell, the clergyman, had the original house, which stretched across the garden almost to the chapel, pulled down because people bothered him, asking to see Shakespeare's house. And there (between the window and the wall) was the room he died in. A mulberry reputes to be the scion of the tree that grew outside Shakespeare's window. Great cushions of blue, yellow, white flowers in the garden, which is open, so that the living go on walking and sitting there.

* Word illegible.

Friday, May 18th

I broke off, after sticking my Irish papers into the old book, and felt I suppose a little shiver. Can't be anything I said to myself after all that holiday; but it was—the flu. So I had to resign all ideas—all flood of *Pargiters* and the glorious and difficult end of that book: all was blotted by the damp sponge; and now it is precisely a week since I went to bed, and here we are for Whitsun at Monks. What's more amazing is that I write this with a gold Waterman, and have some thoughts of supplanting steel Woolworth. It is a sunny voluptuous day, the birds all rasping on their nests, I suppose, and cawing on the trees and early in the morning giving loud and continued bursts of songs to which I lie listening. I hear L. going about the garden with Percy. All is calm and profoundly comfortable, owing to the absence for ever even in the background of grumbling Nelly and her replacement by the steady silent unselfish Mabel. Yes, we do without a char; we are free, serene, matter of fact, oh what a relief! So if I can pull my head out of the bog, I may go back on Tuesday to the three months immersion. But I take a day or two more to rest myself. How infinitely modest and disillusioned and without ambition of any sort I became, all because of influenza. Couldn't believe that anyone would come and see me, let alone that I could ever again string a dozen words. Now self confidence, conceit, the blessed illusion by which we live begin to return; very gently. Smooth serenity is the first stage which I will not interrupt by writing.

Tuesday, May 22nd

At last today, which is Tuesday, after striking the match on the box despairingly, sterilely—oh I was so overcome with rigidity and nothingness—a little flame has come. Perhaps I'm off. This refers to the devilish difficulty of starting Part 7 again after the 'flu. Elvira and George, or John, talking in her room. I'm still miles outside them, but I think I got into the right tone of voice this morning. I make this note by way of warning. What is important now is to go very slowly; to stop in the middle of the flood; never to press on; to lie back and let the

soft subconscious world become populous; not to be urging
foam from my lips. There's no hurry. I've enough money to
last a year. If this book comes out next June year it's time
enough. The last chapters must be so rich, so resuming, so weav-
ing together that I can only go on by letting my mind brood
every morning on the whole book. There's no longer any need
to forge ahead, as the narrative part is over. What I want is to
enrich and stabilise. This last chapter must equal in length
and importance and volume the first book: and must in fact
give the other side, the submerged side of that. I shan't, I think,
re-read; I shall summon it back—the tea-party, the death, Oxford and so on, from my memory. And as the whole book depends on bringing this off, I must be very leisurely and patient
and nurse my rather creaking head and dandle it with French
and so on as cunningly as possible.

Monday, June 11th

That hopeful page reads rather too credulous now, since
I went back and again on Friday following shivered, and ached,
was stiff as a rod, talking to Elizabeth Bowen: 101: bed: influenza: and so lay all that week, till last Sunday to be accurate: and then went to Rodmell; and there began the chapter
again and had a sudden fuse of ideas and then there was the
opera, the nightingale singing in the ilex tree, Christabel *
and Mr. Olaf Hambro telling stories about the Queen and
Prince: and a very hot concert yesterday, so I cannot, no I cannot, write today. Patience, as Carlyle would say (in Italian).
But consider—the whole system is so strained over this end,
that one tiny grit, one late night, one too tiring day—takes away
all rush, all fusing. And just as I saw it clear before me: the
very intricate scenes: all contrasting; building up: so wait
till tomorrow.

Monday, June 18th

Very very hot: day altered so as to go out after tea. A drought
over the world. In flood with *Here and Now,* praise be. Yet

* Lady Aberconway.

very wary: only just now I made up the scene with Ray and Maggie: a sign I am fertilising, for I should be doing French for Janie, who comes at 5.

Friday, July 27th

Ah hah—but now, having despatched that entirely disagreeable day, Worthing and Mr. Fears, representing Rodmell Labour Party for an hour after dinner, I'm free to begin the last chapter; and by a merciful Providence the well is full, ideas are rising and if I can keep at it widely, freely, powerfully, I shall have two months of complete immersion. Odd how the creative power at once brings the whole universe to order. I can see the day whole, proportioned—even after a long flutter of the brain such as I've had this morning it must be a physical, moral, mental necessity, like setting the engine off. A wild windy hot day—a tearing wind in the garden; all the July apples on the grass. I'm going to indulge in a series of quick sharp contrasts: breaking my moulds as much as ever I like. Trying every kind of experiment. Now of course I can't write diary or letters or read because I am making up all the time. Perhaps Bob T. was right in his poem when he called me fortunate above all—I mean in having a mind that can express —no, I mean in having mobilised my being—learnt to give it complete outcome—I mean, that I have to some extent forced myself to break every mould and find a fresh form of being, that is of expression, for everything I feel or think. So that when it is working I get the sense of being fully energised— nothing stunted. But this needs constant effort, anxiety and rush. Here in *Here and Now* I am breaking the mould made by *The Waves*.

Thursday, August 2nd

I'm worried too with my last chapters. Is it all too shrill and voluble? And then the immense length, and the perpetual ebbs and flows of invention. So divinely happy one day; so jaded the next.

Monday, August 7th

A rather wet Bank Holiday. Tea with Keynes. Maynard had had teeth out but was very fertile. For instance: Yes, I've been 3 weeks in America. An impossible climate. In fact it has collected all the faults of all the climates. This carries out my theory about climate. Nobody could produce a great work in America. One sweats all day and the dirt sticks to one's face. The nights are as hot as the days. Nobody sleeps. Everyone is kept on the go all day long by the climate. I used to dictate articles straight off. I felt perfectly well until I left. "So to German politics." They're doing something very queer with their money. I can't make out what. It may be the Jews are taking away their capital. Let me see, if 2,000 Jews were each to take away £2,000—Anyhow, they can't pay their Lancashire bill. Always the Germans have bought cotton from Egypt, had it spun in Lancashire; it's a small bill, only ½ a million, but they can't pay. Yet they're buying copper all the time. What's it for? Armaments no doubt. That's one of the classic examples of international trade. 20,000 people out of work. But of course there's something behind it. What is the cause of the financial crisis? They're doing something foolish. No Treasury control of the soldiers.

(But I am thinking all the time of what is to end *Here and Now*. I want a chorus, a general statement, a song for four voices. How am I to get it? I am now almost within sight of the end, racing along: becoming more and more dramatic. And how to make the transition from the colloquial to the lyrical, from the particular to the general?)

Friday, August 17th

Yes, I think owing to the sudden rush of two wakeful nights, making up early mornings rather, I think I see the end of *Here and Now* (or *Music* or *Dawn* or whatever I shall call it): it's to end with Elvira going out of the house and saying What did I make this knot in my handkerchief for? and all the coppers rolling about—

It's to be all in speeches—no play. I have now made a sketch of what everyone is to say; and it ends with a supper party in the downstairs room. I think the back is broken. It will run to something like 850 of my rough pages I imagine: which is at 200, 170,000 and I shall sweat it down to 130,000.

Tuesday, August 21st

The lesson of *Here and Now* is that one can use all kinds of "forms" in one book. Therefore the next might be poem, reality, comedy, play; narrative, psychology all in one. Very short. This needs thinking over also, a play about the Parnells, or a biography of Mrs. P.

Thursday, August 30th

If I can't even write here, owing to making up the last scenes, how can I possibly read Dante? Impossible. After three days' grind, getting back, I am I think floated again. Robson comes to tea today; and the Wolves tomorrow; and . . . another lapse making up Elvira's speech . . . "D'you know what I've been clasping in my hand all the evening? Coppers."

Well anyhow, I've enough in stock to last out this chapter; I daresay another two or three weeks. Yesterday I found a new walk, and a new farm, in the fold between Asheham and Tarring Neville. Very lovely, all alone, with the down rising behind. Then I walked back by a rough broad overflowing grey river. The porpoise came up and gulped. It rained. All ugliness was dissolved. An incredibly eighteenth century landscape, happily making me think less of Wilmington.

A tremendous hailstorm after tea; like white ice; broken up: lanced, lashing; like the earth being whipped. This happened several times; black clouds while we played Brahms. No letters at all this summer. But there will be many next year, I predict. And I don't mind; the day, yesterday to be exact, being so triumphant: writing; the walk; reading, Leeson, a   *
Saint Simon, Henry James's preface to *P. of a Lady*—very clever,   * but one or two things I recognise; then Gide's Journal, again full of startling recollection—things I could have said myself.

* Illegible.

Sunday, September 2nd

I don't think I have ever been more excited over a book than I am writing the end of—shall it be *Dawn?* Or is that too emphatic, sentimental. I wrote like a—forget the word—yesterday; my cheeks burn; my hands tremble. I am doing the scene where Peggy listens to their talking and bursts out. It was this outburst that excited me so. Too much perhaps. I can't make the transition to E.'s speech easily.

Wednesday, September 12th

Roger died on Sunday. Tomorrow we go up, following some instinct, to the funeral. I feel dazed; very wooden. Women cry, L. says: but I don't know why I cry—mostly with Nessa. And I'm too stupid to write anything. My head all stiff. I think the poverty of life now is what comes to me; and this blackish veil over everything. Hot weather; a wind blowing. The substance gone out of everything. I don't think this is exaggerated. It'll come back I suppose. Indeed I feel a great wish, now and then, to live more all over the place, to see people, to create, only for the time one can't make the effort. And I can't write to Helen, but I must now shut this and try.

Maupassant, on writers (true I think). "En lui aucun sentiment simple n'existe plus. Tout ce qu'il voit, ses joies, ses plaisirs, ses souffrances, ses désespoirs, deviennent instantanément des sujets d'observation. Il analyse malgré tout, malgré lui, sans fin, les coeurs, les visages, les gestes, les intonations."

Remember turning aside at mother's bed, when she had died, and Stella * took us in, to laugh, secretly, at the nurse crying. She's pretending, I said, aged 13, and was afraid I was not feeling enough. So now.

The writer's temperament.

"Ne jamais souffrir, penser, aimer, sentir, comme tout le monde, bonnement, franchement, simplement, sans s'analyser soi-même après chaque joie et après chaque sanglot."

Sur l'eau 116

* Stella Duckworth, V. W.'s half-sister.

Saturday, September 15th

I was glad we went to the service on Thursday. It was a very hot summer's day. And all very simple and dignified. Music. Not a word spoken. We sat there, before the open doors that lead into the garden. Flowers and strollers which Roger would have liked. He lay under an old red brocade with two branches of very bright many coloured flowers. It is a strong instinct to be with one's friends. I thought of him too, at intervals. Dignified and honest and large—"large sweet soul"—something ripe and musical about him—and then the fun and the fact that he had lived with such variety and generosity and curiosity. I thought of this.

Tuesday, September 18th

I like writing this morning because it takes off the strain on the lips. A cold dull day after all this blaze. Now we have Graham, and Mrs. W., but then, perhaps, peace: and an end to the book? O if that could be! But I feel 10 miles distant—far away—detached, very jaded now.

I had a notion that I could describe the tremendous feeling at R.'s funeral: but of course I can't. I mean the universal feeling; how we all fought with our brains, loves and so on; and *must* be vanquished. Then the vanquisher, this outer force became so clear; the indifferent, and we so small, fine, delicate. A fear then came to me, of death. Of course I shall lie there too before that gate and slide in; and it frightened me. But why? I mean, I felt the vainness of this perpetual fight, with our brains and loving each other against the other thing; if Roger could die.

But then, next day, today, which is Thursday, one week later, the other thing begins to work—the exalted sense of being above time and death which comes from being again in a writing mood. And this is not an illusion, so far as I can tell. Certainly I have a strong sense that Roger would be all on one's side in this excitement, and that whatever the invisible force does, we thus get outside it. A nice letter from Helen. And today we go to Worthing—

Sunday, September 30th

The last words of the nameless book were written 10 minutes ago, quite calmly too. 900 pages: L. says 200,000 words. Lord God what an amount of re-writing that means! But also, how heavenly to have brought the pen to a stop at the last line, even if most of the lines have now to be rubbed out. Anyhow the design is there. And it has taken a little less than 2 years: some months less indeed, as *Flush* intervened; therefore it has been written at a greater gallop than any of my books. The representational part accounts for the fluency. And I should say—but do I always say this?—with greater excitement: not, I think, of the same kind quite. For I have been more general, less personal. No "beautiful writing"; much easier dialogue; but a great strain, because so many more faculties had to keep going at once, though none so pressed upon. No tears and exaltation at the end; but peace and breadth, I hope. Anyhow, if I die tomorrow, the line is there. And I am fresh; and shall re-write the end tomorrow. I don't think I'm fresh enough, though, to go on "making up." That was the strain—the invention: and I suspect that the last 20 pages have slightly flagged. Too many odds and ends to sweep up. But I have no idea of the whole—

Tuesday, October 2nd

Yes, but my head will never let me glory sweepingly; always a tumble. Yesterday morning the old rays of light set in; and then the sharp, the very sharp pain over my eyes; so that I sat and lay about till tea; had no walk, had not a single idea of triumph or relief. L. bought me a little travelling ink pot, by way of congratulation. I wish I could think of a name. *Sons and Daughters?* Probably used already. There's a mass to be done to the last chapter, which I shall, I hope, d.v., as they say in some circles, I suppose, still, begin tomorrow; while the putty is still soft.

So the summer is ended. Until 9th of September, when Nessa came across the terrace—how I hear that cry He's dead —a very vigorous, happy summer. Oh the joy of walking! I've never felt it so strong in me. Cowper Powys, oddly enough, expresses the same thing: the trance like, swimming, flying through the air; the current of sensations and ideas; and the slow, but fresh change of down, of road, of colour; all this churned up into a fine thin sheet of perfect calm happiness. It's true I often painted the brightest pictures on the sheet and often talked aloud. Lord how many pages of *Sons and Daughters*—perhaps *Daughters and Sons* would give a rhythm more unlike *Sons and Lovers,* or *Wives and Daughters*—I made up, chattering them in my excitement on the top of the down, in the folds. Too many buildings, alas; and gossip to the effect that Christie and the Ringmer Building Co. are buying Botten's Farm to build on. Sunday I was worried, walking to Lewes, by the cars and the villas. But again, I've discovered the ghostly farm walk; and the Piddinghoe walk; and such variety and loveliness—the river lead and silver; the ship—Servic of London—going down: the bridge opened. Mushrooms and the garden at night: the moon, like a dying dolphin's eye; or red orange, the harvest moon; or polished like a steel knife; or lambent; sometimes rushing across the sky; sometimes hanging among the branches. Now in October the thick wet mist has come, thickening and blotting. On Sunday we had Bunny and Julian.

Books read or in reading.

Shakespeare: *Troilus*
Pericles
Taming of Shrew
Cymbeline

Maupassant
de Vigny   only
St. Simon   scraps
Gide

Library books: Powys
Wells
Lady Brooke
Prose. Dobree
Alice James

Many MSS.
none worth keeping

Thursday, October 4th

A violent rain storm on the pond. The pond is covered with little white thorns; springing up and down: the pond is bristling with leaping white thorns, like the thorns on a small porcupine; bristles; then black waves; cross it; black shudders; and the little water thorns are white; a helter skelter rain and the elms tossing it up and down; the pond overflowing on one side; lily leaves tugging; the red flower swimming about; one leaf flapping; then completely smooth for a moment; then prickled; thorns like glass; but leaping up and down incessantly; a rapid smirch of shadow. Now light from the sun; green and red; shiny; the pond a sage green; the grass brilliant green; red berries on the hedges; the cows very white; purple over Asheham.

Thursday, October 11th

A brief note. In today's *Lit. Sup.*, they advertise *Men Without Art,* by Wyndham Lewis: chapters on Eliot, Faulkner, Hemingway, Virginia Woolf . . . Now I know by reason and instinct that this is an attack; that I am publicly demolished; nothing is left of me in Oxford and Cambridge and places where the young read Wyndham Lewis. My instinct is not to read it. And for that reason: Well, I open Keats and find: "Praise or blame has but a momentary effect on the man whose love of beauty in the abstract makes him a severe critic on his own works. My own domestic criticism has given me pain beyond what Blackwood or Quarterly could possibly inflict . . . This is a mere matter of the moment—I think I shall be among the English poets after my death. Even as a matter of present interest the attempt to crush me in the Quarterly has only brought me more into notice."

Well: do I think I shall be among the English novelists after my death? I hardly ever think about it. Why then do I shrink from reading W. L.? Why am I sensitive? I think vanity: I dislike the thought of being laughed at: of the glow of satisfaction that A., B. and C. will get from hearing V. W. demolished: also it will strengthen further attacks: perhaps I feel uncertain of my own gifts: but then, I know more about them than W L.: and anyhow I intend to go on writing. What I shall do is craftily to gather the nature of the indictment from talk and reviews; and, in a year perhaps, when my book is out, I shall read it. Already I am feeling the calm that always comes to me with abuse: my back is against the wall: I am writing for the sake of writing, etc.; and then there is the queer disreputable pleasure in being abused—in being a figure, in being a martyr, and so on.

Sunday, October 14th

The trouble is I have used every ounce of my creative writing mind in *The Pargiters*. No headache (save what Elly calls typical migraine—she came to see L. about his strain yesterday). I cannot put spurs in my flanks. It's true I've planned the romantic chapter of notes: but I can't set to. This morning I've taken the arrow of W. L. to my heart: he makes tremendous and delightful fun of B. and B.: * calls me a peeper, not a looker; a fundamental prude; but one of the four or five living (so it seems) who is an artist. That's what I gather the flagellation amounts to: (Oh I'm underrated, Edith Sitwell says). Well: this gnat has settled and stung: and I think (12:30) the pain is over. Yes. I think it's now rippling away. Only I can't write. When will my brain revive? In 10 days I think. And it can read admirably: I began *The Seasons* last night . . . Well: I was going to say, I'm glad that I need not and cannot write, because the danger of being attacked is that it makes one answer back—a perfectly fatal thing to do. I mean, fatal to arrange *The P.s* so as to meet his criticisms. And I think my revelation two years ago stands me in sublime stead: to adventure and discover and allow no rigid poses: to be supple and naked to the truth. If there is truth in W. L., well, face it: I've no doubt I'm prudish and peeping. Well then live more boldly, but for God's sake don't try to bend my writing one way or the other. Not that one can. And there is the odd pleasure too of being abused and the feeling of being dismissed into obscurity is also pleasant and salutary.

* Mr. Bennett and Mrs. Brown.

Tuesday, October 16th

Quite cured today. So the W. L. illness lasted two days. Helped off by old Ethel's bluff affection and stir yesterday by buying a blouse; by falling fast asleep after dinner.

Writing away this morning.

I am so sleepy. Is this age? I can't shake it off. And so gloomy. That's the end of the book. I looked up past diaries—a reason for keeping them, and found the same misery after *Waves*—after *Lighthouse*. I was, I remember, nearer suicide, seriously, than since 1913. It is after all natural. I've been galloping now for three months—so excited I made a plunge at my paper—well, cut that all off—after the first divine relief, of course some terrible blankness must spread. There's nothing left of the people, of the ideas, of the strain, of the whole life in short that has been racing round my brain: not only the brain; it has seized hold of my leisure; think how I used to sit still on the same railway lines—running on my book. Well, so there's nothing to be done the next two or three or even four weeks but dandle oneself; refuse to face it; refuse to think about it. This time Roger makes it harder than usual. We had tea with Nessa yesterday. Yes, his death is worse than Lytton's. Why, I wonder? Such a blank wall. Such a silence: such a poverty. How he reverberated!

Monday, October 29th

Reading *Antigone*. How powerful that spell is still—Greek, an emotion different from any other. I will read Plotinus: Herodotus: Homer I think.

Thursday, November 1st

Ideas that came to me last night dining with Clive; talking to Aldous * and the Kenneth Clarks.

About Roger's life: that it should be written by different people to illustrate different stages.

Youth, by Margery †
Cambridge, by Wedd?

* Aldous Huxley.   † Margery Fry.

Early London life . . .
          Clive
          Sickert
Bloomsbury, Desmond
          V. W.
Later life,   Julian
          Blunt
          Heard   and so on.

all to be combined say by Desmond and me together. About novels: the different strata of being: the upper, under. This is a familiar idea, partly tried in the Pargiters. But I think of writing it out more closely; and now, particularly, in my critical book: showing how the mind naturally follows that order in thinking: how it is illustrated by literature.

I must now do biography and autobiography.

Friday, November 2nd

Two teeth out with a new anaesthetic: hence I write here, not seriously. And this is another pen. And my brain is very slightly frozen, like my gums. Teeth become like old roots that one breaks off. He broke and I scarcely felt. My brain frozen thinks of Aldous and the Clarks: thinks vaguely of biography; thinks am I reviewed anywhere—can't look—thinks it is a fine cold day.

I went upstairs to rinse my bleeding gum—the cocaine lasts ½ an hour; then the nerves begin to feel again—and opened the *Spectator* and read W. L. on me again. An answer to Spender. "I am not malicious. Several people call Mrs. W. Felicia Hemans." This I suppose is another little scratch of the cat's claws: to slip that in, by the way—"I don't say it—others do." And so they are supercilious on the next page about Sickert; and so—Well L. says I should be contemptible to mind. Yes: but I do mind for 10 minutes: I mind being in the light again, just as I was sinking into my populous obscurity. I must take a pull on myself. I don't think this attack will last more than two days. I think I shall be free from the infection by Monday. But what a bore it all is. And how many sudden shoots into nothingness open before me. But wait one moment. At the worst, should I be a quite negligible writer, I enjoy writing: I think I am an honest observer. Therefore the world will go on providing me with excitement whether I can use it or not. Also, how am I to balance W. L.'s criticism with Yeats —let alone Goldie and Morgan? Would they have felt anything if I had been negligible? And about two in the morning I am possessed of a remarkable sense of (driving eyeless) strength. And I have L. and there are his books; and our life together. And freedom, now, from money paring. And . . . if only for a time I could completely forget myself, my reviews, my fame, my sink in the scale—which is bound to come now and to last about 8 or 9 years—then I should be what I mostly am: very rapid, excited, amused, intense. Odd, these extravagant ups and downs of reputation; compare the Americans in the *Mercury* . . . No, for God's sake don't compare: let all praise and blame sink to the bottom or float to the top and let me go my ways indifferent. And care for people. And let fly, in life, on all sides.

These are very sensible sayings I think. And it's all forgotten and over.

What is uppermost now is (1) the question of writing R.'s * life. Helen † came. Says both she and M.‡ wish it. So I wait. What do I feel about it? If I could be free, then here's the chance of trying biography; a splendid, difficult chance—better than trying to find a subject—that is, if I *am* free.

Wednesday, November 14th

And am now, 10:30 on Thursday morning, November 15th, about to tackle re-reading and re-writing *The Pargiters:* an awful moment.

12:45. Well, that horrid plunge has been made and I've started re-writing the *Ps.* Lord, Lord! Ten pages a day for 90 days. Three months. The thing is to contract: each scene to be a scene: much dramatised: contrasted: each to be carefully dominated by one interest: some generalised. At any rate this releases the usual flood and proves that only creating can

* Roger Fry's.   † Helen Anrep.   ‡ Margery Fry.

bring about proportion: now, damnably disagreeable, as I see it will be—compacting the vast mass—I am using my faculties again, and all the flies and fleas are forgotten.

A note: despair at the badness of the book: can't think how I ever could write such stuff—and with such excitement: that's yesterday: today I think it good again. A note, by way of advising other Virginias with other books that this is the way of the thing: up down up down—and Lord knows the truth.

Wednesday, November 21st

Margery Fry to tea on Sunday. A long debate about the book on Roger: not very conclusive. She says she wants a study by me, reinforced with chapters on other aspects. I say, Well, but those books are unreadable. Oh of course I want you to be quite free, she says. I should have to say something about his life, I say. The family—Now there of course I'm afraid I should have to ask you to be careful, she says. The upshot of all of which is that she's to write to the *N.S.* asking for letters; that I'm to go through them; that we're then to discuss—so it will drag on these many months, I suppose. And I plan working at *Ps:* and getting in reading time with Roger's papers, so that by October next I could write, if that's the decision. But what?

Monday, December 2nd

Isn't it odd? Some days I can't read Dante at all after revising *The Ps.:* other days I find it very sublime and helpful. Raises one out of the chatter of words. But today (doing the scene at the Lodge) I'm too excited. I think it a good book today. I'm in the thick again. But I will stop at the end of the funeral scene and calm my brain. That is I will write the play for Christmas: *Freshwater* a farce—for a joke. And rig up my Contemporary Criticism article; and look around. David Cecil on fiction: a good book for readers, not for writers—all so elementary; but some good points made, from the outside. I've done though with that sort of criticism. And he's often wrong: gets W. H. wrong, I think; wants to have a profound theory. We—Bloomsbury—are dead; so says Joad. I snap my fingers

at him. Lytton and I the two distractions. Poor Francis * lies
in a hotel bedroom in Russell Square this rainy morning. I
went in and sat with him. Quite himself with a lump on his
forehead. And is aware of it all. May die under another operation, or slowly stiffen into complete paralysis. His brain may
go. All this he knows; and there it was between us, as we joked.
He came to the verge of it once or twice. But I can't feel any
more at the moment—not after Roger. I cannot go through that
again. That's my feeling. I kissed him. "This is the first time
—this chaste kiss," he said. So I kissed him again. But I must
not cry, I thought, and so went.

Wednesday, December 18th

Talk with Francis yesterday. He is dying: but makes no
bones about it. Only his expression is quite different. Has no
hope. The man says he asks every hour how long will this go
on, and hopes for the end. He was exactly as usual; no wandering, no incoherence. A credit to Athens. The soul deserves to
be immortal, as L. said. We walked back, glad to be alive,
numb somehow. I can't use my imagination on that theme.
What would it be like to lie there, expecting death? and how
odd and strange a death. I write hurriedly, going to Angelica's
concert this fine soft day.

Sunday, December 30th

Since I forgot to bring my writing book, I must fill up here,
on loose sheets. End the year: with these cursed dogs barking:
and I am sitting in my new house; and it is, of all hours, 3:10;
and it is raining; and the cow has the sciatica; and we are taking her into Lewes to catch a train to London; after which we
have tea at Charleston, act the play and dine there. It has been
the wettest Christmas, I should say, drawing a bow at a ven-
ture, on record. Only yesterday did I manage my phantom
farm walk; but pray God, with Christmas over, the rain will
stop falling, Miss Emery's dogs barking.

It was stupid to come without a book, seeing that I end
every morning with a head full of ideas about *The Pargiters*.

* Francis Birrell.

NINETEEN THIRTY-FOUR   227

It is very interesting to write out. I am re-writing considerably. My idea is to contract the scenes; very intense, less so; then drama; then narrative. Keeping a kind of swing and rhythm through them all. Anyhow it admits of great variety—this book. I think it shall be called *Ordinary People*. I finished, more or less, Maggie and Sarah, the first scene, in the bedroom: with what excitement I wrote it! And now hardly a line of the original is left. Yes, but the spirit is caught I think. I write perhaps 60 pages before I catch that. And coming back I see it hopping like a yellow canary on its perch. I want to make both S. and M. bold characters, using character dialogue. Then we go on to Martin's visit to Eleanor: then the long day that ends with the King's death. I have sweated off 80 or 90 pages, mostly due to a fault in paging though.

End of the year: and Francis transacting his death at that nursing home in Collingham Place. The expression on his face is what I see: as if he were facing a peculiar lonely sorrow. One's own death—think of lying there alone, looking at it, at 45 or so: with a great desire to live. "And so the *New Statesman's* going to be the best paper that ever was, is it?" "He's dead though," (of Brimley Johnson) spoken with a kind of bitterness. None of these words are exactly right.

And here we are, chafed by the cow's lame leg and the dogs; yet as usual very happy I think: ever so full of ideas. L. finishing his *Quack Quack* of a morning: the Zet * crawling from one chair to the other—picking at his head.

And Roger dead. And am I to write about him? And the stirring of the embers—I mean the wish to make up as much of a fire as possible. So to get ready for the wet drive. Dogs still barking.

* A marmoset.

1935

Tuesday, January 1st

The play rather tosh; * but I'm not going to bother about making a good impression as a playwright. And I had a lovely old year's walk yesterday round the rat farm valley, by a new way and met Mr. Freeth, and talked about road making; and then into Lewes to take the car to Martin's and then home and read St. Paul and the papers. I must buy the Old Testament. I am reading the Acts of the Apostles. At last I am illuminating that dark spot in my reading. What happened in Rome? And there are seven volumes of Renan. Lytton calls him "mellifluous." Yeats and Aldous agreed, the other day, that their great aim in writing is to avoid the "literary." Aldous said how extraordinary the "literary" fetish had been among the Victorians. Yeats said that he wanted only to use the words that real people say. That his change had come through writing plays. And I said, rashly, that all the same his meaning was very difficult. And what is "the literary." That's rather an interesting question. Might go into that, if I ever write my critical book. But now I want to write On being despised. My mind will go on pumping up ideas for that. And I must finish *Ordinary People:* and then there's Roger and writing despised. Begin Roger in October 1935. Is that possible? Publish *O.P.* in October; and work at these two during 1936. Lord knows! But I must press a good deal of work in—remembering 53— 54—55 are on me. And how excited I get over my ideas! And there's people to see.

---

* *Freshwater, A Comedy.* This was a play written by Virginia Woolf to be acted at a party on January 18th. It was acted by Vanessa Bell, Julian and Angelica Bell, Adrian Stephen and Leonard Woolf.

Friday, January 11th

This spring will be on us all of a clap. Very windy; today; a dumb misted walk two days ago to Piddinghoe. Now the men are threshing. Nessa and Angelica and Eve yesterday. We talk a great deal about the play. An amusing incident. And I shall hire a donkey's head to take my call in—by way of saying This is a donkey's work. I make out that I shall reduce *The Caravan* (so called suddenly) to 150,000: and shall finish re-typing in May. I wonder. It is compressed I think. And sometimes my brain threatens to split with all the meaning I think I could press into it. The discovery of this book, it dawns upon me, is the combination of the external and the internal. I am using both, freely. And my eye has gathered in a good many externals in its time.

Saturday, January 19th

The play came off last night, with the result that I am dry-brained this morning and can only use this book as a pillow. It was said, inevitably, to be a great success; and I enjoyed—let me see what? Bunny's praise; Oliver's; * but not much Christabel's or the standing about pumping up vivacities with David, Cory, Elizabeth Bowen: yet on the whole it is good to have an unbuttoned laughing evening once in a way. Roger's ghost knocked at the door—his portrait of Charlie Sanger was delivered in the thick of the rehearsal. And how Francis would have enjoyed this, Leonard said. These are our ghosts now. But they would applaud the attempt. So to sleep: and now, God bless my soul, as Tennyson would say, I must rinse and freshen my mind and make it work soberly on something hard. There's my Dante; and Renan. And the horrid winter lap begins; the pale unbecoming days, like an aging woman seen at 11 o'clock. However, L. and I shall go for a walk this afternoon; and that seems to me an enormous balance at the Bank! solid happiness.

I have an idea for a "play." Summer's night. Someone on a seat. And voices speaking from the flowers.

* Oliver Strachey.

Wednesday, January 23rd

Yes, I ought to have explained why I wrote the Sickert. I always think of things too late. I am reading *The Faery Queen* —with delight. I shall write about it. I took Angelica shopping. "Do you mind if I read *The Heir of Redcliffe?*" she said at tea, amusing me. What a curious sense the clothes sense is! Buying her coat, mine, hearing the women talk, as of race horses, about new skirts. And I am fluttered because I must lunch with Clive tomorrow in my new coat. And I can't think out what I mean about *conception:* the idea behind *F.Q.* How to express a kind of natural transition from state to state. And the air of natural beauty. It is better to read the originals. Well, Clive's lunch will jump me out of this. And now that the play is over, we must begin to see people here: and go to *Hamlet* and plan our spring journey. I am taking a fortnight off fiction. My mind became knotted. I think of making The-resa *sing:* and so lyricise the argument. Get as far from T (so called after my Sarah and Elvira provisionally). But oh heavens the duck squashy—this is from the pressed duck Jack once gave us: all juice; one squab of juice. I am reading *Point Counterpoint.* Not a good novel. All raw, uncooked, protesting. A descendant, oddly enough, of Mrs. H. Ward: interest in ideas; makes people into ideas. A man from America returns my letters and says he is glad to see me as I am.

Friday, February 1st

And again this morning, Friday, I'm too tired to go on with *Ps.* Why? Talking too much I daresay. I thought, though, I wanted "society": and saw Helen, Mary, Gillett. Ann tonight. I think *The Ps.* however a promising work. Only nerve vigour wanted. A day off today.

Wednesday, February 20th

Sara is the real difficulty: I can't get her into the main stream, yet she is essential. A very difficult problem; this transi-tion business. And the burden of something that I won't call propaganda. I have a horror of the Aldous novel: that must be avoided. But ideas are sticky things: won't coalesce: hold up

the creative, subconscious faculty; that's it I suppose. I've written the chophouse scene I don't know how many times.

Tuesday, February 26th
   A very fine skyblue day, my windows completely filled with
blue for a wonder. Mr. Riley has just mended them. And I
have been writing and writing and rewriting the scene by the
Round Pond. What I want to do is to reduce it all so that each
sentence, though perfectly natural dialogue, has a great pressure of meaning behind it. And the most careful harmony and
contrast of scene—the boats colliding etc.—has also to be arranged. Hence the extreme difficulty. But I hope perhaps
tomorrow to have done, and then the dinner party and Kitty
in the country should go quicker. At least I find the upper
air scenes much simpler; and I think it's right to keep them so.
But Lord what a lot of work still to do! It won't be done before
August. And here I am plagued by the sudden wish to write an
anti-Fascist pamphlet.

Wednesday, February 27th
   And I've just written it all over again. But it must do this
time, I say to myself. Yet I know that I must put the screw
on and write some pages again. It's too jerky: too   *
It's obvious that one person sees one thing and another another; and that one has to draw them together. Who was it
who said through the unconscious one comes to the conscious,
and then again to the unconscious?
   I now feel a strong desire to stop reading *F.Q.*: to read
Cicero's letters, and the Chateaubriand Memoirs. As far as I
can see, this is the natural swing of the pendulum. To particu-
larise after the generalisation of romantic poetry.

Monday, March 11th
   How I should like, I thought some time on the drive up
this afternoon, to write a sentence again! How delightful to
feel it form and curve under my fingers! Since October 16th

* Word omitted.

I have not written one new sentence, but only copied and typed.
A typed sentence somehow differs; for one thing it is formed
out of what is already there: it does not spring fresh from the
mind. But this copying must go on, I see, till August. I am
only now in the first war scene: with luck I shall get to E. in
Oxford Street before we go in May: and spend June and July
on the grand orchestral finale. Then in August I shall write
again.

Saturday, March 16th

I have had three severe swingeings lately: Wyndham Lewis;
Mirsky; and now Swinnerton. Bloomsbury is ridiculed; and I
am dismissed with it. I didn't read W. L.: and Swinnerton only
affected me as a robin affects a rhinoceros—except in the depths
of the night. How resilient I am; and how fatalistic now; and
how little I mind and how much; and how good my novel is;
and how tired I am this morning; and how I like praise; and
how full of ideas I am; and Tom and Stephen * came to tea,
and Ray † and William ‡ dine; and I forgot to describe my
interesting talk with Nessa about my criticising her children;
and I left out—I forget what. My head is numb today and I
can scarcely read Osbert on Brighton, let alone Dante.

In last week's *Time and Tide* St. John Ervine called Lytton
"that servile minded man . . . that Pandar" or words to that
effect. I'm thinking whether, if I write about Roger, I shall
include a note, a sarcastic note, on the Bloomsbury baiters. No,
I suppose not. Write them down—that's the only way.

Monday, March 18th

The only thing worth doing in this book is to stick it out:
stick to the idea and don't lower it an inch, in deference to
anyone. What's so odd is the way the whole thing dissolves in
company and then comes back with a rush; and Swinnerton's
sneers and Mirsky's—making me feel that I'm hated and despised and ridiculed—well, this is the only answer: to stick to
my ideas. And I wish I need never read about myself or think

* Stephen Spender.   † Ray Strachey.   ‡ William Plomer.

about myself, anyhow till it's done, but look firmly at my object and think only of expressing it. Oh what a grind it is embodying all these ideas and having perpetually to expose my mind, opened and intensified as it is by the heat of creation, to the blasts of the outer world. If I didn't feel so much, how easy it would be to go on.

Having just written a letter about Bloomsbury I cannot control my mind enough to go on with *The Ps.* I woke in the night and thought of it. But whether to send it or not, I don't know. But now I *must* think of something else. Julian and Helen last night.

L. advised me *not* to send the letter and after two seconds I see he is right. It is better, he says, to be able to say we don't answer. But we suggest a comic guide to Bloomsbury by Morgan and he nibbles.

Thursday, March 21st

Too jaded again to tackle that very difficult much too crowded raid chapter. In fact I am on the verge of the usual headache—for one thing yesterday was such a scramble.

I have resolved to leave that blasted chapter here and do nothing at Rodmell. Yet, as I see, I cannot read; my mind is all tight like a ball of string. A most unpleasant variety of headache; but I think soon over. Only a little change needed. Not a real bad headache. Why make this note? Because reading is beyond me and writing is like humming a song. But what a worthless song! And it is the spring.

Monday, March 25th

And this morning, in spite of being in a rage, I wrote the whole of that d——d chapter again, in a spasm of desperation and, I think, got it right, by breaking up, the use of thought skipping and parentheses. Anyhow that's the hang of it. And I cut from 20 to 30 pages.

Wednesday, March 27th

I see I am becoming a regular diariser. The reason is that I cannot make the transition from *Pargiters* to Dante without some bridge. And this cools my mind. I am rather worried about the raid chapter: afraid if I compress and worry that I shall spoil. Never mind. Forge ahead and see what comes next.

Yesterday we went to the Tower, which is an impressive murderous bloody grey raven haunted military barrack prison dungeon place; like the prison of English splendour; the reformatory at the back of history; where we shot and tortured and imprisoned. Prisoners scratched their names, very beautifully, on the walls. And the crown jewels blazed, very tawdry, and there were the orders, like Spinks or a Regent Street jewellers. And we watched the Scots Guards drill: and an officer doing a kind of tiger pace up and down—a wax faced barbers block officer trained to a certain impassive balancing. The sergeant major barked and swore. All in a hoarse bark: the men stamped and wheeled like—machines: then the officer also barked: all precise, inhuman, showing off. A degrading, stupefying sight. But in keeping with the grey walls, the cobbles, the executioner's block. People sitting on the river bank among old cannon. Steps etc. very romantic: a dungeon like feeling.

Monday, April 1st

At this rate I shall never finish the *Purgatorio*. But what's the use of reading with half one's mind running on Eleanor and Kitty. Oh that scene wants compacting. It's too thin run. But I shall finish it before I go away. We think of three weeks in Holland and France; a week in Rome, flying there. We went to Kew yesterday and if vegetable notes are needed this is to signify that yesterday was the prime day for cherry blossom, pear trees and magnolia. A lovely white one with black cups to the flowers; another purple tinted, just falling. Another and another. And the yellow bushes and the daffodils in the grass. So to walk through Richmond—a long walk by the ponds. I verified certain details.

Tuesday, April 9th

I met Morgan in the London Library yesterday and flew into a passion.

"Virginia, my dear," he said. I was pleased by that little affectionate familiar tag.

"Being a good boy and getting books on Bloomsbury?" I said.

"Yes. You listen. Is my book down?", he asked Mr. Mannering.

"We were just posting it," said Mr. M.

"And, Virginia, you know I'm on the Committee here," said Morgan. "And we've been discussing whether to allow ladies"—It came over me that they were going to put me on: and I was then to refuse: "Oh but they do," I said. "There was Mrs. Green."

"Yes, yes. There was Mrs. Green. And Sir Leslie Stephen said never again. She was so troublesome. And I said haven't ladies improved? But they were all quite determined. No, no, no, ladies are quite impossible. They wouldn't hear of it."

See how my hand trembles. I was so angry (also very tired) standing. And I saw the whole slate smeared. I thought how perhaps M. had mentioned my name, and they had said no no no: ladies are impossible. And so I quieted down and said nothing and this morning in my bath I made up a phrase in my book *On Being Despised* which is to run—a friend of mine, who was offered . . . one of those prizes—for her sake the great exception was to be made—who was in short to be given an honour—I forget what . . . She said And they actually thought I would take it. They were, on my honour, surprised, even at my very modified and humble rejection. You didn't tell them what you thought of them for daring to suggest that you should rub your nose in that pail of offal? I remarked. Not for a hundred years, she observed. And I will bring in M. Pattison: and I will say sympathy uses the same face required to lay 700 bricks. And I will show how you can't sit on committees if you also pour out tea—that by the way Sir L. S. spent his evenings with widow Green: yes, these flares up are very good for my book: for they simmer and become transparent: and I see how I can transmute them into beautiful clear reasonable ironical prose. God damn Morgan for thinking I'd have

taken that . . . And dear old Morgan comes to tea today and
then sits with Berry who's had cataract.

The veil of the temple—which, whether university or cathedral, academic or ecclesiastical, I forget—was to be raised
and as an exception she was to be allowed to enter in. But
what about my civilisation? For 2,000 years we have done
things without being paid for doing them. You can't bribe me
now. Pail of offal? No: I said while very deeply appreciating
the hon. . . . In short one must tell lies, and apply every
emollient in our power to the swollen skin of our brothers' so
terribly inflamed vanity. Truth is only to be spoken by those
women whose fathers were pork butchers and left them a share
in the pig factory.

Friday, April 12th

This little piece of rant won't be very intelligible in a year's
time. Yet there are some useful facts and phrases in it. I rather
itch to be at that book. But I have been skirmishing round a
headache, and can't pull my weight in the morning.

Saturday, April 13th

Let me make a note that it would be much wiser not to
attempt to sketch a draft of *On Being Despised,* or whatever it
is to be called, until *The Ps.* is done with. I was vagrant this
morning and made a rash attempt, with the interesting discovery that one can't propagate at the same time as write fiction.
And as this fiction is dangerously near propaganda, I must keep
my hands clear.

It's true I'm half asleep, after the Zoo and Willy. But he
threw some coals on my fire: the horror of the legal profession:
its immense wealth: its conventions: a Royal Commission now
sitting: its hidebound hoariness and so on: worth going into
one of these days: and the medical profession and the osteo-
paths—worth a fling of laughter. But oh dear, not now. Now
for Alfieri and Nash and other notables: so happy I was reading alone last night. We saw the great dumb fish at the Zoo
and the gorillas: storms of rain, cloud: and I read Annie S.

Swan on her life with considerable respect. Almost always this comes from autobiography: a liking, at least some imaginative stir: for no doubt her books, which she can't count, and has no illusions about, but she can't stop telling stories, are wash, pigs', hogs'—any wash you choose. But she is a shrewd capable old woman.

Saturday, April 20th

The scene has now changed to Rodmell, and I am writing at the table L. made (supported on a cushion) and it is raining. Good Friday was a complete fraud—rain and more rain. I tried walking along the bank and saw a mole, running on the meadow—it glides rather—is like an elongated guinea pig. Pinka * went and nuzzled it and then it managed to slide into a hole. At the same time through the rain I heard the cuckoo's song. Then I came home and read and read—Stephen Spender: too quick to stop to think: shall I stop to think? read it again? It has considerable swing and fluency; and some general ideas; but peters out in the usual litter of an undergraduate's table: wants to get everything in and report and answer all the chatter. But I want to investigate certain questions: why do I always fight shy of my contemporaries? What is really the woman's angle? Why does so much of this seem to me in the air? But I recognise my own limitation: not a good ratiocinator, Lytton used to say. Do I instinctively keep my mind from analysing, which would impair its creativeness? I think there's something in that. No creative writer can swallow another contemporary. The reception of living work is too coarse and partial if you're doing the same thing yourself. But I admire Stephen for trying to grapple with these problems. Only of course he has to hitch them round—to use his own predicament as a magnet and thus the pattern is too arbitrary: if you're not in his predicament. But as I say, I read it at a gulp without screwing my wits tight to the argument. This is a method I find very profitable: then go back and screw.

* A spaniel.

Saturday, April 27th

All desire to practise the art of a writer has completely left me. I cannot imagine what it would be like: that is, more accurately, I cannot curve my mind to the line of a book; no, nor of an article. It's not the writing but the architecting that strains. If I write this paragraph, then there is the next and then the next. But after a month's holiday I shall be as tough and springy as—say heather root: and the arches and the domes will spring into the air as firm as steel and light as cloud—but all these words miss the mark. Stephen Spender demands a letter of criticism; can't write it. Nor can I describe with any certainty Mrs. Collett, with whom both L. and I fell in love yesterday. A whippet woman; steel blue eyes; silver spotted jersey; completely free, edged, outspoken, the widow of the Lord Mayor's son, who was killed before her eyes flying. After that she broke down and the only cure she said was to go to Hong Kong and stay with Bella. From that we did not expect anything much, to tell the truth; whereas she ridiculed the Jubilee, the Lord Mayor and told us all about life in the Mansion House. The L.M. spends £20,000 out of his own pocket on his year of office; 10,000 on his sheriffdom; then buys an ermine coat for £1,000 in which to admit the King to Temple Bar. It rains; the King flashes past and the coat is spoilt. Her mother in law is a perfectly natural sensible woman who goes buying fish with a bag. The Queen gave her as a token of esteem two large shells engraved with the story of George and the Dragon. These mercifully are left at the Mansion House. The L.M. wears a dress that is heavy with bullion. A terrible state of display and ugliness—but she was so nice and unexpected I actually asked her to come and see us—which, had she known it, is a compliment we never never pay even the royal family.

JOURNEY TO HOLLAND, GERMANY, ITALY AND FRANCE

ZUTPHEN. *Monday, May 6th*

Ideas that struck me.

That the more complex a vision the less it lends itself to satire: the more it understands the less it is able to sum up and make linear. For example: Shakespeare and Dostoievsky, neither of them satirise. The age of understanding: the age of destroying—and so on.

Belchamber.

A moving, in its way, completed story. But shallow. A superficial book. But also a finished one. Rounded off. Only possible if you keep one inch below; because the people, like Sainty, have to do things without diving deep; and this runs in the current; which lends itself to completeness. That is, if a writer accepts the conventions and lets his characters be guided by them, not conflict with them, he can produce an effect of symmetry: very pleasant, suggestive; but only on the surface. That is, I can't care what happens: yet I like the design. Also disgust at the cat monkey psychology, to which he is admirably faithful. A sensitive sincere mind—however, doing his embroidery and making his acute observation. Not a snob either.

Thursday, May 9th

Sitting in the sun outside the German Customs. A car with the swastika on the back window has just passed through the barrier into Germany. L. is in the Customs. I am nibbling at *Aaron's Rod.* Ought I to go in and see what is happening? A fine dry windy morning. The Dutch Customs took 10 seconds. This has taken 10 minutes already. The windows are barred. Here they came out and the grim man laughed at Mitzi.* But L. said that when a peasant came in and stood with his hat on, the man said this office is like a church and made him move it. Heil Hitler said the little thin boy opening his bag, perhaps with an apple in it, at the barrier. We become obsequious— delighted that is when the officer smiles at Mitzi—the first stoop in our back.

That a work of art means that one part gets strength from another part.

BRENNER. *Monday, May 13th*

Odd to see the countries change into each other. Beds now made of layers on top. No sheets. Houses building. Austrian,

---

* Our marmoset.

dignified. Winter lasts at Innsbruck till July. No spring. Italy fronts me on a blue bar. The Czecho-Slovaks are in front going to the Customs house.

PERUGIA

Came through Florence today. Saw the green and white cathedral and the yellow Arno dribbling into shallows. A thunderstorm. Irises purple against the clouds. So to Arezzo. A most superb church with dropped hull.

Lake Trasimen: stood in a field of red purple clover: plovers egg lake; grey olives, exquisite, subtle; sea cold, shell green. So on, regretting that we did not stay to Perugia. Brafani where we stayed in 1908. Now all the same. The same ardent sunburnt women. But lace and so on for sale. Better to have stayed at Trasimen. I went into an Albergo yesterday to buy rolls and found a sculptured fireplace, all patriarchal—servants and masters. Cauldron on the fire. Probably not much change since sixteenth century: the people preserve liquids. Men and women scything. A nightingale singing where we sat. Little frogs jumping into the stream.

Brafani: three people watching the door open and shut. Commenting on visitors like fates—summing up, placing. A woman with a hard lined aquiline face—red lips—bird like—perfectly self-satisfied. French pendulous men, a rather poor sister. Now they sit nibbling at human nature. We are rescued by the excellence of our luggage.

Rome: tea. Tea in café. Ladies in bright coats and white hats. Music. Look out and see people like movies. Abyssinia. Children lugging. Café haunters. Ices. Old man who haunts the Greco.

Sunday café: N. and A. drawing. Very cold. Rome a mitigated but perceptible Sunday. Fierce large jowled old ladies. Q. talking about Monaco. Talleyrand. Some very poor black wispy women. The effect of dowdiness produced by wispy hair. The Prime Minister's letter offering to recommend me for the Companion of Honour. No.

Tuesday, May 21st

Oddities of the human brain: woke early and again considered dashing off my book on Professions, to which I had not given a single thought these 7 or 8 days. Why? This vacillates with my novel—how are they both to come out simultaneously. But it is a sign that I must get pen to paper again. Yet at the moment I am going rag marketing with N. and A., who don't come.

Sunday, May 26th

I'm writing at six on a Sunday evening, with a band playing and stopping and children shouting in a too luxurious hotel where the waiters bring one the menu and I mix my French scandalously with odd scraps of painfully acquired Italian. Still I can rattle off Gli Indifferenti lying on my bed for pleasure. Oh the loveliness of the land still here and there—for instance that first morning's drive out of Rome—the sea and the lip of the unviolated land: and the umbrella pines, after Civita Vecchia: then of course all the intense boredom of Genoa and the Riviera, with its geraniums and its bougainvillea and its sense of shoving you between hill and sea and keeping you there in a bright luxury light without room to turn, so steep the vulture neck hills come down. But we slept at Lerici the first night which does the bay, the brimming sea and the green sailing ship and the island and the sparkling fading red and yellow night lamps to perfection. But that kind of perfection no longer makes me feel for my pen. It's too easy. But driving today I was thinking of Roger—Brignolles—Corges—my word, the olives and the rust red earth and the flat green and the trees. But now the band has begun again and we must go down to dine sumptuously off local trout. Off tomorrow and home on Friday. But though I'm impatient for my brain to eat again, I can dally out these last days better than sometimes. Why? Why? I go on asking myself. And feel I could soon polish off those final scenes: a possible amplification of the first paragraph occurred to me. But I don't want to grind at "writing" too hard. To open my net wide. It occurs to me, as we drive, how I'm disliked, how I'm laughed at; and I'm rather proud of my intention to take the fence gallantly. But writing again!

Wednesday, June 5th

Back here * again, and the grim wooden feeling that has made me think myself dead since we came back is softening slightly. It's beginning this cursed dry hand empty chapter again in part. Every time I say it will be the devil! but I never believe it. And then the usual depressions come. And I wish for death. But I am now seeing that the last 200 pages will assert themselves and force me to write a play more or less: all broken up: and I stop to begin making up; also, after the queer interlude, at once life—that is the telephone beginning —starts. So that one is forcibly chafed. (I meant to make a note about the dramatic shape which forces itself upon me.)

Monday, June 10th. Whit Monday

At Monks House. Working very hard. I think I shall rush these scenes off. Yet I cannot write this morning (Tuesday). How can I say, naturally, I have inherited the Rose and the Star!

Thursday, June 13th

In some ways, it's rather like writing *The Waves*—these last scenes. I bring my brain to a state of congestion, have to stop; go upstairs, run into towsled Mrs. Brewster, come back; find a little flow of words. It's the extreme condensation; the contrasts; the keeping it all together. Does this mean that it's good? I feel I have a round of great pillar to set up and can only drag and sweat. It's something like that. It's getting barer and more intense. And then what a relief when I have the upper air scenes—like the one with Eleanor! only they have to be condensed too. It's the proper placing that strains me.

Tuesday, July 16th

A curious sense of complete failure. Margery hasn't written to me about my speech: † according to Janie, Pamela thought the whole thing a failure. And it was for this that I ruined my last pages! I can't write this morning, can't get into the swing.

* London.
† A speech made at Bristol to open a show of Roger Fry's pictures, reprinted in *The Moment* by Virginia Woolf.

Innumerable worries, about getting people to dine and so on, afflict me. My head is all jangled. And I have to get that d——d speech printed, or refuse to. The director has written. Never again, oh never again!

I think though that I can get the last pages right, if I can only dream myself back into them. Yes, but how dream, when I have to see Susie and Ethel, to see Miss Belsher's house, to ring up and write notes and order this and that? Well, be still and ruminate; it's only 16th: there's a fortnight before August. And I'm sure that there is a remarkable shape somewhere concealed there. It's not mere verbiage, I think. If necessary I could put it away. But I think no: merely go on and perhaps write a very rapid short sketch, in ink—that's a good plan. Go back and get the central idea, and then rocket into it. And be very controlled and keep a hand on myself too. And perhaps read a little Shakespeare. Yes, one of the last plays: I think I will do that, so as to loosen my muscles. But oh this anxiety, and the perpetual knocking of the cup out of my hand.

Wednesday, July 17th

Just now I finished my first wild retyping and find the book comes to 740 pages: that is 148,000 words; but I think I can shorten: all the last part is still rudimentary and wants shaping; but I'm too tired in the head to do it seriously this moment. I think all the same I can reduce it; and then—? Dear me. I see why I fled, after *The Waves,* to *Flush.* One wants simply to sit on a bank and throw stones. I want also to read with a free mind. And to let the wrinkles smooth themselves out. Susie Buchan, Ethel, then Julian—so I talked from 4:30 till 1 A.M. with only two hours for dinner and silence.

I think I see that the last chapter should be formed round N.'s speech: it must be much more formal; and I think I see how I can bring in interludes—I mean spaces of silence, and poetry and contrast.

Friday, July 19th

No. I go on getting preliminary headaches. It is no good trying to do the last spurt, which should be much like a breeze in the heavy elms, these last days here: yes, a wind blowing in the trees that are thick with green leaves. For there must be movement as well as some weight, something for the breeze to lift.

Friday, August 16th

I cannot make a single note here, because I am so terrifically pressed re-writing—yes, typing out again at the rate, if possible, of 100 pages a week, this impossible eternal book. I work without looking up till one; which it now is, and therefore I must go in, leaving a whole heap of things unsaid; so many people, so many scenes, and beauty, and a fox and sudden ideas.

Wednesday, August 21st

Up in London yesterday. And I saw this about myself in a book at *The Times*—the most patient and conscientious of artists—which I think is true, considering how I slave at every word of that book. My head is like a like a—pudding is it—something that mildly throbs and can't breed a word at the end of the morning. I begin fresh enough. And I sent off the first 20 pages or so to Mabel yesterday.

Margery Fry comes on Friday with her hands full of papers, she says. Another book. Have I the indomitable courage to start on another? Think of the writing and re-writing. Also there will be joys and ecstasies though. Again very hot. I am going to re-paint this room. Went to Carpenters yesterday and chose chintzes. Is this worth writing? Perhaps.

Thursday, September 5th

I've had to give up writing *The Years*—that's what it's to be called—this morning. Absolutely floored. Can't pump up a word. Yet I can see, just, that something's there; so I shall wait, a day or two, and let the well fill. It has to be damned deep this time. 740 pages in it. I think, psychologically, this is the oddest of my adventures. Half my brain dries completely; but I've only to turn over and there's the other half, I think, ready, quite happily to write a little article. Oh if only anyone knew anything about the brain. And, even today, when I'm desperate, almost in tears looking at the chapter, unable to add to it, I feel I've only got to fumble and find the end of the ball of string—some start off place, someone to look at   * perhaps—no, I don't know—and my head would fill and the tiredness go. But I've been waking and worrying.

Friday, September 6th

I am going to wrap my brain in green dock leaves for a few days: 5, if I can hold out; till the children, L.'s nieces, have gone. If I can—for I think a scene is forming. Why not make an easier transition: Maggie looking at the Serpentine say; and so avoid that abrupt spring? Isn't it odd that this was the scene I had almost a fit to prevent myself writing? This will be the most exciting thing I ever wrote, I kept saying. And now it's the stumbling block. I wonder why? Too personal, is that it? Out of key? But I won't think.

Saturday, September 7th

A heavenly quiet morning reading Alfieri by the open window and not smoking. I believe one could get back to the old rapture of reading if one did not write. The difficulty is, writing makes one's brain so hot it can't settle to read; and then when the heat goes, I'm so tired in the head I can only skirmish. But I've stopped two days now *The Years:* and feel the power to settle calmly and firmly on books coming back at once. John Bailey's life, come today, makes me doubt though. What? Everything. Sounds like a mouse squeaking under a mattress. But I've only just glanced and got the smell of Lit. dinner, *Lit. Sup.,* lit this that and the other—and one remark to the effect that Virginia Woolf of all people has been given Cowper by Desmond and likes it! I, who read Cowper when I was 15— d——d nonsense.

Thursday, September 12th

Mornings which are neither quiet nor heavenly, but mixed of hell and ecstasy: never have I had such a hot balloon in my head as re-writing *The Years:* because it's so long; and the pres-

* Illegible.

sure is so terrific. But I will use all my art to keep my head sane. I will stop writing at 11:30 and read Italian or Dryden and so dandle myself along. To Ethel * at Miss Hudson's yesterday. As I sat in the complete English gentleman's home, I wondered how anybody could tolerate that equipage; and thought how a house should be portable like a snail shell. In future perhaps people will flirt out houses like little fans; and go on. There'll be no settled life within walls. There were endless clean, well repaired rooms. A maid in a cap. Cakes on pagoda trays. A terrible array of glossy brown furniture and books—red sham leather. Many nice old rooms, but the manor house has been embellished and made of course self consciously elaborate. A ballroom; a library—empty. And Miss Hudson all brushed up with her Pekinese, a competent ex-mayor of Eastbourne, with waved grey hair; and all so neat and stout; and the silver frames askew; and the air of order, respectability, commonplace. "I'm going to call on the vicar's wife." Ethel immensely red and stout: churning out, poor old woman, the usual indefatigable egotism about deafness and her Mass. She must have a scene every six months. No. But of course, to go deaf, to be 76—well, back to Charleston with Eve and Angelica.

Friday, September 13th

What a combination for the superstitious! Driving off to visit Margaret and Lilian at Dorking: and I have got into a mild flood I think with *The Years*. The difficulty is always at the beginning of chapters or sections where a whole new mood has to be caught, plumb in the centre. Richmond accepts my Marryat and thanks me for his poor little knighthood!

Wednesday, October 2nd

Yesterday we went to the L.P. meeting at Brighton and, of course, though I have refused to go again this morning, I am so thrown out of my stride that I can't hitch on to *The Years* again. Why? The immersion in all that energy and all that striving for something that is quite oblivious of me; making me feel that I am oblivious of it. No, that's not got it. It was

* Ethel Smyth.

very dramatic. Bevin's attack on Lansbury. Tears came to my eyes as L. spoke. And yet he was posing I felt, acting, unconsciously, the battered Christian man. Then Bevin too acted I suppose. He sank his head in his vast shoulders till he looked like a tortoise. Told L. not to go hawking his conscience round. And what is my duty as a human being? The women delegates were very thin voiced and unsubstantial. On Monday one said It is time we gave up washing up. A thin frail protest but genuine. A little reed piping, but what chance against all this weight of roast beef and beer—which she must cook? All very vivid and interesting; but overlapping: too much rhetoric, and what a partial view: altering the structure of society; yes, but when it's altered? Do I trust Bevin to produce a good world, when he has his equal rights? Had he been born a duke . . . My sympathies were with Salter who preached nonresistance. He's quite right. That should be our view. But then if society is in its present state? Happily, uneducated and voteless, I am not responsible for the state of society. These are some of the murmurs that go round my head, and distract me from what is, after all, my work. A good thing to have a day of disturbance—two days even—but not three. So I didn't go; and can't really write. However I will make myself when I've done this. Odd the enormous susceptibility of my mind to surface impressions: how I suck them in and let them swirl about. And how far does anybody's single mind or work matter? Ought we all to be engaged in altering the structure of society? Louie * said this morning she had quite enjoyed doing for us, was sorry we were going. That's a piece of work too in its way. And yet I can't deny my love of fashioning sentences. And yet . . . L. has gone there and I daresay I'll discuss it with him. He says politics ought to be separate from art. We walked out in the cold over the marsh and discussed this. The fact is too my head easily tires. Yes, too tired to write.

Tuesday, October 15th

Since we came back I have been in such full flush, with *Years* all the morning, Roger between tea and dinner, a walk, and people, that here's a blank. And I only scamp Roger this

* Mrs. Everest who did the house for us.

evening because I wore a hole in my back yesterday; couldn't
write this morning; and must go up and receive Miss Grueber
(to discuss a book on women and fascism—a pure have yer on
as Lottie would say) in ten minutes. Yes, it has been 10 days of
calm full complete bliss. And I thought how I shall hate it.
Not a bit. London is quiet, dry, comfortable. I find my dinner
cooked for me. No children screaming. And the sense of forging ahead, easily, strongly (this petered out today) at *The Years*.
Three days I got into wild excitement over *The Next War*.
Did I say the result of the L.P. at Brighton was the breaking
of that dam between me and the new book, so that I couldn't
resist dashing off a chapter; stopped myself; but have all ready
to develop—the form good I think—as soon as I get time? And
I plan to do this some time this next spring, while I go on
accumulating Roger. This division is by the way perfect and
I wonder I never hit on it before—some book or work for a
book that's quite the other side of the brain between times.
It's the only way of stopping the wheels and making them turn
the other way, to my great refreshment and I hope improvement. Alas, now for Grueber.

Wednesday, October 16th

What I have discovered in writing *The Years* is that you can
only get comedy by using the surface layer—for example, the
scene on the terrace. The question is can I get at quite different layers by bringing in music and painting together with
certain groupings of human beings? This is what I want to
try for in the raid scene: to keep going and influencing each
other: the picture; the music; and the other direction—the
action—I mean character telling a character—while the movement (that is the change of feeling as the raid goes on) continues. Anyhow, in this book I have discovered that there must
be contrast; one strata or layer can't be developed intensively,
as I did I expect in *The Waves*, without harm to the others.
Thus a kind of form is, I hope, imposing itself, corresponding
to the dimensions of the human being; one should be able to
feel a wall made out of all the influences; and this should
in the last chapter close round them at the party so that you

feel that while they go on individually it has completed itself. But I haven't yet got at this. I'm doing Crosby—an upper air scene this morning. The rest of going from one to another seems to me to prove that this is the right sequence for me at any rate. I'm enjoying the sequence, without that strain I had in *The Waves*.

Tuesday, October 22nd

I am again held up in *The Years* by my accursed love of talk. That is to say, if I talk to Rose Macaulay from 4-6:30: to Elizabeth Bowen from 8-12 I have a dull heavy hot mop inside my brain next day and am a prey to every flea, ant, gnat. So I have shut the book—Sal and Martin in Hyde Park—and spent the morning typing out Roger's memoirs. This is a most admirable sedative and refresher. I wish I always had it at hand. Two days rest of that nerve is my prescription; but rest is hard to come by. I think I shall refuse all invitations to chatter parties till I'm done. Could it only be by Christmas! For instance, if I go to Edith Sitwell's cocktail this evening I shall only pick up some exacerbating picture: I shall froth myself into sparklets; and there'll be the whole smoothing and freshening to begin again. But *after The Years* is done *then* I shall go everywhere: and expose every cranny to the light. As it is, who doesn't come here? Every day this week I must talk. But in my own room I'm happier, I think. So I will now plod quietly through the Bridges letters and perhaps begin to arrange all Helen's tangled mass.

Sunday, October 27th

Adrian's birthday, it strikes me. And we asked him to dine. No, I will not hurry this book. I'm going to let every scene shape fully and easily in my hands, before sending it to be typed, even if it has to wait another year. I wonder why time is always allowed to harry one. I think it rather good this morning. I'm doing Kitty's party. And in spite of the terrific curb on my impatience—never have I held myself back so drastically —I'm enjoying this writing more fully and with less strain and —what's the word?—I mean it's giving me more natural pleas-

ure than the others. But I have such a pressure of other books
kicking their heels in the hall it's difficult to go on very slowly.
Yesterday we walked across Ken Wood to Highgate and looked
at the two little old Fry houses. That's where Roger was born
and saw the poppy. I think of beginning with that scene. Yes
that book shapes itself. Then there's my next war—which at
any moment becomes absolutely wild, like being harnessed to
a shark; and I dash off scene after scene. I think I must do it
directly *The Years* is done. Suppose I finish *The Years* in January: then dash off the *War* (or whatever I call it) in six weeks:
and do Roger next summer?

Monday, November 18th

It struck me tho' that I have now reached a further stage
in my writer's advance. I see that there are four? dimensions:
all to be produced, in human life: and that leads to a far richer
grouping and proportion. I mean: I; and the not I; and the
outer and the inner—no I'm too tired to say: but I see it: and
this will affect my book on Roger. Very exciting, to grope on like
this. New combination in psychology and body—rather like
painting. This will be the next novel, after *The Years*.

Thursday, November 21st

Yes, but these upper air scenes get too thin. Reflection
after a morning of Kitty and Edward in Richmond. At first
they're such a relief though after the other that one gets blown
—flies ahead. The thing is to take it quietly: go back: and rub
out detail; too many "points" made; too jerky, and as it were
talking "at." I want to keep the individual and the sense of
things coming over and over again and yet changing. That's
what's so difficult, to combine the two.

Wednesday, November 27th

Too many specimen days—so I can't write. Yet, heaven help
me, have a feeling that I've reached the no man's land that I'm
after; and can pass from outer to inner and inhabit eternity.
A queer very happy free feeling, such as I've not had at the

finish of any other book. And this too is a prodigious long one.
So what does it mean? Another balk this morning; can't get
the start off of the last chapter right. What's wrong I don't
know. But I needn't hurry. And the main thing is to let ideas
blow easily; and come softly pouring. And not to be too emphatic. Of course to step straight into the middle of a new
character is difficult: North: and I'm a little exacerbated;
meant to have a quiet week, and here's Nelly C. and Nan
Hudson both asking to come; and will I ring up; and Nan has
a Turkish friend. But I will *not* be rushed. No.

Saturday, December 28th

It's all very well to write that date in a nice clear hand,
because it begins this new book, but I cannot disguise the fact
that I'm almost extinct, like a charwoman's duster; that is my
brain; what with the last revision of the last pages of *The
Years*. And is it the last revision? And why should I lead the
dance of the days with this tipsy little spin? But in fact I must
stretch my cramped muscles: it's only half past eleven on a
damp grey morning, and I want a quiet occupation for an
hour. That reminds me—I must divine some let down for myself that won't be too sudden when the end is reached. An
article on Gray I think. But how the whole prospect will take
different proportions, once I've relaxed this effort. Shall I ever
write a long book again—a long novel that has to be held in
the brain at full stretch—for close on three years? Nor do I even
attempt to ask if it's worth while. There are mornings so con-
gested I can't even copy out Roger. Goldie depresses me unspeakably. Always alone on a mountain top asking himself
how to live, theorising about life; never living. Roger always
down in the succulent valleys, living. But what a thin whistle
of hot air Goldie lets out through his front teeth. Always live
in the whole, life in the one: always Shelley and Goethe, and
then he loses his hot water bottle; and never notices a face
or a cat or a dog or a flower, except in the flow of the universal.
This explains why his highminded books are unreadable. Yet
he was so charming, intermittently.

Sunday, December 29th

I have in fact just put the last words to *The Years*—rolling, rolling, though it's only Sunday and I allowed myself till Wednesday. And I am not in such a twitter as usual. But then I meant it to end calmly—a prose work. And is it good? That I cannot possibly tell. Does it hang together? Does one part support another? Can I flatter myself that it composes; and is a whole? Well there still remains a great deal to do. I must still condense and point: give pauses their effect, and repetitions, and the run on. It runs in this version to 797 pages: say 200 each (but that's liberal): it comes to roughly 157,000—shall we say 140,000. Yes, it needs sharpening, some bold cuts and emphases. That will take me another—I don't know how long. And I must subconsciously wean my mind from it finally and prepare another creative mood, or I shall sink into acute despair. How odd—that this will all fade away and something else take its place. And by this time next year I shall be sitting here with a vast bundle of press cuttings—no; not in the flesh I hope: but in my mind there will be the usual chorus of what people have said about this mass of scribbled typewriting, and I shall be saying, That was an attempt at that: and now I must do something different. And all the old, or new, problems will be in front of me. Anyhow the main feeling about this book is vitality, fruitfulness, energy. Never did I enjoy writing a book more, I think: only with the whole mind in action: not so intensely as *The Waves*.

Monday, December 30th

And today, no it's no go. I can't write a word: too much headache. Can only look back at *The Years* as an inaccessible Rocky Island; which I can't explore, can't even think of. At Charleston yesterday. The great yellow table with very few places. Reading Roger I became haunted by him. What an odd posthumous friendship—in some ways more intimate than any I had in life. The things I guessed are now revealed; and the actual voice gone.

I had an idea—I wish they'd sleep—while dressing—how to

make my war book *—to pretend it's all the articles editors have asked me to write during the past few years—on all sorts of subjects—Should women smoke: Short skirts: War etc. This would give me the right to wander; also put me in the position of the one asked. And excuse the method: while giving continuity. And there might be a preface saying this, to give the right tone. I think that's got it. A wild wet night—floods out: rain as I go to bed: dogs barking: wind battering. Now I shall slink indoors I think and read some remote book.

* This became *Three Guineas.*

1936

I began the year with three entirely submerged days, head-ache, head bursting, head so full, racing with ideas; and the rain pouring; the floods out; when we stumbled out yesterday the mud came over my great rubber boots; the water squelched in my soles; so this Christmas has been, as far as country is concerned, a failure, and in spite of what London can do to chafe and annoy I'm glad to go back and have, rather guiltily, begged not to stay here another week. Today it is a yellow grey foggy day; so that I can only see the hump, a wet gleam, but no Caburn. I am content though because I think that I have recovered enough balance in the head to begin *The Years*, I mean the final revision on Monday. This suddenly becomes a little urgent, because for the first time for some years, L. says I have not made enough to pay my share of the house, and have to find £70 out of my hoard. This is now reduced to £700 and I must fill it up. Amusing, in its way, to think of economy again. But it would be a strain to think seriously; and worse—a brutal interruption—had I to make money by journalism. The next book I think of calling *Answers to Correspondents* . . . But I must not at once stop and make it up. No. I must find a pa-tient and quiet method of soothing that excitable nerve to sleep until *The Years* is on the table—finished. In February? Oh the relief—as if a vast—what can I say—bony excrescence—bag of muscle—were cut out of my brain. Yet it's better to write that than the other. A queer light on my psychology. I can no longer write for papers. I must write for my own book. I mean I at once adapt what I'm going to say, if I think of a newspaper.

Saturday, January 4th

The weather has improved and we have decided to stay till Wednesday. It will now of course rain. But I will make some good resolutions: to read as few weekly papers, which are apt to prick me into recollection of myself, as possible, until this *Years* is over: to fill my brain with remote books and habits; not to think of *Answers to Correspondents;* and altogether to be as fundamental and as little superficial, to be as physical, as little apprehensive, as possible. And now to do Roger; and then to relax. For, to tell the truth, my head is still all nerves; and one false move means racing despair, exaltation, and all the rest of that familiar misery: that long scale of unhappiness. So I have ordered a sirloin and we shall go for a drive.

Sunday, January 5th

I have had another morning at the old plague. I rather suspect that I have said the thing I meant, and any further work will only muddle. Further work must be merely to tidy and smooth out. This seems likely because I'm so calm. I feel well, that's done. I want to be off on something else. Whether good or bad, I don't know. And my head is quiet today, soothed by reading *The Trumpet Major* last night and a drive to the floods. The clouds were an extraordinary tropical birds wing colour: an impure purple; and the lakes reflected it, and there were droves of plover, black and white; and all very linear in line and pure and subtle in colour. How I slept!

Tuesday, January 7th

I have again copied out the last pages, and I think got the spacing better. Many details and some fundamentals remain. The snow scene for example, and I suspect a good many unfaced passages remain. But I preserve my sense that it's stated; and I need only use my craft, not my creation.

Thursday, January 16th

Seldom have I been more completely miserable than I was about 6:30 last night, reading over the last part of *The Years*. Such feeble twaddle—such twilight gossip it seemed; such a show up of my own decrepitude, and at such huge length. I could only plump it down on the table and rush upstairs with burning cheeks to L. He said: "This always happens." But I felt, No, it has never been so bad as this. I make this note should I be in the same state after another book. Now this morning, dipping in, it seems to me, on the contrary, a full, bustling live book. I looked at the early pages. I think there's something to it. But I must now force myself to begin regular sending to Mabel. 100 pages go tonight I swear.

Tuesday, February 25th

And this will show how hard I work. This is the first moment —this five minutes before lunch—that I've had to write here. I work all the morning: I work from 5 to 7 most days. Then I've had headaches: vanquish them by lying still and binding books and reading *David Copperfield*. I have sworn that the script shall be ready, typed and corrected, on 10th March. L. will then read it. And I've still all the Richmond and El. scene to type out: many corrections in that most accursed raid scene to make: all this to have typed: if I can by the 1st which is Sunday; and then I must begin at the beginning and read straight through. So I'm quite unable either to write here or to do Roger. On the whole, I'm enjoying it—that's odd—though in the ups and downs and with no general opinion.

Wednesday, March 4th

Well, I'm almost through copying the raid scene, I should think for the 13th time. Then it will go tomorrow; and I shall have I think one day's full holiday—if I dare—before re-reading. So I'm in sight of the end: that is in sight of the beginning of the other book which keeps knocking unmercifully at the door. Oh to be able once more to write freely every morning, spinning my own words afresh—what a boon—what a physical relief, rest, delight after these last months—since October year more or less—of perpetual compressing and re-writing always at that one book.

Wednesday, March 11th

Well yesterday I sent off 132 pages to Clark.* We have decided to take this unusual course—that is to print it in galleys before L. sees it, and send it to America.

* R. & R. Clark, Ltd., the printers.

Friday, March 13th

Getting along rather better. So I steal 10 minutes before lunch. Never have I worked so hard at any book. My aim is not to alter a thing in proof. And I begin to suspect there's something there—it hasn't flopped yet. But enough of *The Years*. We walked round Kensington Gardens yesterday discussing politics. Aldous refuses to sign the latest manifesto because it approves sanctions. He's a pacifist. So am I. Ought I to resign. L. says that considering Europe is now on the verge of the greatest smash for 600 years, one must sink private differences and support the League. He's at a special L. Party meeting this morning. This is the most feverish overworked political week we've yet had. Hitler has his army on the Rhine. Meetings taking place in London. So serious are the French that they're—the little Intelligence group—is sending a man to confer here tomorrow: a touching belief in English intellectuals. Another meeting tomorrow. As usual, I think, Oh this will blow over. But it's odd, how near the guns have got to our private life again. I can quite distinctly see them and hear a roar, even though I go on, like a doomed mouse, nibbling at my daily page. What else is there to do—except answer the incessant telephones, and listen to what L. says. Everything goes by the board. Happily we have put off all dinners and so on, on account of *The Years*. A very concentrated, laborious spring this is: with perhaps two fine days: crocuses out: then bitter black and cold. It all seems in keeping: my drudgery: our unsociability: the crisis: meetings: dark—and what it all means, no one knows. Privately . . . no, I doubt that I've seen anyone, or done anything but walk and work—walk for an hour after lunch—and so on.

Monday, March 16th

I ought not to be doing this: but I cannot go on bothering with those excruciating pages any more. I shall come in at 3 and do some: and again after tea. For my own guidance, I have never suffered, since *The Voyage Out*, such acute despair on re-reading, as this time. On Saturday for instance: there I was, faced with complete failure: and yet the book is being printed. Then I set to: in despair; thought of throwing it away: but went on typing. After an hour, the line began to tauten. Yesterday I read it again; and I think it may be my best book. However . . . I'm only at the King's death. I think the change of scene is what's so exhausting: the catching people plumb in the middle: then jerking off. Every beginning seems lifeless—and then I have to retype. I've more or less done 250: and there's 700 to do. A walk down the river and through Richmond Park did more than anything to pump blood in.

Wednesday, March 18th

It now seems to me so good—still talking about *The Years* —that I can't go on correcting. In fact I do think the scene at Witterings is about the best, in that line, I ever wrote. First proofs just come: so there's a cold douche waiting me there. And I can't concentrate this morning—must make up Letter to an Englishman. I think, once more, that is the final form it will take.

Tuesday, March 24th

A very good weekend. Trees coming out: hyacinths; crocuses. Hot. The first spring weekend. Then we walked up to Rat Farm—looked for violets. Still spring here. Am tinkering —in a drowsy state. And I'm so absorbed in *Two Guineas*— that's what I'm going to call it. I must very nearly verge on insanity I think, I get so deep in this book I don't know what I'm doing. Find myself walking along the Strand talking aloud.

Sunday, March 29th

Now it's Sunday and I'm still forging ahead. Done Eleanor in Oxford Street for the 20th time this morning. I've plotted it out now and shall have done by Tuesday 7th April, I tell my-self. And I can't help thinking it's rather good. But no more of that. One bad head this week, lying prostrate.

Thursday, April 9th

Now will come the season of depression, after congestion, suffocation. The last batch was posted to Clark at Brighton yesterday. L. is in process of reading. I daresay I'm pessimistic, but I fancy a certain tepidity in his verdict so far: but then it's provisional. At any rate these are disgusting, racking at the same time enervated days, and must be thrown on the bonfire. The horror is that tomorrow, after this one windy day of respite —oh the cold north wind that has blown ravaging daily since we came, but I've had no ears, eyes, or nose: only making my quick transits from house to room, often in despair—after this one day's despite, I say, I must begin at the beginning and go through 600 pages of cold proof. Why, oh why? Never again, never again. No sooner have I written that, than I make up the first pages of *Two Guineas,* and begin a congenial ramble about Roger. But seriously I think this shall be my last "novel." But then I want to tackle criticism too.

Thursday, June 11th

I can only, after two months, make this brief note, to say at last after two months dismal and worse, almost catastrophic illness—never been so near the precipice to my own feeling since 1913—I'm again on top. I have to re-write, I mean interpolate, and rub out most of *The Years* in proof. But I can't go into that. Can only do an hour or so. Oh but the divine joy of being mistress of my mind again! Back from M.H.* yesterday. Now I am going to live like a cat stepping on eggs till my 600 pages are done. I think I can—I think I can—but must have immense courage and buoyancy to compass it. This, as I say, my first voluntary writing since April 9th, after which I pitched into bed: then to Cornwall—no note of that: then back: saw Elly: then to M.H.: home yesterday for a fortnight's trial. And the blood has mounted to my head. Wrote 1880 this morning.

Sunday, June 21st

After a week of intense suffering—indeed mornings of torture—and I'm not exaggerating—pain in my head—a feeling of complete despair and failure—a head inside like the nostrils after hay fever—here is a cool quiet morning again, a feeling of relief, respite, hope. Just done the Robson: think it good. I am

* Monks House, Rodmell.

living so constrainedly: so repressedly: I can't make notes of life. Everything is planned, battened down. I do half an hour down here: go up, often in despair: lie down: walk round the Square: come back and do another ten lines. Then to Lords yesterday. Always with a feeling of having to repress, control. I see people lying on sofa between tea and dinner. Rose M., Elizabeth Bowen, Nessa. Sat in the Square last night. Saw the dripping green leaves. Thunder and lightning. Purple sky. N. and A. discussing 4/8 time. Cats stealing round. L. dining with Tom and Bella. A very strange, most remarkable summer. New emotions: humility: impersonal joy: literary despair. I am learning my craft in the most fierce conditions. Really reading Flaubert's letters I hear my own voice cry out Oh art! Patience: find him consoling, admonishing. I must get this book quietly, strongly, daringly into shape. But it won't be out till next year. Yet I think it has possibilities, could I seize them. I am trying to cut the characters deep in a phrase: to pare off and compact scenes: to envelop the whole in a medium.

Tuesday, June 23rd

A good day—a bad day—so it goes on. Few people can be so tortured by writing as I am. Only Flaubert I think. Yet I see it now, as a whole. I think I can bring it off, if I only have courage and patience: take each scene quietly: compose: I think it may be a good book. And then—oh when it's finished!

Not so clear today, because I went to dentist and then shopped. My brain is like a scale: one grain pulls it down. Yesterday it balanced: today dips.

Friday, October 30th

I do not wish for the moment to write out the story of the months since I made the last mark here. I do not wish, for reasons I cannot now develop, to analyse that extraordinary summer. It will be more helpful and healthy for me to write scenes; to take up my pen and describe actual events: good practice too for my stumbling and doubting pen. Can I still "write"? That is the question, you see. And now I will try to prove if the gift is dead, or dormant.

Tuesday, November 3rd

Miracles will never cease—L. actually liked *The Years!* He thinks it so far—as far as the wind chapter—as good as any of my books. I will put down the actual facts. On Sunday I started to read the proofs. When I had read to the end of the first section I was in despair: stony but convinced despair. I made myself yesterday read on to Present Time. When I reached that landmark I said, "This is happily so bad that there can be no question about it. I must carry the proofs, like a dead cat, to L. and tell him to burn them unread." This I did. And a weight fell off my shoulders. That is true. I felt relieved of some great pack. It was cold and dry and very grey and I went out and walked through the graveyard with Cromwell's daughter's tomb down through Grays Inn along Holborn and so back. Now I was no longer Virginia, the genius, but only a perfectly magnificent yet content—shall I call it spirit? a body? And very tired. Very old. But at the same time content to join these 100 years with Leonard. So we lunched in a constraint: a grey acceptance: and I said to L. I will write to Richmond and ask for books to review. The proofs will cost I suppose between £200 and £300 which I will pay out of my hoard. As I have £700 this will leave £400. I was not unhappy. And L. said he thought I might be wrong about the book. Then ever so many strange men arrived: Mr. Mumford, mahogany coloured, lean, with a very hard bowler and a cane; whom I put in the drawing room with a cigarette: Mr. —— very heavy and large, who said Pardon me and knocked at the door. And Lord and Lady Cecil rang up to ask us to lunch to meet the Spanish Ambassador. (I am making up *Three Guineas.*) Then, after tea, we went to the *Sunday Times* book show. How stuffy it was! How dead I felt—Oh how infinitely tired! And Miss White came up, a hard little woman with a cheery wooden face, and talked about her book and reviews. And then Ursula Strachey came across from Duckworths and said You don't know who I am? And I remembered the moonlit river. And then Roger Senhouse tapped me on the shoulder. We went home and L. read and read and said nothing: I began to feel actively depressed; yet could make up *The Years* differently—I've thought of a scheme for

another book—it should be told in the first person. Would that
do as a form for Roger?—and I fell into one of my horrid heats
and deep slumbers, as if the blood in my head were cut off.
Suddenly L. put down his proof and said he thought it extraordinarily good—as good as any of them. And now he is reading
on, and tired out with the exertion of writing these pages I'm
going up to read the Italian book.

Wednesday, November 4th

L. who has now read to the end of 1914, still thinks it extraordinarily good: very strange: very interesting: very sad. We discussed my sadness. But my difficulty is this: I cannot bring
myself to believe that he is right. It may be simply that I exaggerated its badness, and therefore he now, finding it not so bad,
exaggerates its goodness. If it is to be published, I must at once
sit down and correct: how can I? Every other sentence seemed
to me bad. But I am shelving the question till he has done,
which should be tonight.

Thursday, November 5th

The miracle is accomplished. L. put down the last sheet
about 12 last night; and could not speak. He was in tears. He
says it is "a most remarkable book"—he *likes* it better than
The Waves—and has not a spark of doubt that it must be published. I, as a witness, not only to his emotion but to his absorption, for he read on and on, can't doubt his opinion. What
about my own? Anyhow the moment of relief was divine. I
hardly know yet if I'm on my heels or head, so amazing is the
reversal since Tuesday morning. I have never had such an experience before.

Monday, November 9th

I must make some resolutions about this book. I find it
extremely difficult. I get into despair. It seems so bad. I can
only cling to L.'s verdict. Then I get distracted: I tried, as an
anodyne, to take up an article; a memoir; to review a book
for *The Listener*. They make my mind race. I must fix it upon
The Years. I must do my proofs—send them off. I *must* fix

my mind on it all the morning. I think the only way is to do that, and then let myself do something else between tea and dinner. But immerse in *The Years* all the morning—nothing else. If the chapter is difficult, concentrate for a short time. Then write here. But don't dash off into other writing till after tea. When it is done, we can always ask Morgan.

Tuesday, November 10th

On the whole it has gone better this morning. It's true my brain is so tired of this job it aches after an hour or less. So I must dandle it, and gently immerse it. Yes, I think it's good; in its very difficult way.

I wonder if anyone has ever suffered so much from a book as I have from *The Years*. Once out I will never look at it again. It's like a long childbirth. Think of that summer, every morning a headache, and forcing myself into that room in my nightgown; and lying down after a page: and always with the certainty of failure. Now that certainty is mercifully removed to some extent. But now I feel I don't care what anyone says so long as I'm rid of it. And for some reason I feel I'm respected and liked. But this is only the haze dance of illusion, always changing. Never write a long book again. Yet I feel I shall write more fiction—scenes will form. But I am tired this morning: too much strain and racing yesterday.

Monday, November 30th

There is no need whatever in my opinion to be unhappy about *The Years*. It seems to me to come off at the end. Anyhow, to be a taut, real, strenuous book. Just finished it; and feel a little exalted. It's different from the others of course: has I think more "real" life in it; more blood and bone. But anyhow, even if there are appalling watery patches, and a grinding at the beginning, I don't think I need lie quaking at nights. I think I can feel assured. This I say sincerely to myself; to hold to myself during the weeks of dull anticipation. Nor need I care much what people say. In fact I hand my compliment to that terribly depressed woman, myself, whose head ached so often; who was so entirely convinced a failure; for in spite of everything I think she brought it off and is to be congratulated. How she did it, with her head like an old cloth, I don't know. But now for rest: and Gibbon.

Thursday, December 31st

There in front of me lie the proofs—the galleys—to go off today, a sort of stinging nettle that I cover over. Nor do I wish even to write about it here.

A divine relief has possessed me these last days—at being quit of it—good or bad. And, for the first time since February I should say my mind has sprung up like a tree shaking off a load. And I've plunged into Gibbon and read and read, for the first time since February, I think. Now for action and pleasure again and going about. I could make some interesting and perhaps valuable notes on the absolute necessity for me of my work. Always to be after something. I'm not sure that the intensiveness and exclusiveness of writing a long book is a possible state: I mean, if ever in future I do such a thing—and I doubt it—I will force myself to vary it with little articles. Anyhow, now I am not going to think Can I write? I am going to rush into unselfconsciousness and work: at Gibbon first; then a few little articles for America; then Roger and *Three Guineas*. Which of the two comes first, how to dovetail, I don't know. Anyhow even if *The Years* is a failure, I've thought considerably and collected a little hoard of ideas. Perhaps I'm now again on one of those peaks where I shall write two or three little books quickly; and then have another break. At least I feel myself possessed of skill enough to go on with. No emptiness. And in proof of this will go in, get my Gibbon notes and begin a careful sketch of the article.

1937

Thursday, January 28th

Sunk once more in the happy tumultuous dream: that is to say began *Three Guineas* this morning and can't stop thinking it. My plan is to write it out now, without more palaver, and think perhaps it might be roughed in by Easter; but I shall allow myself, make myself, scribble a little article or two between whiles. Then I hope to float over the horrid March 15th: wire today to say *Years* haven't reached America. I must plate myself against that sinking and mud. And so far as I can tell, this method is almost too effective.

and ended it
12 Oct. 1937
(provisionally
that is).

Thursday, February 18th

I have now written for three weeks at *Three Guineas* and have done 38 pages. Now I've used up that vein momently and want a few days change. At what? Can't at the moment think.

Saturday, February 20th

I turn my eyes away from the Press as I go upstairs, because there are all the review copies of *The Years* packed and packing. They go out next week: this is my last weekend of comparative peace. What do I anticipate with such clammy coldness? I think chiefly that my friends won't mention it; will turn the conversation rather awkwardly. I think I anticipate considerable lukewarmness among the friendly reviewers—respectful tepidity; and a whoop of Red Indian delight from the Grigs who will joyfully and loudly announce that this is the longdrawn twaddle of a prim prudish bourgeois mind, and say that now no one can take Mrs. W. seriously again. But violence I shan't so much mind. What I think I shall mind most is the awkwardness when I go, say to Tilton or Charleston, and they don't know what to say. And since we

I suppose what
I expect is that
they'll say now
Mrs. W. has written a long book
all about nothing.

shan't get away till June I must expect a very full exposure to this damp firework atmosphere. They will say it's a tired book; a last effort . . . Well, now that I've written that down I feel that even so I can exist in that shadow. That is if I keep hard at work. And there's no lack of that. I discussed a book of illustrated incidents with Nessa yesterday; we are going to produce 12 lithographs for Christmas, printed by ourselves. As we were talking, Margery Fry rang up to ask me to see Julian Fry about Roger. So that begins to press on me. Then L. wants if possible to have *Three Guineas* for the autumn: and I have my Gibbon, my broadcast, and a possible leader on Biography to fill in chinks. I plan to keep out of literary circles till the mild boom is over. And this, waiting, under consideration, is after all the worst. This time next month I shall feel more at ease. And it's only now and then I mind now.

Sunday, February 21st

I'm off again, after five days lapse (writing *Faces and Voices*) on *Three Guineas:* after a most dismal hacking got a little canter and hope now to spin ahead. Odd that one sometimes does a transition quite quickly. A quiet day for a wonder—no one seen yesterday: so I went to Caledonian Market, couldn't find spoon shop: bought yellow gloves 3/- and stockings 1/- and so home. Started reading French again: *Misanthrope* and Colette's memoirs given me last summer by Janie: when I was in the dismal drowse and couldn't fix on that or anything. Today the reviewers (oh d——n this silly thought) have their teeth fixed in me; but what care I for a goosefeather bed, etc. In fact, once I get into the canter over *Three Guineas* I think I shall see only the flash of the white rails and pound along to the goal.

Sunday, February 28th

I'm so entirely imbued with *Three Guineas* that I can hardly jerk myself away to write here. (Here in fact I again dropped my pen to think about my next paragraph—universities)—how will that lead to professions and so on. It's a bad habit.

Sunday, March 7th

As will be seen on the last page my spiritual temperature went up with a rush; why I don't know, save that I've been having a good gallop at *Three Guineas*. Now I have broached the fatal week and must expect a sudden drop. It's going to be pretty bad, I'm certain; but at the same time I am convinced that the drop needn't be fatal: that is, the book may be damned, with faint praise; but the point is that I my- self know why it's a failure, and that its failure is deliberate. I also know that I have reached my point of view, as writer, as being. As writer I am fitted out for another two books—*Three Guineas* and Roger (let alone articles): as being the interest and safety of my present life are unthrowable. This I have, honestly, proved this winter. It's not a gesture. And honestly the diminution of fame, that people aren't any longer enthu- siastic, gives me the chance to observe quietly. Also I am in a position to hold myself aloof. I need never seek out anyone. In short either way I'm safe, and look forward, after the un- avoidable tosses and tumbles of the next ten days, to a slow, dark, fruitful spring, summer and autumn. This is set down I hope once and for all. And please to remember it on Friday when the reviews come in.

We have sold 5,300 before publication.

Friday, March 12th

Oh the relief! L. brought the *Lit. Sup.* to me in bed and said It's quite good. And so it is; and *Time and Tide* says I'm a first rate novelist and a great lyrical poet. And I can already hardly read through the reviews: but feel a little dazed, to think then it's *not* nonsense; it does make an effect. Yet of course not in the least the effect I meant. But now, my dear, after all that agony, I'm free, whole; round: can go full ahead. And so stop this cry of content and sober joy. Off to M.H. Julian back today. I use my last five minutes before lunch to note that though I have slipped the gall and fret and despair even of the past few weeks wholly today, and shan't I think renew them; I have once more loaded myself with the strain of *Three Guineas,* at which I have been writing hard and laboriously. So now I'm straining to draw that cart across the rough ground. It seems therefore that there is no rest; no sense of It's finished. One always harnesses oneself by instinct; and can't live without the strain. Now *The Years* will completely die out from my mind.

Car mended. But rain pouring.

Sunday, March 14th

I am in such a twitter owing to two columns in the *Observer* praising *The Years* that I can't, as I foretold, go on with *Three Guineas.* Why I even sat back just now and thought with pleasure of people reading that review. And when I think of the agony I went through in this room, just over a year ago . . . when it dawned on me that the whole of three years' work was a complete failure: and then when I think of the mornings here when I used to stumble out and cut up those proofs and write three lines and then go back and lie on my bed—the worst summer in my life, but at the same time the most illuminating—it's no wonder my hand trembles. What most pleases me though is the obvious chance now since de Selincourt sees it, that my intention in *The Years* may be not so entirely muted and obscured as I feared. The *T.L.S.* spoke as if it were merely the death song of the middle classes: a series of exquisite impressions: but he sees that it is a creative, a constructive book. Not that I've yet altogether read him: but he has pounced on some of the key sentences. And this means that it will be debated; and this means that *Three Guineas* will strike very sharp and clear on a hot iron: so that my immensely careful planning won't be baulked by time of life etc. as I had made certain. Making certain however was an enormous discovery for me, though.

Friday, March 19th

Now this is one of the strangest of my experiences—"they" say almost universally that *The Years* is a masterpiece. *The*

Times says so. Bunny etc.: Howard Spring. If somebody had told me I should write this, even a week ago, let alone six months ago, I should have given a jump like a shot hare. How entirely and absolutely incredible it would have been! The praise chorus began yesterday: by the way I was walking in Covent Garden and found St. Pauls, C.G., for the first time, heard the old char singing as she cleaned the chairs in the ante hall; then went to Burnets; chose stuff; bought the *Evening Standard* and found myself glorified as I read it in the Tube. A calm quiet feeling, glory: and I'm so steeled now I don't think the flutter will much worry me. Now I must begin again on *Three Guineas*.

Something about a masterpiece and how Mrs. W. has more to give us than any living novelist . . . astonishing fertility.

Saturday, March 27th

No, I am not going to titivate Gibbon—that is condense by a thousand words. Too much screw needed, and my brain unstrung. Merely scribbling here: over a log fire, on a cold but bright Easter morning; sudden shafts of sun, a scatter of snow on the hills early; sudden storms, ink black, octopus pouring, coming up; and the rooks fidgeting and pecking on the elm trees. As for the beauty, as I always say when I walk the terrace after breakfast, too much for one pair of eyes. Enough to float a whole population in happiness, if only they would look. Curiously a combination, this garden, with the church, and the cross of the church black against Asheham Hill. That is all the elements of the English brought together, accidentally. We came down on Thursday, packed in the rush in London; cars spinning all along the roads: yesterday at last perfect freedom from telephones and reviews, and no one rang up. I began *Lord Ormont and his Aminta* and found it so rich, so knotted, so alive, and muscular after the pale little fiction I'm used to, that, alas, it made me wish to write fiction again. Meredith underrated. I like his effort to escape plain prose. And he had humour and some insight too—more than they allow him now. Also Gibbon. And so I'm well fitted out; but can't write more than this without the old tightening and throbbing at the back of the head.

Friday, April 2nd

How I interest myself! Quite set up and perky today with a mind brimming because I was so damnably depressed and smacked on the cheek by Edwin Muir in the *Listener* and by Scott James in the *Life and Letters* on Friday. They both gave me a smart snubbing: E. M. says *The Years* is dead and disappointing. So in effect did S. James. All the lights sank; my reed bent to the ground. Dead and disappointing—so I'm found out and that odious rice pudding of a book is what I thought it—a dank failure. No life in it. Much inferior to the bitter truth and intense originality of Miss Compton Burnett. Now this pain woke me at 4 A.M. and I suffered acutely. All day driving to Janet and back I was under the cloud. But about 7 it lifted; there was a good review, of 4 lines, in the *Empire Review*. The best of my books: did that help? I don't think very much. But the delight of being exploded is quite real. One feels braced for some reason; amused; round; combative; more than by praise.

Saturday, April 3rd

Now I have to broadcast on 29th. It will go like this: can't be a craft of words. Am going to disregard the title and talk about words: why they won't let themselves be made a craft of. They tell the truth: they aren't useful. That there should be two languages: fiction and fact. Words are inhuman . . . won't make money—need privacy. Why. For their embraces, to continue the race. A dead word. The purists and the impurists. These are only impressions, not fixations. I respect words too. Associations of words. Felicity brings in absent thee. We can easily make new words. Squish squash: crick crack. But we can't use them in writing.

Sunday, April 4th

Another curious idiosyncrasy. Maynard thinks *The Years* my best book: thinks one scene, E. and Crosby, beats Tchekov's

Cherry Orchard—and this opinion though from the centre, from a very fine mind, doesn't flutter me as much as Muir's blame; it sinks in slowly and deeply. It's not a vanity feeling; the other is; the other will die as soon as the week's number of the *Listener* is past. L. went to Tilton and had a long quiet cronies talk. Maynard said that he thought *The Years* very moving: more tender than any of my books: did not puzzle him like *The Waves;* symbolism not a worry; very beautiful; and no more said than was needed; hadn't yet finished it. But how compose the two opinions; it's my most human book; and most inhuman? Oh to forget all this and write—as I must tomorrow.

Friday, April 9th

"Such happiness wherever it is known is to be pitied for tis surely blind." Yes, but my happiness isn't blind. That is the achievement, I was thinking between 3 and 4 this morning, of my 55 years. I lay awake so calm, so content, as if I'd stepped off the whirling world into a deep blue quiet space and there open eyed existed, beyond harm; armed against all that can happen. I have never had this feeling before in all my life; but I have had it several times since last summer: when I reached it, in my worst depression, as if I stepped out, throwing aside a cloak, lying in bed, looking at the stars, these nights at Monks House. Of course it ruffles, in the day, but there it is. There it was yesterday when old Hugh came and said nothing about *The Years*.

MONKS HOUSE. *Monday, June 1st*

I have at last got going with *Three Guineas*—after five days' grind, re-copying, to some extent re-writing; my poor old brain hums again—largely I think because I had a good long walk yesterday and so routed the drowse—it was very hot. At any rate I must use this page as a running ground—for I can't screw all the three hours; I must relax and race here the last hour. That's the worst of writing—its waste. What can I do with the last hour of my morning? Dante again. But oh how my heart leaps up to think that never again shall I be harnessed

to a long book. No. Always short ones in future. The long book
still won't be altogether downed—its reverbera-
tions grumble. Did I say—no, the London days
were too tight, too hot, and distracted for this
book—that H. Brace wrote and said they were
happy to find that *The Years* is the best-selling
novel in America? This was confirmed by my
place at the head of the list in the *Herald Tribune.*
They have sold 25,000—my record, easily. (Now
I am dreaming of *Three Guineas.*) We think if we make money
of buying perhaps an annuity. The great de-
sirable is not to have to earn money by writing. I am doubtful if I shall ever write another novel. Certainly not unless under great
compulsion such as *The Years* inspired in
me. Were I another person, I would say to
myself, Please write criticism; biography; invent a new form for both; also write some
completely unformal fiction: short: and poetry. Fate has here
a hand in it, for when I've done *Three Guineas*
—which I hope to have written, not yet for
publication though, in August—I intend to
put the script aside and write Roger. What I
think best would be to work hard at *Three
Guineas* for a month—June: then begin read-
ing and re-reading my Roger notes. By the way, I have been
sharply abused in *Scrutiny* who, L. says, calls
me a cheat in *The Waves* and *The Years;* most
intelligently (and highly) praised by F. Faulkner
in America—and that's all. (I mean that's all I
need I think write about reviews now: I suspect the clever young man is going to enjoy
downing me—so be it: but in private Sally Graves and Stephen
Spender approve: so, to sum up, I don't know, this is honest,
where I stand; but intend to think no more of it. Gibbon was
rejected by the *N. Republic,* so I shall send no more to America. Nor will I write articles at all except for the *Lit. Sup.* for
whom I am going now to do Congreve.)

Monday,
June 14th.
The Years
still
is top of
the list.

Monday
July 12th.
The Years is
still top of
the list and
has been weekly.

August 23rd.
Years now
2nd or 3rd.
9 editions.

Yesterday,
October 22nd,
it was last on
the list.

Tuesday, June 22nd

Isn't it shameful to write here first thing, not to tackle Congreve? But my brain after talking to Miss Sarton, to Murray, to Ann gave out after dinner, so that I couldn't read *Love for Love*. And I won't do *Three Guineas* till Monday—till I've had a quiet breather. Then the Prof. Chapter: then the final. So now to draw the blood off that brain to another part—according to H. Nicolson's prescription, which is the right one. I would like to write a dream story about the top of a mountain. Now why? About lying in the snow; about rings of colour; silence; and the solitude. I can't though. But shan't I, one of these days, indulge myself in some short releases into that world? Short now for ever. No more long grinds: only sudden intensities. If I could think out another adventure. Oddly enough I see it now ahead of me—in Charing Cross Road yesterday—as to do with books: some new combination. Brighton? A round room on the pier—and people shopping, missing each other—a story Angelica told in the summer. But how does this make up with criticism? I'm trying to get the four dimensions of the mind . . . life in connection with emotions from literature. A day's walk—a mind's adventure; something like that. And it's useless to repeat my old experiments: they must be new to be experiments.

Wednesday, June 23rd

It's ill writing after reading *Love for Love*—a masterpiece. I never knew how good it is. And what exhilaration there is in reading these masterpieces. This superb hard English! Yes, always keep the classics at hand to prevent flop. I can't write out my feeling, though; must decant it tomorrow in an article. But neither can I settle to read poor Rosemary's verses, as I should with a view to this evening. How could L. S. in *D.N.B.* deny C. feeling, pain—more in that one play than in all Thackeray: and the indecency often honesty. But enough—I went shopping, whitebait hunting, to Selfridges yesterday and it grew roasting hot and I was in black—such astonishing chops and changes this summer—often one's caught in a storm, frozen or roasted. As I reached 52, a long trail of fugitives—like a

caravan in a desert—came through the square: Spaniards flying
from Bilbao, which has fallen, I suppose. Somehow brought
tears to my eyes, though no one seemed surprised. Children
trudging along; women in London cheap jackets with gay
handkerchiefs on their heads, young men, and all carrying
either cheap cases, and bright blue enamel kettles, very large,
and canisters, fitted I suppose with gifts from some charity—
a shuffling trudging procession, flying—impelled by machine
gun in Spanish fields to trudge through Tavistock Square,
along Gordon Square, then where?—clasping their enamel
kettles. A strange spectacle. They went on, knowing which
way: I suppose someone directed them. One boy was chatting,
the others absorbed, like people on the trek. A reason why we
can't write like Congreve I suppose.

Sunday, July 11th

A gap: not in life, but in comment. I have been in full
flood every morning with *Three Guineas*. Whether I shall
finish by August becomes doubtful. But I am in the middle
of my magic bubble. Had I time I would like to describe
the curious glance of the world—the pale disillusioned world
—that I get so violently now and then, when the wall thins—
either I'm tired or interrupted. Then I think of Julian near
Madrid: and so on. Margaret Ll. Davies writes that Janet *
is dying, and will I write on her for *The Times*—a curious
thought, rather: as if it mattered who wrote, or not. But this
flooded me with the idea of Janet yesterday. I think writing,
my writing, is a species of mediumship. I become the person.

Monday, July 19th

Just back from M.H. but I *can't* and *won't* write anything
—too bothered and dithered. Also, I screwed my head tight
—too tight—knocking together a little obituary of Janet for
The Times. And couldn't make it take the folds well: too stiff
and mannered. She died. Three notes from Emphie † this
morning. She died on Thursday, shut her eyes and "looks so

* Janet Case, an old friend, who taught Virginia Woolf Greek.
† Janet's sister.

beautiful." Today they are cremating her, and she had had
printed a little funeral service—with the death day left blank.
No words: an adagio from Beethoven and a text about gentle-
ness and faith which I would have included had I known. But
what does my writing matter? There is something fitting and
complete about the memory of her, thus consummated. Dear
old harum scarum Emphie will have her solitary moments to
herself. To us she will always be a scatterbrain; yet to me very
touching and I remember that phrase in her letter, how she
ran into Janet's room at midnight, and they had a nice little
time together. She was always running in. Janet was the stead-
fast contemplative one, anchored in some private faith which
didn't correspond with the world's. But she was oddly inarticulate. No hand for words. Her letters, save that the last
began "My beloved Virginia," always cool and casual. And how
I loved her, at Hyde Park Gate: and how I went hot and cold
going to Windmill Hill: and how great a visionary part she has
played in my life, till the visionary became a part of the fictitious, not of the real life.

Friday, August 6th

Will another novel ever swim up? If so, how? The only hint
I have towards it is that it's to be dialogue: and poetry: and
prose; all quite distinct. No more long closely written books.
But I have no impulse; and shall wait; and shan't mind if the
impulse never formulates; though I suspect one of these days
I shall get that old rapture. I don't want to write more fiction.
I want to explore a new criticism. One thing I think proved,
I shall never write to "please," to convert; now am entirely
and for ever my own mistress.

Tuesday, August 17th

Not much to say. It's true, the only life this summer is in
the brain. I get excited writing. Three hours pass like 10 minutes. This morning I had a moment of the old rapture—think
of it!—over copying *The Duchess and the Jeweller* for Chambrun, N.Y. I had to send a synopsis. I expect he'll regret the

synopsis. But there was the old excitement, even in that little extravagant flash—more than in criticism I think.

Happily—if that's the word—I get these electric shocks— Cables asking me to write. Chambrun offer £500 for a 9,000 word story. And I at once begin makir g up adventures—ten days of adventures—a man rowing with black knitted stockings on his arms. Do I ever write, even here, for my own eye? If not, for whose eye? An interesting question, rather.

LONDON. *Tuesday, October 12th*

Yes, we are back at Tavistock Square; and I've never writ- ten a word since September 27th. That shows how every morn- ing was crammed to the margin with *Three Guineas*. This is the first morning I write, because at 12, ten minutes ago, I wrote what I think is the last page of *Three Guineas*. Oh how violently I have been galloping through these mornings! It has pressed and spurted out of me. If that's any proof of virtue, like a physical volcano. And my brain feels cool and quiet after the expulsion. I've had it sizzling now since—well I was think- ing of it at Delphi I remember. And then I forced myself to put it into fiction first. No, the fiction came first. *The Years*. And how I held myself back, all through the terrible depres- sion, and refused, save for some frantic notes, to tap it until *The Years*—that awful burden—was off me. So that I have de- served this gallop. And taken time and thought too. But whether it is good or bad, how can I tell? I must now add the bibliog- raphy and notes. And have a week's respite.

Tuesday, October 19th

It came over me suddenly last night as I was reading *The Shooting Party*—the story that I'm to send to America, H. B.— that I saw the form of a new novel. It's to be first the state- ment of the theme: then the restatement: and so on: repeating the same story: singling out this and then that, until the central idea is stated.

This might also lend itself to my book of criticism. But how I don't know, being very jaded in the brain, try to discover. What happened was this: when I finished the *S.P.*, I thought, now that the woman has called a taxi; I will go on to meet, say, Christabel, at T. Square who tells the story again: or I will expatiate upon my own idea in telling the story; or I will find some other person at the *S.P.* whose life I will tell: but all the scenes must be controlled and radiate to a centre. I think this is a possible idea; and would admit of doing it in short bursts: could be a concentrated small book: could contain many varieties of mood. And possibly criticism. I must keep the idea at the back of my mind for a year or two, while I do Roger etc.

1938

Sunday, January 9th

Yes, I will force myself to begin this cursed year. For one thing I have "finished" the last chapter of Three Guineas and for the first time since I don't know when have stopped writing in the middle of the morning.

Friday, February 4th

A ten minutes spin here. L. gravely approves *Three Guineas.* Thinks it an extremely clear analysis. On the whole I'm content. One can't expect emotion, for as he says, it's not on a par with the novels. Yet I think it may have more practical value. But I'm much more indifferent, that's true: feel it a good piece of donkeywork, and don't think it affects me either way as the novels do.

Tuesday, April 11th

Anyhow, on April 1st I think, I started *Roger:* and with the help of his memoirs have covered the time till Clifton. Much of it donkey work; and I suppose to be rewritten. Still there is 20 pages put down, after being so long put off. And it is an immense solace to have this sober drudgery to take to instantly and so tide over the horrid anticlimax of *Three Guineas.* I didn't get so much praise from L. as I hoped. He had to swallow the notes at a gulp though. And I suspect I shall find the page proofs (due tomorrow) a chill bath of disillusionment. But I wanted—how violently—how persistently, pressingly, compulsorily I can't say—to write this book: and have a quiet composed feeling: as if I had said my say: take it or leave it: I'm quit of that: free for fresh adventures—at the age of 56. Last night I began making up again: summers night: a complete whole: that's my idea. *Roger* surrounds me: and then to

278

M.H. on Thursday, and that infernal bundle of proofs. Am I right though in thinking that it has some importance—*Three Guineas*—as a point of view: shows industry; fertility; and is, here and there, as "well written" (considering the technical problems—quotations, arguments etc.) as any of my rather skimble skamble works! I think there's more to it than to a *Room:* which, on rereading, seems to me a little egotistic, flaunting, sketchy: but has its brilliance—its speed. I'm suspicious of the vulgarity of the notes: of a certain insistence.

Tuesday, April 26th

We had our Easter at M.H.: but as for the sun, it never shone; was colder than Christmas; a grudging lead-coloured sky; razor wind; winter clothes; proofs; much acute despair; curbed however by the aid of divine philosophy; a joy in discovering Mandeville's *Bees* (this really a fruitful book; the very book I want). Then Q. rings up; to warn you: Have you had a letter from Pipsy? * Ottoline is dead. They told her P. might die, and the shock killed her: and he's asking you to write about her (with Mr. Wicks and Mr. Mussell exploring the attics for the new room). So I had to write; and the horrid little pellet screwed my brain; leaves it giddy. Yet in spite of that here am I sketching out a new book; only don't please impose that huge burden on me again, I implore. Let it be random and tentative: something I can blow of a morning, to relieve myself of *Roger:* don't, I implore, lay down a scheme; call in all the cosmic immensities; and force my tired and diffident brain to embrace another whole—all parts contributing—not yet awhile. But to amuse myself, let me note: Why not *Poyntzet Hall:* † a centre: all literature discussed in connection with real little incongruous living humour: and anything that comes into my head; but "I" rejected: "We" substituted: to whom at the end there shall be an invocation? "We" . . . the composed of many different things . . . we all life, all art, all waifs and strays—a rambling capricious but somehow unified whole—the present state of my mind? And English country;

* Philip Morrell.   † Became *Between the Acts.*

and a scenic old house—and a terrace where nursemaids walk
—and people passing—and a perpetual variety and change from
intensity to prose, and facts—and notes; and—but eno'! I must
read *Roger:* and go to Ott's memorial service, representing also
T. S. Eliot at his absurd command. 2:30 at Martin's in the
Fields.

Ottoline's burial service. Oh dear, oh dear the lack of intensity; the wailing and mumbling; the fumbling with bags;
the shuffling; the vast brown mass of respectable old South
Kensington ladies. And then the hymns; and the clergyman
with a bar of medals across his surplice; and the orange and
blue windows; and a toy Union Jack sticking from a cranny.
What all this had to do with Ottoline, or our feelings? Save
that the address was to the point: a critical study, written presumably by Philip and delivered, very resonantly, by Mr.
Speaight the actor: a sober, and secular speech, which made
one at least think of a human being, though the reference to
her beautiful voice caused one to think of that queer nasal
moan: however that too was to the good in deflating immensities. P.'s secretary buttonholed me and told me to sit high up.
The pew was blocked by a vast furred lady who said, "I'm
afraid I can't move"—as indeed seemed the fact. So I stationed
myself rather behind: near enough though to see the very well
set up back of P. in his thick coat; and his red ram's head
turned now and then looking along the ranks; also I pressed
his hand, simulated, I fear, more emotion than I felt when he
asked me, had I liked the address? and so slowly moved out on
to the steps—past Jack and Mary, Sturge Moores, Molly etc.:
Gertler having tears in his eyes; various household staffs: was
then pounced on and pinioned by Lady Oxford: who was hard
as whipcord; upright; a little vacant in the eye, in spite of
make up which made it shine. She said she had expostulated
with Ott. about the voice; Mere affectation. But a wonderful
woman. Tell me, though, why did her friends quarrel with her?
Pause. She was *exigeante,* Duncan volunteered at last. And so
Margot refused to ask further; and modulated into stories of
Symonds and Jowett, when I bantered her on her obituary.

Mine, of Ott. for *The Times,* has not appeared, nor do I much regret. . . .

Walked in Dulwich yesterday and lost my brooch by way of a freshener when confronted with the final proofs just today (April 26th) done: and to be sent this afternoon: a book I shall never look at again. But I now feel entirely free. Why? Have committed myself, am afraid of nothing. Can do anything I like. No longer famous, no longer on a pedestal: no longer hawked in by societies: on my own, forever. That's my feeling: a sense of expansion, like putting on slippers. Why this should be so, why I feel myself enfranchised till death, and quit of all humbug, when I daresay it's not a good book and will excite nothing but mild sneers; and how very inconsequent and egotistical V. W. is—why, why I can't analyse: being fluttered this morning.

The difficulty is that I get so absorbed in this fantastic *Pointz Hall* I can attend to *Roger.* So what am I to do? This however is only my first day of freedom: and I have been rendered self-conscious by a notice of *Three Guineas* on the front page of the new bloated *T.L.S.* Well it can't be helped; and I must cling to my "freedom"—that mysterious hand that was reached out to me about four years ago.

Thursday, May 5th

Pouring now; the drought broken; the worst spring on record; my pens diseased, even the new box; my eyes ache with *Roger* and I'm a little appalled at the prospect of the grind this book will be. I must somehow shorten and loosen; I *can't* (remember) stretch it to a long painstaking literal book: later I must generalise and let fly. But then, what about all the letters? How can one cut loose from facts, when there they are, contradicting my theories? A problem. But I'm convinced I can't, physically, strain after an R.A. portrait. What was I going to say with this defective nib?

Tuesday, May 17th

I'm pleased this morning because Lady Rhondda writes that she is profoundly excited and moved by *Three Guineas.* Theo

Bosanquet who has a review copy read her extracts. And she thinks it may have a great effect, and signs herself my grateful outsider. A good omen; because this shows that certain people will be stirred; will think; will discuss; it won't altogether be frittered away. Of course Lady R. is already partly on my side; but again as she's highly patriotic and citizenlike she might have been roused to object. It's on the cards that it will make more splash among the inkpots than I thought—feeling very dim and cold these last weeks, and indifferent too; and oblivious of the great excitement and intensity with which (certainly) I wrote. But as the whole of Europe may be in flames—it's on the cards. One more shot at a policeman and the Germans, Czechs, French will begin the old horror. The 4th of August may come next week. At the moment there is a lull. L. says K. Martin says we say (The P.M.) that we will fight this time. Hitler therefore is chewing his little bristling moustache. But the whole thing trembles: and my book may be like a moth dancing over a bonfire—consumed in less than one second.

Friday, May 20th

Time and again I have meant to write down my expectations, dreads and so on, waiting the publication on—I think June 2nd—of *Three Guineas:* but haven't, because what with living in the solid world of *Roger* and then (again this morning) in the airy world of *Poyntz Hall* I feel extremely little. And don't want to rouse feeling. What I'm afraid of is the taunt charm and emptiness. The book I wrote with such violent feeling to relieve that immense pressure will not dimple the surface. That is my fear. Also I'm uneasy at taking this role in the public eye—afraid of autobiography in public. But the fears are entirely outbalanced (this is honest) by the immense relief and peace I have gained and enjoy this moment. Now I am quit of that poison and excitement. Nor is that all. For having spat it out, my mind is made up. I need never recur or repeat. I am an outsider. I can take my way: experiment with my own imagination in my own way. The pack may howl, but it shall never catch me. And even if the pack—reviewers, friends, enemies—pays me no attention or sneers, still I'm free. This is the actual result of that spiritual conversion (I can't

bother to get the right words) in the autumn of 1933 or 4—
when I rushed through London buying, I remember, a great
magnifying glass, from sheer ecstasy, near Blackfriars: when I
gave the man who played the harp half a crown for talking to
me about his life in the tube station. The omens are mixed:
L. is less excited than I hoped: Nessa highly ambiguous: Miss
Hepworth and Mrs. Nicholls say, "Women owe a great deal to
Mrs. Woolf" and I have promised Pippa to supply books. Now
for R.'s letters. Monk's House at the moment windy and cold.

Friday, May 27th

It's odd to be working at half cock after all those months of
high pressure. The result is half an hour every day to write
here. *Roger* I'm retyping: and shall then sketch Walpole. I
have just been signing in bright green ink those circulars. But
I will not expatiate on the dreariness of doing things one ought
to do. A letter, grateful, from Bruce Richmond, ending my 30
years connection with him—the *Lit Sup*. How pleased I used
to be when L. called me "You're wanted by the Major Journal!" and I ran down to the telephone to take my almost weekly
orders at Hogarth House! I learnt a lot of my craft writing for
him: how to compress; how to enliven; and also was made to
read with a pen and notebook, seriously. I am now waiting for
today week—when that's over, my swell will subside. And can't
I prophesy? On the whole I shall get more pain than pleasure;
I shall mind the sneers more than I shall enjoy Lady Rhondda's
enthusiasm. There'll be many sneers—some very angry letters.
Some silences. And then—three weeks yesterday—we shall be
off. And by July 7th when we come back—or sooner, for we
dread too many hotels—it will be over, almost entirely; and
then for two years I think I shall publish nothing, save American articles. And this week of waiting is the worst, and it's not
very bad—nothing in the least comparable to the horror of *The
Years*: (that deadened into indifference, so sure was I of failure).

Tuesday, May 31st

A letter from Pippa. She is enthusiastic. So this is the last
load off my mind—which weighed it rather heavy, for I felt if
I had written all that, if it was not to her liking I should have

to brace myself pretty severely in my own private esteem. But she says it's the very thing for which they have panted: and the poison is now drawn. Now I can face the music, or donkeys bray or geeses cackle of the Reviews so indifferently that (truthfully) I find myself forgetting that they'll all be out this weekend. Never have I faced review day so composedly. Also I don't much mind my Cambridge friends either. Maynard may have a gibe; but what care I?

RODMELL. *Friday, June 3rd*

This is the coming out day of *Three Guineas.* And the *Lit. Sup.* has two columns and a leader; and the *Referee* a great black bar Woman declares sex war, or some such caption. And it makes so much less difference than any other cackle on coming out day that I've written quietly at *Poyntz Hall:* haven't even troubled to read R. Lynd, nor look at the Ref. nor read through *The Times* article. It's true I have a sense of quiet and relief. But no wish to read reviews, or hear opinions.

I wonder why this is? Because it's a fact I want to communicate rather than a poem? I daresay something of the kind. Mercifully we have 50 miles of felt between ourselves and the din. It is sunny, warm, dry and like a June day but will rain later. Oh it pleased me that the *Lit. Sup.* says I'm the most brilliant pamphleteer in England. Also that this book may mark an epoch if taken seriously. Also that the *Listener* says I am scrupulously fair, and puritanically deny myself flights. But that's about all.

Anyhow that's the end of six years floundering, striving, much agony, some ecstasy: lumping the *Years* and *Three Guineas* together as one book—as indeed they are. And now I can be off again, as indeed I long to be. Oh to be private, alone, submerged.

Sunday, June 5th

This is the mildest childbirth I have ever had. Compare it with *The Years!* I wake knowing the yap will begin and never bother my head. Yesterday I had *Time and Tide,* and various London obscurities: today *Observer:* Selincourt. A terrible indictment. *Sunday Times, New Statesman* and *Spectator*, reserved for next week presumably. So the temperature remains steady. I foretell a great many letters on Tuesday night: some anonymous and abusive. But I have already gained my point: I'm taken seriously, not dismissed as a charming prattler as I feared. *The Times* yesterday had a paragraph headed "Mrs. Woolf's call to women" a serious challenge that must be answered by all thinkers—or something like that: prefacing the *Lit. Sup.* advt: unknown before I think; and must be some serious intention behind it.

BALDOCK. *Thursday, June 16th*
Stop to light a pipe on the Icknield Way, a scrubby street of yellow villas. Now St. James Deeping. After Croyland, a magnificent moulded Church. Now very hot: flat; an old gent. fishing. Spread out and exposed. River above road level. On now to Gainsborough. Lunch at Peterborough: factory chimneys. Railway gate opened; off again. Gainsborough. A red Venetian palace rising among bungalows: in a square of unkempt grass. Long windows, leaning walls. A maze of little lanes. A strange forgotten town. Sunday at Housesteads. Thorn trees: sheep. The wall and white headed boys in front. Miles and miles of lavender campagna. One thread coloured frail road crossing the vast uncultivated lonely land. Today all cloud and blue and wind. The wall is a wave with a sharp crest, as of a wave drawn up to break. Then flat. Bogs under the crest. Waiting now for the rain to stop, for it blew and rained that day on the wall. Now a few miles from Corbridge waiting in the middle of the moor. Very black. Larks singing. Lunch deferred. A party of ninety lunching at the Inn at Piercebridge. A sense of local life eighteenth century inn diners to celebrate some sport. So on to a Manse in a garden: a very solid private house that takes in residents. Hot ham and fruit, but real cream, looking over an ugly range. The country early today was fen Wash country. Then the Pennines. These are shrouded in a heat mist. Larks singing. L. now looking for water for Sally * (but this should precede the wall). Sunday. Sitting by the road under the Roman

* A spaniel.

wall while L. cleans sparking plugs. And I have been reading translations of Greek verse and thinking idly. When one reads the mind is like an aeroplane propeller invisibly quick and unconscious—a state seldom achieved. Not a bad Oxford introduction, trying to be in touch, up to date: scholarly but Oxford. Cows moving to the top of the hill by some simultaneous sympathy. One draws the others. Wind rocks the car. Too windy to climb up and look at the lake. Reason why the hills are still Roman—the landscape immortal . . . what they saw I see. The wind, the June wind, the water, and snow. Sheep bedded in the long turf like pearls. No shade, no shelter. Romans looking over the border. Now nothing comes.

Tuesday. Now in Midlothian. Stopping for petrol. On the way to Stirling. Scotch mist driven across the trees. Normal Scots weather. Great hills. Ugly puritanical houses. The Hydro built 90 years ago. A woman called and said she had seen Mrs. Woolf walking in Melrose on Saturday. Second sight as I was not there. Galashiels a manufacturing town. Hideous. Fragments of talk overheard at the Hydro Melrose. Soft voiced old Scotch ladies sitting in their accredited places by the fire under the window. "I was wondering why you walked about with an umbrella." One who is stitching, "I wonder if I should wash it and begin again. I'm working on a dirty ground." Here I interpose: We stopped at Dryburgh to see Scott grave. It is under the broken palanquin of a ruined chapel. Just enough roof to cover it. And there he lies—Sir Walter Scott, Baronet. In a caddy made of chocolate blancmange with these words cut large and plain on the lid. As Dame Charlotte who is buried beside him is covered with the same chocolate slab it must have been his taste. And there's something fitting in it. For the Abbey is impressive and the river running at the bottom of the field. And all the old Scots ruins standing round him. I picked a white syringa in memory but lost it. An airy place but Scott is much pressed together. The col. by his side and Lockhart his son in law at his feet. Then there's Haig's stuck about with dark red poppies. But the old ladies are discussing Dr. John Brown whose brother was a doctor in Melrose. Soon one's head would ache and one's senses fuddle. One would eat too many cakes at tea and there's a huge dinner at 7. "I think he's very nice—her husband. She's got a personality of her own. A very nice cir-r-cle. Where do they live? Retired to Perthshire. . . . I'm three stitches out . . . Miss Peace came along to the reading room with her friend and wanted a fire. Couldn't she have rung the bell or something? Out you come! (unpicking the knitting). There so much opened up now. Two years ago was the Centenary (of Dryburgh?). I went to the meeting. There was a service—most interesting. All the Ministers. Five on the platform. Possibly the Moderator. At any rate it was very nice and it was a beautiful day and the place was very full. The birds joined in the music. Alan Haig's birthday. There was a service at Dryburgh. I like D. I've not been to Jedburgh—awfully pretty." No, I don't think I can write it all out. The old creatures are sitting on a sofa not much older than I am I daresay. Yes, they're about 65. "Edinburgh's nice—I like it. We have to go away before we appreciate it. You have to go away from your birthplace. Then when you go back everything changed. A year does it—two years do it. I should leave it (of the work) and see the effect afterwards. What church d'you go to? Church of Scotland—not to St. Giles. It used to be the Tron. We go to St. Giles. It was St. George's parish—my husband was an elder in St. George's parish Charlotte Square. D'you like Waugh? I like him in a way I don't *hear* him, and it's a common complaint. He gives very hard sermons—you can't take anything away. The choir's beautiful. I can't get a sitting from which you can hear. I feel it infra dig rushing with the crowd. The crowd hasn't reached—I've just got to sit still—I'm having a service—I hear the prayers, the young men the music. It was pretty well where they come in from the Thistle chapel. They passed me bang. I rose and moved along. There are some seats the people never come to, and often the best seats. I like St. Giles, a lovely old place. The old lady whose seat I had told me the church was all renovated. Chambers did it, and when it came to the opening not a seat retained for the Chambers family. Badly arranged. Someone provided seats for them. A stupid thing. Always some higher church alteration. I like the episcopal. If it be episcopal let it

be: if Church of Scotland, let it be Church of Scotland. Dr.
Waugh's brother is at Dundee. He would like Roseneath. Someone said that the minister at Roseneath is delicate."

Wind rages: trees leafless: bannocks and a blue pound note
the only changes. Glencoe. Menaching. Leaf green hills, islands
floating. A moving string of cars; no inhabitants, only tourists
. . . Ben Nevis with stripes of snow. The sea. Little boats: feeling of Greece and Cornwall. Yellow flags and great foxgloves:
no farms, villages or cottages: a dead land over-run with insects. An old man who could not get up from his chair. Two
other ladies, her legs overflowing her shoes. All dress for dinner, and sit in the drawing room. This was the good inn at
Crianlarich. Lake with hanging stalactites green trees in the
middle. Bowl of the hills. Hills with velvet leaf green. The
Bannington of Eaton Place. She had found winter green for
her father-in-law, a botanist. Sky light at 11. Bad review of
Three Guineas by G. M. Young. Pain lasted ten minutes: over
then. Loch Ness swallowed Mrs. Hambro. She was wearing
pearls.

And then, sick of copying, I tore the rest of it up—a lesson,
next journey, not to make endless pencil notes that need copying. Some too I regret. Some Boswell experiments in inns. Also
the woman whose grandmother worked for the Wordsworths
and remembered him as an old man in a cloak with a red lining muttering poetry. Sometimes he would pat the children on
the head but never spoke to them. On the other hand, H.
Coleridge was always drinking at the pub with the men.

Thursday, July 7th

Oh the appalling grind of getting back to *Roger*, after these
violent oscillations, *Three Guineas* and *P.H.* How can I concentrate upon minute facts in letters? This morning I have
forced myself back to Failand in 1888. But Jumbo * last night
threw cold water on the whole idea of biography of those who
have no lives. Roger had, she says, no life that can be written.
I daresay this is true. And here am I sweating over minute
facts. It's all too minute and tied down—documented. Is it to

* Marjorie Strachey.

be done on this scale? Is he interesting to other people in that light? I think I will go on doggedly till I meet him myself—1909—and then attempt something more fictitious. But must plod on through all these letters till then. I think contrast the two all the time. My view: his—and other people's. And then his books.

Saturday, August 7th

Rather enjoy doing *P.H.* That's something, for it won't please anyone, if anyone should ever read it. Ann Watkins, by the way, says the *Atlantic* readers haven't read enough of Walpole to understand my article. Refused.

Wednesday, August 17th

No I won't go on doing *Roger*—abstracting with blood and sweat from the old Articles—right up to lunch. I will steal 25 minutes. In fact I've been getting absorbed in *Roger*. Didn't I say I wouldn't? Didn't L. say there's no hurry? Except that I'm 56; and think that Gibbon then allowed himself 12 years, and died instantly. Still why always chafe and urge and strain at the leash? What I want is a season of calm weather. Contemplation. I get this sometimes about 3 A.M. when I always wake, open my window and look at the sky over the apple trees. A tearing wind last night. Every sort of scenic effect—a prodigious toppling and clearing and massing, after the sunset that was so amazing L. made me come and look out of the bathroom window—a flurry of red clouds; hard; a water colour mass of purple and black, soft as a water ice; then hard slices of intense green stone; blue stone and a ripple of crimson light. No: that won't convey it: and then there were the trees in the garden; and the reflected light: our hot pokers burning on the edge of the steep. So, at supper, we discussed our generation: and the prospects of war. Hitler has his million men now under arms. Is it only summer manœuvres or—? Harold broadcasting in his man of the world manner hints it may be war. That is the complete ruin not only of civilisation in Europe, but of our last lap. Quentin conscripted etc. One ceases to think about it —that's all. Goes on discussing the new room, new chair, new

books. What else can a gnat on a blade of grass do? And I
would like to write *P.H.:* and other things.

Sunday, August 28th

The character of this summer is extreme drought. Brooks
dry. Not a mushroom yet. Sunday is the devil's own day at
M.H.: dogs, children, bells . . . there they go for evensong.
I can't settle anywhere. Beaten after three hard fights at bowls.
Bowls is our mania. Reading rather scamped. I'm strung into a
ball with *Roger:* got him, very stiffly, to the verge of America.
I shall take a dive into fiction: then compose the chapter that
leads to the change. But is it readable—and Lord to think of
the further compressing and leavening. Ding dong bell . . .
ding dong—why did we settle in a village? And how deliberately we are digging ourselves in! And at any moment the
guns may go off and explode us. L. is very black. Hitler has his
hounds only very lightly held. A single step—in Czechoslovakia
—like the Austrian Archduke in 1914—and again it's 1914.
Ding dong ding dong. People all strolling up and down the
fields. A grey close evening.

Thursday, September 1st

A very fine clear September day. Sybil threatens to dine,
but may put us off—should a Cabinet Minister crop up. Politics
marking time. A violent attack on *Three Guineas* in *Scrutiny*
by Q. Leavis. I don't think it gave me an entire single thrill of
horror. And I didn't read it through. A symbol though of what
wiggings are to come. But I read enough to see that it was all
personal—about Queenie's own grievances and retorts to my
snubs. Why I don't care more for praise or wigging I don't
know. Yet it's true. A slight distaste for my biography of Roger
this morning: too detailed and flat. But I must take it up tomorrow, and lay aside *P.H.* I fear. Quentin over to finish his
table. We have settled to keep the roof Cornish cream colour.
I found a new walk down Telscombe Valley to the river yesterday.

Oh Queenie was at once cancelled by a letter from Jane

Walker—a thousand thanks . . . *Three Guineas* ought to be in the hands of every English speaking man and woman etc.

Monday, September 5th

It's odd to be sitting here, looking up little facts about Roger and the M.M. in New York, with a sparrow tapping on my roof this fine September morning when it may be 3rd August 1914 . . . What would war mean? Darkness, strain: I suppose conceivably death. And all the horror of friends: and Quentin: . . . All that lies over the water in the brain of that ridiculous little man. Why ridiculous? Because none of it fits: encloses no reality. Death and war and darkness representing nothing that any human being from the pork butcher to the Prime Minister cares one straw about. Not liberty, not life. Merely a housemaid's dream, and we woke from that dream and had the Cenotaph to remind us of the fruits. Well, I can't spread my mind wide enough to take it in, intelligibly. If it were real, one could make something of it. But as it is it merely grumbles, in an inarticulate way, behind reality. We may hear his mad voice vociferating tonight. Nuremberg rally begun: but it goes on for another week. And what will be happening this time 10 days? Suppose we skim across, still at any moment any accident may suddenly bring out the uproar. But this time everyone's agog. That's the difference. And as we're all equally in the dark we can't cluster and group: we are beginning to feel the herd impulse: everyone asks everyone Any news? What d'you think? The only answer is Wait and see.

Old Mr. Thompsett meanwhile after driving horses to the brooks and about the fields for 74 years had died in the hospital. And L. is to read his will on Wednesday.

Saturday, September 10th

I don't feel that the crisis is real—not so real as Roger in 1910 at Gordon Square, about which I've just been writing; and now switch off with some difficulty to use the last 20 minutes that are over before lunch. Of course we may be at war this time next week. The papers each in turn warn Hitler in the same set, grim but composed words, dictated by the Government presumably, that if he forces us we shall fight. They are all equally calm and good tempered. Nothing is to be said to provoke. Every allowance is to be made. In fact we are simply marking time as calmly as possible until Monday or Tuesday, when the oracle will speak. And we mean him to know what we think. The only doubt is whether what we say reaches his own much cumbered long ears. (I'm thinking of Roger not of Hitler—how I bless Roger and wish I could tell him so, for giving me himself to think of—what a help he remains in this welter of unreality.) All these grim men appear to me like grown ups staring incredulously at a child's sand castle which for some inexplicable reason has become a real vast castle, needing gunpowder and dynamite to destroy it. Nobody in their senses can believe in it. Yet nobody must tell the truth. So one forgets. Meanwhile the aeroplanes are on the prowl, crossing the downs. Every preparation is made. Sirens will hoot in a particular way when there's the first hint of a raid. L. and I no longer talk about it. Much better to play bowls and pick dahlias. They're blazing in the sitting room, orange against the black last night. Our balcony is now up.

Tuesday, September 20th

Since I'm too stale to work—rather headachy—I may as well write a sketch roughly of the next chapter.* (I've been rather absorbed in *P.H.,* hence headache. Note: fiction is far more a strain than biography—that's the excitement.)

Suppose I make a break after H.'s † death (madness). A separate paragraph quoting what R. himself said. Then a break. Then begin definitely with the first meeting. That is the first impression: a man of the world, not professor or Bohemian. Then give facts in his letters to his mother. Then back to the second meeting. Pictures: talk about art: I look out of window. His persuasiveness—a certain density—wished to persuade you to like what he liked. Eagerness, absorption, stir—a kind of vibration like a hawkmoth round him. Or shall I make a scene here—at Ott.'s? Then Cple. ‡ Driving out: getting things in: his deftness in combining. Then quote the letters to R.

* *Roger Fry.*   † Helen Fry.   ‡ Constantinople.

The first 1910 show.
The ridicule. Quote W. Blunt.
Effect on R. Another close-up.
The letter to MacColl. His own personal liberation.
Excitement. Found his method (but this wasn't lasting. His letters to V. show that he was swayed too much by her.)
Love. How to say that he never was in love?
Give the pre-war atmosphere. Ott. Duncan. France.
Letter to Bridges about beauty and sensuality. His exactingness. Logic.

Thursday, September 22nd

By mistake I wrote some pages of *Roger* here; a proof, if proof is needed, as I'm in the habit of saying, that my books are in a muddle. Yes, at this moment, there are packets of letters to V. B. 1910-1916—packets of testimonials for the Oxford Slade—endless folders, each containing different letters, press cuttings and extracts from books. In between come my own, now numerous, semiofficial *Three Guineas* letters (now sold 7,017 . . .) No sober silent weeks of work alone all day as we'd planned, when the Bells went. I suppose one enjoys it. Yet I was just getting into the old, very old, rhythm of regular reading, first this book then that: *Roger* all the morning; walk from 2 to 4; bowls 5 to 6:30; then Madame de Sévigné; get dinner 7:30; read *Roger;* listen to music; bind Eddie's *Candide;* read Siegfried Sassoon; and so bed at 11:30 or so. A very good rhythm; but I can only manage it for a few days it seems. Next week all broken.

Thursday, October 6th

Another 10 minutes. I'm taking a frisk at *P.H.* at which I can only write for one hour. Like the *Waves.* I enjoy it intensely: head screwed up over *Roger.* A violent storm two days ago. No walking. Apples down. Electric light cut off. We used the four 6d. candlesticks bought at Woolworths. Dinner cooked, and smoked, on dining room fire. Men now staining boards. The room will be done actually this week. Politics now a mere "I told you so . . . You did. I didn't." I shall cease to read the papers. Sink at last into contemplation. Peace for our lifetime: why not try to believe it? Can't make a push and go to S. Remy. Want to: don't want to. Long for change: love reading Sévigné even by candlelight. Long for London and lights; long for vintage; long for complete solitude. All this discussed with L. walking to Piddinghoe yesterday.

Friday, October 14th

Two things I mean to do when the long dark evenings come: to write, on the spur of the moment, as now, lots of little poems to go into *P.H.*: as they may come in handy: to collect, even bind together, my innumerable *T.L.S.* notes: to consider them as material for some kind of critical book: quotations? comments? ranging all through English literature as I've read it and noted it during the past 20 years.

Tuesday, November 1st

Max * like a Cheshire cat. Orbicular. Jowled. Blue eyed. Eyes grow vague. Something like Bruce Richmond—all curves. What he said was, I've never been in a group. No, not even as a young man. It was a serious fault. When you're a young man you ought to think There's only one right way. And I thought This is very profound, but you mayn't realise it. "It takes all sorts to make a world." I was outside all the groups. Now dear Roger Fry who liked me, was a born leader. No one so "illuminated." He looked it. Never saw anyone look it so much. I heard him lecture, on the Aesthetics of Art. I was disappointed. He kept on turning the page—turning the page . . . Hampstead hasn't yet been spoilt. I stayed at Jack Straw's Castle some years ago. My wife had been having influenza. And the barmaid, looking over her shoulder, said—my wife had had influenza twice—"Quite a greedy one aren't you?" Now that's immortal. There's all the race of barmaids in that. I suppose I've been ten times into public houses. George Moore never used his eyes. He never knew what men and women think. He got it all out of books. Ah I was afraid you would remind me of *Ave atque Vale*. Yes; that's beautiful. Yes, it's true he used his eyes

* Max Beerbohm.

then. Otherwise it's like a lovely lake, with no fish in it. *The Brook Kerith* . . . Coulson Kernahan? (I told how C. K. stopped me in Hastings. Are you Edith Sitwell? No, Mrs. W. And you? Coulson Kernahan.) At this Max gobbled. Instantly said he had known him in Yellow Book days. He wrote *God and the Ant*. Sold 12 million copies. And a book of reminiscences. How I visited Lord Roberts . . . The great man rose from his chair. His eyes—were they hazel? were they blue? were they brown—no they were just soldier's eyes. And he wrote, Celebrities I have not met, Max Beerbohm.

About his own writing: dear Lytton Strachey said to me: first I write one sentence: then I write another. That's how I write. And so I go on. But I have a feeling writing ought to be like running through a field. That's your way. Now how do you go down to your room, after breakfast—what do you feel? I used to look at the clock and say oh dear me, it's time I began my article . . . No, I'll read the paper first. I never wanted to write. But I used to come home from a dinner party and take my brush and draw caricature after caricature. They seemed to bubble up from here . . . he pressed his stomach. That was a kind of inspiration, I suppose. What you said in your beautiful essay about me and Charles Lamb was quite true. He was crazy: he had the gift: genius. I'm too like Jack Horner. I pull out my plum. It's too rounded, too perfect . . . I have a public of about 1500. Oh I'm famous, largely thanks to you, and people of importance at the top like you. I often read over my own work. And I have a habit of reading it through the eyes of people I respect. I often read it as Virginia Woolf would read it—picking out the kind of things you would like. You never do that? Oh you should try it.

Isherwood and I met on the doorstep. He is a slip of a wild boy: with quicksilver eyes: nipped: jockeylike. That young man, said W. Maugham, "holds the future of the English novel in his hands." Very enthusiastic. In spite of Max's brilliance, and idiosyncrasy, which he completely realises, and does not overstep, this was a surface evening; as I proved, because I found I could not smoke the cigar which I had brought. That was on the deeper level. All kept to the same surface level by

Sybil's hostesscraft. Stories, compliments. The house: its shell like whites and silvers and greens: its panelling: its old furniture.

Wednesday, November 16th

There are very few mountain summit moments. I mean looking out at peace from a height. I made this reflection going upstairs. That is symbolical. I'm "going upstairs" now, when I write *Biography*. Shall I have a moment on top? Or when I've done Roger? Or tonight, in bed, between 2 and 3? They come spasmodically. Often when I was so miserable about *The Years.*

Viola Tree died last night, of pleurisy: two years younger than I am.

I remember the quality of her skin: like an apricot; a few amber coloured hairs. Eyes blistered with paint underneath. A huge Goddess woman, who was also an old drudge; a big boned striding figure; much got up, of late. Last time I saw her at the Gargoyle Cocktail; when she was in her abundant expansive mood. I never reached any other; yet always liked her. Met her perhaps once a year, about her books. She dined here the night her *Castles in Spain* came out. And I went to tea in Woburn Square, and the butter was wrapped in a newspaper. And there was an Italian double bed in the drawing room. She was instinctive; and had the charm of good actress manners; and their Bohemianism and sentimentality. But I think was a sterling spontaneous mother and daughter; not ambitious; a great hand at life; I suppose harassed for money; and extravagant; and very bold; and courageous—a maker of picturesque surroundings. So strong and large that she should have lived to be 80; yet no doubt undermined that castle, with late hours: I don't know. She could transmit something into words. Her daughter Virginia to be married this week. And think of Viola lying dead. How out of place—unnecessary.

Tuesday, November 22nd

I meant to write Reflections on my position as a writer. I don't want to read Dante; have ten minutes over from rehashing "Lappin and Lapinova," a story written I think at Asheham 20 years ago or more; when I was writing *Night and Day* perhaps.

That's a long stretch. And apparently I've been exalted to a very high position, say about 10 years ago: then was decapitated by W. Lewis, and Miss Stein; am now I think—let me see—out of date, of course; not a patch, with the young, on Morgan: * Yet wrote *The Waves;* yet am unlikely to write anything good again; am a secondrate and likely, I think, to be discarded altogether. I think that's my public reputation at the moment. It is based largely on C. Connolly's cocktail criticism: a sheaf of feathers in the wind. How much do I mind? Less than I expected. But then of course; it's all less than I realised. I mean, I never thought I was so famous; so don't feel the decapitation. Yet it's true that after *The Waves,* or *Flush, Scrutiny* I think found me out. W. L. attacked me. I was aware of an active opposition. Yes I used to be praised by the young and attacked by the elderly. *Three Guineas* has queered the pitch. For the G. M. Youngs and the Scrutineers both attack that. And my own friends have sent me to Coventry over it. So my position is ambiguous. Undoubtedly Morgan's reputation is much higher than my own. So is Tom's.† Well? In a way it is a relief. I'm fundamentally, I think, an outsider. I do my best work and feel most braced with my back to the wall. It's an odd feeling though, writing against the current: difficult entirely to disregard the current. Yet of course I shall. And it remains to be seen if there's anything in *P.H.* In any case I have my critical brain to fall back on.

Monday, December 19th

I will spend the last morning—for tomorrow will be an odious scramble—in summing up the year True, there are 10 days or so to run: but the liberty of this book allows these—I was going to say liberties, but my meticulous conscience bids me look for another word. That raises some questions: but I leave them; questions about my concern with the art of writing. On

* E. M. Forster.　　† T. S. Eliot.

the whole the art becomes absorbing—more? no, I think it's been absorbing ever since I was a little creature, scribbling a story in the manner of Hawthorne on the green plush sofa in the drawing room at St. Ives while the grown ups dined. The last dinner of the year was to Tom.

This year I have worked at *Three Guineas:* and begun, about April 1st. *Roger:* whom I have brought to the year 1919. I have also written Walpole; Lappin Lapinova; and *The Art of Biography.* The reception of *Three Guineas* has been interesting, unexpected—only I'm not sure what I expected. 8,000 sold. Not one of my friends has mentioned it. My wide circle has widened—but I'm altogether in the dark as to the true merits of the book. Is it . . . ? No, I won't even formulate qualities; for, it's true, no one has yet summed it up. Much less unanimity than about *Room of One's Own.* A suspended judgment upon that work then seems fittest. I've written too 120 pages of *Pointz Hall.* I think of making it a 220 page book. A medley. I rush to it for relief after a long pressure of Fry facts. But I think I see a whole somewhere—it was simply seized, one day, about April, as a dangling thread: no notion what page came next. And then they came. To be written for pleasure.

1939

So I take a new nib, after bringing *Roger* to the verge of
Josette with the old one, and spend my last five minutes, this
very fine January morning, in writing the first page of the New
Year. Last five minutes before lunch—how inaugurate this important volume in that time, with this brain? A brain still
running in the rut of the last sentence. Which last sentence
will be rewritten a dozen times, too. So the dominant theme
is work: *Roger:* the others the usual Rodmell themes. That is,
I've let the frost go too far away. We came down 14 or 15 days
ago and found all pipes frozen. There was snow for five days—
bitter cold: wind. We staggered for one hour through the bliz-
zard. Chains were on our wheels. We ground over to Charleston
and Tilton on Christmas day. Then, two days later, woke to
find green grass everywhere. The long spikes of ice that hung
down the kitchen window had drops on their noses. They
melted. The pipes thawed. Now it's a June morning with an
east wind. And time's up. But the book's begun anyhow. And
perhaps I shall get a clearer head and say 10 minutes tomorrow.

Now that I have brought my brain to the state of an old
washerwoman's flannel over *Roger*—Lord the Josette chapter
—and it's all too detailed, too tied down—I must expand, first
on this irresponsible page and then, for four days I swear, before we go back on Sunday, in fiction. Though I've ground
out most wish to write, even fiction. Rodmell is a grind on the
brain: in winter especially. I write three solid hours: walk two:
then we read, with intervals for cooking dinner, music, news,
till 11:30. I've thus read ever so many packets of R.'s letters;
and some Sévigné; Chaucer—and some nonsense books.

Thursday, January 18th

It is undoubtedly a great freshener to have my story taken by Harpers. I heard this morning. A beautiful story, enchanted to have it. 600 dollars made then. But the encouragement, I must note, by way of supplying my theories that one should do without encouragement, is a warmer, a reviver. I can't deny it. I was, perhaps partly on that account, in full flood this morning with *P.H.* I think I have got at a more direct method of summarising relations; and then the poems (in meter) ran off the prose lyric vein, which, as I agree with Roger, I overdo. That was, by the way, the best criticism I've had for a long time: that I poetise my inanimate scenes, stress my personality; don't let the meaning emerge from the matière.

Tuesday, February 28th

It is unfortunate for truth's sake that I never write here except when jangled with talk. I only record the dumps and the dismals and them very barely. A holiday from *Roger*. And one day's happiness with *P.H.* Then too many parcels; books coming out; and a head numb at the back. As usual, when I'm prone, all the gnats settle. The usual ones. I needn't specify. I have to "speak" to polytechnics; and engagements multiply. Innumerable refugees to add to the tangle. There—I've recorded them when I said I wouldn't.

Saturday, March 11th

Yesterday, that is Friday 10th, I set the last word to the first sketch of *Roger*. And now I have to begin—well not even to begin, but to revise and revise. A terrible grind to come: and innumerable doubts, of myself as biographer: of the possibility of doing it at all: all the same I've carried through to the end; and may allow myself one moment's mild gratification. There are the facts more or less extracted. And I've no time to go into all the innumerable horrors. There may be a flick of life in it—or is it all dust and ashes?

Tuesday, April 11th

I am reading Dickens; by way of a refresher. How he lives: not writes: both a virtue and a fault. Like seeing something emerge; without containing mind. Yet the accuracy and even sometimes the penetration—into Miss Squeers and Miss Price and the farmer for example—remarkable. I can't dip my critical mind, even if I try to. Then I'm reading Sévigné, professionally, for that quick amalgamation of books that I intend. In future, I'm to write quick, intense, short books, and never be tied down. This is the way to keep off the settling down and refrigeration of old age. And to float all preconceived theories. For more and more I doubt if enough is known to sketch even probable lines, all too emphatic and conventional. Maurice, the last of the Ll. Davies brothers, is dead; and Margaret lives —lives too carefully of life, I used to feel Why drag on, always measuring and testing one's little bit of strength and setting it easy tasks so as to accumulate years? Also I'm reading Rochefoucauld. That's the real point of my little brown book—that it makes me read—with a pen—following the scent; and read the good books: not the slither of MSS and the stridency of the young chawking—the word expresses callow bills agape and chattering—for sympathy. Chaucer I take at need. So if I had any time—but perhaps next week will be more solitudinous—I should, if it weren't for the war—glide my way up and up into that exciting layer so rarely lived in: where my mind works so quick it seems asleep; like the aeroplane propellers. But I must retype the last Clifton passage; and so be quit for tomorrow and clear the decks for Cambridge. Rather good, I expect it is: condensed and moulded.

Thursday, April 13th

Two days of influenza after that, mild but sucking one's head as usual, so I'm out here this morning only to drone my way through a few Roger letters. I finished my first 40 pages— childhood etc.—well under the week; but then they were largely autobiography; Now politics impend. Chamberlain's statement in the House today. War I suppose not tomorrow, but nearer.

I read about 100 pages of Dickens yesterday, and see something vague about the drama and fiction; how the emphasis, the caricature of these innumerable scenes, forever forming character, descend from the stage. Literature—that is the shading, suggesting, as of Henry James, hardly used. All bold and

coloured. Rather monotonous; yet so abundant, so creative: yes,
but not *highly* creative: not suggestive. Everything laid on the
table. Nothing to engender in solitude. That's why it's so rapid
and attractive. Nothing to make one put the book down and
think. But these are influenza musings; and I'm so muddled
I shall take Sir Edward into the house and extract him over the
fire.

Saturday, April 15th

I've done rather well at *Roger* considering: I don't think I
shall take two weeks over each chapter. And it's rather amusing—dealing drastically with this year's drudgery. I think I
see how it shapes: and my compiling method was a good one.
Perhaps it's too like a novel. I don't bother. No letters; no
news; and my head too staked for reading. L. galloping through
his book. I should like a holiday—a few days in France—or a
run through the Cotswolds. But considering how many things
I have that I like—What's odd—(I'm always beginning like this)
is the severance that war seems to bring: everything becomes
meaningless: can't plan: then there comes too the community
feeling: all England thinking the same thing—this horror of
war—at the same moment. Never felt it so strong before. Then
the lull and one lapses again into private separation.

But I must order macaroni from London.

Wednesday, April 26th

I've done a quarter—100 pages of *Roger* which I shall have
by tomorrow. As there are 400 pages, and one hundred takes
three weeks (oh but I was interrupted)—it will take nine weeks
to finish. Yes, I ought to have finished it by the end of July.
Only we may go away. Say August. And have it all typed in
September . . . Well—then it will be out this time next year.
And I shall be free in August—What a grind it is; and I suppose of little interest except to six or seven people. And I shall
be abused.

Thursday, June 29th

The grind of doing *Roger* and P I P makes my head spin
and I let it reel itself off for 10 minutes here. I wonder why;

and if I shall ever read this again. Perhaps if I go on with my memoirs, also a relief from *R.*, I shall make use of it. A dismal day yesterday: shoe hunting in Fortnums. A sale, but only of the unsaleable. And the atmosphere, British upper classes; all tight and red nailed; myself a figure of fun—whips my skin: I fidget: but recoup myself walking in the rain through the Parks. Come home and try to concentrate on Pascal. I can't. Still it's the only way of tuning up, and I get a calm, if not understanding. These pin points of theology need a grasp beyond me. Still I see Lytton's point—my dear old serpent. What a dream life is to be sure—that he should be dead, and I reading him: and trying to make out that we indented ourselves in the world; whereas I sometimes feel it's been an illusion— gone so fast; lived so quickly; and nothing to show for it, save these little books. But that makes me dig my feet in and squeeze the moment. So after dinner I walked to the Clinic with L.; waited outside with Sally tugging; watched the evening sight: oh and the purple grey clouds above Regents Park with the violet and yellow sky signs made me leap with pleasure.

Monday, August 7th

I am now going to make the rash and bold experiment of breaking off, from condensing *Vision and Design;* to write here for 10 minutes instead of revising, as I ought, my morning's grind.

Oh yes, I thought of several things to write about. Not exactly diary. Reflections. That's the fashionable dodge. Peter Lucas and Gide both at it. Neither can settle to creative art. (I think, sans *Roger,* I could.) It's the comment—the daily interjection—that comes handy in times like these. I too feel it. But what was I thinking? I have been thinking about Censors. How visionary figures admonish us. That's clear in an MS I'm reading.

If I say this, So-and-so will think me sentimental. If that . . . will think me bourgeois. All books now seem to me surrounded by a circle of invisible censors. Hence their selfconsciousness, their restlessness. It would be worth while trying to discover what they are at the moment. Did Wordsworth have them? I doubt it. I read "Ruth" before breakfast. Its stillness, its unconsciousness, its lack of distraction, its concentration and the resulting "beauty" struck me. As if the mind must be allowed to settle undisturbed over the object in order to secrete the pearl.

That's an idea for an article.

The figurative expression is that all the surroundings of the mind have come much closer. A child crying in the field brings poverty: my comfort; to mind. Ought I to go to the village sports? "Ought" thus breaks into my contemplation.

Oh and I thought, as I was dressing, how interesting it would be to describe the approach of age, and the gradual coming of death. As people describe love. To note every symptom of failure: but why failure? To treat age as an experience that is different from the others; and to detect every one of the gradual stages towards death which is a tremendous experience, and not as unconscious, at least in its approaches, as birth is.

I must now return to my grind, I think rather refreshed.

Wednesday, August 9th

My grind has left me dazed and depressed. How on earth to bring off this chapter? God knows.

Thursday, August 24th

Perhaps it is more interesting to describe "the crisis" than R.'s love affairs. Yes we are in the very thick of it. Are we at war? At one I'm going to listen in. It's very different, emotionally, from last September. In London yesterday there was indifference almost. No crowd in the train—we went by train. No stir in the streets. One of the removers called up. It's fate, as the foreman said. What can you do against fate? Complete chaos at 37.* Ann † met in graveyard. No war, of course now, she said. John said ‡ "Well I don't know what to think." But as a dress rehearsal it's complete. Museums shut. Searchlight on Rodmell Hill. Chamberlain says danger imminent. The Russian pact a disagreeable and unforeseen surprise. Rather

* 37 Mecklenburgh Square into which we were moving.
† Ann Stephen, V. W.'s niece.
‡ John Lehmann.

like a herd of sheep we are. No enthusiasm. Patient bewilder-
ment. I suspect some desire "to get on with it." Order double
supplies and some coal. Aunt Violet in refuge at Charleston.
Unreal. Whiffs of despair. Difficult to work. Offer of £200 from
Chambers for a story. Haze over the marsh. Aeroplanes. One
touch on the switch and we shall be at war. Danzig not yet
taken. Clerks cheerful. I add one little straw to another, waiting to go in, palsied with writing. There's no cause now to
fight for, said Ann. Communists baffled. Railway strike off.
Lord Halifax broadcasts in his country gentleman voice. Louie
says will clothes be dear? Underneath of course wells of pes-
simism. Young men torn to bits: mothers like Nessa two years
ago. But again, some swerve to the right may come at any moment. The common feeling covers the private, then recedes.
Discomfort and distraction. And all mixed with the mess at 37.

Wednesday, September 6th

Our first air raid warning at 8:30 this morning. A warbling
that gradually insinuates itself as I lay in bed. So dressed and
walked on the terrace with L. Sky clear. All cottages shut.
Breakfast. All clear. During the interval a raid on Southwark.
No news. The Hepworths came on Monday. Rather like a sea
voyage. Forced conversation. Boredom. All meaning has run
out of everything. Scarcely worth reading papers. The B.B.C.
gives any news the day before. Emptiness. Inefficiency. I may
as well record these things. My plan is to force my brain to
work on Roger. But Lord this is the worst of all my life's experiences. It means feeling only bodily feelings: one gets cold
and torpid. Endless interruptions. We have done the curtains.
We have carried coals etc. into the cottage for the 8 Battersea
women and children. The expectant mothers are all quarrelling.
Some went back yesterday. We took the car to be hooded, met
Nessa, were driven to tea at Charleston. Yes, it's an empty
meaningless world now. Am I a coward? Physically I expect
I am. Going to London tomorrow I expect frightens me. At a
pinch enough adrenalin is secreted to keep one calm. But my
brain stops. I took up my watch this morning and then put it
down. Lost. That kind of thing annoys me. No doubt one can

conquer this. But my mind seems to curl up and become unde-
cided. To cure this one had better read a solid book like
Tawney. An exercise of the muscles. The Hepworths are travelling books in Brighton. Shall I walk? Yes. It's the gnats and
flies that settle on non-combatants. This war has begun in cold
blood. One merely feels that the killing machine has to be set
in action.

So far, the *Athenia* has been sunk. It seems entirely meaningless—a perfunctory slaughter. Like taking a jar in one hand,
a hammer in the other. Why must this be smashed? Nobody
knows. This feeling is different from any before. And all the
blood has been let out of common life. No movies or theatres
allowed. No letters, except strays from America. *Reviewing* rejected by Atlantic. No friends write or ring up. Yes, a long sea
voyage, with strangers making conversation, and lots of small
bothers and arrangements, seems the closest I can get. Of
course all creative power is cut off. Perfect summer weather.

It's like an invalid who can look up and take a cup of tea.
Suddenly one can take to the pen with relief. Result of a walk
in the heat, clearing the fug and setting the blood working.
This book will serve to accumulate notes, the first of such
quickenings. And for the hundredth time I repeat—any idea is
more real than any amount of war misery. And what one's
made for. And the only contribution one can make—this little
pitter patter of ideas is my whiff of shot in the cause of freedom. So I tell myself. Thus bolstering up a figment—a phantom: recovering that sense of something pressing from outside
which consolidates the mist, the non-existent.

I conceived the idea, walking in the sunbaked marsh where
I saw one clouded yellow, of making an article out of these 15
odd diaries. This will be an easy slope of work: not the steep
grind of Roger. But shall I ever have a few hours to read in?
I must. Tonight the Raid has diminished from a raid on
Southwark; on Portsmouth; on Scarborough, to an attempt on
the East Coast without damage. Tomorrow we go up.

Monday, September 11th

I have just read 3 or 4 characters of Theophrastus, stumbling
from Greek to English, and may as well make a note of it. Try-

ing to anchor my mind on Greek. Rather successful. As usual, how Greek sticks, darts, eels in and out! No Latin would have noted that a boor remembers his loans in the middle of the night. The Greek has his eye on the object. But it's a long distance one has to roll away to get at Theophrastus and Plato. But worth the effort.

Thursday, September 28th

No, I'm not sure of the date. And Vita is lunching here. I'm going to stop *R.* at 12, then read something real. I'm not going to let my brain addle. Little sharp notes. For somehow my brain is not very vigorous at the end of a book though I could dash off fiction or an article merrily enough. Why not relieve it then? Wasn't it my conscientious grind at *The Years* that killed it. So I whizz off to Stevenson—Jekyll and Hyde—not much to my liking. Very fine clear September weather. Windy but lovely light. And I can't form letters.

Friday, October 6th

Well I have succeeded in despite of distractions to belong to other nations in copying out again the whole of *Roger.* Needless to say, it's still to be revised, compacted, vitalised. And can I ever do it? The distractions are so incessant. I compose articles on Lewis Carroll and read a great variety of books—Flaubert's life, R.'s lectures, out at last, a life of Erasmus and Jacques Blanche. We are asked to lunch with Mrs. Webb, who so often talks of us. And my hand seems as tremulous as an aspen. I have composed myself by tidying my room. Can't quite see my way now as to the next step in composition. Tom this weekend. I meant to record a Third Class Railway Carriage conversation. The talk of business men. Their male detached lives. All politics. Deliberate, well set up, contemptuous and indifferent of the feminine. For example: one man hands the *Evening Standard,* points to a woman's photograph. "Women? Let her go home and bowl her hoop," said the man in blue serge with one smashed eye. "She's a drag on him," another fragment. The son is going to lectures every night. Odd to look into this cool man's world: so weather tight: insurance clerks all on top of their work; sealed up; self-sufficient; admirable; caustic; laconic; objective; and completely provided for. Yet thin, sensitive: yet schoolboys; yet men who earn their livings. In the early train they said, "Can't think how people have time to go to war. It must be that the blokes haven't got jobs." "I prefer a fool's paradise to a real hell." "War's lunacy. Mr. Hitler and his set are gangsters. Like Al Capone." Not a chink through which one can see art, or books. They play crosswords when insurance shop fails.

Saturday, October 7th

It's odd how those first days of complete nullity when war broke out have given place to such a pressure of ideas and work that I feel the old throb and spin in my head more of a drain than ever. The result partly of taking up journalism. A good move, I daresay; for it compacts; and forces me to organise. I'm masterfully pulling together those diffuse chapters of *R.* because I know I must stop and do an article. Ideas for articles obsess me. Why not try the one for *The Times?* No sooner said than I'm ravaged by ideas. Have to hold the *Roger* fort—for I will have the whole book typed and in Nessa's hands by Christmas—by force.

Thursday, November 9th

How glad I am to escape to my free page. But I think I'm nearing the end of my trouble with *Roger*. Doing once more, the last pages: and I think I like it better than before. I think the idea of breaking up the last chapter into sections was a good one. If only I can bring that end off. The worst of journalism is that it distracts, like a shower on the top of the sea.

Reviewing * came out last week; and was not let slip into obscurity as I expected. *Lit. Sup.* had a tart and peevish leader; the old tone of voice I know so well—rasped and injured. Then Y. Y. polite but aghast in the *N.S.* And then my answer—why an answer should always make me dance like a monkey at the Zoo, gibbering it over as I walk, and then re-writing, I don't know. It wasted a day. I suppose it's all pure waste: yet if one's

* A pamphlet by Virginia Woolf.

an outsider, be an outsider. Only don't for God's sake attitudi-
nise and take up the striking, the becoming attitude.

Thursday, November 30th

Very jaded and tired and depressed and cross, and so take
the liberty of expressing my feelings here. *R.* a failure—and
what a grind . . . no more of that. I'm brain fagged and must
resist the desire to tear up and cross out—must fill my mind
with air and light; and walk and blanket it in fog. Rubber
boots help. I can flounder over the marsh. No, I will write a
little memoir.

Saturday, December 2nd

Tiredness and dejection give way if one day off is taken
instantly. I went in and did my cushion. In the evening my
pain in my head calmed. Ideas came back. This is a hint to be
remembered. Always turn the pillow. Then I become a swarm
of ideas. Only I must hive them till *R.* is done. It was annoying to get on to the surface and be so stung with my pamphlet.
No more controversy for a year, I vow. Ideas: about writers'
duty. No, I'll shelve that. Began reading Freud last night; to
enlarge the circumference: to give my brain a wider scope: to
make it objective; to get outside. Thus defeat the shrinkage of
age. Always take on new things. Break the rhythm etc. Use this
page, now and then, for notes. Only they escape after the morning's grind.

Saturday, December 16th

The litter in this room is so appalling that it takes me five
minutes to find my pen. *R.* all unsewn in bits. And I must
take 50 pages, should be 100, up on Monday. Can't get the marriage chapter right. Proportion all wrong. Alteration, quotation, makes it worse. But it's true I don't fuss quite so much as
over a novel. I learned a lesson in re-writing *The Years* which I
shall never forget. Always I say to myself Remember the horror
of that. Yesterday I was, I suppose, cheerful. Two letters from
admirers of *Three Guineas:* both genuine: one a soldier in the
trenches; the other a distracted middle class woman.

Monday, December 18th

Once more, as so often, I hunt for my dear old red-covered book, with what an instinct I'm not quite sure. For what the point of making these notes is I don't know; save that it becomes a necessity to uncramp, and some of it may interest me later. But what? For I never reach the depths; I'm too surface blown. And always scribble before going in—look quickly at my watch. Yes, 10 minutes left—what can I say. Nothing that needs thought; which is provoking; for I often think. And think the very thought I could write here. About being an outsider. About my defiance of professional decency. Another allusion of a tart kind to Mrs. W., and her desire to kill reviewers in the *Lit. Sup.* yesterday. Frank Swinnerton is the good boy and I'm the bad little girl. And this is trivial, compared with what? Oh the *Graf Spee* is going to steam out of Monte Video today into the jaws of death. And journalists and rich people are hiring aeroplanes from which to see the sight. This seems to me to bring war into a new angle; and our psychology. No time to work out. Anyhow the eyes of the whole world (B.B.C.) are on the game; and several people will lie dead tonight, or in agony. And we shall have it served up for us as we sit over our logs this bitter winter night. And the British Captain has been given a K.C.B. and *Horizon* is out; and Louie has had her teeth out; and we ate too much hare pie last night; and I read Freud on Groups; and I've been titivating *Roger:* and this is the last page; and the year draws to an end; and we've asked Plomer for Christmas; and—now time's up as usual. I'm reading Ricketts diary—all about the war—the last war; and the Herbert diaries and . . . yes, Dadie's *Shakespeare,* and notes overflow into my two books.

1940

Saturday, January 6th

An obituary: Humbert Wolfe. Once I shared a packet of choc. creams with him, at Eileen Powers. An admirer sent them. This was a fitting tribute. A theatrical looking glib man. Told me he was often asked if I were his wife. Volunteered that he was happily married, though his wife lived—Geneva? I forget. Remember thinking, Why protest? What's worrying you? Oh it was the night Arnold Bennett attacked me in the *Evening Standard.* Orlando? I was going to meet him at Sybil's next day. There was a queer histrionic look in him, perhaps strain in him. Very self assured, outwardly. Inwardly lacerated by the taunt that he wrote too easily and deified satire; that's my salvage from an autobiography of him—one of many, as if he were dissatisfied and must always draw and redraw his own picture. I suppose the origin of many of the new middle aged autos. So the inspirer of these vague winter night memories —he who sends for the last time a faint film across my tired head—lies with those blackberry eyes shut in that sulphurous cavernous face. (If I were writing I should have to remove either lies or eyes. Is this right? Yes, I think for me; nor need it spoil the run: only one must always practise every style: it's the only way to keep on the boil: I mean the only way to avoid crust is to set a faggot of words in a blaze. That phrase flags. Well, let it. These pages only cost a fraction of a farthing, so that my exchequer isn't imperilled.) Mill I should be reading. Or *Little Dorrit,* but both are gone stale, like a cheese that's been cut and left. The first slice is always the best.

Friday, January 26th

These moments of despair—I mean glacial suspense—a painted fly in a glass case—have given way as they so often do

311

to ecstasy. Is it that I have thrown off those two dead pigeons—
my story, my Gas at Abbotsford (printed today)—and so ideas
rush in. I began one night, absolutely submerged, throttled,
held in a vice with my nose rubbed against *Roger*—no way out—
all hard as iron—to read Julian. And off winged my mind along
those wild uplands. A hint for the future. Always relieve pressure by a flight. Always violently turn the pillow: hack an outlet. Often a trifle does. A review offered of Marie Corelli by the
Listener. These are travellers notes which I offer myself should
I again be lost. I think the last chapter must be sweated from
20,000 to 10,000. This is an attempt at the first words:

"Transformation is the title that Roger Fry gave to his last
book of essays. And it seems natural enough, looking back at
the last ten years of his life, to choose it by
way of title for them too.

But transformation
must express not
only change, but
achievement.

"They were years not of repose and stagnation, but of perpetual experiment and
experience. His position as a critic became
established. 'At the time of his death,'
writes Howard Hannay, 'Roger Fry's position in the English
art world was unique, and the only parallel to it is that of
Ruskin at the height of his reputation.'

"But that position was the result of the freedom and the
vigour with which he carried on his intellectual life; and with
which he extended and enlarged his views. Nor was he less
adventurous in the other life. And these two transformations
resulted in something permanent. As Sir K. Clark says, 'Although he was remarkably consistent in the main outlines of
his beliefs, his mind was invincibly experimental and ready for
any adventure, however far it might lead him beyond the bound-
aries of academic tradition.'

"Physically, the strain was very great. His health had suffered
from the long years at the Omega."

No, I cannot reel it off at all. How queer the change is from
private writing to public writing. And how exhausting. My
little fund of gossip and comment is dried up. What was I

going to say? Oh that the lyric mood of the winter—its intense spiritual exaltation—is over. The thaw has set in; and rain and wind; and the marsh is soggy and patched with white, and two very small lambs were staggering in the east wind. One dead ewe was being carted off; and shirking the horror I crept back by the hangar. Nor have I spent a virtuous evening, hacking at these phrases. I'm enjoying Burke though, and shall tune up on the French Revolution.

Friday, February 2nd

Only the fire sets me dreaming—of all the things I mean to write. The break in our lives from London to country is a far more complete one than any change of house. Yes, but I haven't got the hang of it altogether. The immense space suddenly becomes vacant: then illuminated. And London, in nips, is cramped and creased. Odd how often I think with what is love I suppose of the City: of the walk to the Tower: that is my England: I mean, if a bomb destroyed one of those little alleys with the brass bound curtains and the river smell and the old woman reading, I should feel—well, what the patriots feel.

Friday, February 9th

For some reason hope has revived. Now what served as bait? A letter from Joe Ackerly approving my Corelli? Not much. Tom dining with us? No. I think it was largely reading Stephen's autobiography: though it gave me a pang of envy, by its youth and its vigour, and some good novelist's touches— I could pick holes though. But it's odd—reading that and *South Riding* both mint new, gives me a fillip after all the evenings I grind at Burke and Mill. A good thing to read one's contemporaries, even rapid twinkling slice of life novels like poor W. H.'s. And then, I've polished off, to the last gaiter button, the three d——d chapters for London on Monday; and got my teeth I think firm into the last Transformations: and though of course I shall get the black shivers when I re-read, let alone submit to Nessa and Margery, I can't help thinking I've caught a good deal of that iridescent man in my oh so laborious but-

terfly net. I daresay I've written every page—certainly the last
—10 or 15 times over. And I don't think I've killed: I think I've
brisked. Hence an evening glow. Yet the wind cuts like a
scythe; the dining room carpet is turning to mould; and John
Buchan has fallen on his head and is apparently dying. Monty
Shearman is also dead; and Campbell. L.'s absurd nice old parson friend—his bachelor Buffy friend. Now the wind rises:
something rattles, and thank God I'm not on the North Sea,
nor taking off to raid Heligoland. Now I'm going to read
Freud. Yes, Stephen gave me three hours of continuous illusion—and if one can get that still, there's a world—what's the
quotation?—there's a world outside? No. From *Coriolanus?*

Sunday, February 11th

By way of postponing the writing of cheques—the war, by
the way, has tied up my purse strings again, as in the old days
of 11/- a week pocket money—I write here: and note that the
authentic glow of finishing a book is on me. Does this mean
it's good; or only that I have delivered my mind successfully?
Anyhow, after shivering yesterday, today I made a stride, and
shall I think finish this week at 37. It's tight and conscientious
anyhow. So, walking this mildish day, up to Telscombe I invented pages and pages of my lecture: which is to be full and
fertile. The idea struck me that the Leaning Tower school is
the school of auto-analysis after the suppression of the nineteenth century. Quote Stevenson. This explains Stephen's
autobiography: Louis MacNeice etc. Also I get the idea of
cerebration: poetry that is not unconscious, but stirred by surface irritation, to which the alien matter of politics, that can't
be fused, contributes. Hence the lack of suggestive power. Is
the best poetry that which is most suggestive—is it made of the
fusion of many different ideas, so that it says more than is ex-
plicable? Well, that's the line; and it leads to Public Libraries:
and the supersession of aristocratic culture by common readers:
also to the end of class literature: the beginning of character
literature: new words from new blood; and the comparison
with the Elizabethans. I think there's something in the psycho-
analysis idea: that the Leaning Tower writer couldn't describe

society: had therefore to describe himself, as the product, or victim: a necessary step towards freeing the next generation of repressions. A new conception of the writer needed: and they have demolished the romance of "genius" of the great man, by diminishing themselves. They haven't explored, like H. James, the individual: they haven't deepened; they've cut the outline sharper. And so on. L. saw a grey heraldic bird: I only saw my thoughts.

Sunday, February 18th

This diary might be divided into London diary and country. I think there is a division. Just back from the London chapter. Bitter cold. This shortened my walk, which I meant to be through crowded streets. Then the dark—no lighted windows, depressed me. Standing in Whitehall, I said to my horses "Home, John" and drove back in the grey dawn light, the cheerless spectral light of fading evening in houses—so much more cheerless than the country evening—to Holborn, and so to the bright cave, which I liked better, having shifted the chairs. How silent it is there—and London silent: a great dumb ox lying couchant.

Monday, February 19th

I may as well make a note I say to myself: thinking sometimes who's going to read all this scribble? I think one day I may brew a tiny ingot out of it—in my memoirs. Lytton is hinted as my next task by the way. And *Three Guineas* a dead failure in U.S.A.; but enough.

Wednesday, March 20th

Yes, another attack,* in fact two other attacks: one Sunday week—101 with Angelica there to put me to bed; t'other last Friday, 102 after lunch. So to bed up here in L.'s room, and Dr. Tooth, who keeps me in bed (where I sit up with L. reading proofs) till tomorrow. That's the boring history. What they call recurring with slight bronchitis. Yes. One Sunday

---

* Of influenza.

(the 101 Sunday) L. gave me a very severe lecture on the first half. We walked in the meadows. It was like being pecked by a very hard strong beak. The more he pecked the deeper, as always happens. At last he was almost angry that I'd chosen "what seems to me the wrong method. It's merely analysis, not history. Austere repression. In fact dull to the outsider. All those dead quotations." His theme was that you can't treat a life like that; must be seen from the writer's angle, unless the liver is himself a seer, which R. wasn't. It was a curious example of L. at his most rational and impersonal: rather impressive: yet so definite, so emphatic, that I felt convinced: I mean of failure; save for one odd gleam, that he was himself on the wrong tack, and persisting for some deep reason—dissympathy with R.? lack of interest in personality? Lord knows. I note this plaited strand in my mind; and even while we walked and the beak struck deeper, deeper, had this completely detached interest in L.'s character. Then Nessa came; disagreed; Margery's letter "Very alive and interesting"; then L. read the second half; thought it ended on the doorstep at Bernard Street: then N.'s note "I'm crying can't thank you"— then N. and D. to tea up here; forbid me to alter anything; then Margery's final letter "It's *him* . . . unbounded admiration." There I pause. Well, I think I re-write certain passages, have even in bed sketched them, but how in time for this spring? That I shelve till tomorrow. Great relief all the same.

Thursday, March 21st

Here is the Good Friday festival beginning. How one can sense that in a garden, with flowers and birds only, I can't say. Now for me begins the twilight hour, the emerging hour, of disagreeable compromise. Up to lunch. In the sitting room for tea. You know the dreary, messy, uncomfortable paper strewn, picking at this and that, frame of mind. And with *R.* hanging over me. Walk out as soon as possible and keep on reading Hervey's memoirs. And so come to the top slowly. I'm thinking of some articles. Sidney Smith. Madame de Staël. Virgil. Tolstoy, or perhaps Gogol. Now I'll get L. to find a life of Smith in the Lewes Library. A good idea. I'll ring up Nessa about

sending Helen that chapter, and establish an engagement. I
read Tolstoy at breakfast—Goldenweiser that I translated with
Kot in 1923 and have almost forgotten. Always the same reality—like touching an exposed electric wire. Even so imper-
fectly conveyed—his rugged short cut mind—to me the most,
not sympathetic, but inspiring, rousing: genius in the raw.
Thus more disturbing, more "shocking," more of a thunder-
clap, even on art, even on literature, than any other writer. I
remember that was my feeling about *War and Peace,* read in
bed at Twickenham.* Old Savage † picked it up, "Splendid
stuff!" and Jean ‡ tried to admire what was a revelation to me.
Its directness, its reality. Yet he's against photographic realism.
Sally is lame and has to go to the vet. Sun coming out. One
bird pierces like a needle. All crocuses and squills out. No
leaves or buds on trees. I'm quoted, about Russian, in *Lit. Sup.*
leader, oddly enough.

Friday, March 29th
What shall I think of that liberating and freshening? I'm in
the mood when I open my window at night and look at the
stars. Unfortunately it's 12:15 on a grey dull day, the aeroplanes are active, Botten § is to be buried at 3; and I'm brain
creased after Margery, after John and after Q. But it's the little
antlike nibblings of M. that infect me—ants run in my brain—
emendations, tributes, feelings, dates—and all the detail that
seems to the non-writer so easy—("just to add this about Joan"
etc.) and to me is torture. Thumbing those old pages—and copying into the carbon. Lord, lord! And influenza damped. Well
I recur, what shall I think of? The river. Say the Thames at
London Bridge: and buying a notebook; and then walking
along the Strand and letting each face give me a buffet; and
each shop; and perhaps a Penguin. For we're up in London on
Monday. Then I think I'll read an Elizabethan—like swinging
from bough to bough. Then back here I'll saunter . . . oh yes
and we'll travel our books round the Coast—and have tea in

* A nursing home at Twickenham.   † Sir George Savage, V. W.'s doctor.
‡ Miss Thomas, who kept the nursing home.
§ A Rodmell farmer.

a shop and look at antiques; and there'll be a lovely farmhouse
—or a new lane—and flowers; and bowls with L., and reading
very calmly for *C.R.s.* but no pressure; and May coming and
asparagus and butterflies. Perhaps I'll garden a little; oh and
print; and change my bedroom furniture. Is it age, or what,
that makes life here alone, no London, no visitors, seem a long
trance of pleasure. . . . I'm inducing a state of peace and
sensation feeling—not idea feeling. The truth is we've not seen
spring in the country since I was ill at Asheham—1914—and
that had its holiness in spite of the depression. I think I'll also
dream a poet-prose book; perhaps make a cake now and then.
Now, now—never any more future skirmishing or past regretting. Relish the Monday and the Tuesday, and don't take
on the guilt of selfishness feeling: for in God's name I've done
my share, with pen and talk, for the human race. I mean young
writers can stand on their own feet. Yes, I deserve a spring—I
owe nobody nothing. Not a letter I need write (there are the
poems in MS all waiting) nor need I have week-enders. For
others can do that as well as I can, this spring. Now being
drowned by the flow of running water, I will read Whymper
till lunch time.

Sunday, March 31st

I would like to tell myself a nice little wild improbable story
to spread my wings after this cramped ant-like morning—which
I will not detail—for details are the death of me. Thank God,
this time next week I shall be free—free of entering M.'s corrections and my own into margins. The story? Oh, about the
life of a bird, its cheep cheep—its brandishing of a twig by my
window—its sensations. Or about Botten becoming one with
the mud—the glory fading—the million tinted flowers sent by
the doleful mourners. All black like a moving pillar box the
woman was—or the man in a black cardboard casing. A story
doesn't come. No, but I may unfurl a metaphor—No. The windows very dove grey and dim blue islanded—a rust red on L.
and V.* and the marsh green and dark like the floor of the sea.

* Refers to two elm trees in the garden.

At the back of my head the string is still wound tight. I will
unwind it playing bowls. To carry the virtues of the sketch—its
random reaches, its happy finds—into the finished work is
probably beyond me. Sydney Smith did in talk.

Saturday, April 6th

I spent one afternoon at the L.L.,* looking up quotes. Another buying silk for vests. And we did not dine with the
Hutchinsons to meet Tom and Desmond. And how glad I
was of the drowsy evening. And so at 12:45 yesterday handed
L. the two MSS † and we drove off as happy as Bank Holiday
clerks. That's off my shoulders! Good or bad—done. So I felt
wings on my shoulders: and brooded quietly till the tyre
punctured: we had to jackal in midroad; and I was like a stalk,
all crumpled, when we got here. And it's a keen spring day;
infinitely lit and tinted and cold and soft: all the groups of
daffodils yellow along the bank; lost my three games, and want
nothing but sleep.

Monday, May 13th

I admit to some content, some closing of a chapter and peace
that comes with it, from posting my proofs today. I admit—
because we're in the third day of "the greatest battle in history." It began (here) with the 8 o'clock wireless announcing
as I lay half asleep the invasion of Holland and Belgium. The
third day of the Battle of Waterloo. Apple blossom snowing
the garden. A bowl lost in the pond. Churchill exhorting all
men to stand together. "I have nothing to offer but blood and
tears and sweat." These vast formless shapes further circulate.
They aren't substances: but they make everything else minute.
Duncan saw an air battle over Charleston—a silver pencil and
a puff of smoke. Percy has seen the wounded arriving in their
boots. So my little moment of peace comes in a yawning hollow. But though L. says he has petrol in the garage for suicide
should Hitler win, we go on. It's the vastness, and the small-
ness, that makes this possible. So intense are my feelings (about

* London Library.
† The manuscript of *Roger Fry: A Biography.*

Roger); yet the circumference (the war) seems to make a hoop round them. No, I can't get the odd incongruity of feeling intensely and at the same time knowing that there's no importance in that feeling. Or is there, as I sometimes think, more importance than ever?

Monday, May 20th

This idea was meant to be more impressive. It bobbed up I suppose in one of the sentient moments. The war is like a desperate illness. For a day it entirely obsesses: then the feeling faculty gives out; next day one is disembodied, in the air. Then the battery is re-charged and again—what? Well, the bomb terror. Going to London to be bombed. And the catastrophe—if they break through: Channel this morning said to be their objective. Last night Churchill asked us to reflect, when being bombed, that we were at least drawing fire from the soldiers, for once. Desmond and Moore * are at this moment reading— i.e. talking under the apple trees. A fine windy morning.

Saturday, May 25th

Then we went up to what has been so far the worst week in the war. And so remains. On Tuesday evening, after my freshener, before Tom and Wm. P.† came, the B.B.C. announced the taking of Amiens and Arras. The French P.M. told the truth and knocked all our "holding" to atoms. On Monday they broke through. It's tedious picking up details. It seems they raid with tanks and parachutists: roads crammed with refugees can't be bombed. They crash on. Now are at Boulogne. But it also seems these occupations aren't altogether solid. What are the great armies doing to let this 25 mile hole stay open? The feeling is we're outwitted. They're agile and fearless and up to any new dodge. The French forgot to blow up bridges. The Germans seem youthful, fresh, inventive. We plod behind. This went on the three London days.

Rodmell burns with rumours. Are we to be bombed, evacu-

---

* Desmond MacCarthy and Professor G. E. Moore, O.M.
† William Plomer.

ated? Guns that shake the windows. Hospital ships sunk. So it comes our way.

Today's rumour is the Nun in the bus who pays her fare with a man's hand.

Tuesday, May 28th

And today at 8, the French P.M. broadcast the treachery of the Belgian King. The Belgians have capitulated. The Government is not capitulating. Churchill to broadcast at 4. A wet dull day.

Wednesday, May 29th

But hope revives. I don't know why. A desperate battle. The Allies holding. How sick one gets of the phrase—how easy to make a Duff Cooper speech about valour; and history, where one knows the end of the sentence. Still it cheers, somehow. Poetry as Tom said is easier to write than prose. I could reel off patriotic speeches by the dozen. L. has been in London. A great thunderstorm. I was walking on the marsh and thought it was the guns on the channel ports. Then, as they swerved, I conceived a raid on London; turned on the wireless; heard some prattler; and then the guns began to lighten; then it rained. Began *P.H.** again today and threshed and threshed till perhaps a little grain can be collected. I sent off my Walpole too. After dinner I began Sydney Smith; plan being to keep short flights going; *P.H.* in between. Oh yes—one can't plan, any more, a long book. H. Brace cable that they accept *Roger*—whom, which, I'd almost forgotten. So that's a success: where I'd been expecting failure. It can't be so bad as all that. 250 advance. But we shall I suppose certainly postpone. Reading masses of Coleridge and Wordsworth letters of a night—curiously untwisting and burrowing into that plaited nest.

Thursday, May 30th

Walking today (Nessa's birthday) by Kingfisher pool saw my first hospital train—laden, not funereal but weighty, as if not

* *Between the Acts.*

to shake bones: something—what is the word I want—grieving
and tender and heavy laden and private—bringing our wounded
back carefully through the green fields at which I suppose
some looked. Not that I could see them. And the faculty for
seeing in imagination always leaves me so suffused with something partly visual, partly emotional, I can't, though it's very
pervasive, catch it when I come home—the slowness, cadaver-
ousness, grief of the long heavy train, taking its burden through
the fields. Very quietly it slid into the cutting at Lewes. Instantly wild duck flights of aeroplanes came over head; ma-
noeuvred; took up positions and passed over Caburn.

Friday, May 31st
Scraps, orts and fragments, as I said in *P.H.*, which is now
bubbling. I'm playing with words: and think I owe some dex-
terity to finger exercises here—but the scraps: Louie has seen
Mr. Westmacott's man. "It's an eyesore"—his description of
fighting near Boulogne. Percy weeding: "I shall conquer 'em
in the end. If I was sure of our winning the other battle . . ."
Raid, said to be warned, last night. All the searchlights in extreme continual vibration: they have blots of light, like beads
of dew on a stalk. Mr. Hanna "stood by" half the night. Rumour,
very likely: rumour, which has transported the English in
Belgium who, with their golf sticks, ball and some nets in a
car coming from Flanders, were taken for parachutists: con-
demned to death; released; and returned to Seaford. Rumour,
via Percy, transplanted them to "somewhere near Eastbourne"
and the villagers armed with rifles, pitchforks etc. Shows what
a surplus of unused imagination we possess. We—the educated
—check it; as I checked my cavalry on the down at Telscombe
and transformed them into cows drinking. Making up again.
So that I couldn't remember, coming home, if I'd come by the
mushroom path or the field. How amazing that I can tap that
old river again: and how satisfying. But will it last? I made
out the whole of the end: and need only fill in: the faculty,
dormant under the weight of *Roger,* springs up. And to me it's
the voice on the scent again. "Any waste paper?" Here I was
interrupted by the jangling bell. Small boy in white sweater

come, I suppose, for Scouts, and Mabel says they pester us daily at 37; and make off with the spoils. Desperate fighting. The same perorations. Coming through Southease I saw Mrs. Cockell in old garden hat weeding. Out comes a maid in muslin apron and cap tied with blue riband. Why? To keep up standards of civilisation?

Friday, June 7th

Just back * this roasting hot evening. The great battle which decides our life or death goes on. Last night an air raid here. Today battle sparks. Up till 2:30 this morning.

Sunday, June 9th

I will continue—but can I? The pressure of this battle wipes out London pretty quick. A gritting day. As sample of my present mood, I reflect: capitulation will mean All Jews to be given up. Concentration camps. So to our garage. That's behind correcting *Roger*, playing bowls. One taps any source of comfort—Leigh Ashton at Charleston yesterday for instance. But today the line is bulging. Last night aeroplanes (G.?) over: shafts of light following. I papered my windows. Another reflection: I don't want to go to bed at midday: this refers to the garage. What we dread (it's no exaggeration) is the news that the French Government have left Paris. A kind of growl behind the cuckoos and t'other birds. A furnace behind the sky. It struck me that one curious feeling is, that the writing "I" has vanished. No audience. No echo. That's part of one's death. Not altogether serious, for I correct *Roger*, send finally I hope tomorrow: and could finish *P.H.* But it is a fact—this disparition of an echo.

Monday, June 10th

A day off. I mean one of those odd lapses of anxiety which may be false. Anyhow they said this morning that the line is unbroken—save at certain points. And our army has left Norway and is going to their help. Anyhow—it's a day off—a coal

* From London.

gritty day. L. breakfasted by electric light. And cool mercifully
after the furnace. Today, too, I sent off my page proofs, and
then have read my *Roger* for the last time. The Index remains.
And I'm in the doldrums; a little sunk, and open to the suggestion, conveyed by the memory of Leonard's coolness, en-
forced by John's * silence, that it's one of my failures.

Saturday, June 22nd

Waterloo I suppose. And the fighting goes on in France; and
the terms aren't yet public; and it's a heavy grey day, and I've
been beaten at bowls, feel depressed and irritated and vow I'll
play no more, but read my book. My book is Coleridge: Rose
Macaulay; the Bessborough letters—rather a foolish flight inspired by Hary-o: I would like to find one book and stick to it.
But can't. I feel, if this is my last lap, oughtn't I to read Shakespeare? But can't. I feel oughtn't I to finish off *P.H.:* oughtn't
I to finish something by way of an end? The end gives its vividness, even its gaiety and recklessness to the random daily life.
This, I thought yesterday, may be my last walk. On the down
above Baydean I found some green glass tubes. The corn was
glowing with poppies in it. And I read my Shelley at night.
How delicate and pure and musical and uncorrupt he and
Coleridge read, after the Left Wing Group. How lightly and
firmly they put down their feet, and how they sing; and how
they compact; and fuse and deepen. I wish I could invent a
new critical method—something swifter and lighter and more
colloquial and yet intense: more to the point and less composed; more fluid and following the flight; than my *C.R.* essays.
The old problem: how to keep the flight of the mind, yet be
exact. All the difference between the sketch and the finished
work. And now dinner to cook. A role. Nightly raids in the
east and south coast. 6, 3, 22 people killed nightly.

A high wind was blowing: Mabel, Louie picking currants
and gooseberries. Then a visit to Charleston threw another
stone into the pond. And at the moment, with *P.H.* only to fix
upon, I'm loosely anchored. Further, the war—our waiting
while the knives sharpen for the operation—has taken away

* John Lehmann.

the outer wall of security. No echo comes back. I have no surroundings. I have so little sense of a public that I forget about
Roger coming or not coming out. Those familiar circumvolu-
tions—those standards—which have for so many years given
back an echo and so thickened my identity are all wide and wild
as the desert now. I mean, there is no "autumn," no winter.
We pour to the edge of a precipice . . . and then? I can't conceive that there will be a 27th June 1941. This cuts away
something even at tea at Charleston. We drop another afternoon into the millrace.

Wednesday, July 24th

Yes, there are things to write about: but I want at the moment, the eve of publication moment, to discover my emotions.
They are fitful: thus not very strong—nothing like so strong
as before *The Years*—oh dear, nothing like. Still they twinge. I
wish it were this time next week. There'll be Morgan and
Desmond. And I fear Morgan will say—just enough to show he
doesn't like, but is kind. D. will certainly depress. The *Times
Lit. Sup.* (after its ill temper about *Reviewing*) will find chinks.
T. and T. will be enthusiastic. And—that's all. I repeat that
two strains, as usual, will develop: fascinating; dull: life-like;
dead. So why do I twinge? Knowing it almost by heart. But not
quite. Mrs. Lehmann enthusiastic. John silent. I shall of course
be sneered at by those who sniff at Bloomsbury. I'd forgotten
that. But as L. is combing Sally I can't concentrate. No room
of my own. For 11 days I've been contracting in the glare of
different faces. It ended yesterday with the W.I.: my talk—it
was talked—about the Dreadnought. A simple, on the whole
natural, friendly occasion. Cups of tea: biscuits; and Mrs.
Chavasse, in a tight dress, presiding: out of respect for me, it
was a Book tea. Miss Gardner had *Three Guineas* pinned to
her frock: Mrs. Thompsett *Three Weeks:* and someone else a
silver spoon. No I can't go on to Ray's * death, about which I
know nothing, save that that very large woman, with the shock
of grey hair, and the bruised lip; that monster, whom I re-

* Ray Strachey.

member typical of young womanhood, has suddenly gone. She
had a kind of representative quality, in her white coat and
trousers; wall building; disappointed, courageous, without—
what?—imagination?

Lady Oxford said that there was no virtue in saving, more in
spending. She hung over my neck in a spasm of tears. Mrs.
Campbell has cancer. But in a twinkling she recovered, began
to spend. A cold chicken, she said, was always under cover on
the sideboard at my service. The country people used butter.
She was beautifully dressed in a rayed silk, with a dark blue
tie; a dark blue fluted Russian cap with a red flap. This was
given her by her milliner: the fruit of spending.

All the walls, the protecting and reflecting walls, wear so
terribly thin in this war. There's no standard to write for: no
public to echo back; even the "tradition" has become transparent. Hence a certain energy and recklessness—part good part
bad I daresay. But it's the only line to take. And perhaps the
walls, if violently beaten against, will finally contain me. I feel
tonight still veiled. The veil will be lifted tomorrow when my
book comes out. That's what may be painful: may be cordial.
And then I may feel once more round me the wall I've missed—
or vacancy? or chill? I make these notes, but am tired of notes,
tired of Gide, tired of de Vigny notebooks. I want something
sequacious now and robust. In the first days of the war I could
read notes only.

Thursday, July 25th

I'm not very nervous at the moment: indeed at worst it's only
a skin deep nervousness; for after all, the main people approve:
still I shall be relieved if Morgan approves. That I suppose I
shall know tomorrow. The first review (Lynd) says: "deep
imaginative sympathy . . . makes him an attractive figure (in
spite of wild phrases): There is little drama . . . at the same
time those interested in modern art will find it of absorbing
interest . . ."

What a curious relation is mine with Roger at this moment
—I who have given him a kind of shape after his death. Was he
like that? I feel very much in his presence at the moment; as if

I were intimately connected with him: as if we together had given birth to this vision of him: a child born of us. Yet he had no power to alter it. And yet for some years it will represent him.

Friday, July 26th

I think I have taken, say a good second, judging from the *Lit. Sup.* review. No Morgan. *Times* say it takes a very high place indeed among biographies. *Times* say I have a genius for the relevant. *Times* (art critic I gather) goes on to analyse Roger's tones, etc. *Times* intelligent, but not room for more. It's a nice quiet feeling now. With my Coleridge beneath me, and this over, as it really very nearly (how I hate that clash) is, I'm aware of something permanent and real in my existence. By the way, I'm rather proud of having done a solid work. I am content, somehow. But when I read my post it's like putting my hand in a jar of leeches and so I've a mint of dull dreary letters to write. But it's an incredibly lovely—yes lovely is the word—transient, changing, warm, capricious summer evening. Also I won two games. A large hedgehog was found drowned in the lily pool; L. tried to resuscitate it. An amusing sight. 2/6 is offered by the Government for live hedgehogs. I'm reading Ruth Benedict with pressure of suggestions—about culture patterns—which suggests rather too much. Six volumes of Aug. Hare also suggest—little articles. But I'm very peaceful, momentarily, this evening. Saturday I suppose a no-review day. Immune is again the right word. No, John hasn't read it. When the twelve planes went over, out to sea, to fight, last evening, I had I think an individual, not communal B.B.C. dictated feeling. I almost instinctively wished them luck. I should like to be able to take scientific notes of reactions. Invasion may be tonight: or not at all—that's Joubert's summing up. And—I had something else to say—but what? And dinner to get ready.

Friday, August 2nd

Complete silence surrounds that book. It might have sailed into the blue and been lost. "One of our books did not return" as the B.B.C. puts it. No review by Morgan: no review at all.

No letter. And though I suspect Morgan has refused, finding it unpalatable, still I remain—yes, honestly—quiet minded and prepared to face a complete, lasting silence.

Sunday, August 4th

Just time, while Judith and Leslie * finish their game, to record on a great relief—Desmond's review really says all I wanted said. The book delights friends and the younger generation say Yes, yes, we know him: and it's not only delightful but important. That's enough. And it gave me a very calm rewarded feeling—not the old triumph, as over a novel, but the feeling I've done what was asked of me, given my friends what they wanted. Just as I'd decided I'd given them nothing but the materials for a book I hadn't written. Now I can be content: needn't worry what people think: for Desmond is a good bell-ringer; and will start the others—I mean, the talk among intimates will follow, more or less, his lines. Herbert Read and Maccoll have bit their hardest; put their case; now only Morgan remains, and perhaps a personal dart from W. Lewis.

Tuesday, August 6th

Yes, I was very happy again when I saw Clive's blue envelope at breakfast (with John) this morning. It's Clive almost—what? —devout: no, quiet, serious, completely without sneer, approving. As good in its way as the best of my books—the best biography for many years—the first part as good as the last and no break. So I'm confirmed in what I felt, even when I had that beak pecking walk in March with a temperature of 101 with Leonard—confirmed in what I feel—that the first part is really more generally interesting, though less complex and intensified than the last. I'm sure it was necessary—as a solid pavement for the whole to stand on.

Saturday, August 10th

And then Morgan slightly damped me: but I was damp already from Leslie hum haw the night before and the day before

* Judith Stephen and Leslie Humphrey.

and again tomorrow. So Morgan and Vita slightly damped: and Bob slightly elated and Ethel, and some old boy in the *Spectator*, attacking Read. But God's truth, that's the end of it all. No more reviews and if I had solitude—no men driving stakes, digging pink gun emplacements, and no neighbours, doubtless I could expand and soar—into *P.H.*, into Coleridge; but must first—damn John—re-write the *L.P.** Incessant company is as bad as solitary confinement.

Friday, August 16th

Third edition ordered. L. said, at 37 on Wednesday "It's booming." The boom is dulled by our distance. And why does a word of tepidity depress more than a word of praise exalts? I don't know. I refer to Waley: I don't refer to Pamela—great work of art etc. Well, it's taking its way. It's settling. It's done. And I'm writing *P.H.*, which leaves a spare hour. Many air raids. One as I walked. A haystack was handy. But walked on, and so home. All clear. Then sirens again. Then Judith and Leslie. Bowls. Then Mrs. Ebbs etc. to borrow table. All clear. I must make a stopgap for the last hour, or I shall dwindle, as I'm doing here. But *P.H.* is a concentration—a screw. So I will go in; and read Hare and write to Ethel. Very hot, even out here.

They came very close. We lay down under the tree. The sound was like someone sawing in the air just above us. We lay flat on our faces, hands behind head. Don't close your teeth, said L. They seemed to be sawing at something stationary. Bombs shook the windows of my lodge. Will it drop I asked? If so, we shall be broken together. I thought, I think, of nothingness—flatness, my mood being flat. Some fear I suppose. Should we take Mabel to garage. Too risky to cross the garden, L. said. Then another came from Newhaven. Hum and saw and buzz all round us. A horse neighed in the marsh. Very sultry. Is it thunder? I said. No, guns, said L., from Ringmer, from Charleston way. Then slowly the sound lessened. Mabel in kitchen said the windows shook. Air raid still on: distant

* *Letter to a Young Poet.*

planes; Leslie playing bowls. I well beaten. My books only gave
me pain, Charlotte Brontë said. Today I agree. Very heavy,
dull and damp. This must at once be cured. The all clear.
5 to 7. 144 down last night.

Monday, August 19th

Yesterday, 18th, Sunday, there was a roar. Right on top of
us they came. I looked at the plane, like a minnow at a roaring shark. Over they flashed—three I think. Olive green. Then
pop pop pop—German? Again pop pop pop, over Kingston.
Said to be five bombers hedge hopping on their way to London. The closest shave so far. 144 brought down—no that was
last time. And no raid (so far) today. Rehearsal. I cannot read
Remorse. Why not say so?

Friday, August 23rd

Book flopped. Sales down to 15 a day since air raid on London. Is that the reason? Will it pick up?

Wednesday, August 28th

How I should like to write poetry all day long—that's the
gift to me of poor X, who never reads poetry because she hated
it at school. She stayed from Tuesday to Sunday night, to be
exact: and almost had me down. Why? Because (partly) she has
the artist's temperament without being an artist. She's tempera-
mental, but has no outlet. I find her charming: individual:
honest and somehow pathetic. Her curious obtusity, her stale-
ness of mind, is perceptible to her. And she hesitates. Ought
one to make up? Y. says yes—I say no. The truth is she has no
instinct for colour: no more than for music or pictures. A great
deal of force and spirit and yet always at the leap something
balks her. I can imagine her crying herself to sleep. So, having
brought no rations, or book, she floundered on here. I called
her, to mitigate her burden. My good dog. My Afghan hound—
with her long too thick legs and her long body; and the shock
of wild unbrushed hair on top. I'm glad I'm so nice looking,
she said. And she is. But well, it taught me, that week of un-
intermittent interruptions, bowls, tea parties, droppings in,

what public school is like—no privacy. A good rub with a
coarse towel for my old mind, no doubt. And Judith and Leslie
are about to play bowls. This is why, my first solitary morning,
after London and the protracted air raid—from 9:30 to 4 A.M.
—I was so light, so free, so happy I wrote what I call *P.H.* poetry.
Is it good? I suppose not, very. I should say, to placate V. W.
when she wishes to know what was happening in August, 1940
—that the air raids are now at their prelude. Invasion, if it
comes, must come within three weeks. The harrying of the
public is now in full swing. The air saws: the wasps drone; the
siren—it's now Weeping Willie in the papers—is as punctual
as the vespers . . . We've not had our raid yet, we say. Two
in London. One caught me in the London Library. There I
saw reading in *Scrutiny* that Mrs. W. after all was better than
the young. At this I was pleased. John Buchan—"V. W. is our
best critic since M. Arnold and wiser and juster—" also pleased
me. I must write to Pamela. Sales a little better.

P.S. to the last page. We went out on to the terrace; began
playing. A large two decker plane came heavily and slowly.
L. said a Wellesley something. A training plane said Leslie.
Suddenly there was pop pop from behind the church. Practising we said. The plane circled slowly out over the marsh
and back, very close to the ground and to us. Then a whole
volley of pops (like bags burst) came together. The plane swung
off, slow and heavy and circling towards Lewes. We looked.
Leslie saw the German black cross. All the workmen were
looking. It's a German: that dawned. It was the enemy. It
dipped among the fir trees over Lewes and did not rise. Then
we heard the drone. Looked up and saw two planes very high.
They made for us. We started to shelter in the lodge. But
they wheeled and Leslie saw the English sign. So we watched
—they side slipped, glided, swooped and roared for about five
minutes round the fallen plane as if identifying and making
sure. Then made off towards London. Our version is that it
was a wounded plane, looking for a landing. "It was a Jerry
sure enough," the men said: the men who are making a gun
hiding by the gate. It would have been a peaceful matter of fact

death to be popped off on the terrace playing bowls this very
fine cool sunny August evening.

Saturday, August 31st

Now we are in the war. England is being attacked. I got this
feeling for the first time completely yesterday; the feeling of
pressure, danger, horror. The feeling is that a battle is going
on—a fierce battle. May last four weeks. Am I afraid? Intermittently. The worst of it is one's mind won't work with a spring
next morning. Of course this may be the beginning of invasion. A sense of pressure. Endless local stories. No—it's no
good trying to capture the feeling of England being in a battle.
I daresay if I write fiction and Coleridge and not that infernal
bomb article for U.S.A. I shall swim into quiet water.

Monday, September 2nd

There might be no war, the past two days. Only one raid
warning. Perfectly quiet nights. A lull after the attacks on
London.

Thursday, September 5th

Hot, hot, hot. Record heat wave, record summer if we kept
records this summer. At 2:30 a plane zooms: 10 minutes later
air raid sounds; 20 later, all clear. Hot, I repeat; and doubt if
I'm a poet. H. P. hard labour. Brain w— no, I can't think of
the word—yes, wilts. An idea. All writers are unhappy. The
picture of the world in books is thus too dark. The wordless
are the happy: women in cottage gardens: Mrs. Chavasse. Not
a true picture of the world; only a writer's picture. Are musi-
cians, painters, happy? Is their world happier?

Tuesday, September 10th

Back from half a day in London—perhaps our strangest visit.
When we got to Gower Street a barrier with diversion on it. No
sign of damage. But coming to Doughty Street a crowd. Then
Miss Perkins at the window. Meck. S.* roped off. Wardens there.
Not allowed in. The house about 30 yards from ours struck at

* Mecklenburgh Square.

one in the morning by a bomb. Completely ruined. Another
bomb in the square still unexploded. We walked round the
back. Stood by Jane Harrison's house. The house was still
smouldering. That is a great pile of bricks. Underneath all the
people who had gone down to their shelter. Scraps of cloth
hanging to the bare walls at the side still standing. A looking
glass I think swinging. Like a tooth knocked out—a clean cut.
Our house undamaged. No windows yet broken—perhaps the
bomb has now broken them. We saw Bernal with an arm band
jumping on top of the bricks. Who lived there? I suppose the
casual young men and women I used to see from my window;
the flat dwellers who used to have flower pots and sit in the balcony. All now blown to bits. The garage man at the back—
blear eyed and jerky—told us he had been blown out of
his bed by the explosion: made to take shelter in a church.
"A hard cold seat," he said, "and a small boy lying in my
arms. I cheered when the all clear sounded. I'm aching all
over." He said the Jerries had been over for three nights
trying to bomb Kings Cross. They had destroyed half Argyll
Street, also shops in Grays Inn Road. Then Mr. Pritchard
ambled up. Took the news as calm as a grig. "They actually
have the impertinence to say this will make us accept peace
. . . !" he said: he watches raids from his flat roof and sleeps
like a hog. So, after talking to Miss Perkins, Mrs. Jackson—but
both serene—Miss P. had slept on a camp bed in her shelter—
we went on to Grays Inn. Left the car and saw Holborn. A vast
gap at the top of Chancery Lane. Smoking still. Some great shop
entirely destroyed: the hotel opposite like a shell. In a wine
shop there were no windows left. People standing at the tables
—I think drink being served. Heaps of blue green glass in the
road at Chancery Lane. Men breaking off fragments left in the
frames. Glass falling. Then into Lincoln's Inn. To the *N.S.*
office: windows broken, but house untouched. We went over it.
Deserted. Wet passages. Glass on stairs. Doors locked. So back
to the car. A great block of traffic. The Cinema behind Madame
Tussaud's torn open: the stage visible; some decoration swinging. All the R. Park houses with broken windows, but undamaged. And then miles and miles of orderly ordinary streets—all

Bayswater, and Sussex Square as usual—streets empty—faces set and eyes bleared. In Chancery Lane I saw a man with a barrow of music books. My typist's office destroyed. Then at Wimbledon a siren: people began running. We drove, through almost empty streets, as fast as possible. Horses taken out of the shafts. Cars pulled up. Then the all clear. The people I think of now are the very grimy lodging house keepers, say in Heathcote Street: with another night to face: old wretched women standing at their doors; dirty, miserable. Well—as Nessa said on the phone, it's coming very near. I had thought myself a coward for suggesting that we should not sleep two nights at 37. I was greatly relieved when Miss P. telephoned advising us not to stay, and L. agreed.

Wednesday, September 11th

Churchill has just spoken. A clear, measured, robust speech. Says the invasion is being prepared. It's for the next two weeks apparently if at all. Ships and barges massing at French ports. The bombing of London of course preparatory to invasion. Our majestic City—etc., which touches me, for I feel London majestic. Our courage etc. Another raid last night on London. Time bomb struck the Palace. John rang up. He was in Mecklenburgh Square the night of the raid: wants the Press moved at once. L. is to go up on Friday. Our windows are broken, John says. He is lodging out somewhere. Mecklenburgh Square evacuated. A plane shot down before our eyes just before tea: over the racecourse; a scuffle; a swerve; then a plunge; and a burst of thick black smoke. Percy says the pilot bailed out. We count now on an air raid about 8:30. Anyhow, whether or not, we hear the sinister sawing noise about then, which loudens and fades; then a pause; then another comes. "They're at it again" we say as we sit, I doing my work. L. making cigarettes. Now and then there's a thud. The windows shake. So we know London is raided again.

Thursday, September 12th

A gale has risen. Weather broken. Armada weather. No sound of planes today, only wind. Terrific air traffic last night. But the raid beaten off by new London barrage. This is cheer-

ing. If we can hold out this week—next week—week after—if the
weather's turned—if the force of the raids on London is broken
—we go up tomorrow to see John about moving Press; to patch
the windows, rescue valuables and get letters—if, that is, we're
allowed in the Square. Oh, blackberrying I conceived, or re-
moulded, an idea for a Common History book—to read from
one end of literature including biography; and range at will,
consecutively.

Friday, September 13th

A strong feeling of invasion in the air. Roads crowded with
army wagons, soldiers. Just back from hard day in London.
Raid, unheard by us, started outside Wimbledon. A sudden
stagnation. People vanished. Yet some cars went on. We decided
to visit lavatory on the hill: shut. So L. made use of tree. Pouring. Guns in the distance. Saw a pink brick shelter. That was
the only interest of our journey—our talk with the man, woman
and child who were living there. They had been bombed at
Clapham. Their house unsafe; so they hiked to Wimbledon.
Preferred this unfinished gun emplacement to a refugee over-
crowded house. They had a roadman's lamp; a saucepan and
could boil tea. The nightwatchman wouldn't accept their tea;
had his own; someone gave them a bath. In one of the Wimbledon houses there was only a caretaker. Of course they couldn't
house us. But she was very nice—gave them a sit down. We all
talked. Middleclass smartish lady on her way to Epsom regretted
she couldn't have the child. But we
wouldn't part with her, they said—the
man a voluble emotional Kelt, the
woman placid Saxon. As long as she's
all right we don't mind. They sleep on
some shavings. Bombs had dropped on
the Common. He a housepainter. Very
friendly and hospitable. They liked
having people in to talk. What will they
do? The man thought Hitler would
soon be over. The lady in the cocks hat said Never. Twice we
left: more guns: came back. At last started, keeping an eye on
shelters and people's behaviour. Reached Russell Hotel. No

He laid rather a thin
rug on the step for me
to sit on. An officer
looked in. "Making
ready for the invasion,"
said the man, as if it
were going off in
about ten minutes.

John. Loud gunfire. We sheltered. Started for Mecklenburgh
Square; met John, who said the Square still closed; so lunched
in the hotel: decided the Press emergency—to employ Garden
City Press—in 20 minutes. Raid still on. Walked to Mecklenburgh Square.

Saturday, September 14th

A sense of invasion—that is lorries of soldiers and machines
—like cranes—walloping along to Newhaven. An air raid is on.
A little pop rattle which I take to be machine gun, just gone
off. Planes roaring and roaring. Percy and L. say some are English. Mabel comes out and looks: asks if we want fish fried or
boiled.

The great advantage of this page is that it gives me a fidget
ground. Fidgets: caused by losing at bowls and invasion: caused
by another howling banshee, by having no book I must read:
and so on. I am reading Sévigné: how recuperative last week;
gone stale a little with that mannered and sterile Burney now:
even through the centuries his acid dandified somehow supercilious well what?—can't find the word—this manner of his, this
character penetrates; and moreover reminds me of someone
I dislike. Is it Logan? There's a ceremony in him that reminds
me of Tom. There's a parched artificial cruelty
and—oh the word! the word! Am I oversensi-
tive to character in writing? I think we mod-
erns lack love. Our torture makes us writhe.
But I can't go into that—a phrase that brings in Old Rose, to
whom I mean to write. One always thinks there's a landing place
coming. But there aint. A stage, a branch, an end. I dislike writing letters of thanks about *Roger*. I've said it so many times. I
think I will begin my new book by reading Ifor Evans, 6d. Penguin.

I suggest supercilious.

Monday, September 16th

Well, we're alone in our ship. A very wet stormy day. Mabel *
stumped off, with her bunions, carrying her bags at 10. Thank
you for all your kindness; she said the same to us both. Also

* The cook, who had decided to go and live with her sister.

would I give her a reference? "I hope we shall meet again," I said. She said "Oh no doubt" thinking I referred to death. So that 5 years' uneasy mute but very passive and calm relation is over: a heavy unsunned pear dropped from a twig. And we're freer, alone. No responsibility: for her. The house solution is to have no residents. But I'm stupid; have been dallying with Mr. Williamson's confessions appalled by his egocentricity. Are all writers as magnified in their own eyes? He can't move an inch from the glare of his own personality—his fame. And I've never read one of those immortal works. To Charleston this afternoon, after provisioning for our siege in Lewes. Last night we saw tinsel sparks here and there in the sky over the flat. L. thought they were shells bursting from the London barrage. Great air traffic all night. Some loud explosions. I listened for church bells, thinking largely, I admit, of finding ourselves prisoned here with Mabel. She thought the same. Said that if one is to be killed one will be killed. Prefers death in a Holloway shelter playing cards—naturally—to death here.

Tuesday, September 17th

No invasion. High wind. Yesterday in the Public Library I took down a book of X.'s criticism. This turned me against writing my book. London Library atmosphere effused. Turned me against all literary criticism: these so clever, so airless, so fleshless ingenuities and attempts to prove—that T. S. Eliot for example is a worse critic than X. Is all literary criticism that kind of exhausted air?—book dust, London Library, air. Or is it only that X. is a second hand, frozen fingered, university specialist, don trying to be creative, don all stuffed with books, writer? Would one say the same of the *Common Reader?* I dipped for five minutes and put the book back depressed. The man asked "What do you want, Mrs. Woolf?" I said a history of English literature. But was so sickened I couldn't look. There were so many. Nor could I remember the name of Stopford Brooke.

I continue, after winning two games of bowls. Our island is a desert island. No letters from Meck. No coffee. Papers between 3 and 4. Can't get on to Meck. when we ring up. Some letters

take 5 days coming. Trains uncertain. One must get out at
Croydon. Angelica goes to Hilton via Oxford. So we, L. and I,
are almost cut off. We found a young soldier in the garden last
night, coming back. "Can I speak to Mr. Woolf?" I thought it
meant billeting for certain. No. Could we lend a typewriter?
Officer on hill had gone and taken his. So we produced my portable. Then he said: "Pardon sir. Do you play chess?" He plays
chess with passion. So we asked him to tea on Saturday to play.
He is with the anti-aircraft searchlight on the hill. Finds it dull.
Can't get a bath. A straight good natured young man. Professional soldier? I think the son, say of an estate agent, or small
shopkeeper. Not public school. Not lower class. But I shall investigate. "Sorry to break into your private life" he said. Also
that on Saturday he went to the pictures in Lewes.

Wednesday, September 18th

"We have need of all our courage" are the words that come
to the surface this morning: on hearing that all our windows
are broken, ceilings down, and most of our china smashed at
Mecklenburgh Square. The bomb exploded. Why did we ever
leave Tavistock? What's the good of thinking that? We were
about to start for London, when we got on to Miss Perkins who
told us. The Press—what remains—is to be moved to Letchworth. A grim morning. How can one settle into Michelet and
Coleridge? As I say, we have need of courage. A very bad raid
last night on London—waiting for the wireless. But I did forge
ahead with *P.H.* all the same.

Thursday, September 19th

Less need of courage today. I suppose the impression of Miss
P.'s voice describing the damage wears off.

Wednesday, September 25th

All day—Monday—in London; in the flat; dark; carpets nailed
to windows; ceilings down in patches; heaps of grey dust and
china under kitchen table; back rooms untouched. A lovely
September day—tender—three days of tender weather—John

came. We are moved to Letchworth. The Garden City was moving us that day. *Roger* surprisingly sells. The bomb in Brunswick Square exploded. I was in the baker's. Comforted the agitated worn women.

Sunday, September 29th

A bomb dropped so close I cursed L. for slamming the window. I was writing to Hugh, and the pen jumped from my finger. Raid still on. It's like a sheep dog, chasing a fox out of the fold. You see them yapping and biting and then the marauder, dropping a bone, a bomb towards Newhaven, flies. All clear. Bowls. Villagers at their doors. Cold. All now become familiar. I was thinking (among other things) that this is a lazy life. Breakfast in bed. Read in bed. Bath. Order dinner. Out to Lodge. After rearranging my room (turning table to get the sun: church on right; window left: a new very lovely view) tune up, with cigarette: write till 12: stop: visit L.: look at papers; return; type till 1. Listen in: Lunch. Sore jaw: can't bite. Read papers. Walk to Southease. Back 3. Gather and arrange apples. Tea. Write a letter. Bowls. Type again. Read Michelet or write here. Cook dinner. Music. Embroidery. 9:30 read (or sleep) till 11:30. Bed. Compare with the old London day. Three afternoons someone coming. One night, dinner party. Saturday a walk. Thursday shopping. Tuesday going to tea with Nessa. One City walk. Telephone ringing. L. to meetings. K. M. or Robson bothering. That was an average week: with Friday to Monday here. I think, now we're marooned, I ought to cram in a little more reading. Yet why? A happy, a very free, and disengaged—a life that rings from one simple melody to another. Yes: why not enjoy this after all those years of the other? Yet I compare with Miss Perkins day.

Wednesday, October 2nd

Ought I not to look at the sunset rather than write this? A flush of red in the blue; the haystack on the marsh catches the glow; behind me, the apples are red in the trees. L. is gathering them. Now a plume of smoke goes from the train under Caburn.

And all the air a solemn stillness holds. Till 8:30 when the cadaverous twanging in the sky begins; the planes going to London. Well it's an hour still to that. Cows feeding. The elm tree sprinkling its little leaves against the sky. Our pear tree swagged with pears; and the weathercock above the triangular church tower above it. Why try again to make the familiar catalogue, from which something escapes. Should I think of death? Last night a great heavy plunge of bomb under the window. So near we both started. A plane had passed dropping this fruit. We went on to the terrace. Trinkets of stars sprinkled and glittering. All quiet. The bombs dropped on Itford Hill. There are two by the river, marked with white wooden crosses, still unburst. I said to L.: I don't want to die yet. The chances are against it. But they're aiming at the railway and the power works. They get closer every time. Caburn was crowned with what looked like a settled moth, wings extended—a Messerschmitt it was, shot down on Sunday. I had a nice gallop this morning with Coleridge—Sara. I'm to make £20 with two articles. Books still held up. And Spiras free, and Margot * writes to say "I did it" and adds "a long letter all about yourself and what you believe." What do I? Can't at the moment remember. Oh I try to imagine how one's killed by a bomb. I've got it fairly vivid—the sensation: but can't see anything but suffocating nonentity following after. I shall think—oh I wanted another 10 years—not this—and shan't, for once, be able to describe it. It—I mean death; no, the scrunching and scrambling, the crushing of my bone shade in on my very active eye and brain: the process of putting out the light—painful? Yes. Terrifying. I suppose so. Then a swoon; a drain; two or three gulps attempting consciousness—and then dot dot dot.

Sunday, October 6th

I snatch this page with Anreps and Ruth Beresford imminent to say—what? Will it ever seem strange that L. and I walking on the marsh first look at a bomb crater: then listen

* Lady Oxford.

to the German drone above: then I take two paces nearer L.,
prudently deciding that two birds had better be killed with one
stone? They got Lewes at last yesterday.

Saturday, October 12th

I would like to pack my day rather fuller: most reading must
be munching. If it were not treasonable to say so, a day like this
is almost too—I won't say happy: but amenable. The tune varies,
from one nice melody to another. All is played (today) in such a
theatre. Hills and fields; I can't stop looking; October blooms;
brown plough; and the fading and freshening of the marsh.
Now the mist comes up. And one thing's "pleasant" after another: breakfast, writing, walking, tea, bowls, reading, sweets,
bed. A letter from Rose about her day. I let it almost break
mine. Mine recovers. The globe rounds again. Behind it—oh
yes. But I was thinking I must intensify. Partly Rose. Partly
I'm terrified of passive acquiescence. I live in intensity. In London, now, or two years ago, I'd be owling through the streets.
More pack and thrill than here. So I must supply that—how? I
think book inventing. And there's always the chance of a rough
wave: no, I won't once more turn my magnifying glass on that.
Scraps of memoirs come so coolingly to my mind. Wound up by
those three little articles (one sent today) I unwound a page
about Thoby. Fish forgotten. I must invent a dinner. But it's
all so heavenly free and easy—L. and I alone. I've my rug on
hand too. Another pleasure. And all the clothes drudgery, Sybil
drudgery, society drudgery obliterated. But I want to look back
on these war years as years of positive something or other. L.
gathering apples. Sally barks. I imagine a village invasion. Queer
the contraction of life to the village radius. Wood bought
enough to stock many winters. All our friends are isolated over
winter fires. Chance of interruption small now. No cars. No
petrol. Trains uncertain. And we on our lovely free autumn
island. But I will read Dante, and for my trip through English
literature book. I was glad to see the *C.R.* all spotted with readers at the Free Library to which I think of belonging.

Thursday, October 17th

Our private luck has turned. John says Tavistock Square is no more.* If that's so, I need no longer wake in the night thinking the Wolves luck has taken a downward turn. For the first time they were rash and foolish. Second, an urgent request from Harpers Bazaar for an article or story. So that tree, far from being barren, as I thought, is fruit bearing. And I've spent I don't know how much brain nerve earning 30 gns. with three little articles. But I say, the effort has its reward; for I'm worth, owing to that insect like conscience and diligence, £120 to the U.S.A. A perfect day—a red admiral feasting on an apple day. A red rotten apple lying on the grass; butterfly on it, beyond a soft blue warm coloured down and field. Everything dropping through soft air to rest on the earth. The light is now fading. Soon the siren: then the twang of plucked strings . . . But it's almost forgettable still; the nightly operation on the tortured London. Mabel wants to leave it. L. sawing wood. The funny little cross on the church shows against the downs. We go up tomorrow. A mist is rising; a long fleece of white on the marshes. I must black out. I had so much to say. I am filling my mind slowly with Elizabethans: that is to say letting my mind feed like the Red Admiral—the siren, just as I had drawn the curtains. Now the unpleasant part begins. Who'll be killed tonight? Not us, I suppose. One doesn't think of that—save as a quickener. Indeed I often think our Indian summer was deserved: after all those London years. I mean, this quickens it. Every day seen against a very faint shade of bodily risk. And I returned to *P.H.* today; and am to transfer my habitual note taking I think— what I do on odd days—to random reading. The idea is, accumulate notes. Oh and I've mastered the iron curtain for my brain. Down I shut when I'm tied tight. No reading, no writing. No claims, no "must" I walk—yesterday in the rain over the Piddinghoe down—a new line.

Sunday, October 20th

The most—what?—impressive, no, that's not it—sight in Lon-

* The house which we still had on lease in Tavistock Square was completely destroyed by a bomb.

don on Friday was the queue, mostly children with suitcases, outside Warren Street tube. This was about 11:30. We thought they were evacuees waiting for a bus. But there they were, in a much longer line, with women, men, more bags, blankets, sitting still at 3. Lining up for the shelter in the night's raid— which came of course. Thus, if they left the tube at 6 (a bad raid on Thursday) they were back again at 11. So to Tavistock Square.* With a sigh of relief saw a heap of ruins. Three houses, I should say, gone. Basement all rubble. Only relics an old basket chair (bought in Fitzroy Square days) and Penman's board To Let. Otherwise bricks and wood splinters. One glass door in the next house hanging. I could just see a piece of my studio wall standing: otherwise rubble where I wrote so many books. Open air where we sat so many nights, gave so many parties. The hotel not touched. So to Meck.† All again. Litter, glass, black soft dust, plaster powder. Miss T. and Miss E. in trousers, overalls and turbans, sweeping. I noted the flutter of Miss T.'s hands: the same as Miss Perkins'. Of course friendly and hospitable in the extreme. Jaunty jerky talk. Repetitions. So sorry we hadn't had her card . . . to save you the shock. It's awful . . . Upstairs she propped a leaning bookcase for us. Books all over dining room floor. In my sitting room glass all over Mrs. Hunter's cabinet—and so on. Only the drawing room with windows almost whole. A wind blowing though. I began to hunt out diaries. What could we salvage in this little car? Darwin and the silver, and some glass and china.

Then lunch off tongue, in the drawing room. John came. I forgot *The Voyage of the Beagle*. No raid the whole day. So about 2:30 drove home.

Exhilaration at losing possessions—save at times I want my books and chairs and carpets and beds. How I worked to buy them—one by one—and the pictures. But to be free of Meck., would now be a relief. Almost certainly it will be destroyed— and our queer tenancy of that sunny flat over . . . In spite of the move and the expense, no doubt, if we save our things we shall be cheaply quit—I mean, if we'd stayed at 52 and lost all

* Our house, No. 52, had been destroyed by a bomb.
† Our house, 37 Mecklenburgh Square, wrecked by a bomb.

our possessions. But it's odd—the relief at losing possessions. I
should like to start life, in peace, almost bare—free to go anywhere. Can we be rid of Meck. though?

Friday, November 1st

A gloomy evening, spiritually: alone over the fire—and by
way of conversation, apply to this too stout volume. My *Times*
book for the week is E. F. Benson's last autobiography—in which
he tried to rasp himself clean of his barnacles. I learn there the
perils of glibness. I too can flick phrases. He said, "One must
discover new depths in oneself." Well I don't bother about that
here. I will note, though, the perils of glibness. And add, considering how I feel in my fingers the weight of every word, even
of a review, need I feel guilty?

Sunday, November 3rd

Yesterday the river burst its banks. The marsh is now a sea
with gulls on it. L. and I walked down to the hangar. Water
broken, white, roaring, pouring down through the gap by the
pillbox. A bomb exploded last month; old Thompsett told me
it took a month to mend. For some reason (bank weakened
Everest says by pillbox) it burst again. Today the rain is tremendous. And gale. As if dear old nature were kicking up her
heels. Down to the hangar again. Flood deeper and fuller. Bridge
cut off. Water made road impassable by the farm. So all my
marsh walks are gone—until? Another break in the bank. It
comes over in a cascade: the sea is unfathomable. Yes, now it
has crept up round Botten's haystack—the haystack in the floods
—and is at the bottom of our field. Lovely if the sun were out.
Medieval in the mist tonight. I am happy, quit of my money-
making; back at *P.H.* writing in spurts; covering, I'm glad to
say, a small canvas. Oh the freedom—

Tuesday, November 5th

The haystack in the floods is of such incredible beauty . . .
When I look up I see all the marsh water. In the sun deep blue,
gulls caraway seeds: snowstorms: Atlantic floor: yellow islands:

leafless trees: red cottage roofs. Oh may the flood last for ever.
A virgin lip: no bungalows; as it was in the beginning. Now it's
lead grey with the red leaves in front. Our inland sea. Caburn is
become a cliff. I was thinking: the University fills shells like
H.A.L.F. and Trevelyan. They are their product. Also: Never
have I been so fertile. Also: the old hunger for books is on me:
the childish passion. So that I am very 'happy' as the saying is:
and excited by *P.H.* This diary shorthand comes in useful. A
new style—to mix.

Sunday, November 17th

I observe, as a curious trifle in mental history—I should like
to take naturalist's notes—human naturalist's notes—that it is
the rhythm of a book that, by running in the head, winds one
into a ball; and so jades one. The rhythm of *P.H.* (the last chapter) became so obsessive that I heard it, perhaps used it, in every
sentence I spoke. By reading the notes for memoirs I broke this
up. The rhythm of the notes is far freer and looser. Two days of
writing in that rhythm has completely refreshed me. So I go
back to *P.H.* tomorrow. This I think is rather profound.

Saturday, November 23rd

Having this moment finished the Pageant—or Poyntz Hall?—
(begun perhaps April 1938) my thoughts turn well up, to write
the first chapter of the next book (nameless) Anon, it will be
called. The exact narrative of this last morning should refer to
Louie's interruption, holding a glass jar, in whose thin milk
was a pat of butter. Then I went in with her to skim the milk
off: then I took the pat and showed it to Leonard. This was a
moment of great household triumph.

I am a little triumphant about the book. I think it's an interesting attempt in a new method. I think it's more quintessential
than the others. More milk skimmed off. A richer pat, certainly
a fresher than that misery *The Years*. I've enjoyed writing almost every page. This book was only (I must note) written at
intervals when the pressure was at its highest, during the drudgery of *Roger*. I think I shall make this my scheme: if the new

book can be made to serve as daily drudgery—only I hope to lessen that—anyhow it will be a supported on fact book—then I shall brew some moments of high pressure. I think of taking my mountain top—that persistent vision—as a starting point. Then see what comes. If nothing, it won't matter.

Sunday, December 22nd

How beautiful they were, those old people—I mean father and mother—how simple, how clear, how untroubled. I have been dipping into old letters and father's memoirs. He loved her: oh and was so candid and reasonable and transparent—and had such a fastidious delicate mind, educated, and transparent. How serene and gay even, their life reads to me: no mud; no whirlpools. And so human—with the children and the little hum and song of the nursery. But if I read as a contemporary I shall lose my child's vision and so must stop. Nothing turbulent; nothing involved; no introspection.

Sunday, December 29th

There are moments when the sail flaps. Then, being a great amateur of the art of life, determined to suck my orange, off, like a wasp if the blossom I'm on fades, as it did yesterday—I ride across the downs to the cliffs. A roll of barbed wire is hooped on the edge. I rubbed my mind brisk along the Newhaven road. Shabby old maids buying groceries, in that desert road with the villas; in the wet. And Newhaven gashed. But tire the body and the mind sleeps. All desire to write diary here has flagged. What is the right antidote? I must sniff round. I think Mme. de Sévigné. Writing to be a daily pleasure. I detest the hardness of old age—I feel it. I rasp. I'm tart.

> The foot less prompt to meet the morning dew,
> The heart less bounding at emotion new,
> And hope, once crush'd, less quick to spring again.

I actually opened Matthew Arnold and copied these lines. While doing so, the idea came to me that why I dislike, and like, so many things idiosyncratically now, is because of my growing detachment from the hierarchy, the patriarchy. When Desmond praises *East Coker,* and I am jealous, I walk over the marsh saying, I am I: and must follow that furrow, not copy another. That is the only justification for my writing, living. How one enjoys food now: I make up imaginary meals.

1941

On Sunday night, as I was reading about the Great fire, in a very accurate detailed book, London was burning. Eight of my city churches destroyed, and the Guildhall. This belongs to last year. This first day of the new year has a slice of wind like a circular saw. This book was salvaged from 37: I brought it down from the shop, with a handful of Elizabethans for my book, now called *Turning a Page*. A psychologist would see that the above was written with someone, and a dog, in the room. To add in private: I think I will be less verbose here perhaps—but what does it matter, writing too many pages. No printer to consider. No public.

Thursday, January 9th
A blank. All frost. Still frost. Burning white. Burning blue. The elms red. I did not mean to describe, once more, the downs in snow; but it came. And I can't help even now turning to look at Asheham down, red, purple, dove blue grey, with the cross so melodramatically against it. What is the phrase I always remember—or forget. Look your last on all things lovely. Yesterday Mrs. X. was buried upside down. A mishap. Such a heavy woman, as Louie put it, feasting spontaneously upon the grave. Today she buries the Aunt whose husband saw the vision at Seaford. Their house was bombed by the bomb we heard early one morning last week. And L. is lecturing and arranging the room. Are these the things that are interesting? that recall: that say Stop, you are so fair? Well, all life is so fair, at my age. I mean, without much more of it I suppose to follow. And t'other side of the hill there'll be no rosy blue red snow. I am copying *P.H.*

348

Wednesday, January 15th

Parsimony may be the end of this book. Also shame at my own verbosity, which comes over me when I see the 20 it is—books shuffled together in my room. Who am I ashamed of? Myself reading them. Then Joyce is dead: Joyce about a fortnight younger than I am. I remember Miss Weaver, in wool gloves, bringing *Ulysses* in typescript to our teatable at Hogarth House. Roger I think sent her. Would we devote our lives to printing it? The indecent pages looked so incongruous: she was spinsterly, buttoned up. And the pages reeled with indecency. I put it in the drawer of the inlaid cabinet. One day Katherine Mansfield came, and I had it out. She began to read, ridiculing: then suddenly said, But there's something in this: a scene that should figure I suppose in the history of literature. He was about the place, but I never saw him. Then I remember Tom in Ottoline's room at Garsington saying—it was published then —how could anyone write again after achieving the immense prodigy of the last chapter? He was, for the first time in my knowledge, rapt, enthusiastic. I bought the blue paper book, and read it here one summer I think with spasms of wonder, of discovery, and then again with long lapses of intense boredom. This goes back to a pre-historic world. And now all the gents are furbishing up their opinions, and the books, I suppose, take their place in the long procession.

We were in London on Monday. I went to London Bridge. I looked at the river; very misty; some tufts of smoke, perhaps from burning houses. There was another fire on Saturday. Then I saw a cliff of wall, eaten out, at one corner; a great corner all smashed; a Bank; the Monument erect: tried to get a bus; but such a block I dismounted; and the second bus advised me to walk. A complete jam of traffic; for streets were being blown up. So by Tube to the Temple; and there wandered in the desolate ruins of my old squares: gashed; dismantled; the old red bricks all white powder, something like a builder's yard. Grey dirt and broken windows. Sightseers; all that completeness ravished and demolished.

Sunday, January 26th

A battle against depression, rejection (by Harpers of my story and Ellen Terry) routed today (I hope) by clearing out kitchen; by sending the article (a lame one) to *N.S.*: and by breaking into *P.H.* two days, I think, of memoir writing. This trough of despair shall not, I swear, engulf me. The solitude is great. Rodmell life is very small beer. The house is damp. The house is untidy. But there is no alternative. Also days will lengthen. What I need is the old spurt. "Your true life, like mine, is in ideas" Desmond said to me once. But one must remember one can't pump ideas. I begin to dislike introspection: sleep and slackness; musing; reading; cooking; cycling: oh and a good hard rather rocky book—viz.: Herbert Fisher. This is my prescription.

There's a lull in the war. Six nights without raids. But Garvin says the greatest struggle is about to come—say in three weeks —and every man, woman, dog, cat, even weevil must girt their arms, their faith—and so on. It's the cold hour, this: before the lights go up. A few snowdrops in the garden. Yes, I was thinking: we live without a future. That's what's queer: with our noses pressed to a closed door. Now to write, with a new nib, to Enid Jones.

Friday, February 7th

Why was I depressed? I cannot remember. We have been to Charlie Chaplin. Like the milk girl we found it boring. I have been writing with some glow. Mrs. Thrale is to be done before we go to Cambridge. A week of broken water impends.

Sunday, February 16th

In the wild grey water after last week's turmoil. I liked the dinner with Dadie best. All very lit up and confidential. I liked the soft grey night at Newnham. We found Pernel in her high ceremonial room, all polished and spectatorial. She was in soft reds and blacks. We sat by a bright fire. Curious flitting talk. She leaves next year. Then Letchworth—the slaves chained to their typewriters, and their drawn set faces and the machines— the incessant more and more competent machines, folding, pressing, gluing and issuing perfect books. They can stamp cloth to imitate leather. Our Press is up in a glass case. No country to look at. Very long train journeys. Food skimpy. No butter, no jam. Old couples hoarding marmalade and grape nuts on their tables. Conversation half whispered round the lounge fire. Elizabeth Bowen arrived two hours after we got back, and went yesterday: and tomorrow Vita; then Enid; then perhaps I shall re-enter one of my higher lives. But not yet.

Wednesday, February 26th

My "higher life" is almost entirely the Elizabethan play. Finished Pointz Hall, the Pageant; the play—finally *Between the Acts* this morning.

Sunday, March 8th

Just back from L.'s speech at Brighton. Like a foreign town: the first spring day. Women sitting on seats. A pretty hat in a teashop—how fashion revives the eye! And the shell encrusted old women, rouged, decked, cadaverous at the teashop. The waitress in checked cotton. No: I intend no introspection. I mark Henry James' sentence: observe perpetually. Observe the oncome of age. Observe greed. Observe my own despondency. By that means it becomes serviceable. Or so I hope. I insist upon spending this time to the best advantage. I will go down with my colours flying. This I see verges on introspection; but doesn't quite fall in. Suppose I bought a ticket at the Museum; biked in daily and read history. Suppose I selected one dominant figure in every age and wrote round and about. Occupation is essential. And now with some pleasure I find that it's seven; and must cook dinner. Haddock and sausage meat. I think it is true that one gains a certain hold on sausage and haddock by writing them down.

GENERAL INDEX

Anrep, Helen, 117, 224
Arnold-Forster, Ka, 56
Asquith, Anthony, 54
Asquith, Margot (Lady Oxford & Asquith), 54, 55, 107, 280, 326

Baring, Maurice, 94, 95, 107, 116
Barnett, Canon S. A., 9-10
Beerbohm, Max, 120, 194, 294, 295
Bell, Clive, 11, 18, 19, 55, 71, 74, 78, 106, 112, 120, 128, 145, 222, 230, 328
Bell, Julian, 62, 117, 228
Bell, Vanessa, 11, 19, 29, 70, 75, 106, 117, 118, 133, 134, 138, 144, 218, 222, 228, 229, 232, 260, 282, 305, 316
Bennett, Arnold, 27, 56, 96, 157, 165, 175, 189
Benson, Stella, 206, 207
Bevin, Ernest, 247
Birrell, Francis, 226, 227, 229
Bridges, Robert, 82
Brooke, Rupert, 3
Butts, Mary, 52, 53
Byron, Lord, 1-4, 44, 45, 151, 152

Case, Janet, 274, 275
Cassis, 71, 72, 150
Cecil, Lord David, 54, 58, 144, 225, 261
Colefax, Lady Sibyl, 55, 95, 116, 122, 145, 206
Congreve, William, 273, 274
Conrad, Joseph, 25-6, 59, 63, 86
Cunard, Lady, 132
Cromer, Lady, 82

Dante, 123, 225
Defoe, 11, 12, 82
Dickens, Charles, 8, 300, 301
Dickinson, G. L. (Goldie), 74, 75, 78, 179, 208, 224, 251

Dickinson, Violet, 19, 42, 52, 195
Don Quixote, 26
Dostoievsky, 49, 56, 129, 203, 239

Eclipse, the, 108-11
Eliot, T. S., 12, 14, 27, 46, 49, 144, 232, 297, 298, 320, 321, 349

Flaubert, 260
Forster, E. M., 11-12, 19, 20, 49, 52, 76, 79, 82, 91, 93, 99, 115, 171, 172, 224, 234-6, 263, 270, 297, 325, 326, 327, 328
Fry, Margery, 224, 225, 244, 266, 316
Fry, Roger, 12, 26, 31, 78, 103, 112, 117, 133, 134, 144, 145, 216, 217, 222-5, 227, 228, 229, 247, 248, 250, 251, 252, 288, 291, 292, 304, 312

Galsworthy, John, 189
Garnett, David (Bunny), 52, 229, 269
Garnett, Mrs. (Angelica Bell), 117, 228
Grant, Duncan, 56, 70, 74, 112, 123, 133, 134, 155, 219, 319

Hardy, Mrs. Thomas, 76, 88-93, 94
Hardy, Thomas, 8, 39, 76, 86, 88-93, 94, 120
Harris, "Bogey," 116
Harrison, Jane, 124
Hunt, Leigh, 35-6
Hutchinson, Mrs. St. John, 85
Hutchinson, St. John, 86
Huxley, Aldous, 26, 93, 183, 222, 228, 257

Isherwood, Christopher, 295

James, Henry, 24, 26, 39, 40, 86, 196, 215

INDEX OF BOOKS
BY VIRGINIA WOOLF